31472400195271

DATE DUE

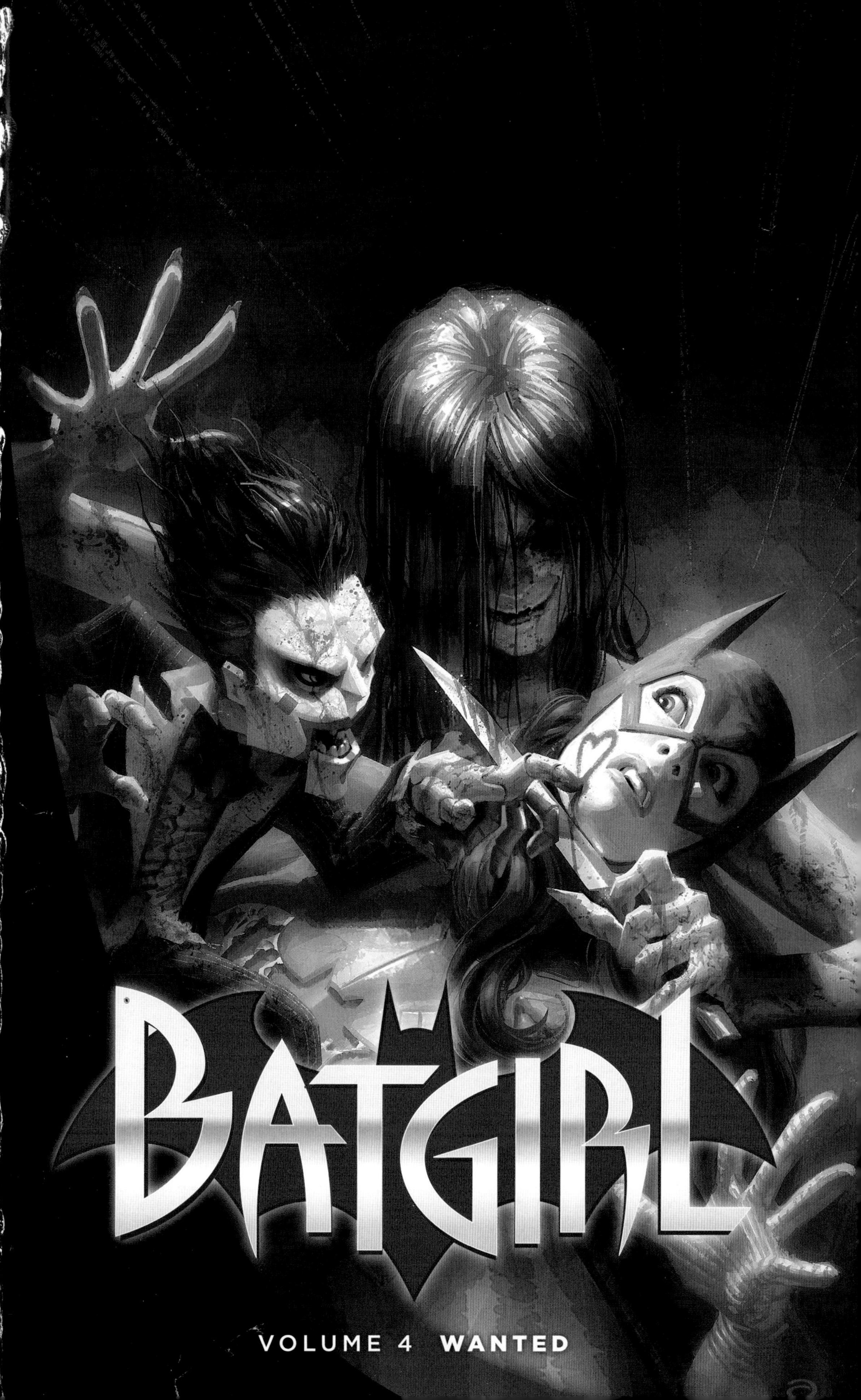
BATGIRL
VOLUME 4 WANTED

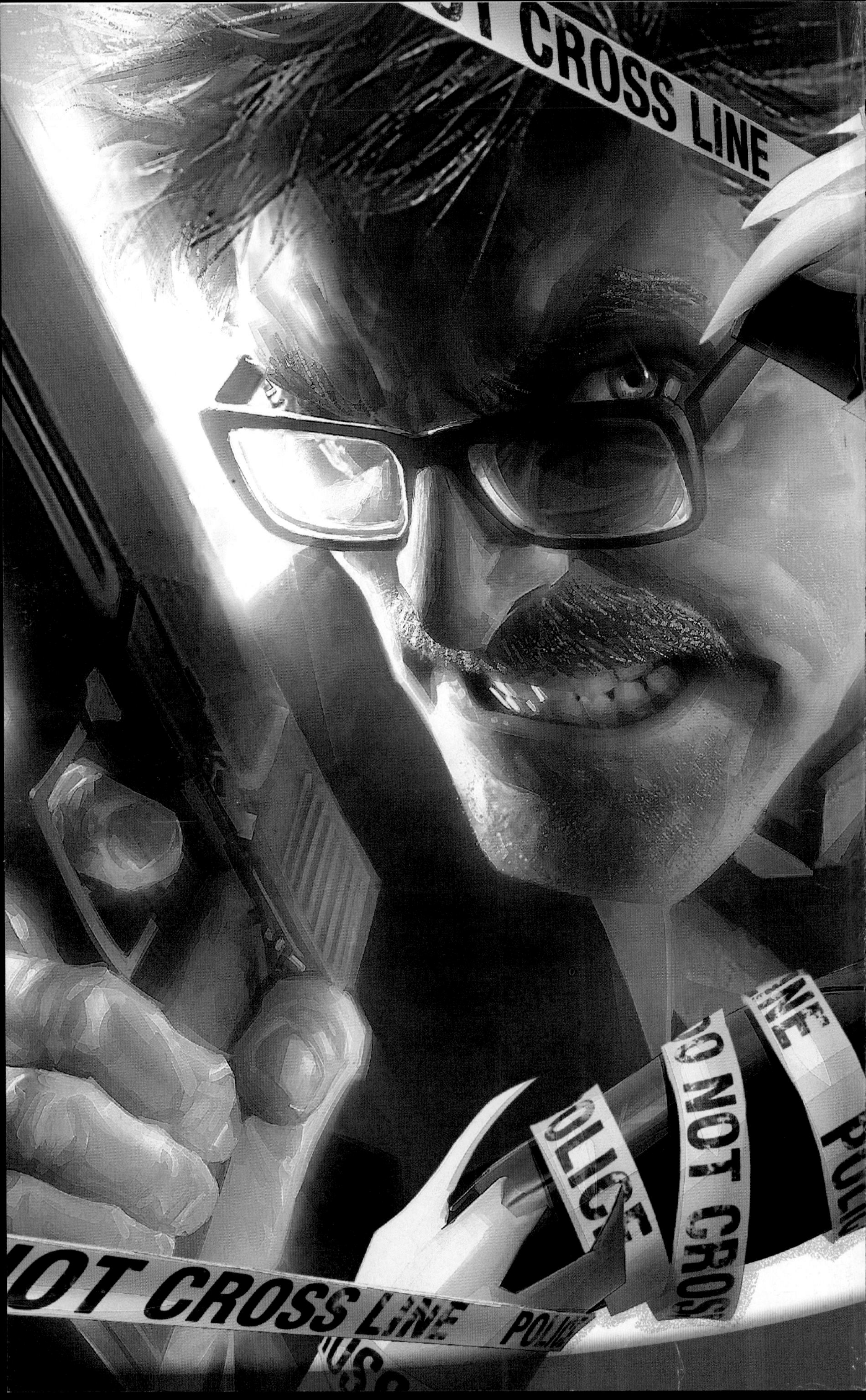

T CROSS LINE
DO NOT CROS
POLICE
OT CROSS LINE
POLICE

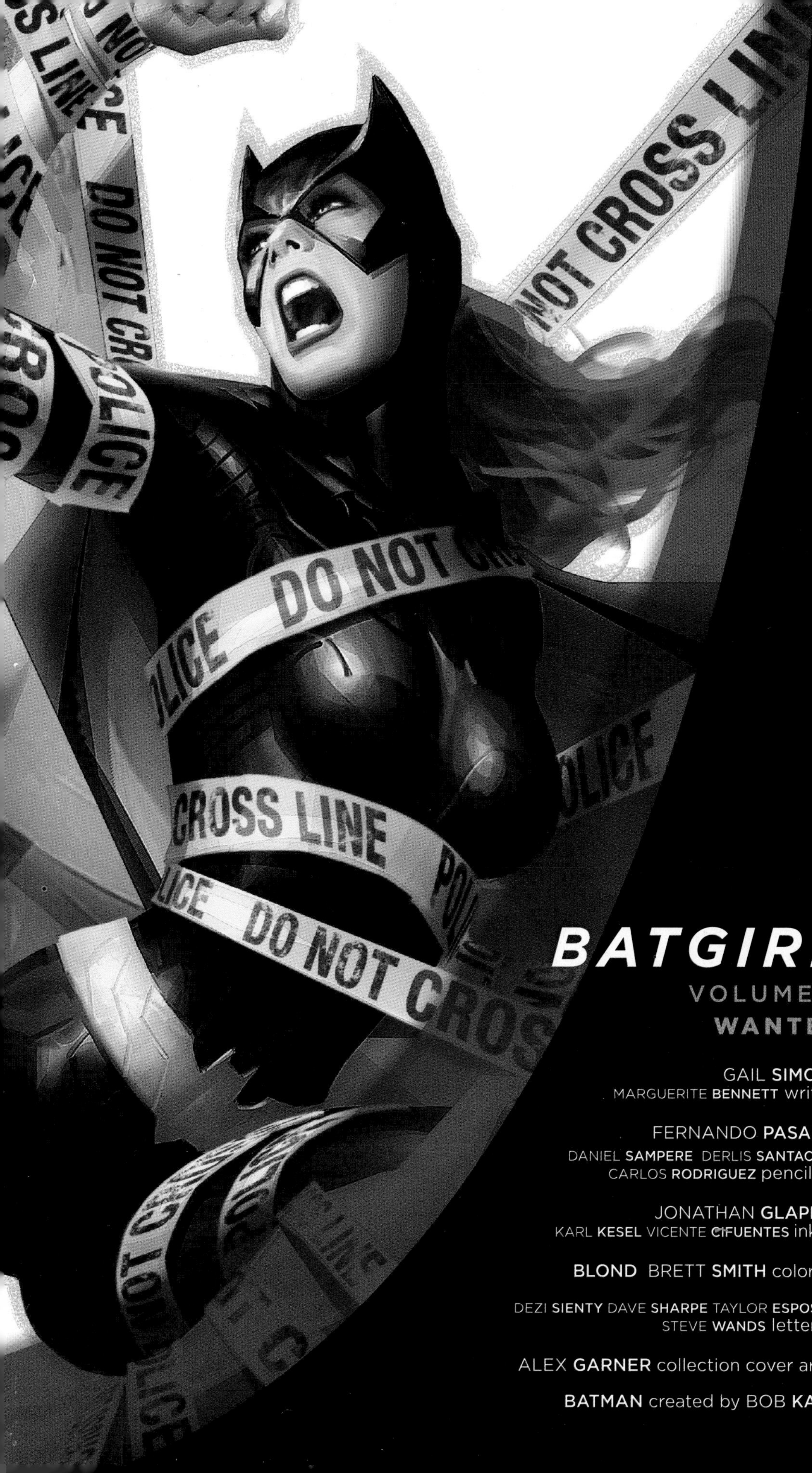
POLICE
DO NOT
CROSS LINE

BATGIRL

VOLUME 4
WANTED

GAIL **SIMONE**
MARGUERITE **BENNETT** writers

FERNANDO **PASARIN**
DANIEL **SAMPERE** DERLIS **SANTACRUZ**
CARLOS **RODRIGUEZ** pencillers

JONATHAN **GLAPION**
KARL **KESEL** VICENTE **CIFUENTES** inkers

BLOND BRETT **SMITH** colorists

DEZI **SIENTY** DAVE **SHARPE** TAYLOR **ESPOSITO**
STEVE **WANDS** letterers

ALEX **GARNER** collection cover artist

BATMAN created by BOB **KANE**

KATIE KUBERT Editor - Original Series ROBIN WILDMAN Editor
ROBBIN BROSTERMAN Design Director - Books ROBBIE BIEDERMAN Publication Design

BOB HARRAS Senior VP - Editor-in-Chief, DC Comics

DIANE NELSON President DAN DIDIO and JIM LEE Co-Publishers GEOFF JOHNS Chief Creative Officer
JOHN ROOD Executive VP - Sales, Marketing and Business Development AMY GENKINS Senior VP - Business and Legal Affairs
NAIRI GARDINER Senior VP - Finance JEFF BOISON VP - Publishing Planning MARK CHIARELLO VP - Art Direction and Design
JOHN CUNNINGHAM VP - Marketing TERRI CUNNINGHAM VP - Editorial Administration
ALISON GILL Senior VP - Manufacturing and Operations HANK KANALZ Senior VP - Vertigo and Integrated Publishing
JAY KOGAN VP - Business and Legal Affairs, Publishing JACK MAHAN VP - Business Affairs, Talent
NICK NAPOLITANO VP - Manufacturing Administration SUE POHJA VP - Book Sales
COURTNEY SIMMONS Senior VP - Publicity BOB WAYNE Senior VP - Sales

BATGIRL VOLUME 4: WANTED

DC Comics, 1700 Broadway, New York, NY 10019
A Warner Bros. Entertainment Company.
Printed by RR Donnelley, Salem, VA, USA. 5/21/14. First Printing.
ISBN: 978-1-4012-4629-7

SUSTAINABLE FORESTRY INITIATIVE

Certified Chain of Custody
At Least 20% Certified Forest Content
www.sfiprogram.org
SFI-01042
APPLIES TO TEXT STOCK ONLY

Library of Congress Cataloging-in-Publication Data

Simone, Gail, author.
Batgirl. Volume 4, Wanted / Gail Simone ; illustrated by Fernando Pasarin ; illustrated by Daniel Sampere.
pages cm. — (The New 52!)
Summary: "Batgirl struggles to continue fighting crime after being emotionally drained by the death of her brother, James, Jr. With her
relationships with Batman and her father strained, Batgirl face one of Batman's most ruthless villains, The Ventriloquist, alone.
— Provided by publisher.
ISBN 978-1-4012-4629-7
1. Graphic novels. I. Pasarin, Fernando, illustrator. II. Sampere, Daniel, 1985- illustrator. III. Title. IV. Title: Wanted.
PN6728.B358S59 2014
741.5'973—dc23
2014000325

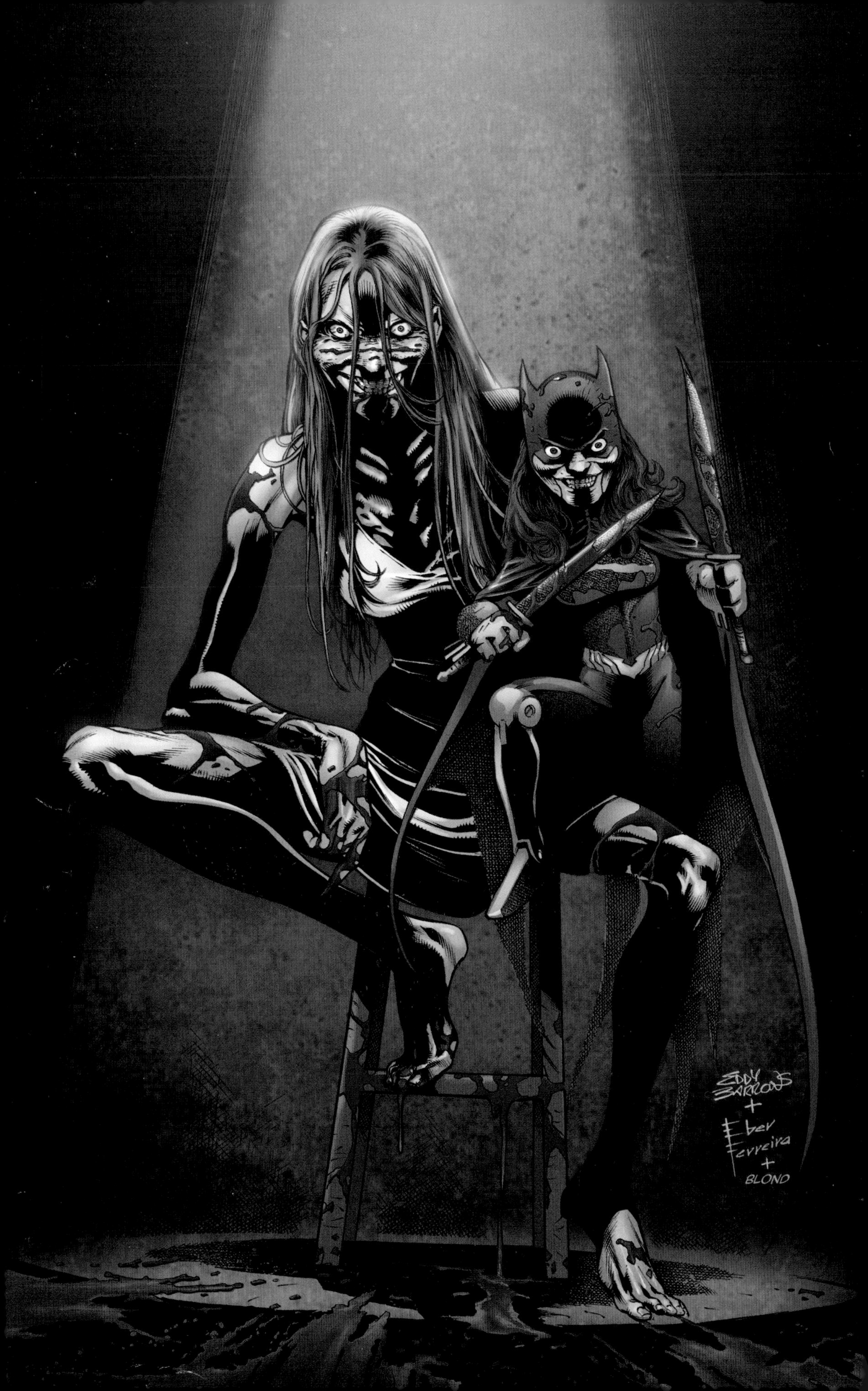
EDDY BARROWS
+
Eber Ferreira
+
BLOND

A SPLINTER WHERE MY HEART SHOULD BE

GAIL SIMONE writer **DANIEL SAMPERE CARLOS RODRIGUEZ** pencillers **JONATHAN GLAPION** inker **VICENTE CIFUENTES** additional finishes
BLOND colorist cover by **EDDY BARROWS, EBER FERREIRA** and **BLOND**

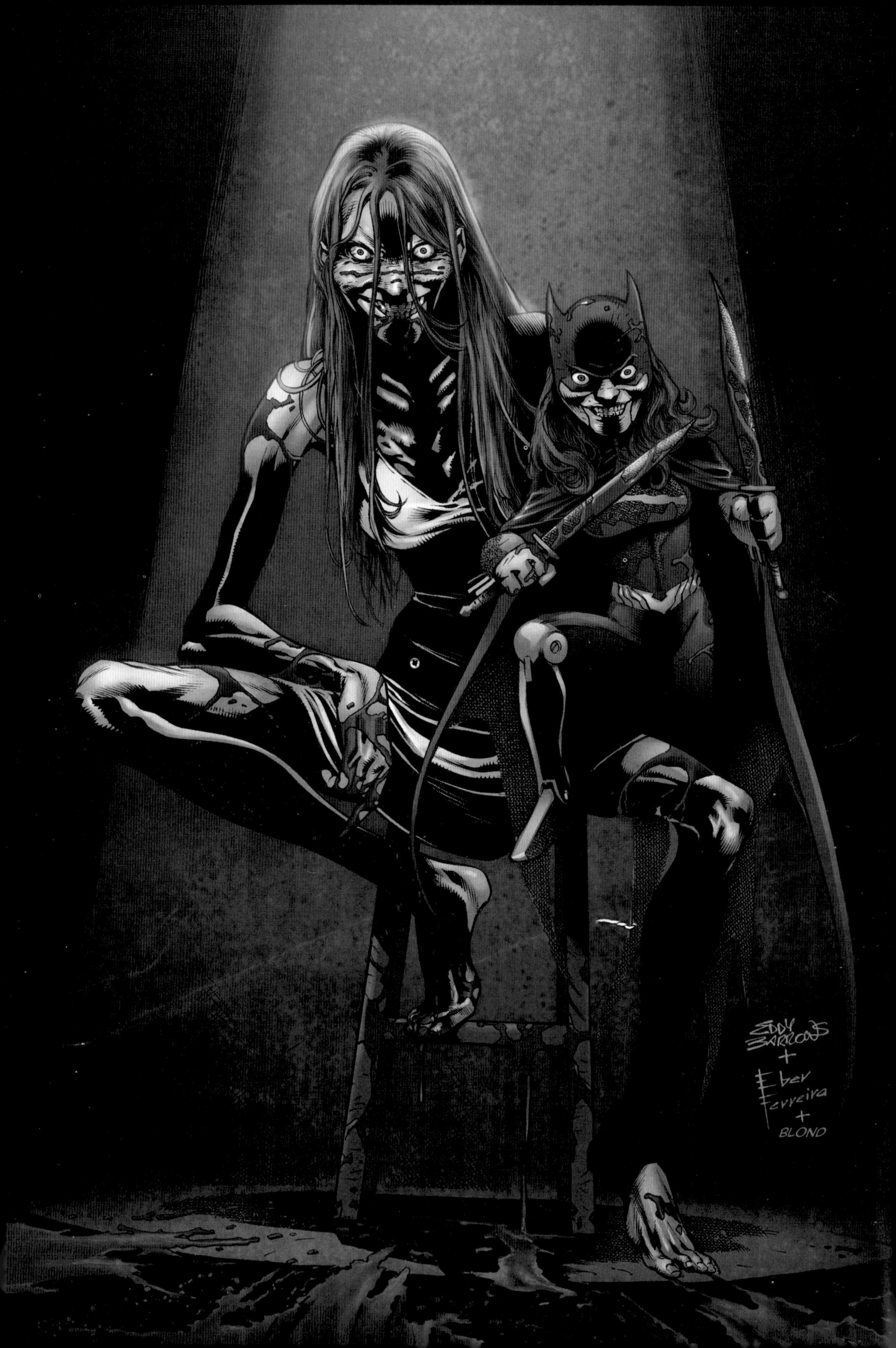
EDDY BARROWS
+
Eber Ferreira
+
BLOND

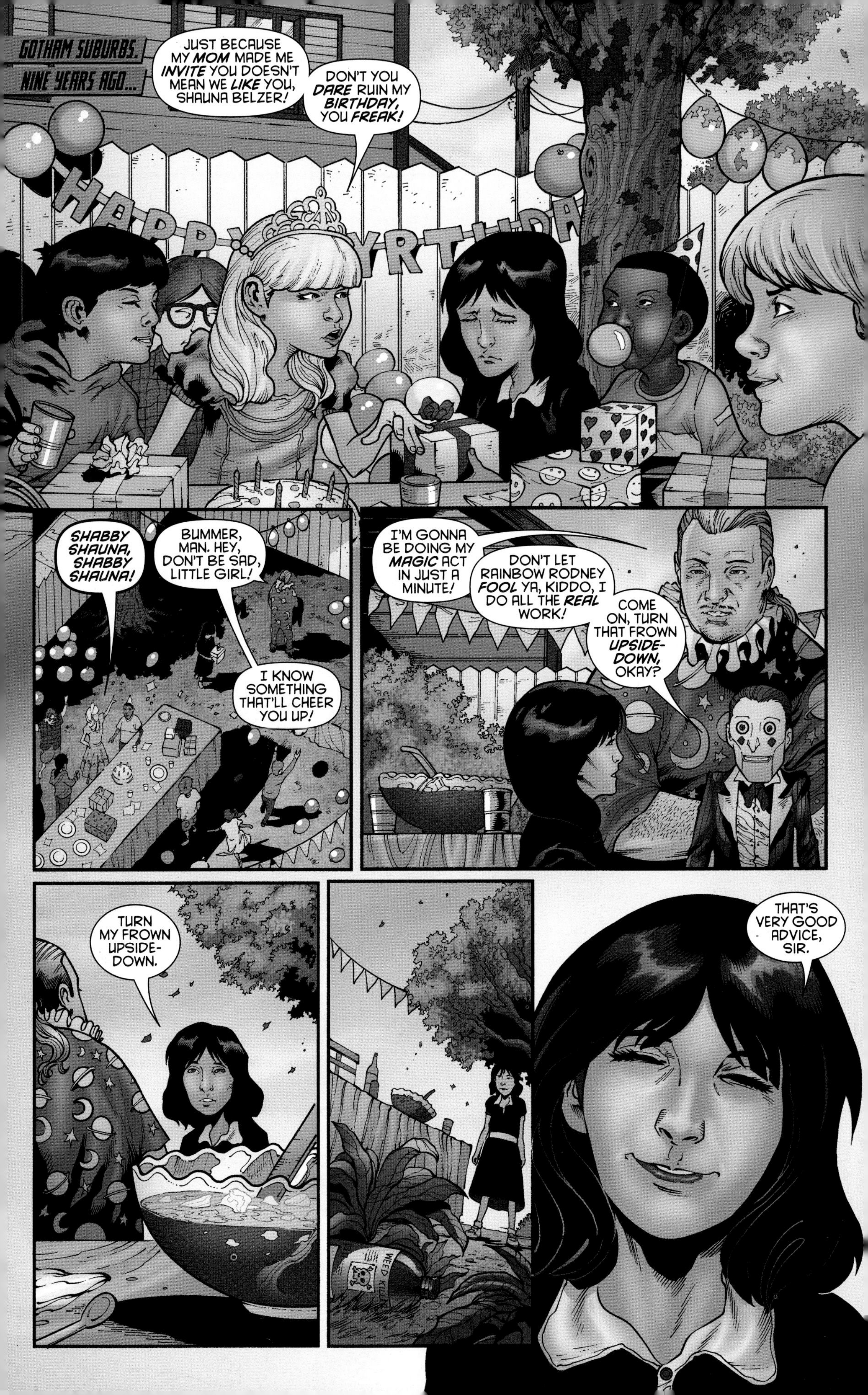

GOTHAM SUBURBS.
NINE YEARS AGO...
JUST BECAUSE MY MOM MADE ME INVITE YOU DOESN'T MEAN WE LIKE YOU, SHAUNA BELZER!
DON'T YOU DARE RUIN MY BIRTHDAY, YOU FREAK!
HAPPY BIRTHDAY
SHABBY SHAUNA, SHABBY SHAUNA!
BUMMER, MAN. HEY, DON'T BE SAD, LITTLE GIRL!
I KNOW SOMETHING THAT'LL CHEER YOU UP!
I'M GONNA BE DOING MY MAGIC ACT IN JUST A MINUTE!
DON'T LET RAINBOW RODNEY FOOL YA, KIDDO, I DO ALL THE REAL WORK!
COME ON, TURN THAT FROWN UPSIDE-DOWN, OKAY?
TURN MY FROWN UPSIDE-DOWN.
WEED KILLER
THAT'S VERY GOOD ADVICE, SIR.

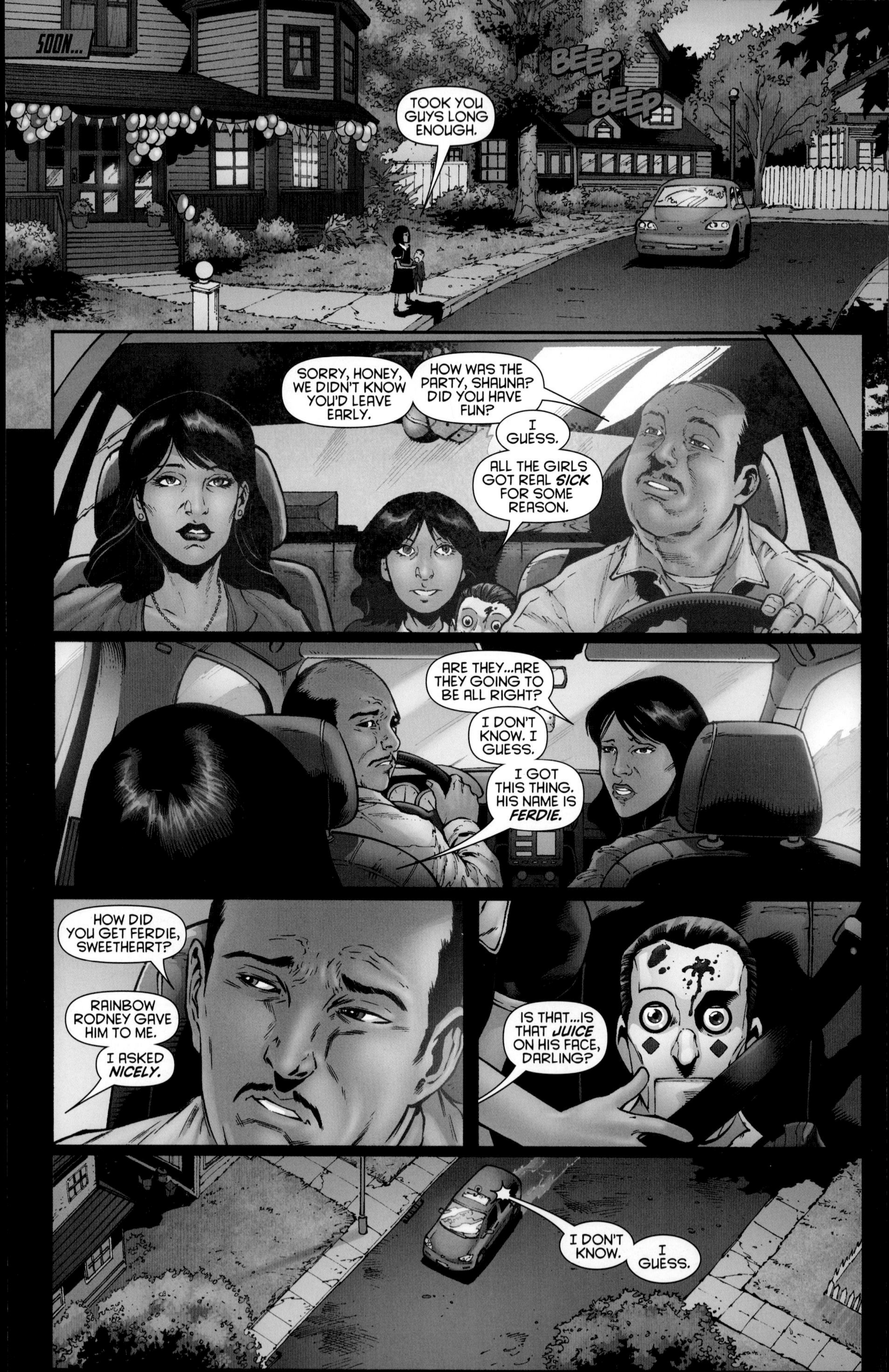
SOON...
BEEP
BEEP
TOOK YOU GUYS LONG ENOUGH.
SORRY, HONEY, WE DIDN'T KNOW YOU'D LEAVE EARLY.
HOW WAS THE PARTY, SHAUNA? DID YOU HAVE FUN?
I GUESS.
ALL THE GIRLS GOT REAL SICK FOR SOME REASON.
ARE THEY...ARE THEY GOING TO BE ALL RIGHT?
I DON'T KNOW. I GUESS.
I GOT THIS THING. HIS NAME IS FERDIE.
HOW DID YOU GET FERDIE, SWEETHEART?
RAINBOW RODNEY GAVE HIM TO ME.
I ASKED NICELY.
IS THAT...IS THAT JUICE ON HIS FACE, DARLING?
I DON'T KNOW.
I GUESS.

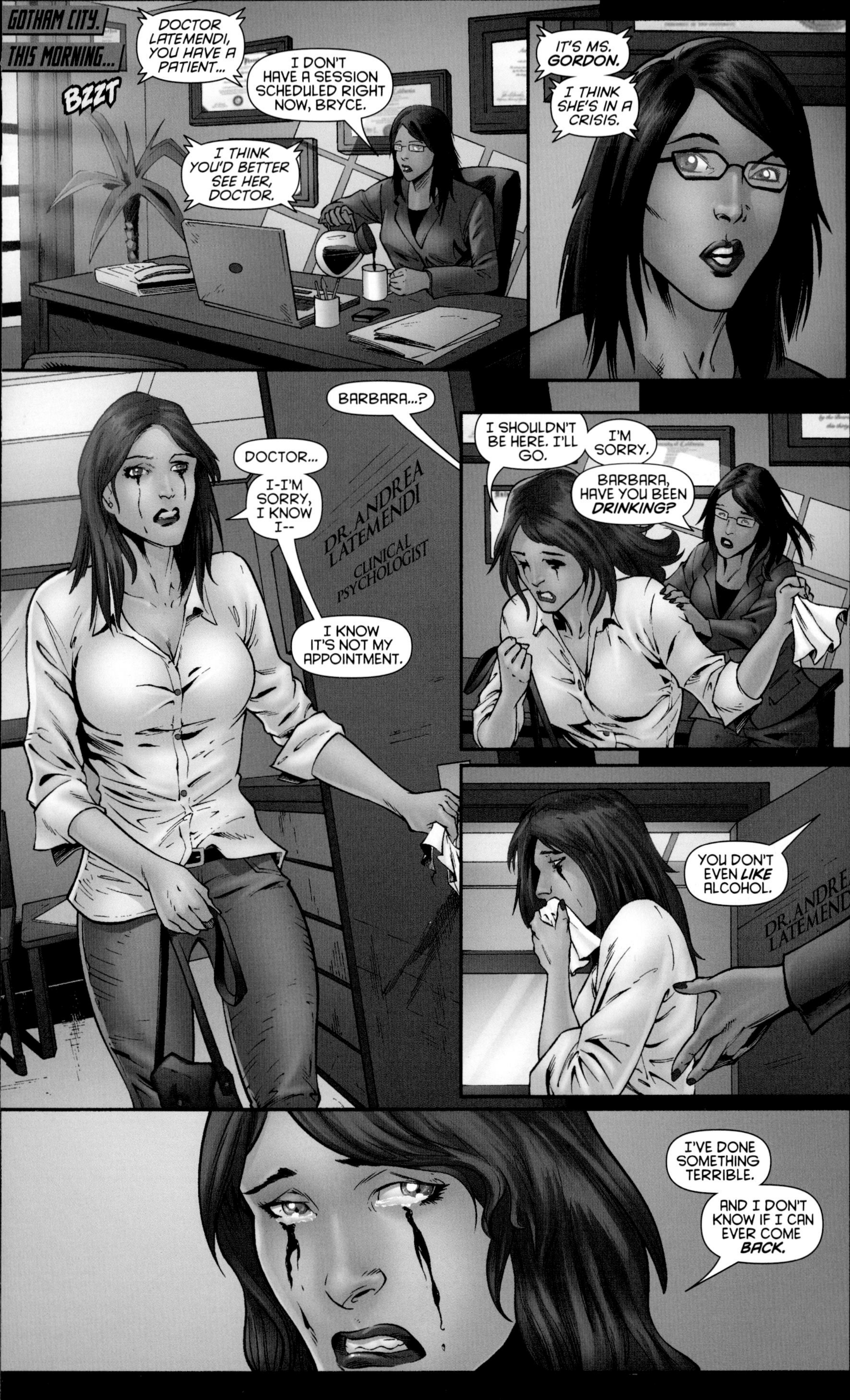
GOTHAM CITY.
THIS MORNING...
DOCTOR LATEMENDI, YOU HAVE A PATIENT...
BZZT
I DON'T HAVE A SESSION SCHEDULED RIGHT NOW, BRYCE.
I THINK YOU'D BETTER SEE HER, DOCTOR.
IT'S MS. GORDON.
I THINK SHE'S IN A CRISIS.
BARBARA...?
DOCTOR...
I-I'M SORRY, I KNOW I--
DR. ANDREA LATEMENDI
CLINICAL PSYCHOLOGIST
I KNOW IT'S NOT MY APPOINTMENT.
I SHOULDN'T BE HERE. I'LL GO.
I'M SORRY.
BARBARA, HAVE YOU BEEN DRINKING?
YOU DON'T EVEN LIKE ALCOHOL.
I'VE DONE SOMETHING TERRIBLE.
AND I DON'T KNOW IF I CAN EVER COME BACK.

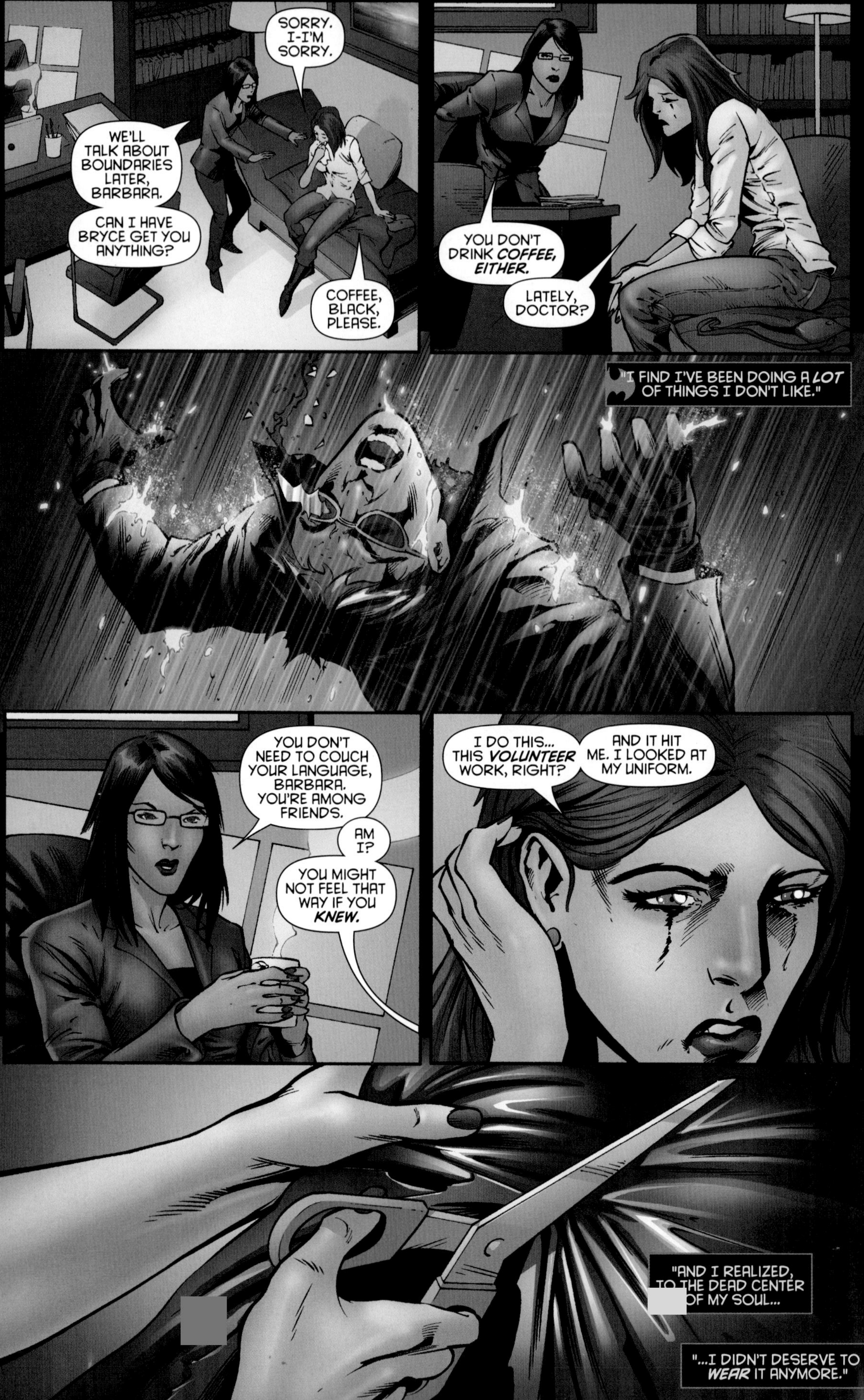
SORRY. I-I'M SORRY.
WE'LL TALK ABOUT BOUNDARIES LATER, BARBARA.
CAN I HAVE BRYCE GET YOU ANYTHING?
COFFEE, BLACK, PLEASE.
YOU DON'T DRINK COFFEE, EITHER.
LATELY, DOCTOR?
"I FIND I'VE BEEN DOING A LOT OF THINGS I DON'T LIKE."
YOU DON'T NEED TO COUCH YOUR LANGUAGE, BARBARA. YOU'RE AMONG FRIENDS.
AM I?
YOU MIGHT NOT FEEL THAT WAY IF YOU KNEW.
I DO THIS... THIS VOLUNTEER WORK, RIGHT?
AND IT HIT ME. I LOOKED AT MY UNIFORM.
"AND I REALIZED, TO THE DEAD CENTER OF MY SOUL...
"...I DIDN'T DESERVE TO WEAR IT ANYMORE."

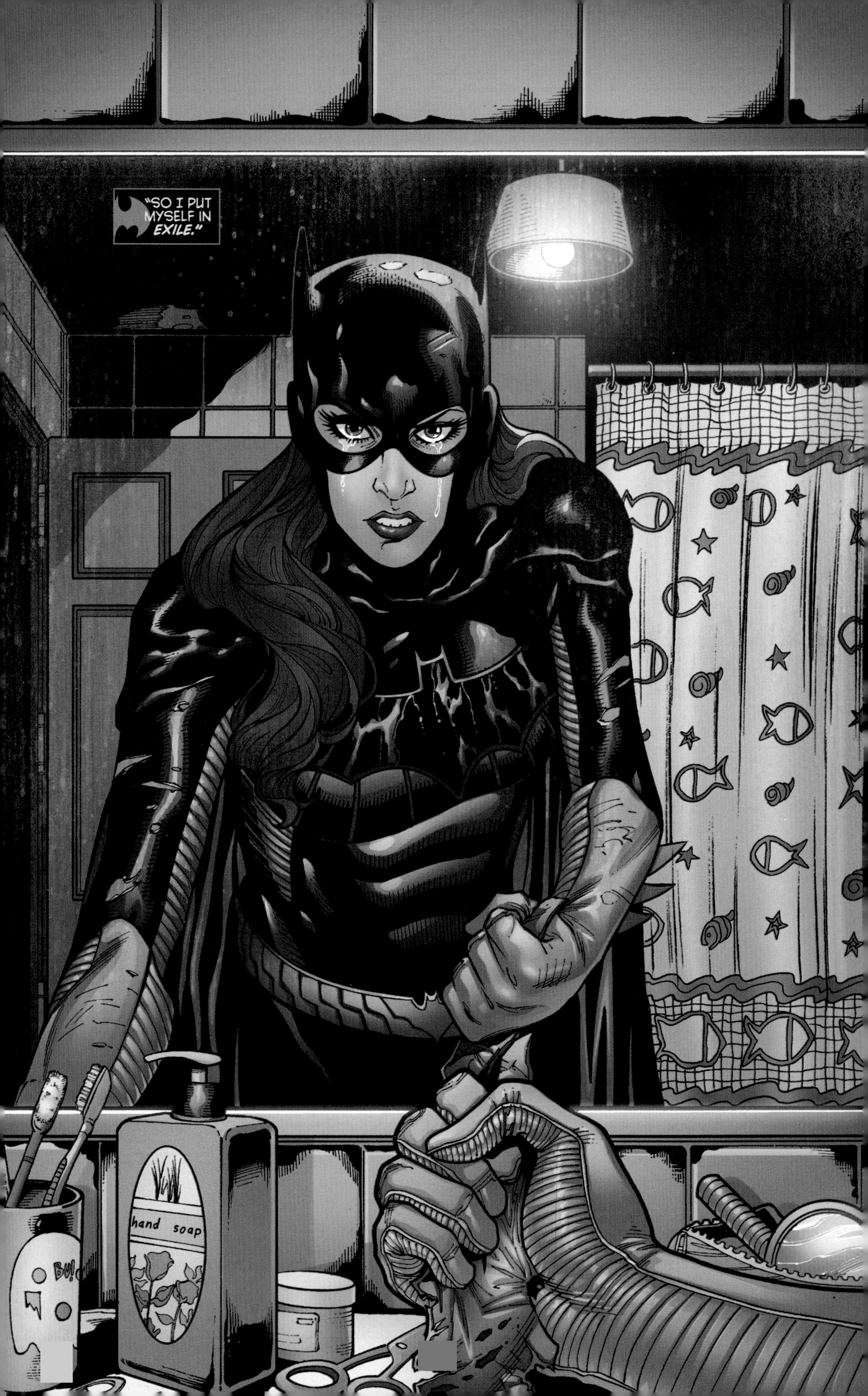
"SO I PUT MYSELF IN EXILE."
hand soap
BU!

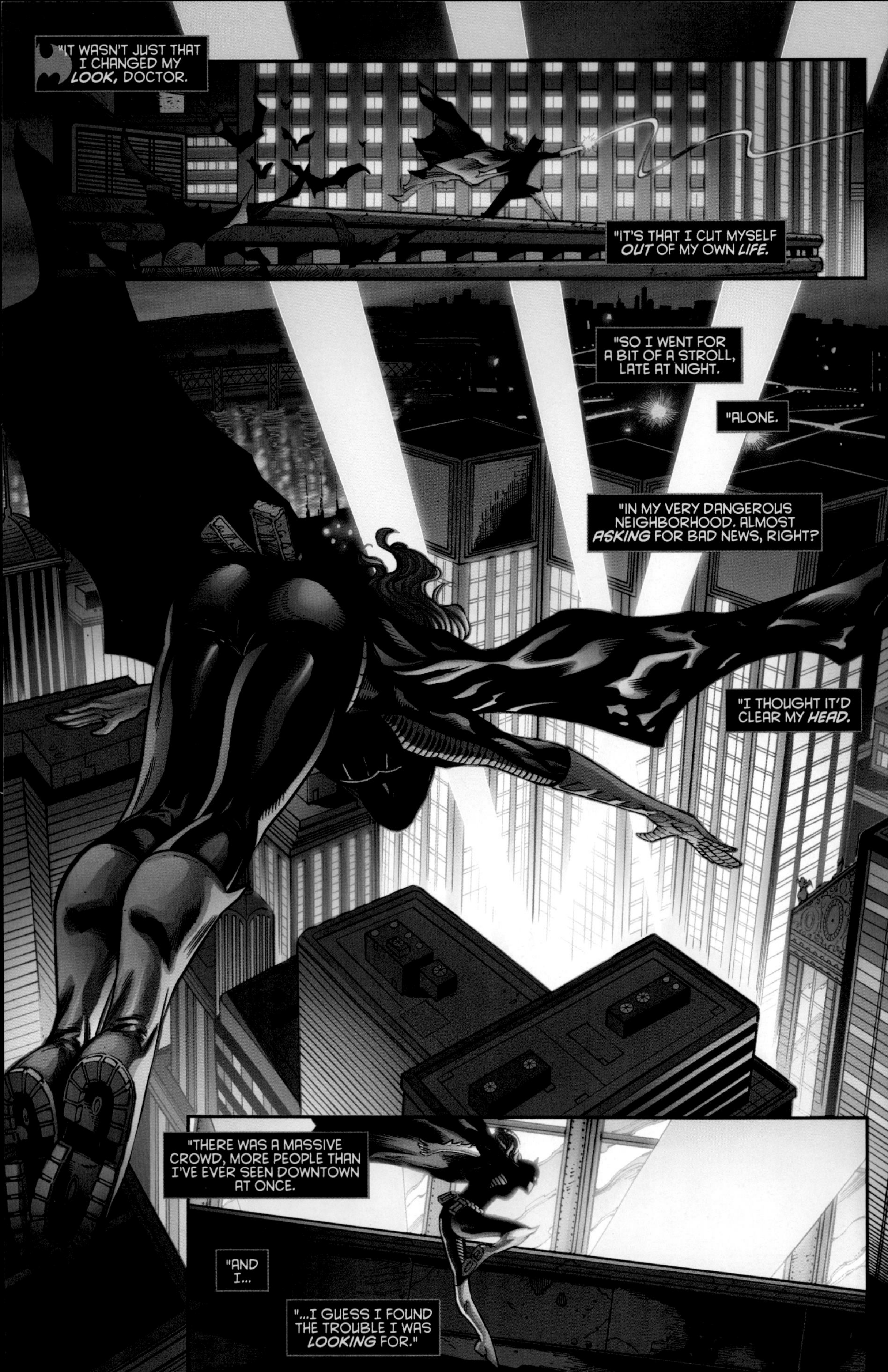
"IT WASN'T JUST THAT I CHANGED MY *LOOK*, DOCTOR.
"IT'S THAT I CUT MYSELF *OUT* OF MY OWN *LIFE*.
"SO I WENT FOR A BIT OF A STROLL, LATE AT NIGHT.
"ALONE.
"IN MY VERY DANGEROUS NEIGHBORHOOD. ALMOST *ASKING* FOR BAD NEWS, RIGHT?
"I THOUGHT IT'D CLEAR MY *HEAD*.
"THERE WAS A MASSIVE CROWD, MORE PEOPLE THAN I'VE EVER SEEN DOWNTOWN AT ONCE.
"AND I...
"...I GUESS I FOUND THE TROUBLE I WAS *LOOKING* FOR."

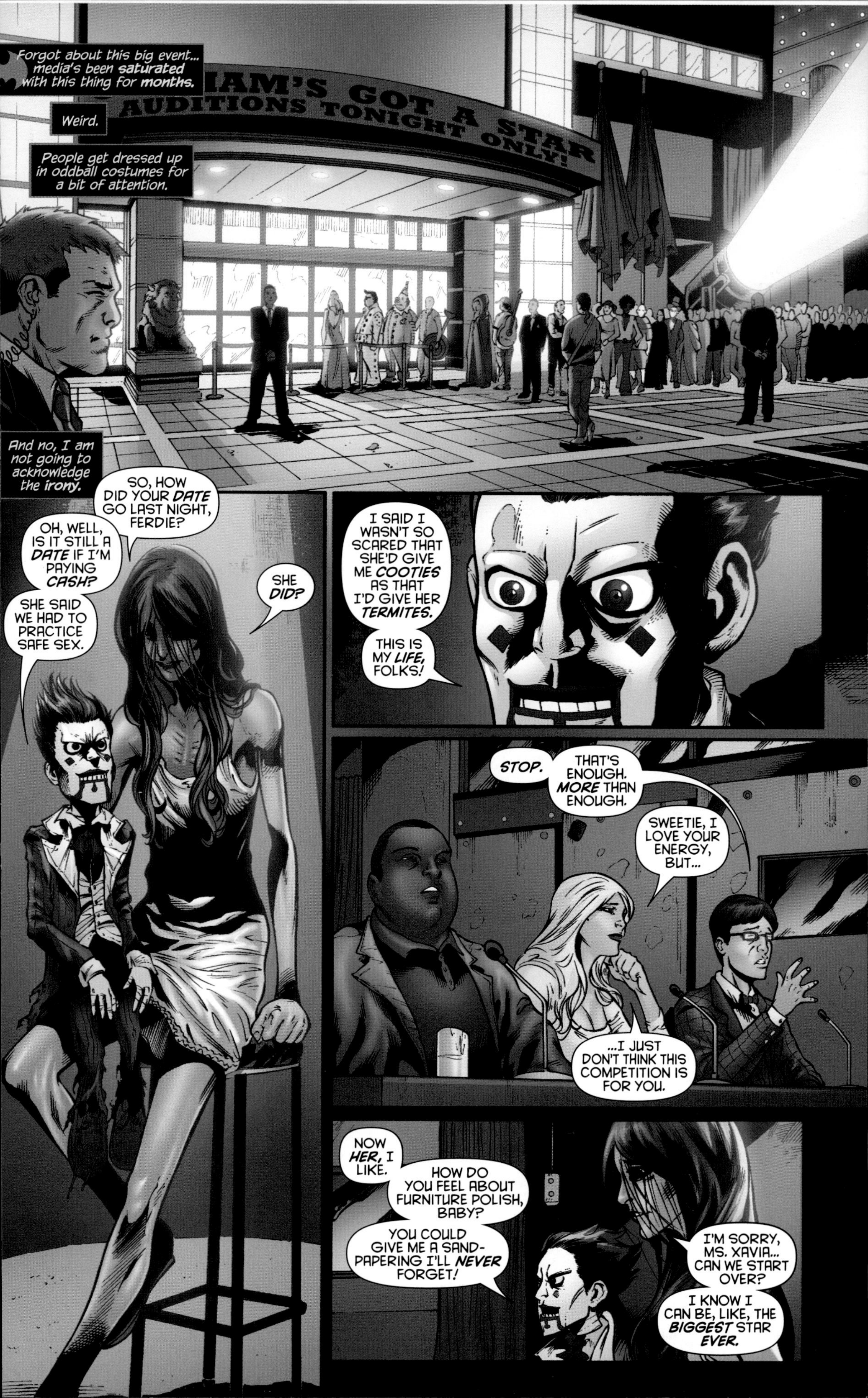

Forgot about this big event... media's been saturated with this thing for months.
Weird.
People get dressed up in oddball costumes for a bit of attention.
...IAM'S GOT A STAR AUDITIONS TONIGHT ONLY!
And no, I am not going to acknowledge the irony.
SO, HOW DID YOUR DATE GO LAST NIGHT, FERDIE?
OH, WELL, IS IT STILL A DATE IF I'M PAYING CASH?
SHE SAID WE HAD TO PRACTICE SAFE SEX.
SHE DID?
I SAID I WASN'T SO SCARED THAT SHE'D GIVE ME COOTIES AS THAT I'D GIVE HER TERMITES.
THIS IS MY LIFE, FOLKS!
STOP.
THAT'S ENOUGH. MORE THAN ENOUGH.
SWEETIE, I LOVE YOUR ENERGY, BUT...
...I JUST DON'T THINK THIS COMPETITION IS FOR YOU.
NOW HER, I LIKE.
HOW DO YOU FEEL ABOUT FURNITURE POLISH, BABY?
YOU COULD GIVE ME A SAND-PAPERING I'LL NEVER FORGET!
I'M SORRY, MS. XAVIA... CAN WE START OVER?
I KNOW I CAN BE, LIKE, THE BIGGEST STAR EVER.

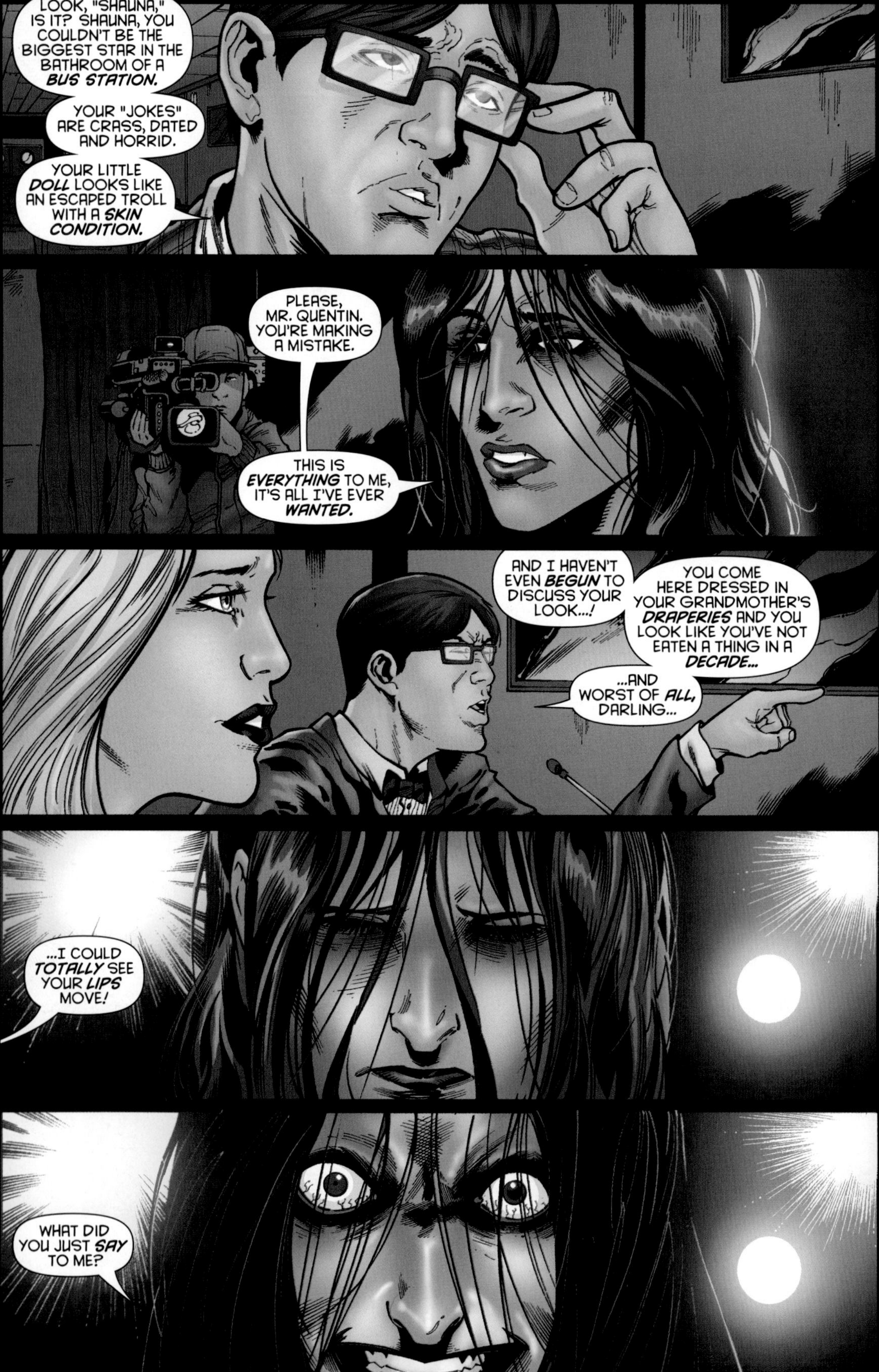
LOOK, "SHAUNA," IS IT? SHAUNA, YOU COULDN'T BE THE BIGGEST STAR IN THE BATHROOM OF A BUS STATION.
YOUR "JOKES" ARE CRASS, DATED AND HORRID.
YOUR LITTLE DOLL LOOKS LIKE AN ESCAPED TROLL WITH A SKIN CONDITION.
PLEASE, MR. QUENTIN. YOU'RE MAKING A MISTAKE.
THIS IS EVERYTHING TO ME, IT'S ALL I'VE EVER WANTED.
AND I HAVEN'T EVEN BEGUN TO DISCUSS YOUR LOOK...!
YOU COME HERE DRESSED IN YOUR GRANDMOTHER'S DRAPERIES AND YOU LOOK LIKE YOU'VE NOT EATEN A THING IN A DECADE...
...AND WORST OF ALL, DARLING...
...I COULD TOTALLY SEE YOUR LIPS MOVE!
WHAT DID YOU JUST SAY TO ME?

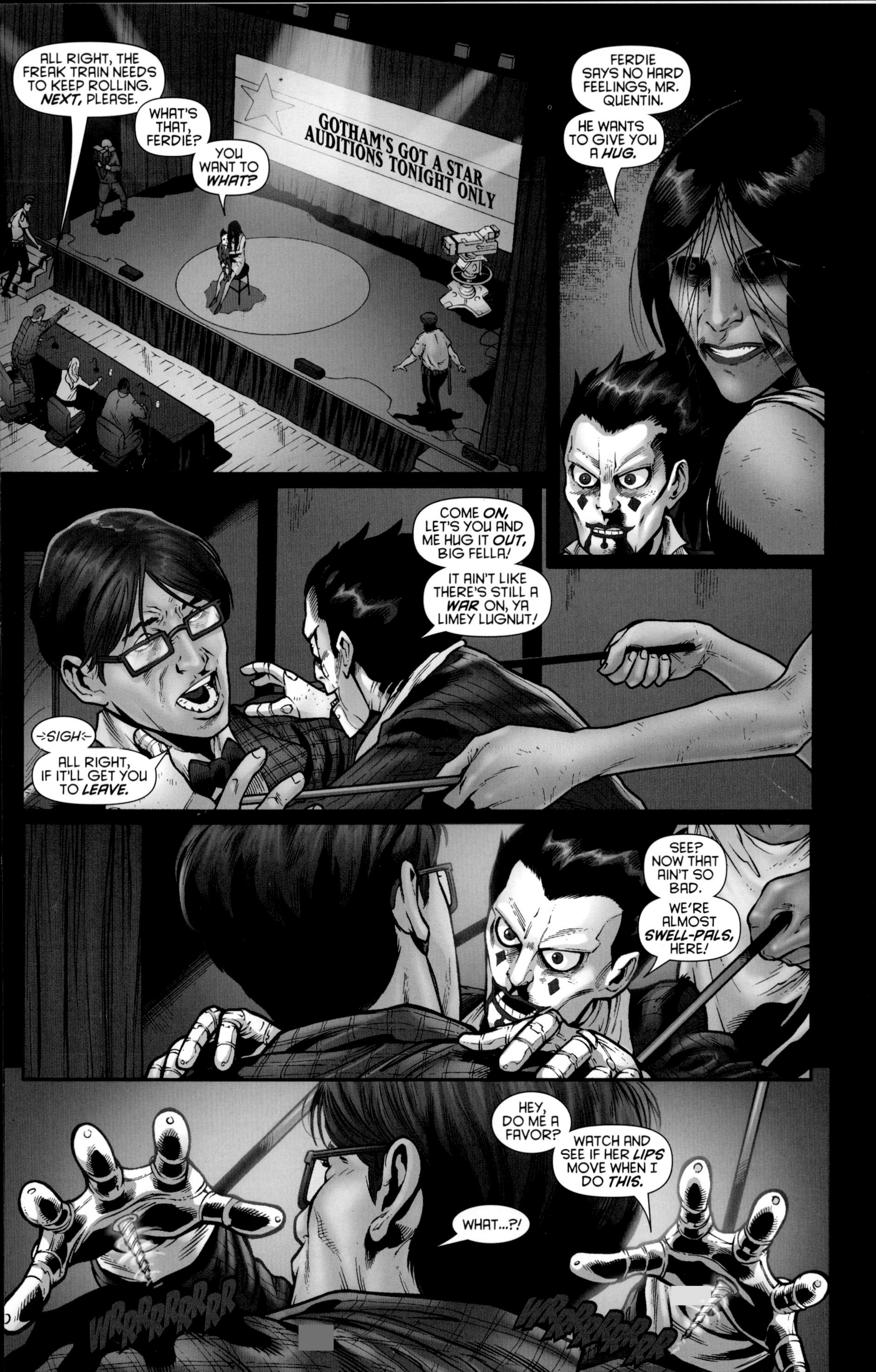
ALL RIGHT, THE FREAK TRAIN NEEDS TO KEEP ROLLING. NEXT, PLEASE.
WHAT'S THAT, FERDIE?
YOU WANT TO WHAT?
GOTHAM'S GOT A STAR
AUDITIONS TONIGHT ONLY
FERDIE SAYS NO HARD FEELINGS, MR. QUENTIN.
HE WANTS TO GIVE YOU A HUG.
COME ON, LET'S YOU AND ME HUG IT OUT, BIG FELLA!
IT AIN'T LIKE THERE'S STILL A WAR ON, YA LIMEY LUGNUT!
-SIGH-
ALL RIGHT, IF IT'LL GET YOU TO LEAVE.
SEE? NOW THAT AIN'T SO BAD.
WE'RE ALMOST SWELL-PALS, HERE!
HEY, DO ME A FAVOR?
WATCH AND SEE IF HER LIPS MOVE WHEN I DO THIS.
WHAT...?!
WRRRRRRRRRR
WRRRRRRRRRR

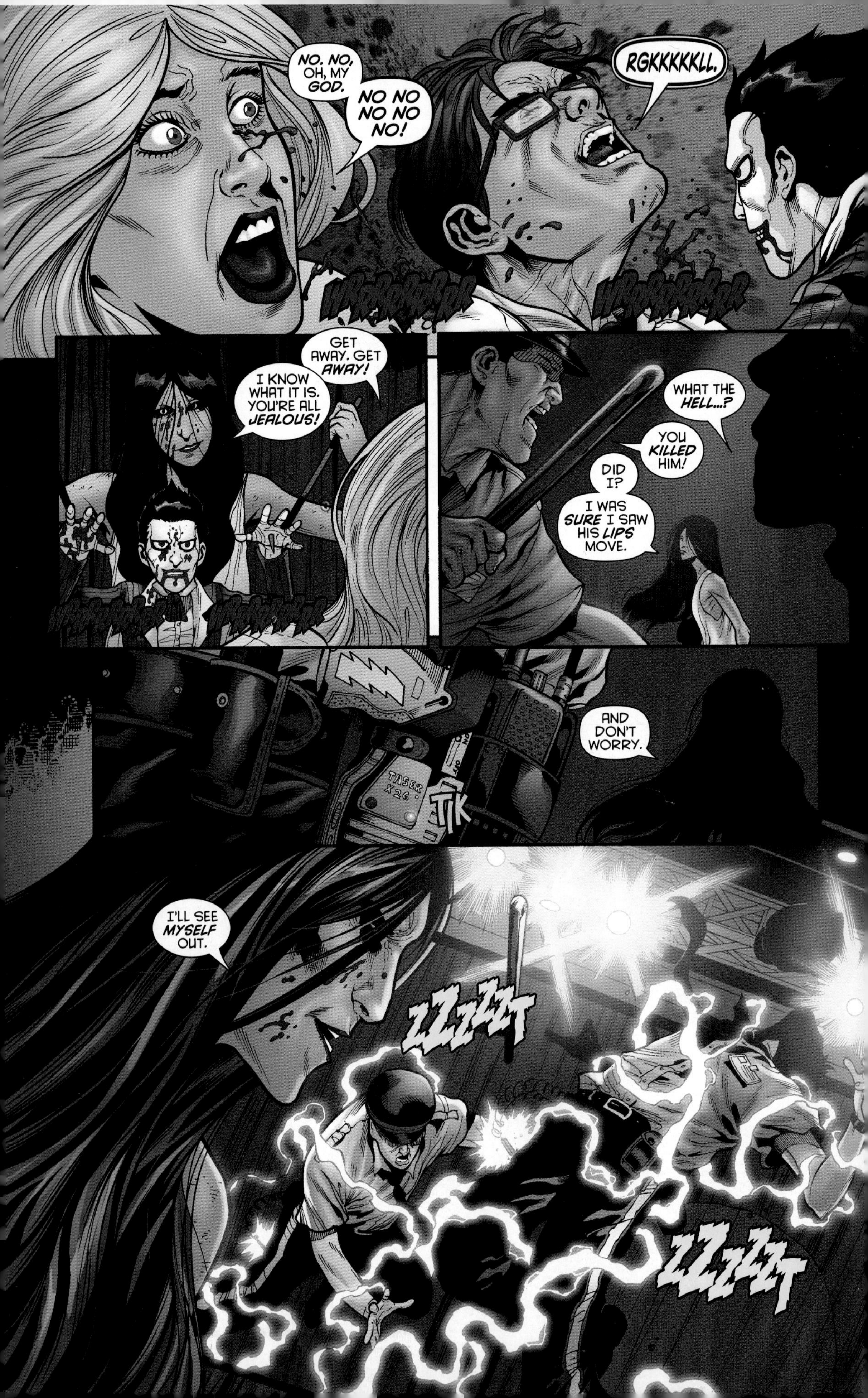
NO, NO, OH, MY GOD.
NO NO NO NO NO!
RGKKKKKLL.
GET AWAY. GET AWAY!
I KNOW WHAT IT IS. YOU'RE ALL JEALOUS!
WHAT THE HELL...?
YOU KILLED HIM!
DID I?
I WAS SURE I SAW HIS LIPS MOVE.
AND DON'T WORRY.
TASER X26
TIK
I'LL SEE MYSELF OUT.
ZZZZZT
ZZZZZZT

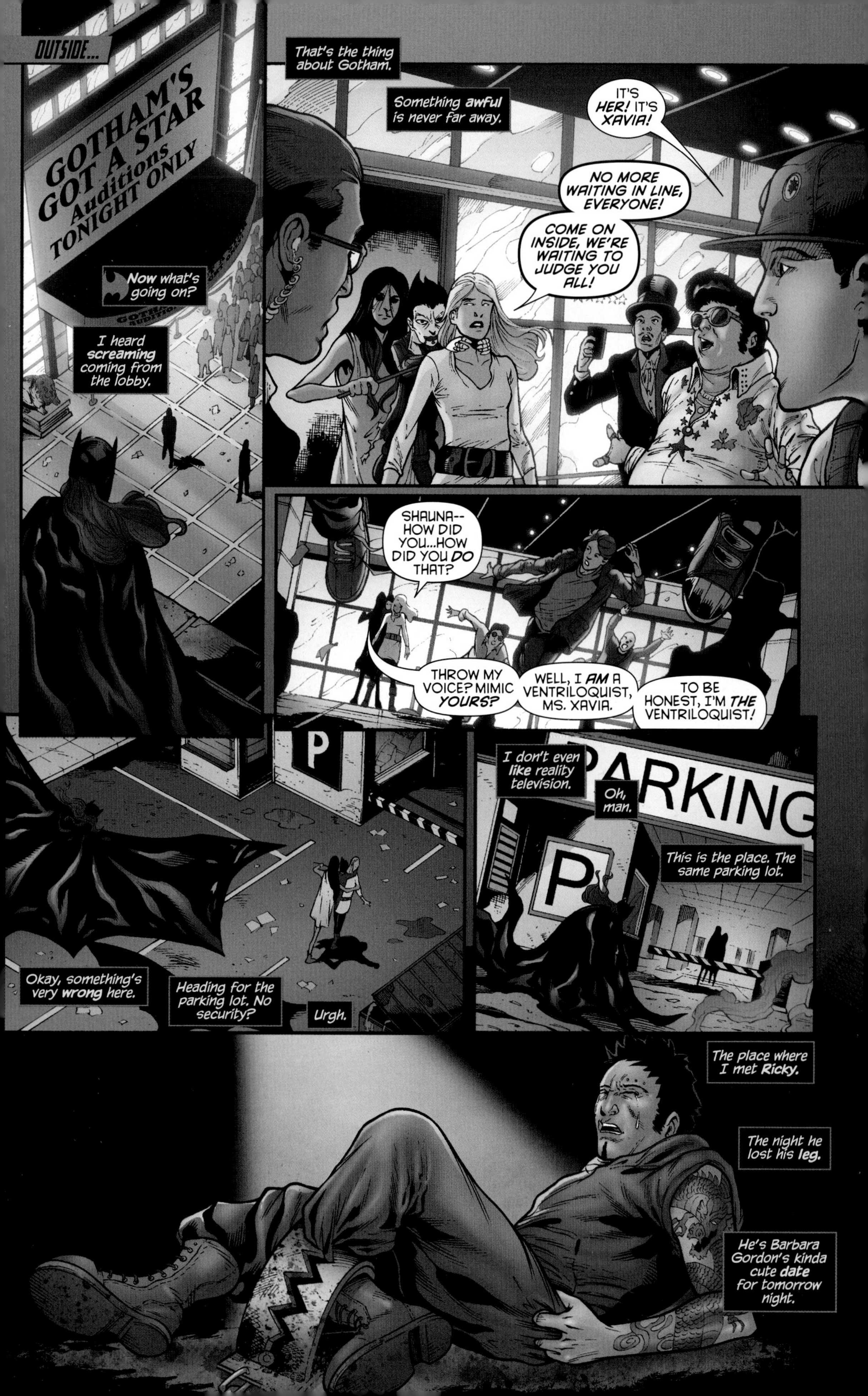
OUTSIDE...
GOTHAM'S GOT A STAR
Auditions
TONIGHT ONLY
Now what's going on?
I heard screaming coming from the lobby.
That's the thing about Gotham.
Something awful is never far away.
IT'S HER! IT'S XAVIA!
NO MORE WAITING IN LINE, EVERYONE!
COME ON INSIDE, WE'RE WAITING TO JUDGE YOU ALL!
SHAUNA-- HOW DID YOU...HOW DID YOU DO THAT?
THROW MY VOICE? MIMIC YOURS?
WELL, I AM A VENTRILOQUIST, MS. XAVIA.
TO BE HONEST, I'M THE VENTRILOQUIST!
P
Okay, something's very wrong here.
Heading for the parking lot. No security?
Urgh.
PARKING
P
I don't even like reality television.
Oh, man.
This is the place. The same parking lot.
The place where I met Ricky.
The night he lost his leg.
He's Barbara Gordon's kinda cute date for tomorrow night.

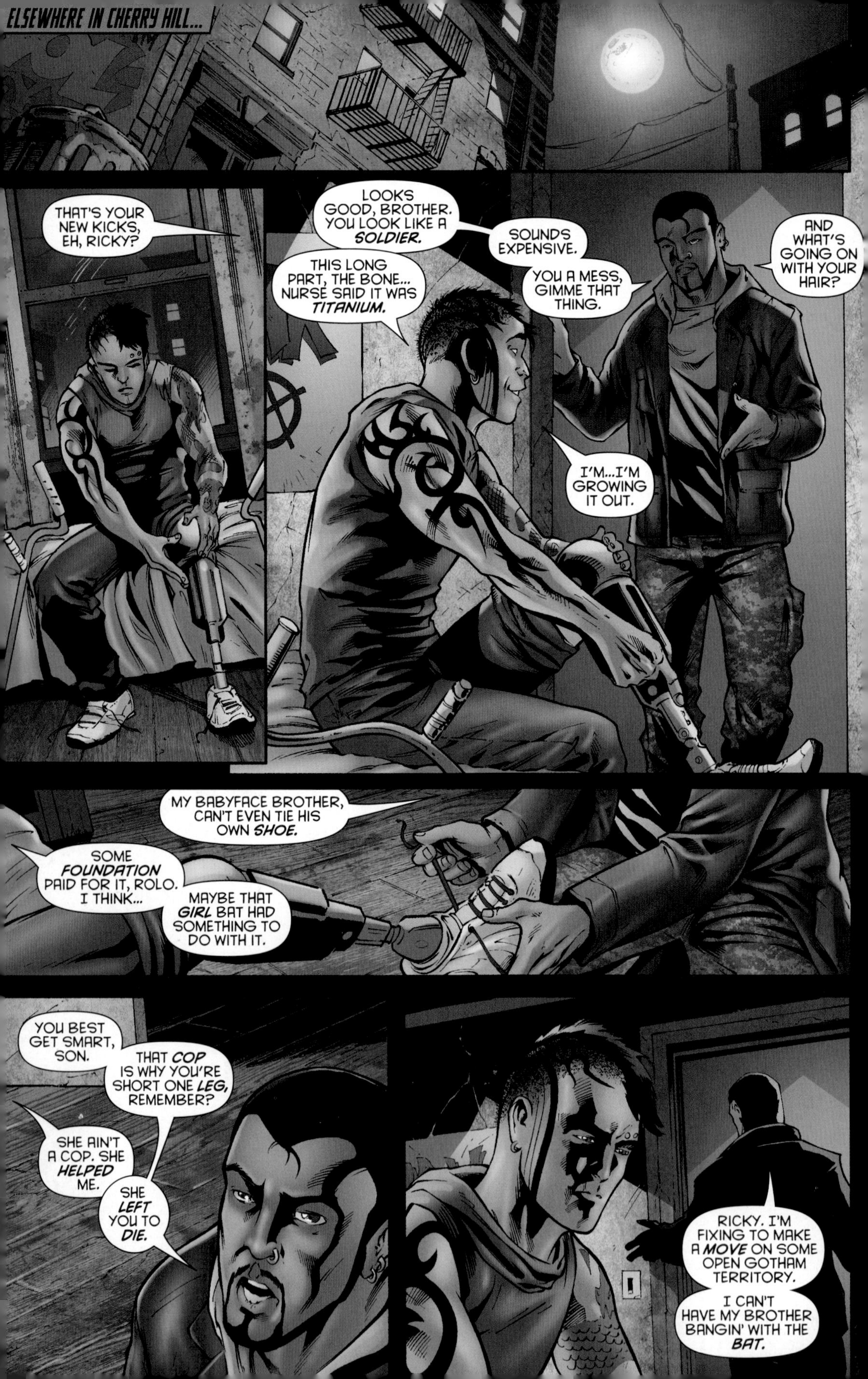
ELSEWHERE IN CHERRY HILL...
THAT'S YOUR NEW KICKS, EH, RICKY?
LOOKS GOOD, BROTHER. YOU LOOK LIKE A SOLDIER.
THIS LONG PART, THE BONE... NURSE SAID IT WAS TITANIUM.
SOUNDS EXPENSIVE.
YOU A MESS, GIMME THAT THING.
AND WHAT'S GOING ON WITH YOUR HAIR?
I'M...I'M GROWING IT OUT.
MY BABYFACE BROTHER, CAN'T EVEN TIE HIS OWN SHOE.
SOME FOUNDATION PAID FOR IT, ROLO. I THINK...
MAYBE THAT GIRL BAT HAD SOMETHING TO DO WITH IT.
YOU BEST GET SMART, SON.
THAT COP IS WHY YOU'RE SHORT ONE LEG, REMEMBER?
SHE AIN'T A COP. SHE HELPED ME.
SHE LEFT YOU TO DIE.
RICKY. I'M FIXING TO MAKE A MOVE ON SOME OPEN GOTHAM TERRITORY.
I CAN'T HAVE MY BROTHER BANGIN' WITH THE BAT.

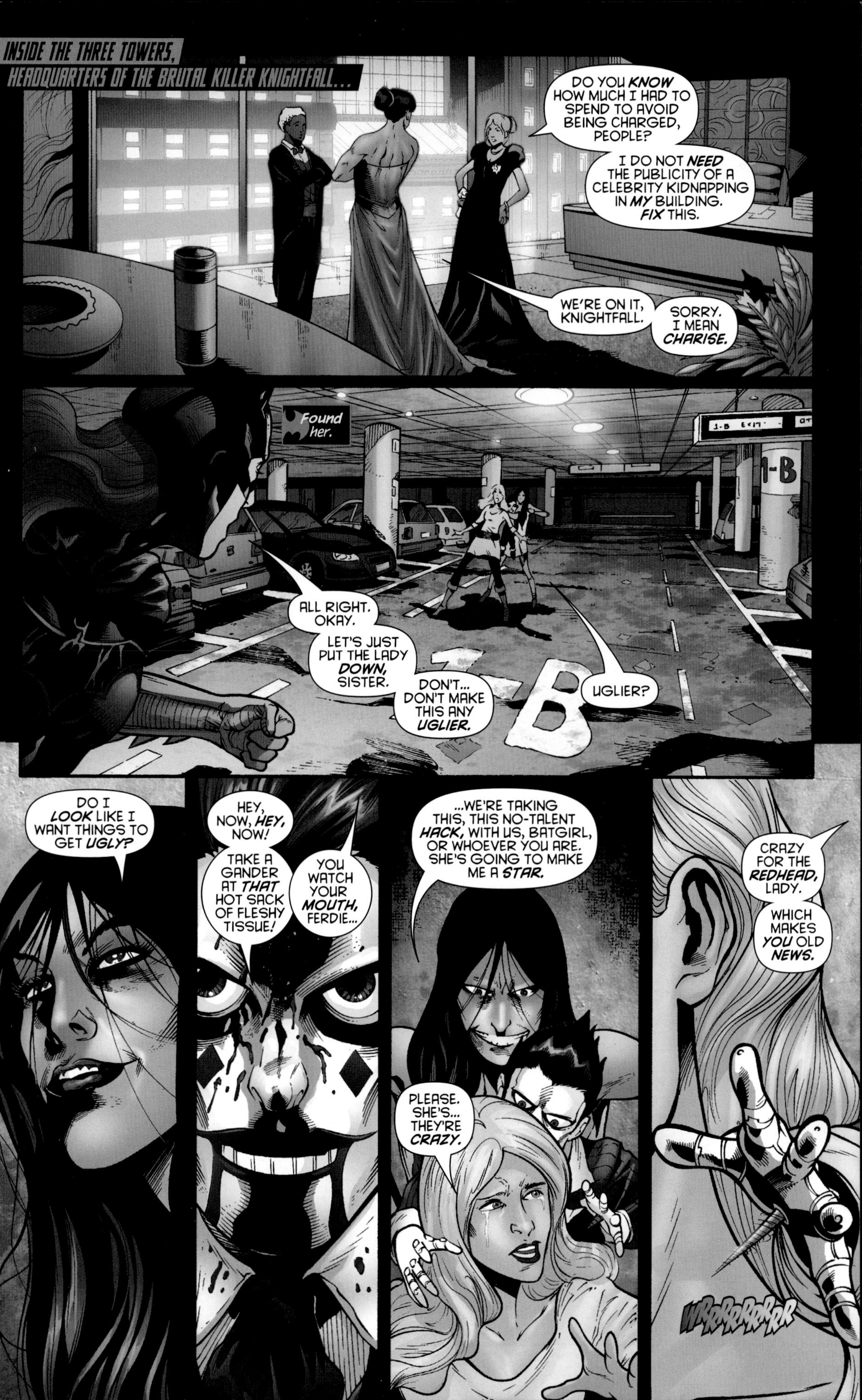
INSIDE THE THREE TOWERS, HEADQUARTERS OF THE BRUTAL KILLER KNIGHTFALL...
DO YOU KNOW HOW MUCH I HAD TO SPEND TO AVOID BEING CHARGED, PEOPLE?
I DO NOT NEED THE PUBLICITY OF A CELEBRITY KIDNAPPING IN MY BUILDING. FIX THIS.
WE'RE ON IT, KNIGHTFALL.
SORRY. I MEAN CHARISE.
Found her.
1-B
ALL RIGHT. OKAY.
LET'S JUST PUT THE LADY DOWN, SISTER.
DON'T... DON'T MAKE THIS ANY UGLIER.
UGLIER?
DO I LOOK LIKE I WANT THINGS TO GET UGLY?
HEY, NOW, HEY, NOW!
TAKE A GANDER AT THAT HOT SACK OF FLESHY TISSUE!
YOU WATCH YOUR MOUTH, FERDIE...
...WE'RE TAKING THIS, THIS NO-TALENT HACK, WITH US, BATGIRL, OR WHOEVER YOU ARE. SHE'S GOING TO MAKE ME A STAR.
PLEASE. SHE'S... THEY'RE CRAZY.
CRAZY FOR THE REDHEAD, LADY.
WHICH MAKES YOU OLD NEWS.
WRRRRRRRR

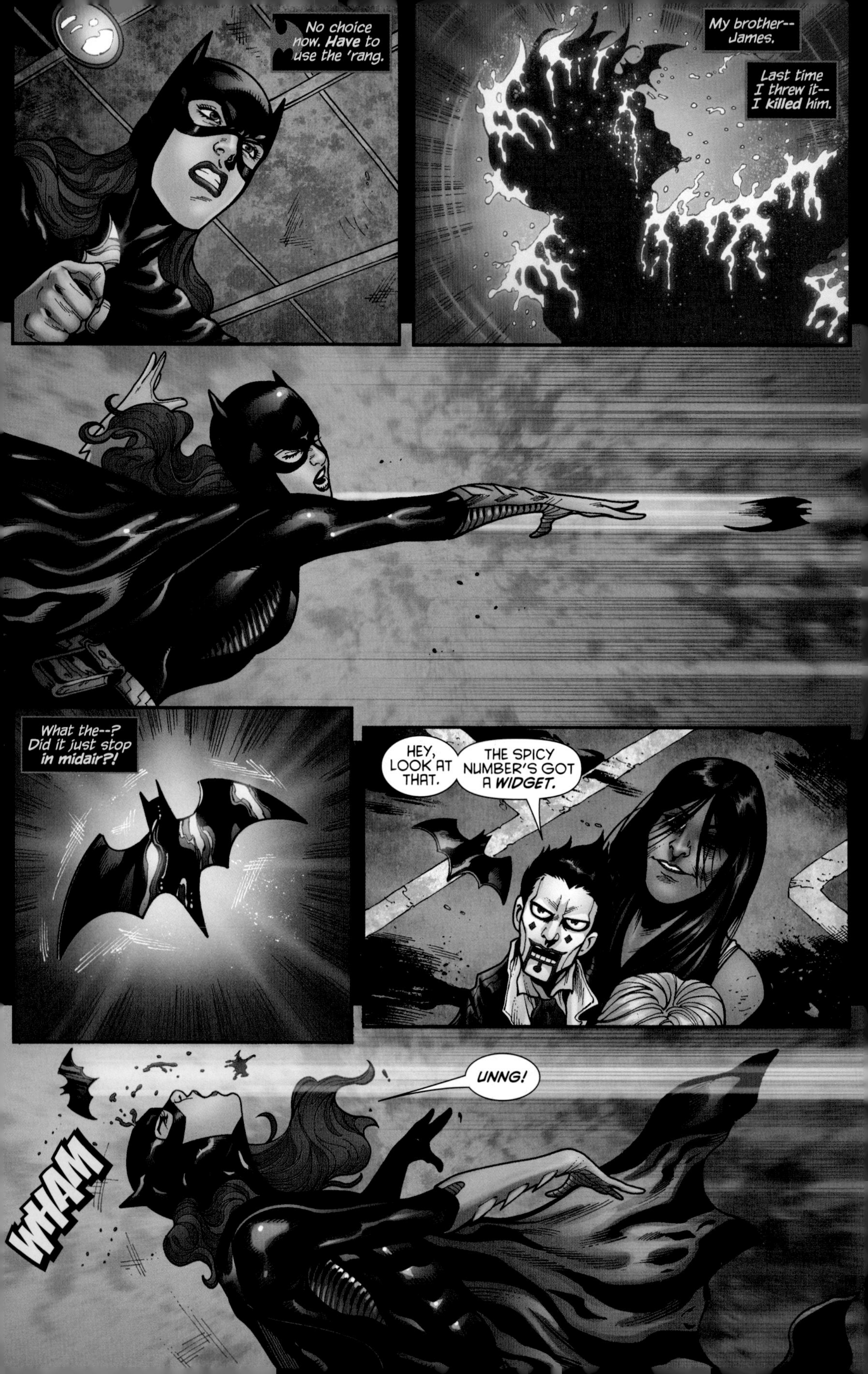
No choice now. Have to use the 'rang.
My brother-- James.
Last time I threw it-- I killed him.
What the--? Did it just stop in midair?!
HEY, LOOK AT THAT.
THE SPICY NUMBER'S GOT A WIDGET.
UNNG!
WHAM

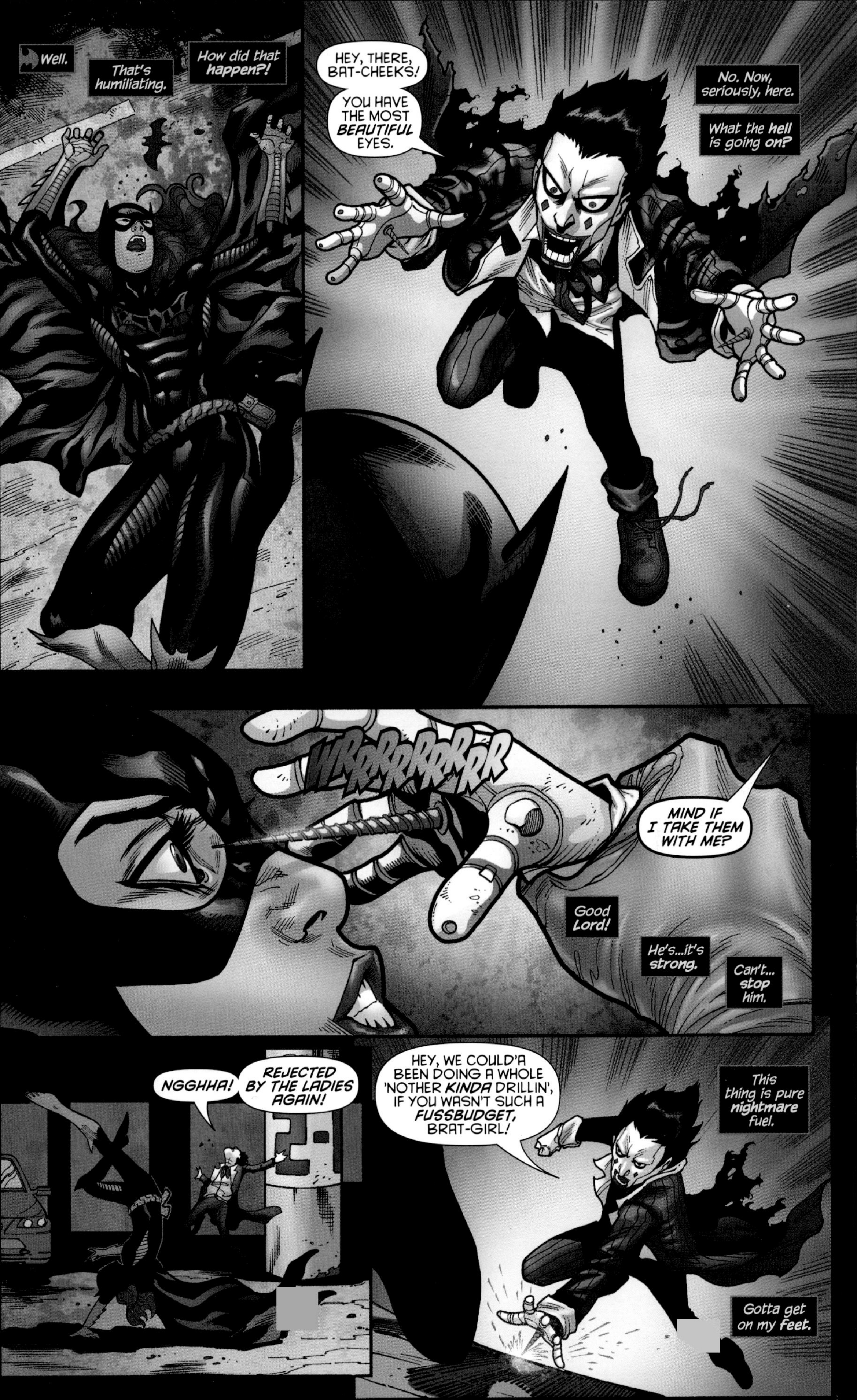
Well.
That's humiliating.
How did that happen?!
HEY, THERE, BAT-CHEEKS!
YOU HAVE THE MOST BEAUTIFUL EYES.
No. Now, seriously, here.
What the hell is going on?
WRRRRRRRRRR
MIND IF I TAKE THEM WITH ME?
Good Lord!
He's...it's strong.
Can't... stop him.
NGGHHA!
REJECTED BY THE LADIES AGAIN!
HEY, WE COULD'A BEEN DOING A WHOLE 'NOTHER KINDA DRILLIN', IF YOU WASN'T SUCH A FUSSBUDGET, BRAT-GIRL!
This thing is pure nightmare fuel.
Gotta get on my feet.

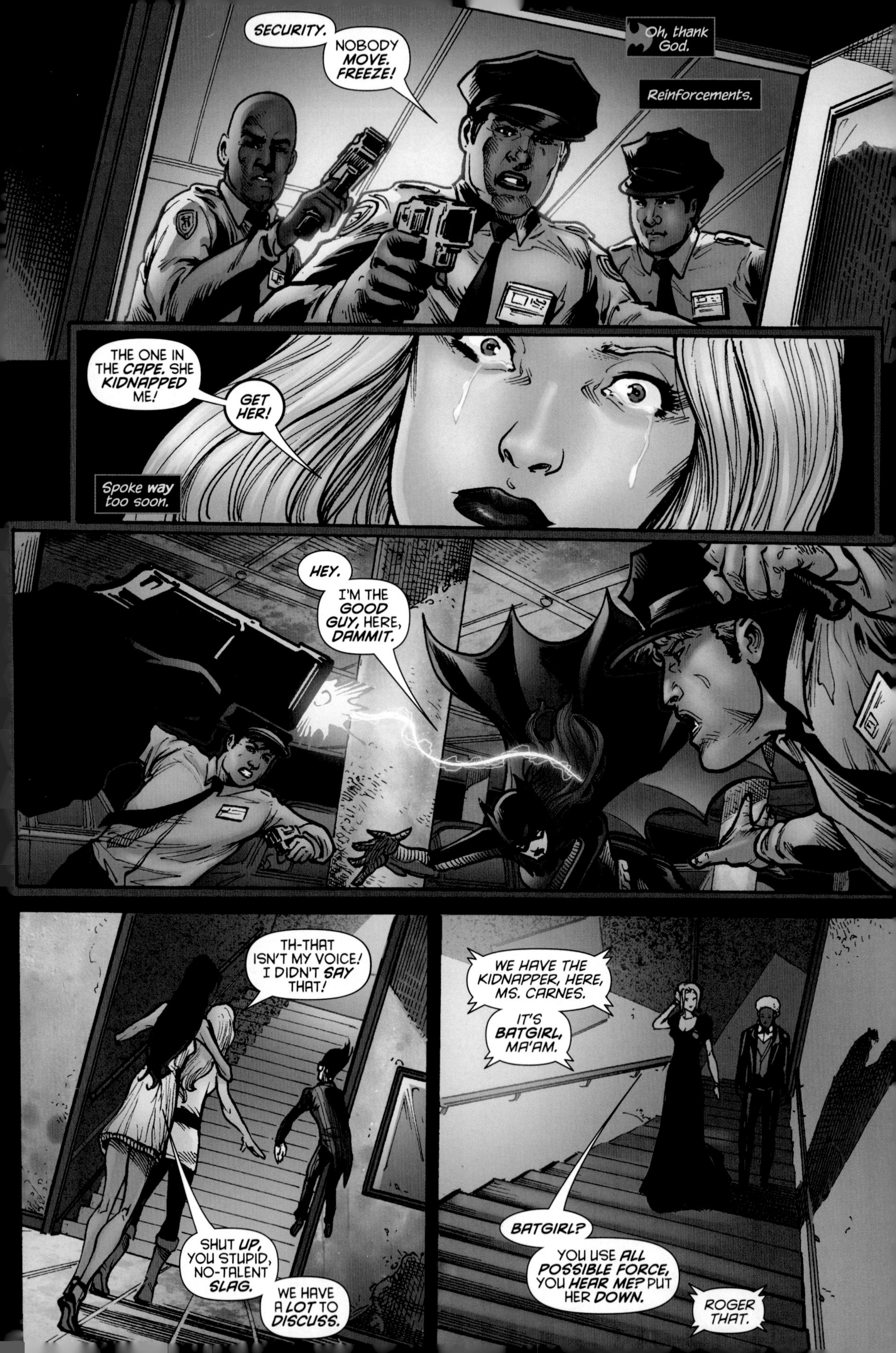
SECURITY.
NOBODY MOVE. FREEZE!
Oh, thank God.
Reinforcements.
THE ONE IN THE CAPE. SHE KIDNAPPED ME!
GET HER!
Spoke way too soon.
HEY.
I'M THE GOOD GUY, HERE, DAMMIT.
TH-THAT ISN'T MY VOICE! I DIDN'T SAY THAT!
SHUT UP, YOU STUPID, NO-TALENT SLAG.
WE HAVE A LOT TO DISCUSS.
WE HAVE THE KIDNAPPER, HERE, MS. CARNES.
IT'S BATGIRL, MA'AM.
BATGIRL?
YOU USE ALL POSSIBLE FORCE, YOU HEAR ME? PUT HER DOWN.
ROGER THAT.

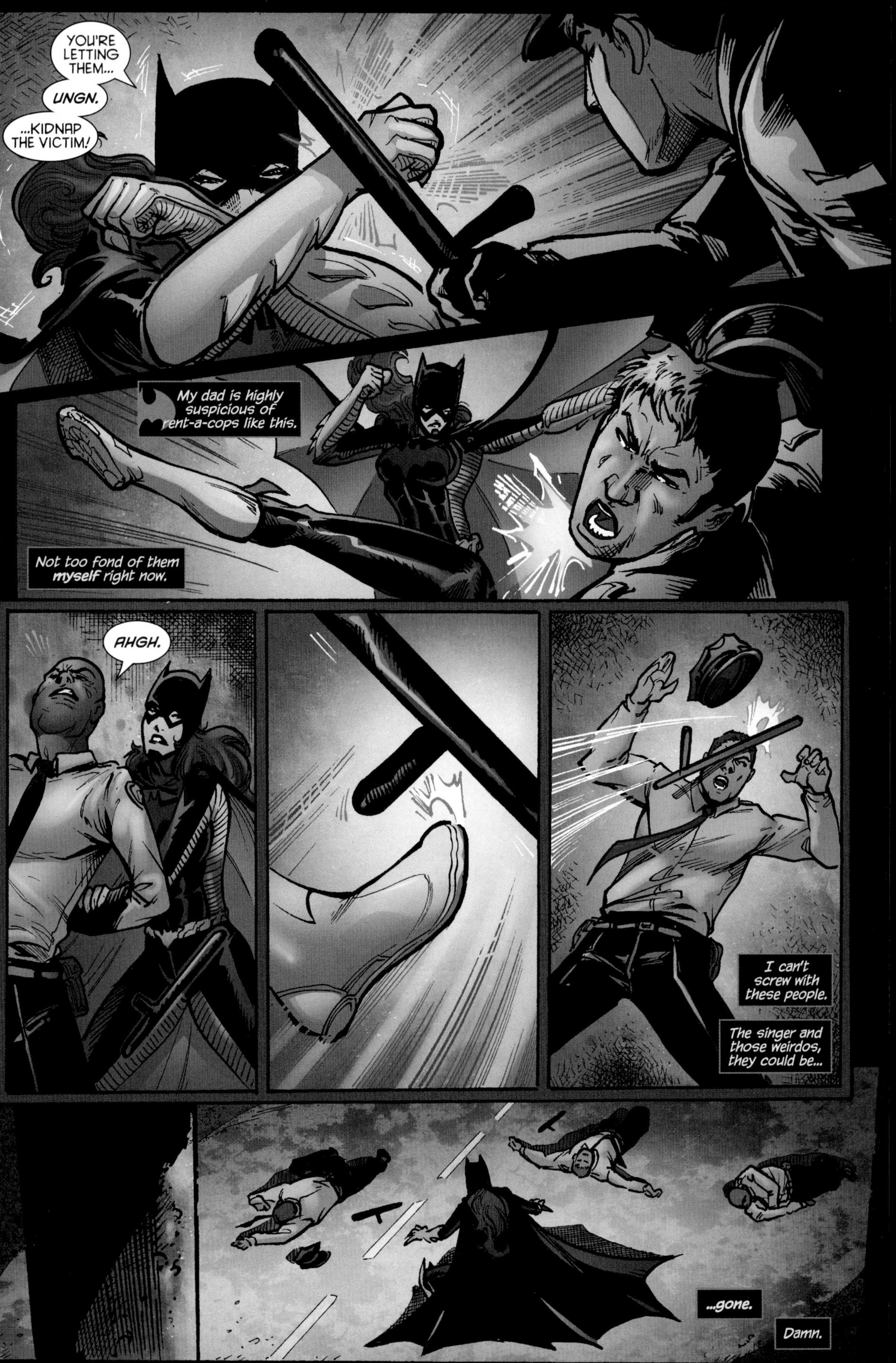
YOU'RE LETTING THEM...
UNGN.
...KIDNAP THE VICTIM!
My dad is highly suspicious of rent-a-cops like this.
Not too fond of them myself right now.
AHGH.
I can't screw with these people.
The singer and those weirdos, they could be...
...gone.
Damn.

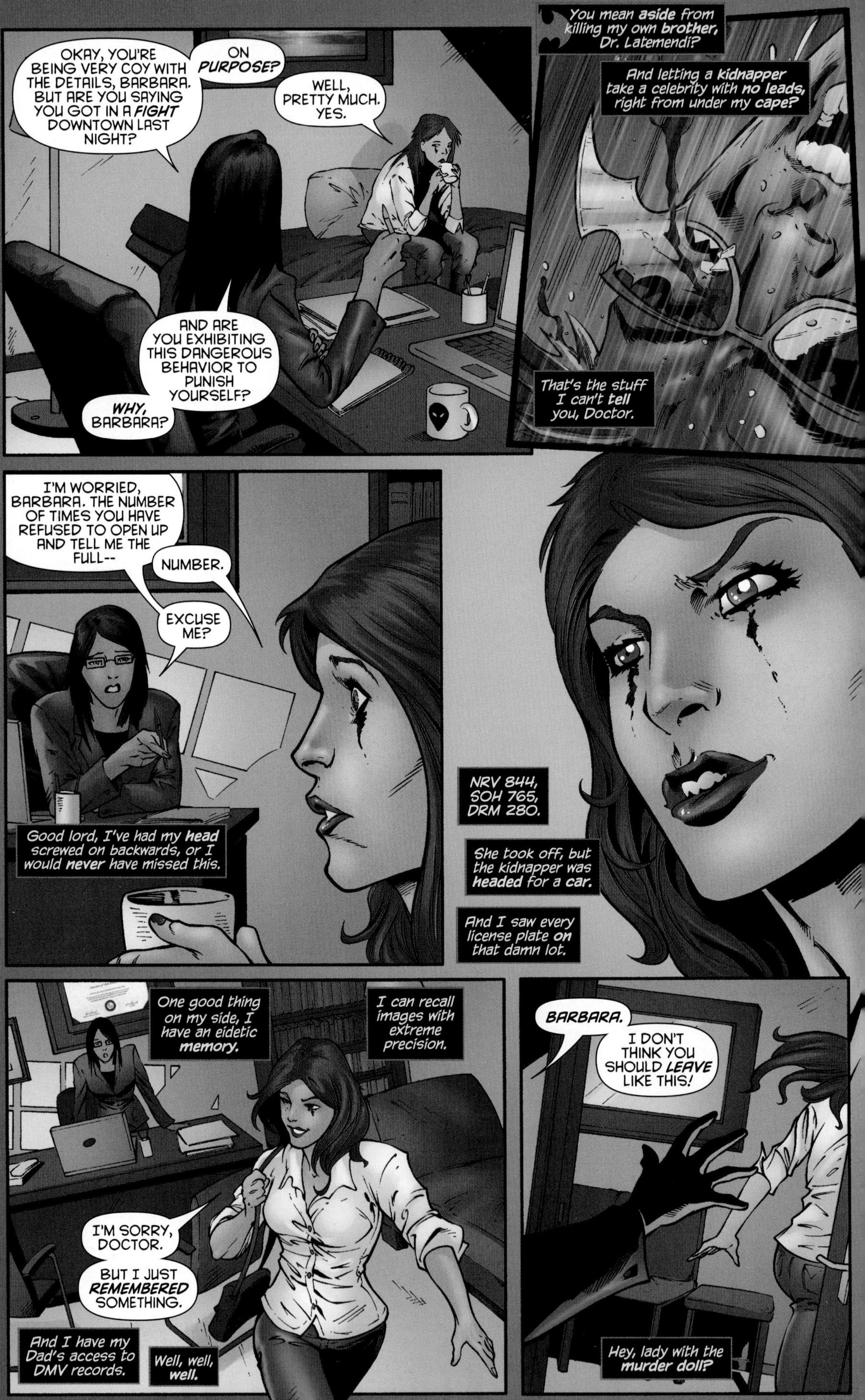

OKAY, YOU'RE BEING VERY COY WITH THE DETAILS, BARBARA. BUT ARE YOU SAYING YOU GOT IN A FIGHT DOWNTOWN LAST NIGHT?
ON PURPOSE?
WELL, PRETTY MUCH. YES.
AND ARE YOU EXHIBITING THIS DANGEROUS BEHAVIOR TO PUNISH YOURSELF?
WHY, BARBARA?
You mean aside from killing my own brother, Dr. Latemendi?
And letting a kidnapper take a celebrity with no leads, right from under my cape?
That's the stuff I can't tell you, Doctor.
I'M WORRIED, BARBARA. THE NUMBER OF TIMES YOU HAVE REFUSED TO OPEN UP AND TELL ME THE FULL--
NUMBER.
EXCUSE ME?
Good lord, I've had my head screwed on backwards, or I would never have missed this.
NRV 844, SOH 765, DRM 280.
She took off, but the kidnapper was headed for a car.
And I saw every license plate on that damn lot.
One good thing on my side, I have an eidetic memory.
I can recall images with extreme precision.
I'M SORRY, DOCTOR.
BUT I JUST REMEMBERED SOMETHING.
And I have my Dad's access to DMV records.
Well, well, well.
BARBARA.
I DON'T THINK YOU SHOULD LEAVE LIKE THIS!
Hey, lady with the murder doll?

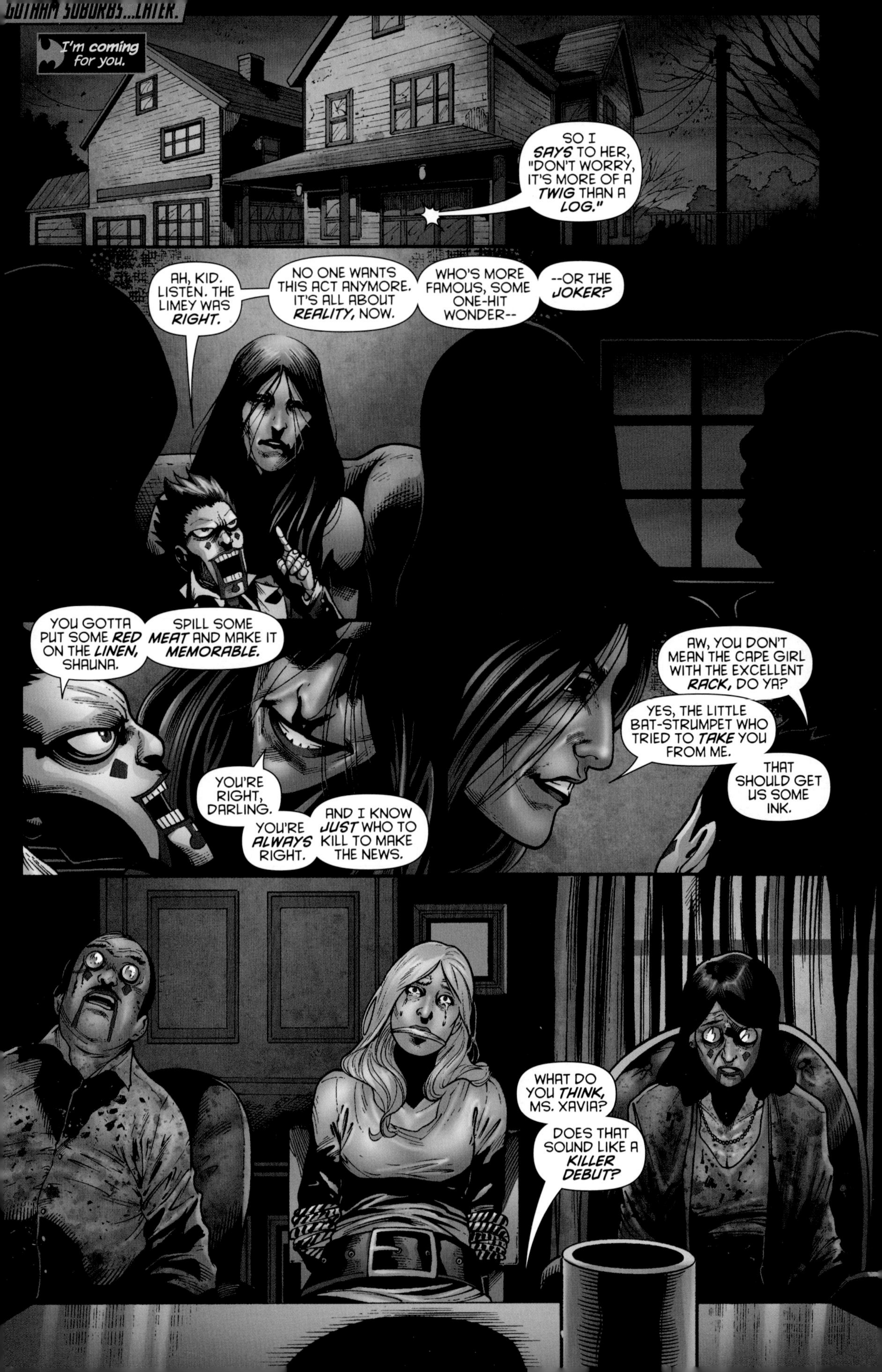
GOTHAM SUBURBS...LATER.
I'm coming for you.
SO I SAYS TO HER, "DON'T WORRY, IT'S MORE OF A TWIG THAN A LOG."
AH, KID. LISTEN. THE LIMEY WAS RIGHT.
NO ONE WANTS THIS ACT ANYMORE. IT'S ALL ABOUT REALITY, NOW.
WHO'S MORE FAMOUS, SOME ONE-HIT WONDER--
--OR THE JOKER?
YOU GOTTA PUT SOME RED ON THE LINEN, SHAUNA.
SPILL SOME MEAT AND MAKE IT MEMORABLE.
YOU'RE RIGHT, DARLING.
YOU'RE ALWAYS RIGHT.
AND I KNOW JUST WHO TO KILL TO MAKE THE NEWS.
AW, YOU DON'T MEAN THE CAPE GIRL WITH THE EXCELLENT RACK, DO YA?
YES, THE LITTLE BAT-STRUMPET WHO TRIED TO TAKE YOU FROM ME.
THAT SHOULD GET US SOME INK.
WHAT DO YOU THINK, MS. XAVIA?
DOES THAT SOUND LIKE A KILLER DEBUT?

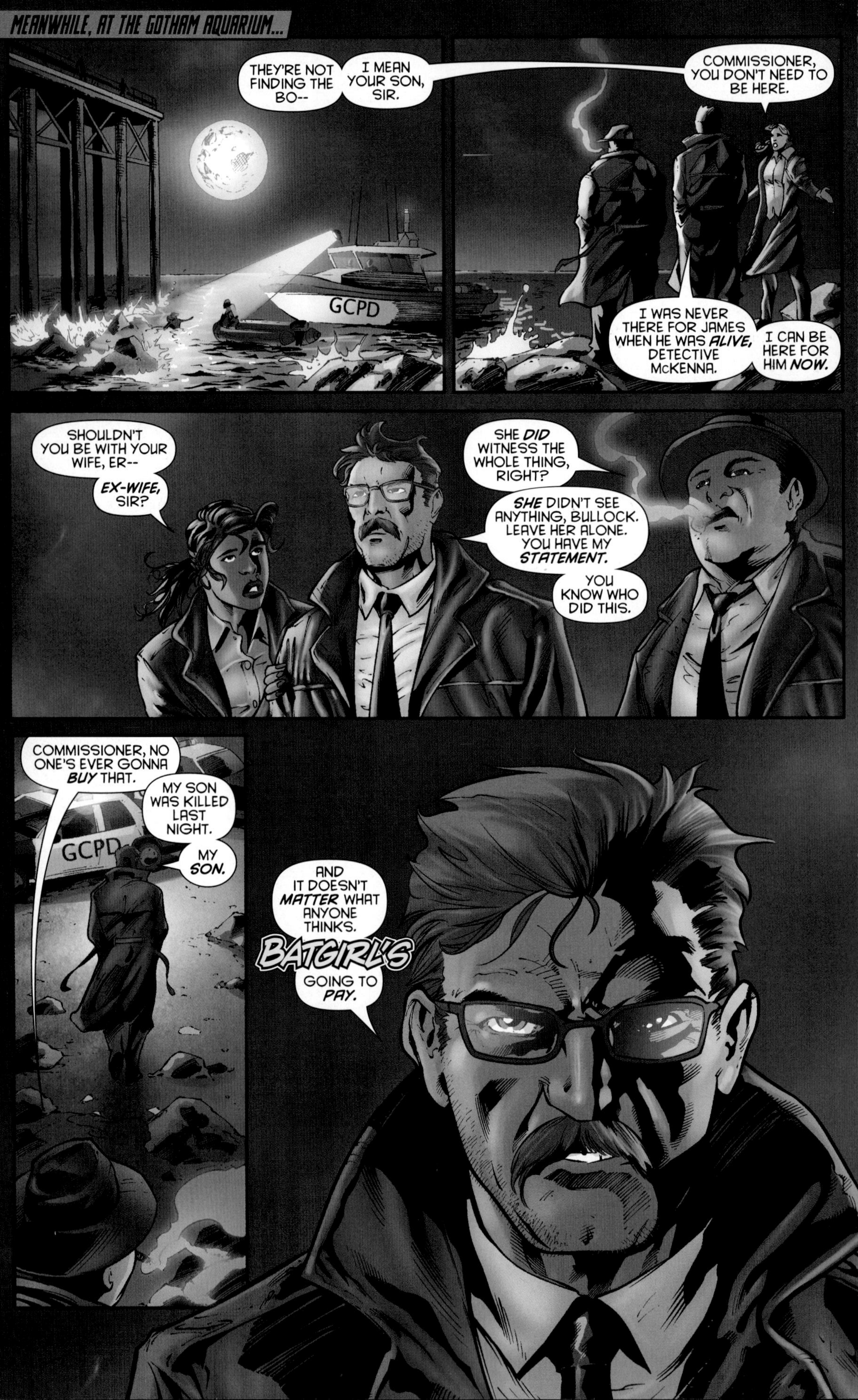
MEANWHILE, AT THE GOTHAM AQUARIUM...
THEY'RE NOT FINDING THE BO--
I MEAN YOUR SON, SIR.
GCPD
COMMISSIONER, YOU DON'T NEED TO BE HERE.
I WAS NEVER THERE FOR JAMES WHEN HE WAS ALIVE, DETECTIVE McKENNA.
I CAN BE HERE FOR HIM NOW.
SHOULDN'T YOU BE WITH YOUR WIFE, ER--
EX-WIFE, SIR?
SHE DID WITNESS THE WHOLE THING, RIGHT?
SHE DIDN'T SEE ANYTHING, BULLOCK. LEAVE HER ALONE. YOU HAVE MY STATEMENT.
YOU KNOW WHO DID THIS.
COMMISSIONER, NO ONE'S EVER GONNA BUY THAT.
MY SON WAS KILLED LAST NIGHT.
MY SON.
GCPD
AND IT DOESN'T MATTER WHAT ANYONE THINKS.
BATGIRL'S GOING TO PAY.

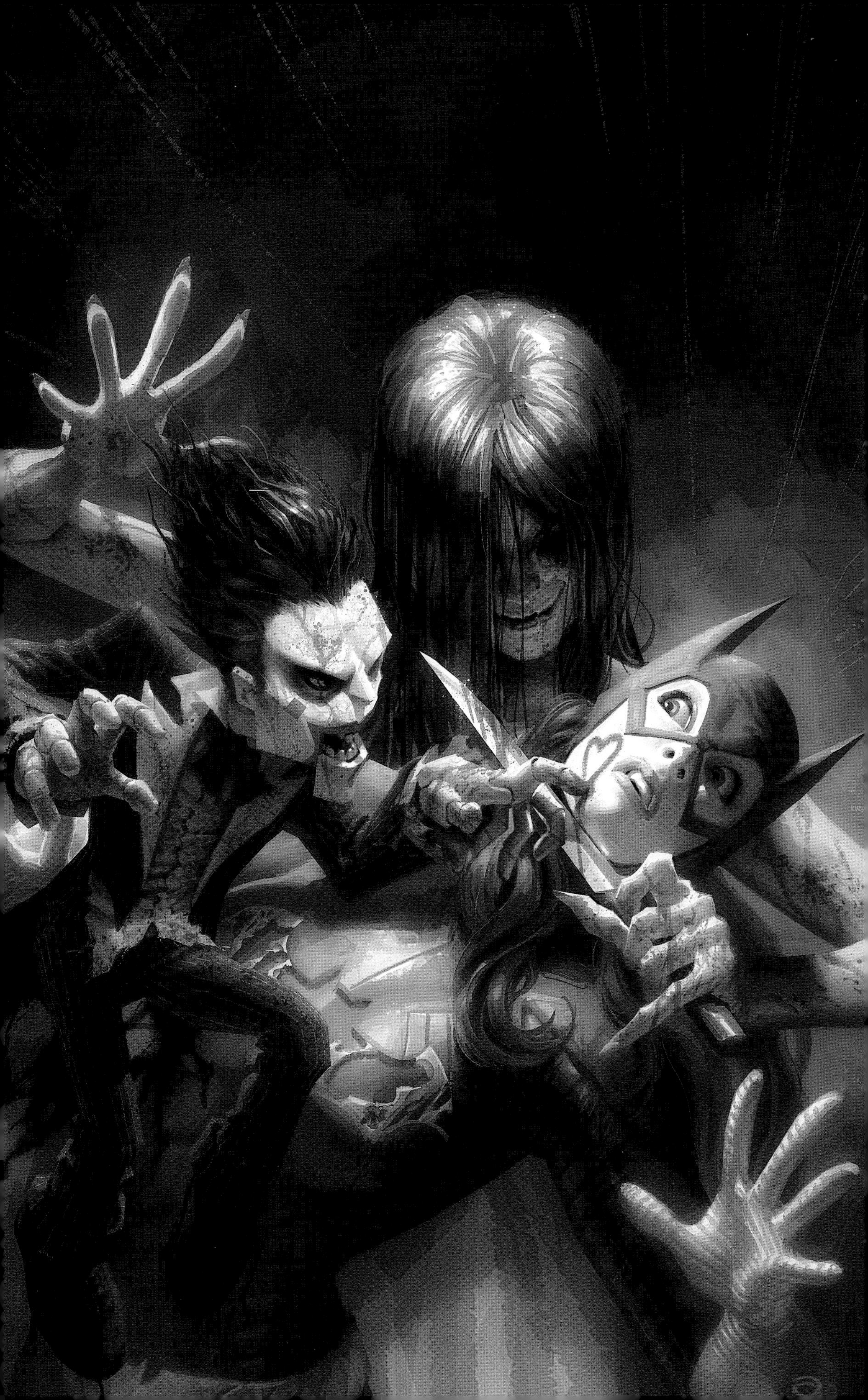

ENCLOSURE

GAIL SIMONE writer **FERNANDO PASARIN** penciller **JONATHAN GLAPION** inker **BLOND** colorist
cover by **ALEX GARNER**

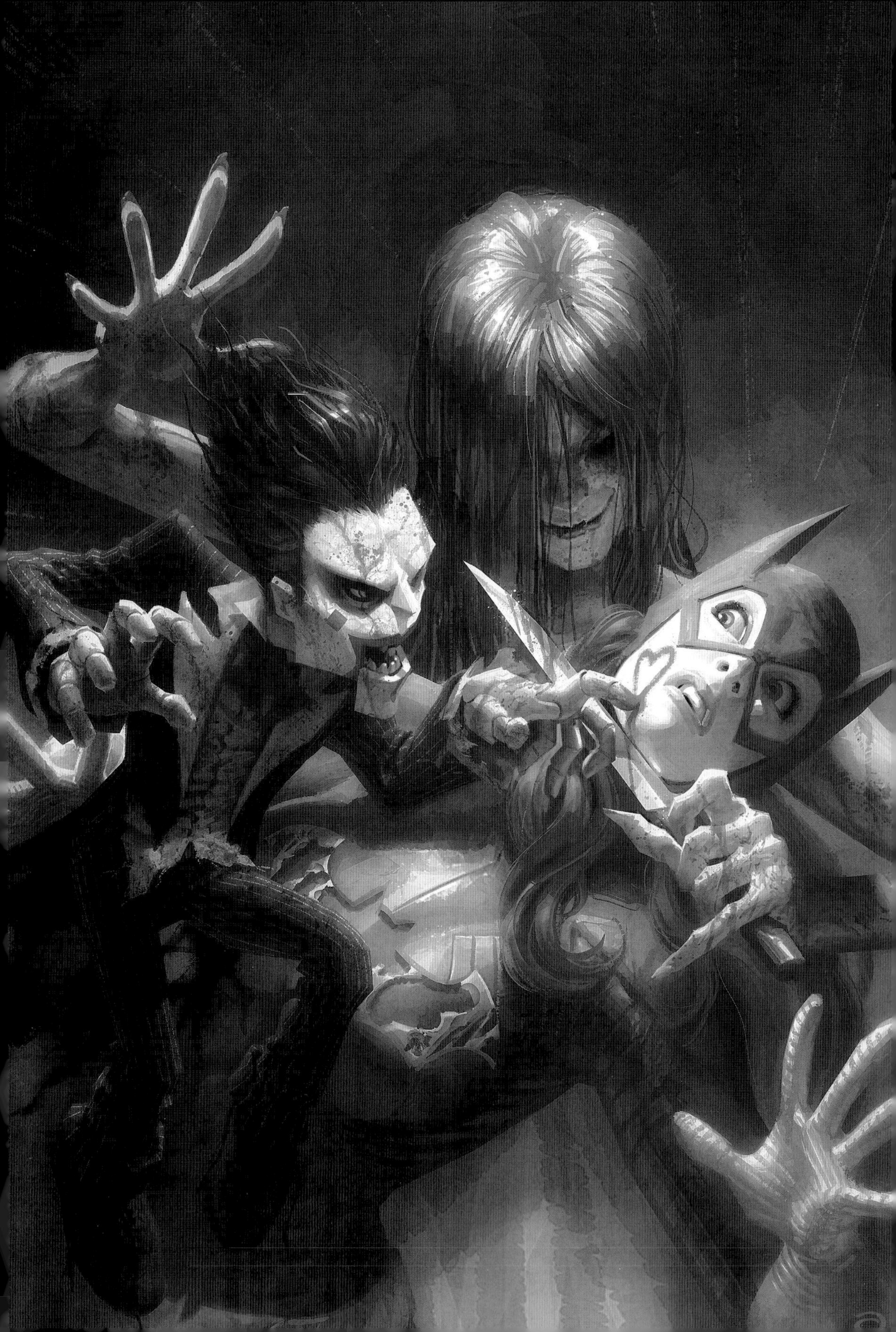

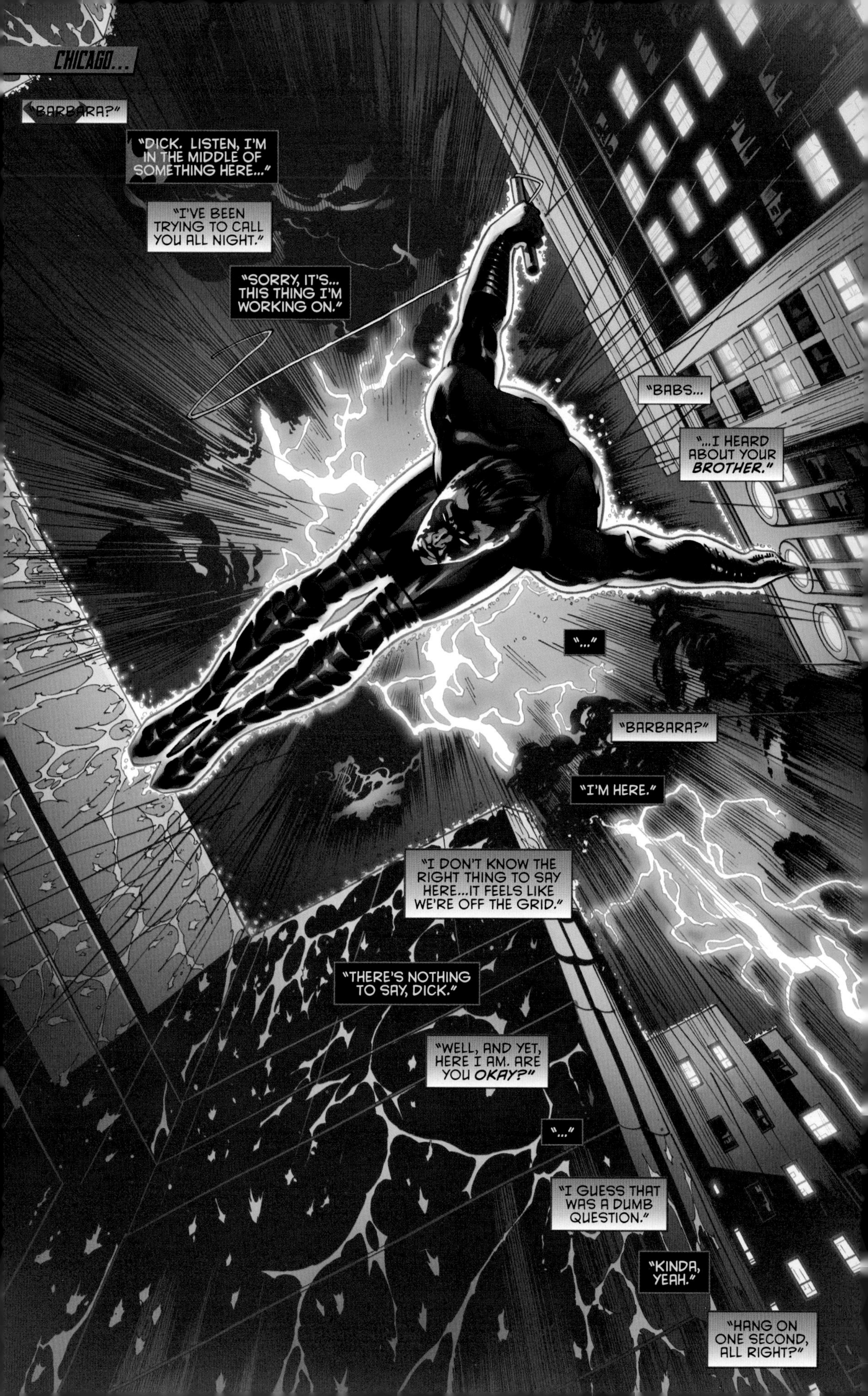
CHICAGO...
"BARBARA?"
"DICK. LISTEN, I'M IN THE MIDDLE OF SOMETHING HERE..."
"I'VE BEEN TRYING TO CALL YOU ALL NIGHT."
"SORRY, IT'S... THIS THING I'M WORKING ON."
"BABS...
"...I HEARD ABOUT YOUR BROTHER."
"..."
"BARBARA?"
"I'M HERE."
"I DON'T KNOW THE RIGHT THING TO SAY HERE...IT FEELS LIKE WE'RE OFF THE GRID."
"THERE'S NOTHING TO SAY, DICK."
"WELL, AND YET, HERE I AM. ARE YOU OKAY?"
"..."
"I GUESS THAT WAS A DUMB QUESTION."
"KINDA, YEAH."
"HANG ON ONE SECOND, ALL RIGHT?"

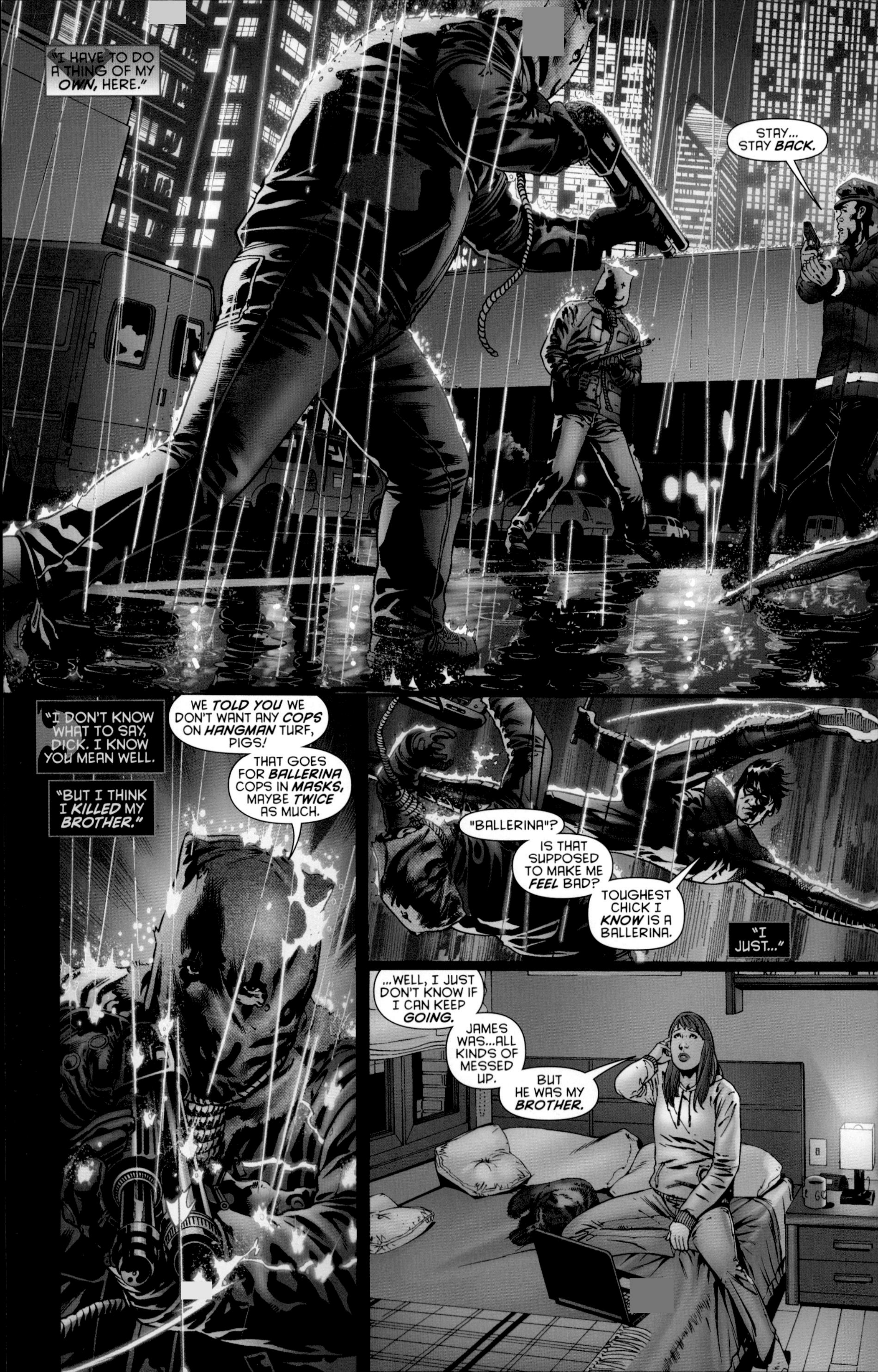
"I HAVE TO DO A THING OF MY OWN, HERE."
STAY... STAY BACK.
"I DON'T KNOW WHAT TO SAY, DICK. I KNOW YOU MEAN WELL.
"BUT I THINK I KILLED MY BROTHER."
WE TOLD YOU WE DON'T WANT ANY COPS ON HANGMAN TURF, PIGS!
THAT GOES FOR BALLERINA COPS IN MASKS, MAYBE TWICE AS MUCH.
"BALLERINA"?
IS THAT SUPPOSED TO MAKE ME FEEL BAD?
TOUGHEST CHICK I KNOW IS A BALLERINA.
"I JUST..."
...WELL, I JUST DON'T KNOW IF I CAN KEEP GOING.
JAMES WAS...ALL KINDS OF MESSED UP.
BUT HE WAS MY BROTHER.

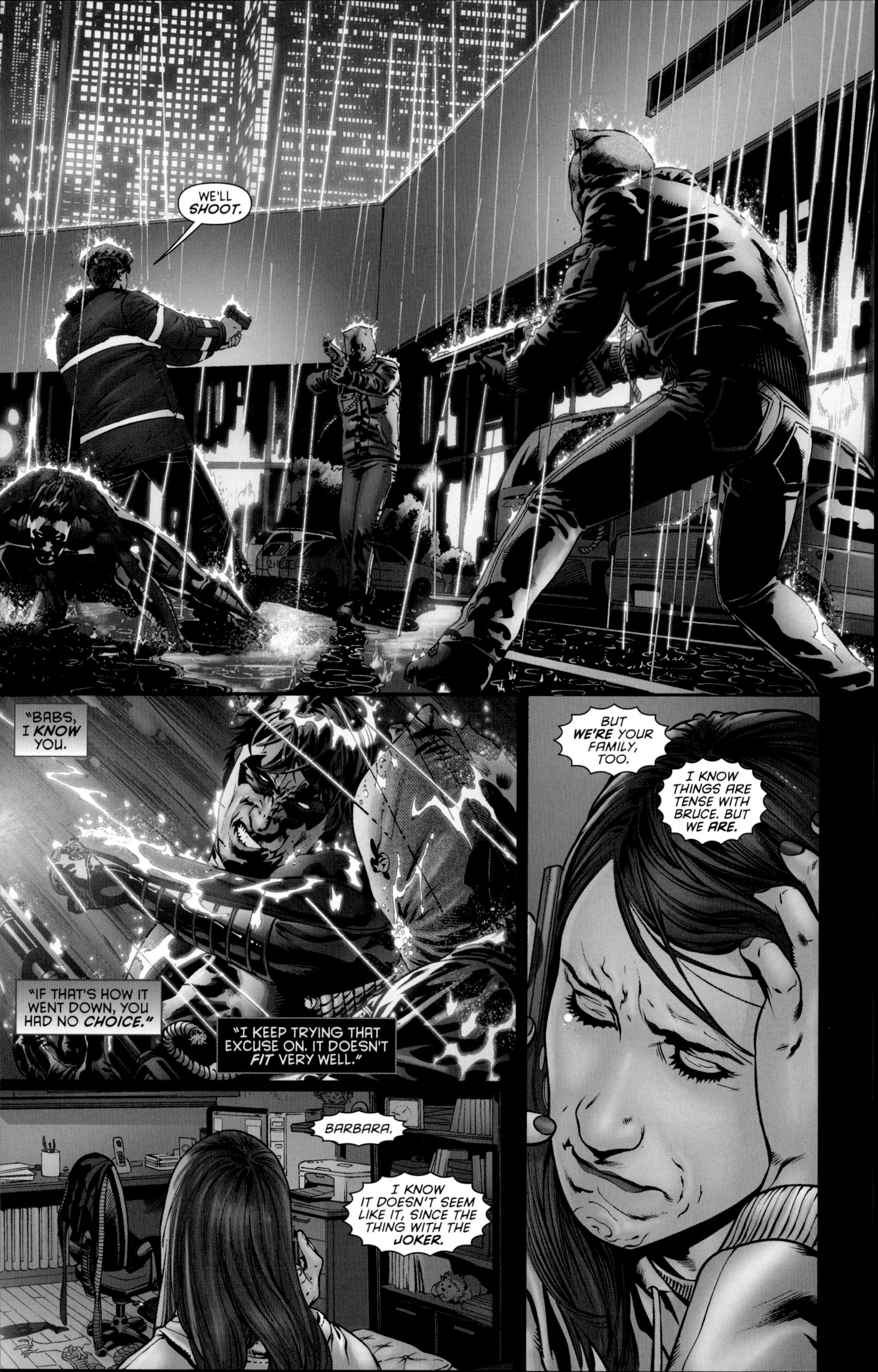
WE'LL SHOOT.
"BABS, I KNOW YOU.
"IF THAT'S HOW IT WENT DOWN, YOU HAD NO CHOICE."
"I KEEP TRYING THAT EXCUSE ON. IT DOESN'T FIT VERY WELL."
BARBARA.
I KNOW IT DOESN'T SEEM LIKE IT, SINCE THE THING WITH THE JOKER.
BUT WE'RE YOUR FAMILY, TOO.
I KNOW THINGS ARE TENSE WITH BRUCE. BUT WE ARE.

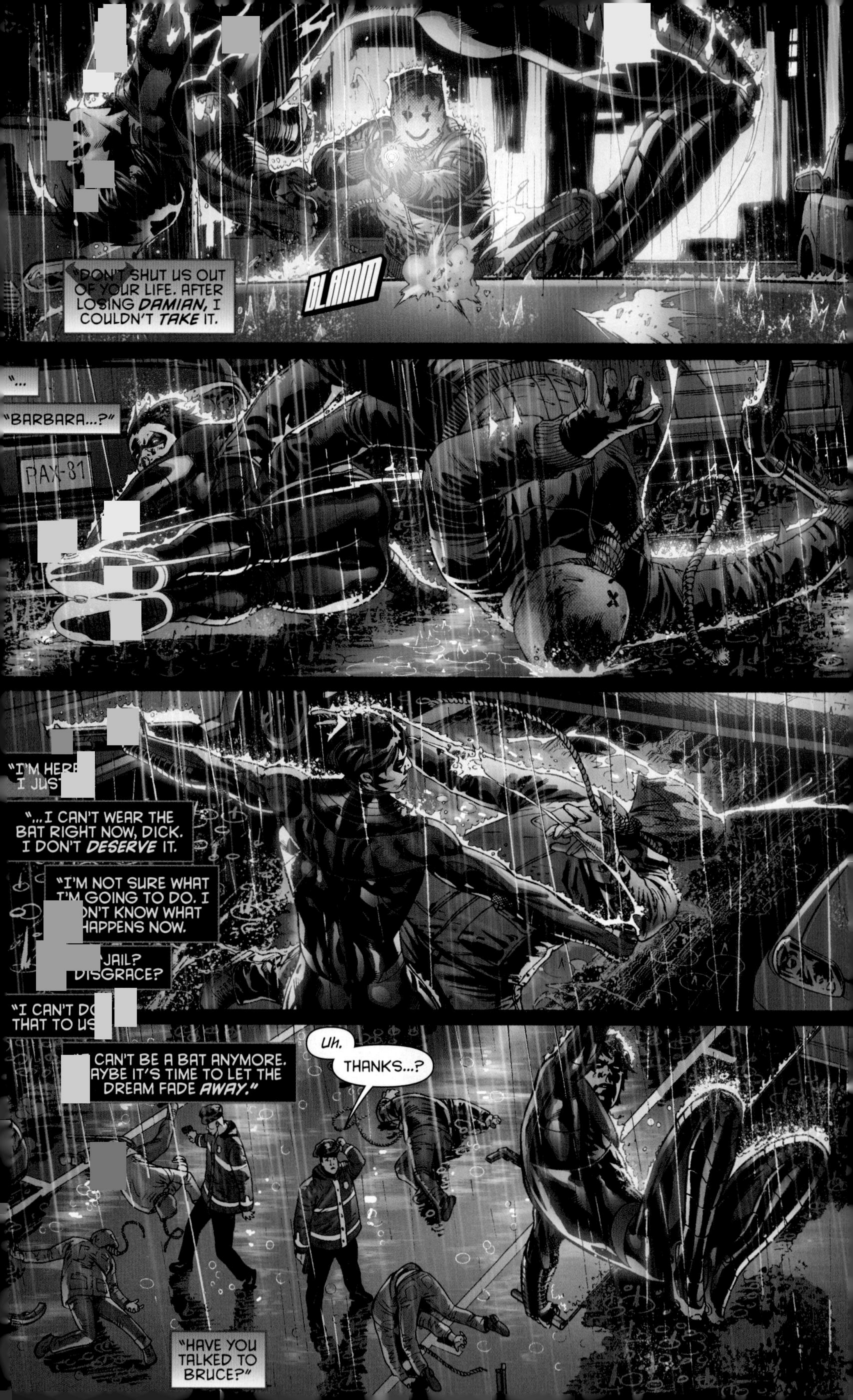
"DON'T SHUT US OUT OF YOUR LIFE. AFTER LOSING DAMIAN, I COULDN'T TAKE IT.
BLAMM
"...
"BARBARA...?"
PAX-81
"I'M HER
I JUS
"...I CAN'T WEAR THE BAT RIGHT NOW, DICK. I DON'T DESERVE IT.
"I'M NOT SURE WHAT I'M GOING TO DO. I
ON'T KNOW WHAT HAPPENS NOW.
JAIL? DISGRACE?
"I CAN'T DO
THAT TO US
CAN'T BE A BAT ANYMORE.
AYBE IT'S TIME TO LET THE DREAM FADE AWAY."
Uh. THANKS...?
"HAVE YOU TALKED TO BRUCE?"

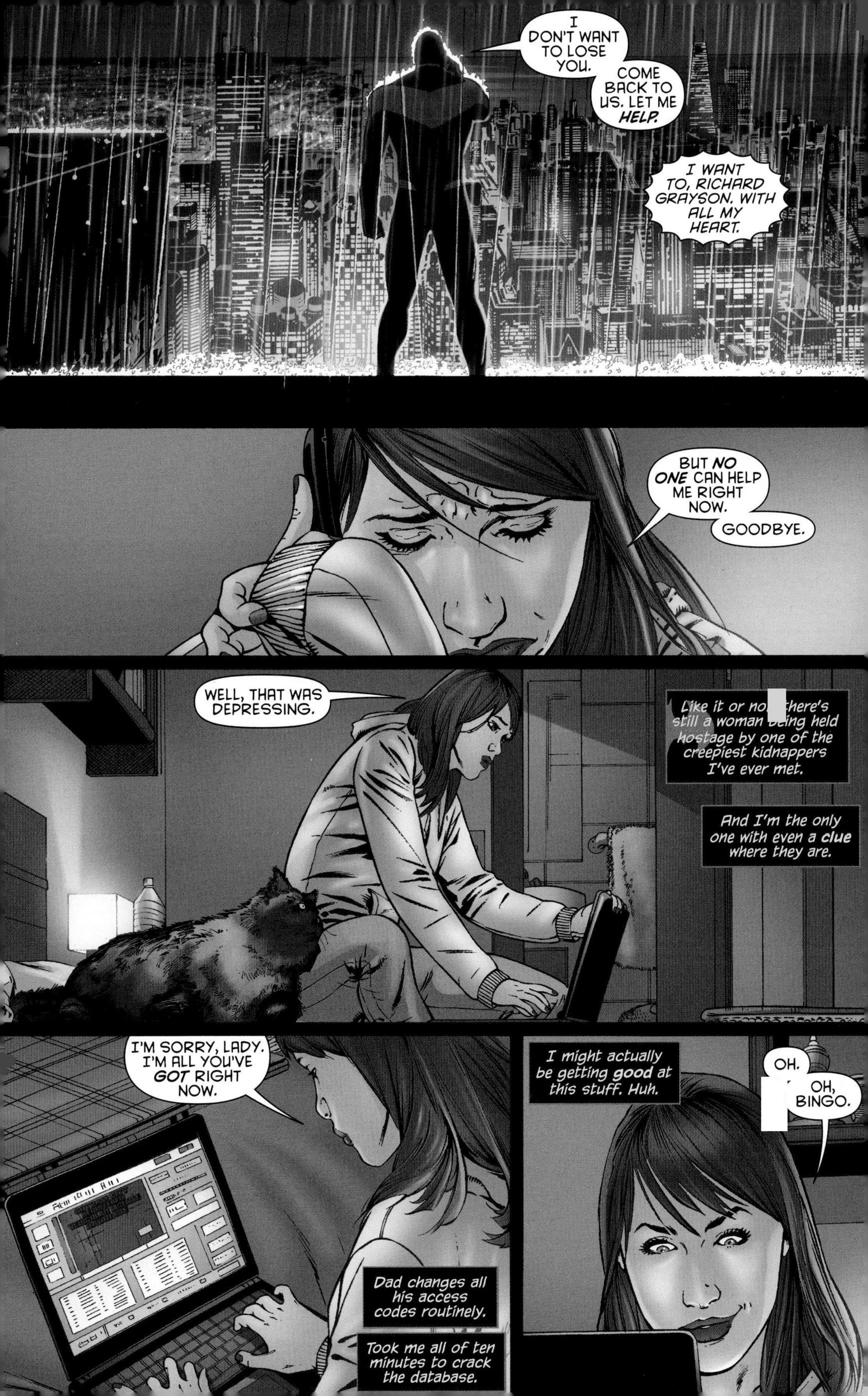
I DON'T WANT TO LOSE YOU.
COME BACK TO US. LET ME HELP.
I WANT TO, RICHARD GRAYSON. WITH ALL MY HEART.
BUT NO ONE CAN HELP ME RIGHT NOW.
GOODBYE.
WELL, THAT WAS DEPRESSING.
Like it or no there's still a woman eing held hostage by one of the creepiest kidnappers I've ever met.
And I'm the only one with even a clue where they are.
I'M SORRY, LADY. I'M ALL YOU'VE GOT RIGHT NOW.
Dad changes all his access codes routinely.
Took me all of ten minutes to crack the database.
I might actually be getting good at this stuff. Huh.
OH.
OH, BINGO.

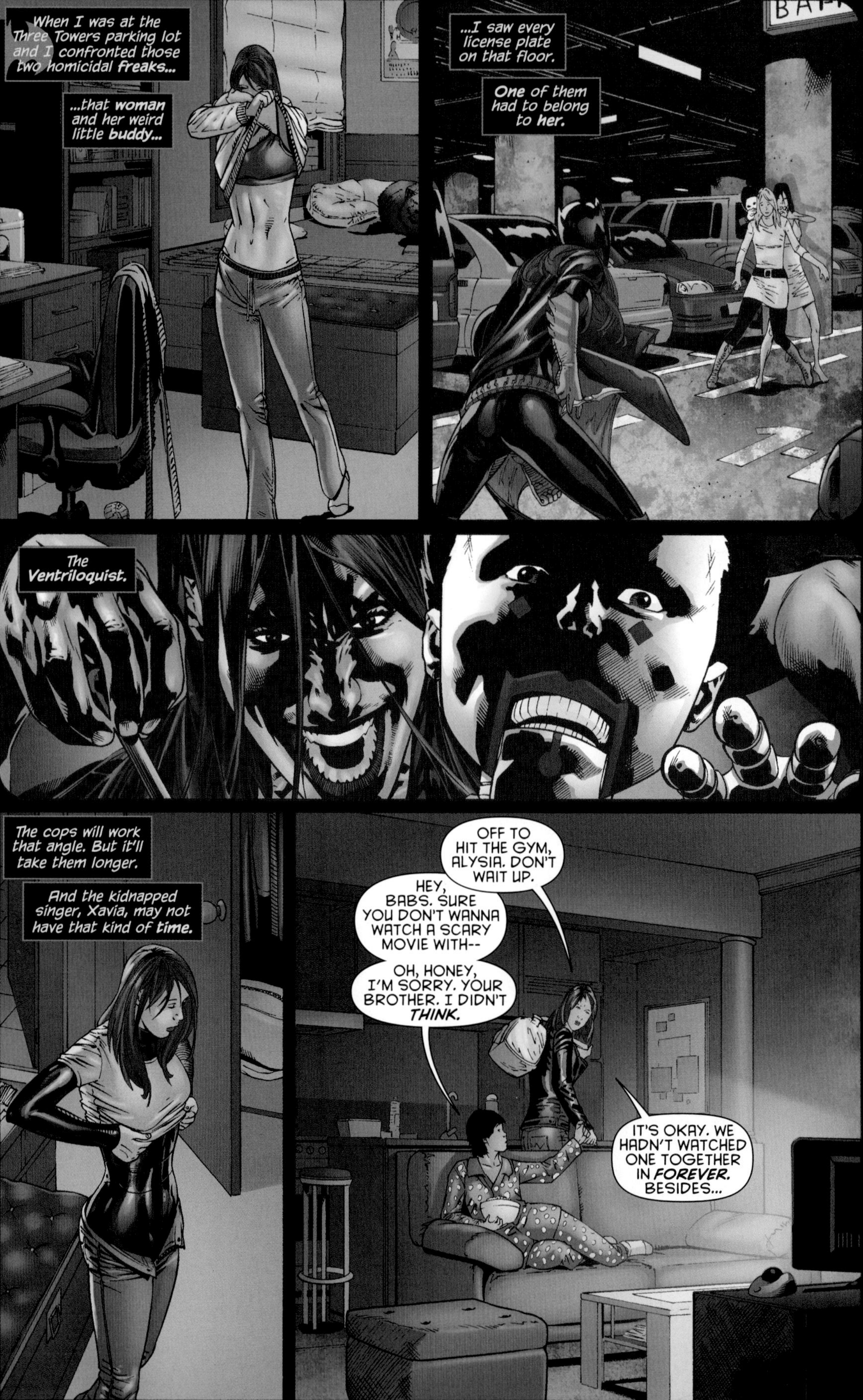
When I was at the Three Towers parking lot and I confronted those two homicidal freaks...
...that woman and her weird little buddy...
...I saw every license plate on that floor.
One of them had to belong to her.
The Ventriloquist.
The cops will work that angle. But it'll take them longer.
And the kidnapped singer, Xavia, may not have that kind of time.
OFF TO HIT THE GYM, ALYSIA. DON'T WAIT UP.
HEY, BABS. SURE YOU DON'T WANNA WATCH A SCARY MOVIE WITH--
OH, HONEY, I'M SORRY. YOUR BROTHER. I DIDN'T THINK.
IT'S OKAY. WE HADN'T WATCHED ONE TOGETHER IN FOREVER. BESIDES...

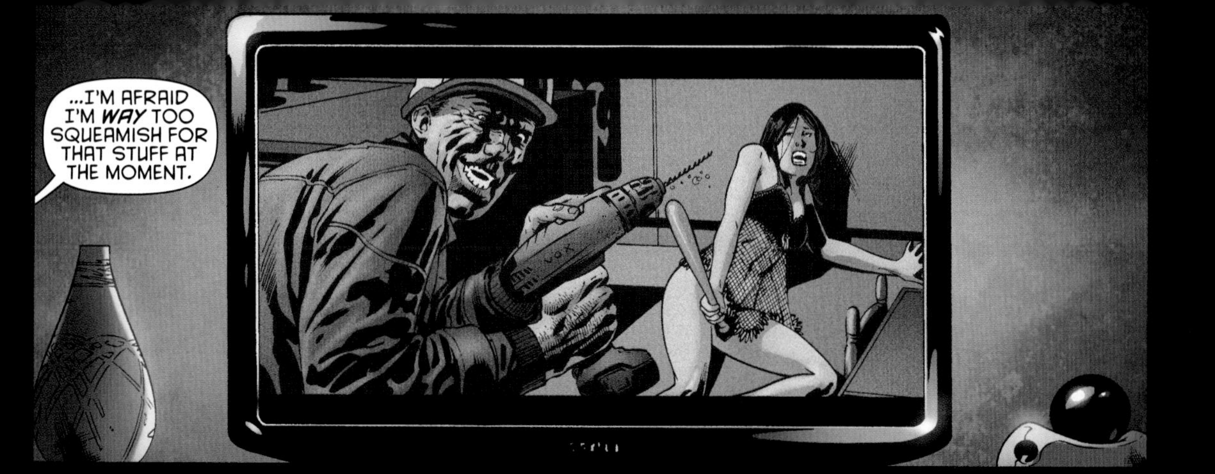
...I'M AFRAID I'M WAY TOO SQUEAMISH FOR THAT STUFF AT THE MOMENT.

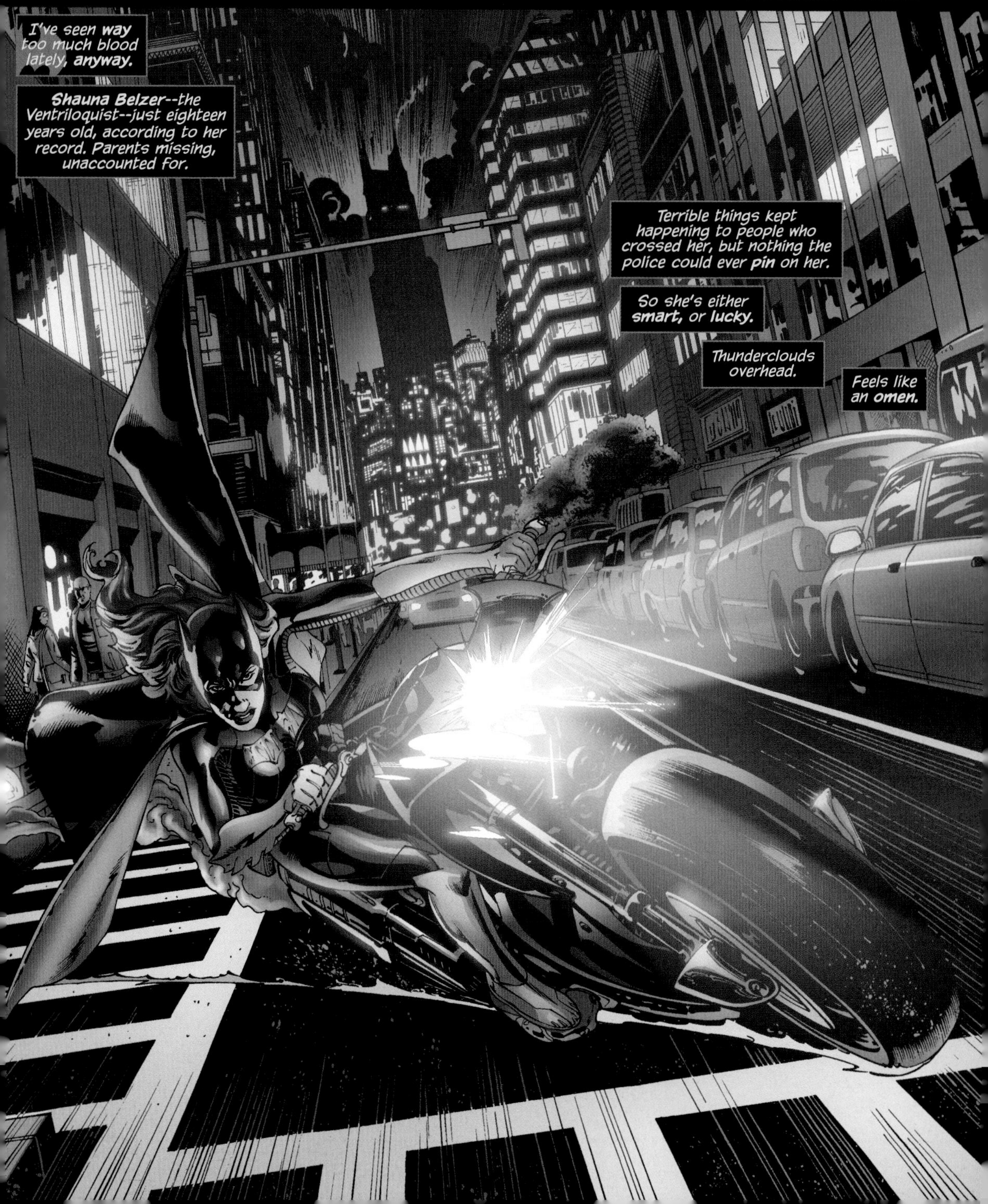
I've seen way too much blood lately, anyway.
Shauna Belzer--the Ventriloquist--just eighteen years old, according to her record. Parents missing, unaccounted for.
Terrible things kept happening to people who crossed her, but nothing the police could ever pin on her.
So she's either smart, or lucky.
Thunderclouds overhead.
Feels like an omen.

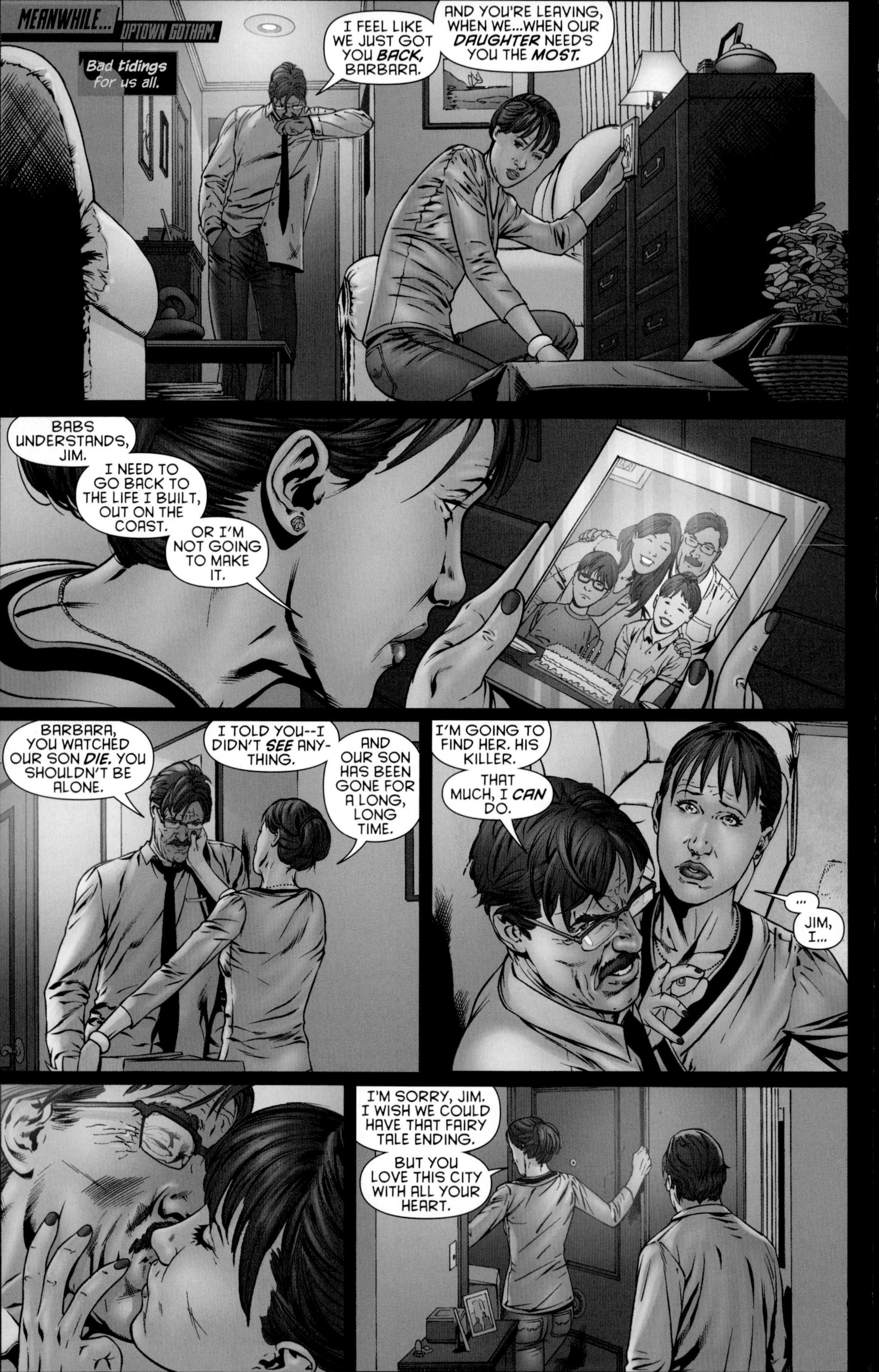
MEANWHILE...
UPTOWN GOTHAM.
Bad tidings for us all.
I FEEL LIKE WE JUST GOT YOU BACK, BARBARA.
AND YOU'RE LEAVING, WHEN WE...WHEN OUR DAUGHTER NEEDS YOU THE MOST.
BABS UNDERSTANDS, JIM.
I NEED TO GO BACK TO THE LIFE I BUILT, OUT ON THE COAST.
OR I'M NOT GOING TO MAKE IT.
BARBARA, YOU WATCHED OUR SON DIE. YOU SHOULDN'T BE ALONE.
I TOLD YOU--I DIDN'T SEE ANY-THING.
AND OUR SON HAS BEEN GONE FOR A LONG, LONG TIME.
I'M GOING TO FIND HER. HIS KILLER.
THAT MUCH, I CAN DO.
...
JIM, I...
I'M SORRY, JIM. I WISH WE COULD HAVE THAT FAIRY TALE ENDING.
BUT YOU LOVE THIS CITY WITH ALL YOUR HEART.

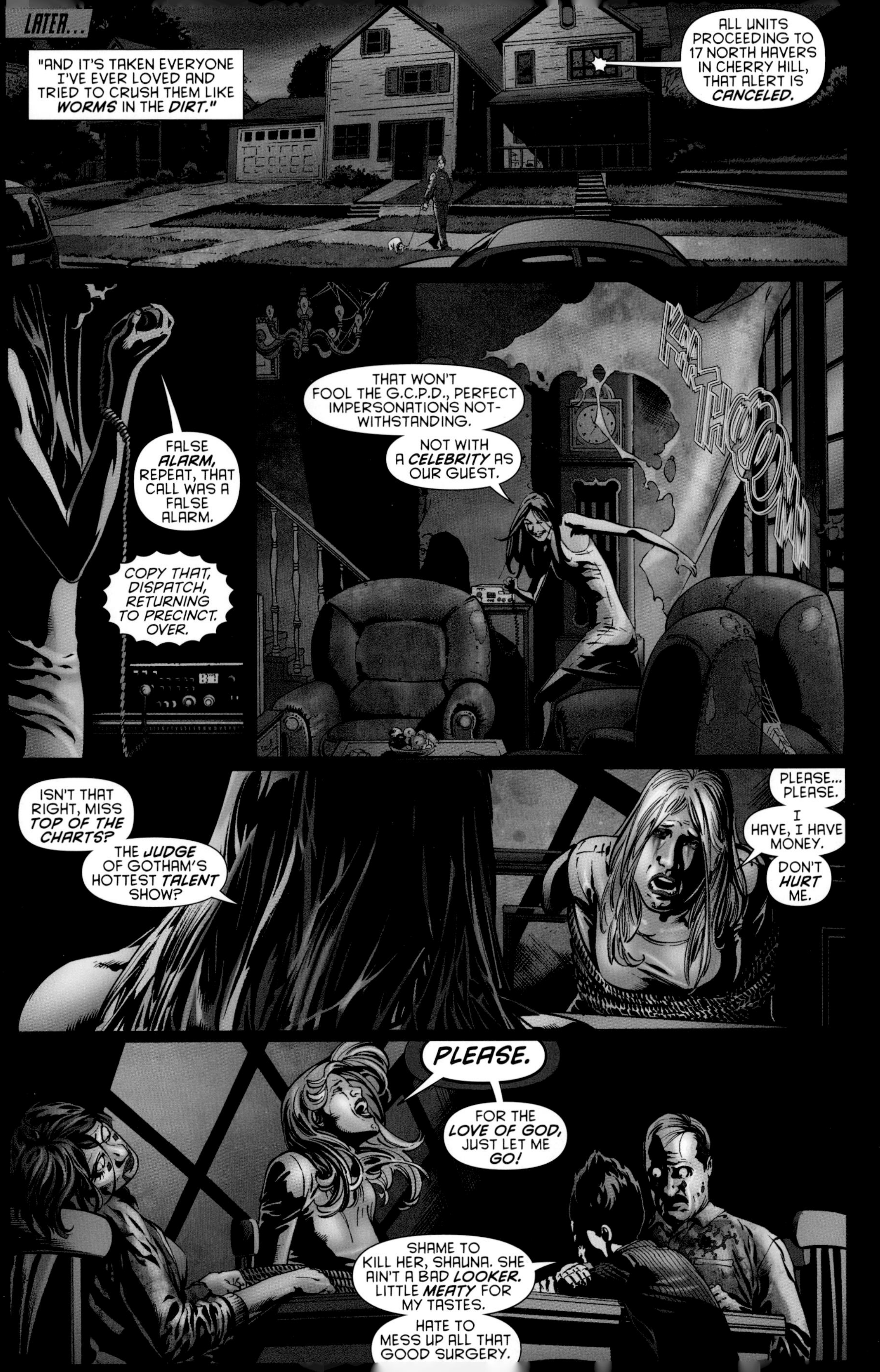
LATER...
"AND IT'S TAKEN EVERYONE I'VE EVER LOVED AND TRIED TO CRUSH THEM LIKE WORMS IN THE DIRT."
ALL UNITS PROCEEDING TO 17 NORTH HAVERS IN CHERRY HILL, THAT ALERT IS CANCELED.
FALSE ALARM, REPEAT, THAT CALL WAS A FALSE ALARM.
COPY THAT, DISPATCH, RETURNING TO PRECINCT. OVER.
THAT WON'T FOOL THE G.C.P.D., PERFECT IMPERSONATIONS NOT-WITHSTANDING.
NOT WITH A CELEBRITY AS OUR GUEST.
KA-THOOOM
ISN'T THAT RIGHT, MISS TOP OF THE CHARTS?
THE JUDGE OF GOTHAM'S HOTTEST TALENT SHOW?
PLEASE... PLEASE.
I HAVE, I HAVE MONEY.
DON'T HURT ME.
PLEASE.
FOR THE LOVE OF GOD, JUST LET ME GO!
SHAME TO KILL HER, SHAUNA. SHE AIN'T A BAD LOOKER. LITTLE MEATY FOR MY TASTES.
HATE TO MESS UP ALL THAT GOOD SURGERY.

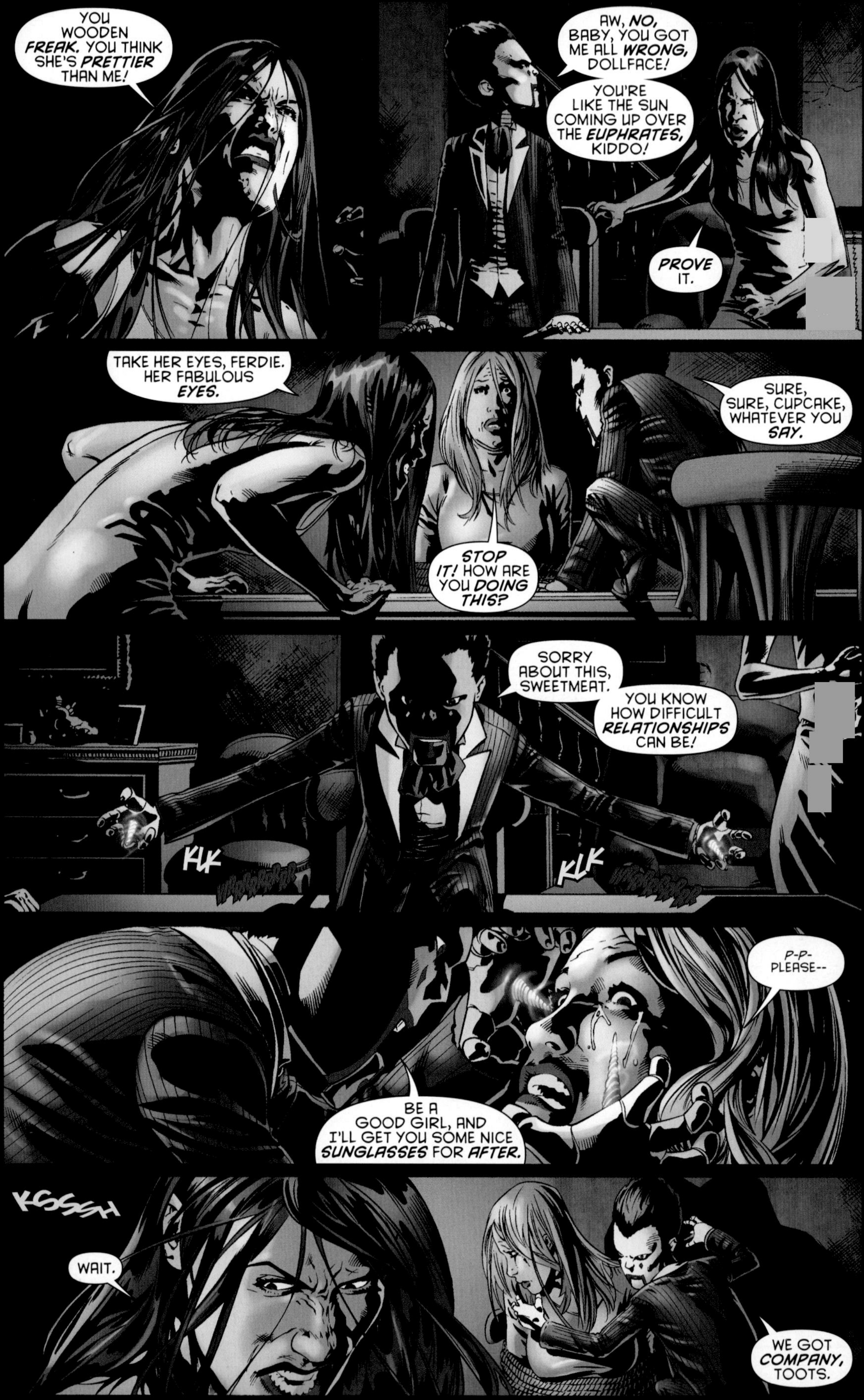
YOU WOODEN FREAK. YOU THINK SHE'S PRETTIER THAN ME!
AW, NO, BABY, YOU GOT ME ALL WRONG, DOLLFACE!
YOU'RE LIKE THE SUN COMING UP OVER THE EUPHRATES, KIDDO!
PROVE IT.
TAKE HER EYES, FERDIE. HER FABULOUS EYES.
SURE, SURE, CUPCAKE, WHATEVER YOU SAY.
STOP IT! HOW ARE YOU DOING THIS?
SORRY ABOUT THIS, SWEETMEAT.
YOU KNOW HOW DIFFICULT RELATIONSHIPS CAN BE!
KLK
KLK
P-P-PLEASE--
BE A GOOD GIRL, AND I'LL GET YOU SOME NICE SUNGLASSES FOR AFTER.
KSSSH
WAIT.
WE GOT COMPANY, TOOTS.

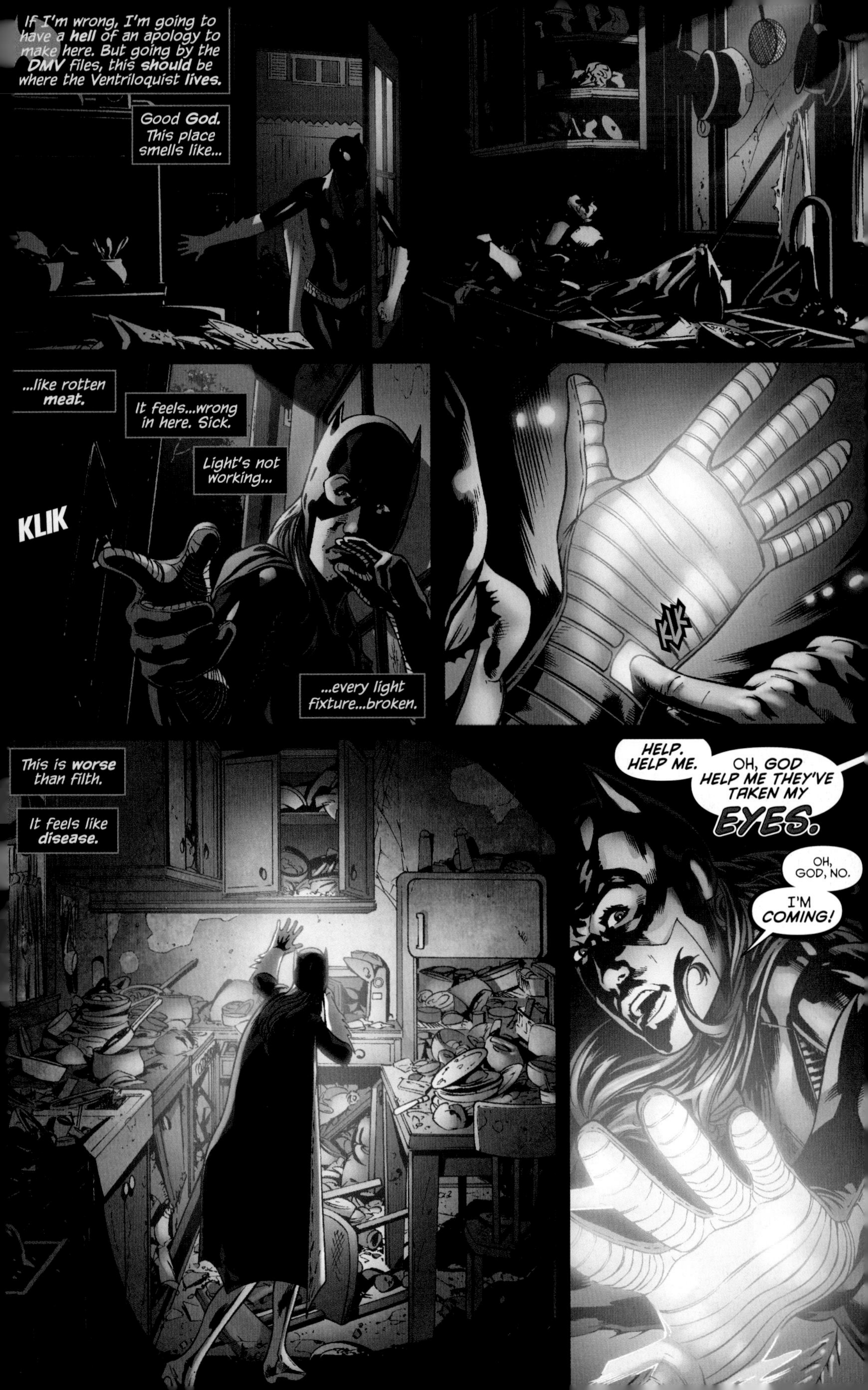
If I'm wrong, I'm going to have a hell of an apology to make here. But going by the DMV files, this should be where the Ventriloquist lives.
Good God. This place smells like...
...like rotten meat.
It feels...wrong in here. Sick.
Light's not working...
KLIK
...every light fixture...broken.
KLIK
This is worse than filth.
It feels like disease.
HELP. HELP ME.
OH, GOD HELP ME THEY'VE TAKEN MY EYES.
OH, GOD, NO.
I'M COMING!

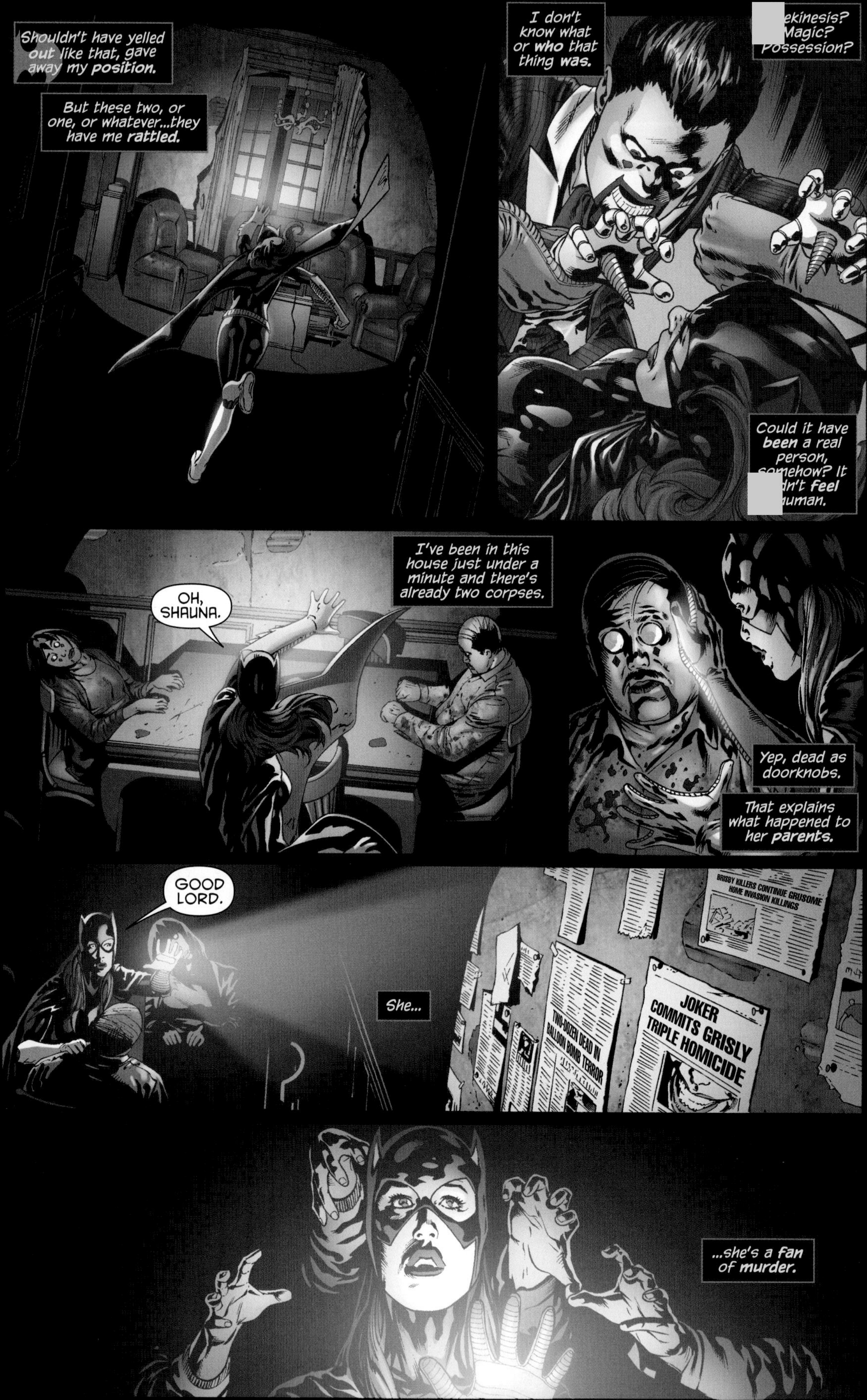

Shouldn't have yelled out like that, gave away my position.
But these two, or one, or whatever...they have me rattled.
I don't know what or who that thing was.
ekinesis? Magic? Possession?
Could it have been a real person, somehow? It dn't feel uman.
I've been in this house just under a minute and there's already two corpses.
OH, SHAUNA.
Yep, dead as doorknobs.
That explains what happened to her parents.
GOOD LORD.
She...
BRISBY KILLERS CONTINUE GRUSOME HOME INVASION KILLINGS
TWO-DOZEN DEAD IN BALLOON BOMB TERROR
JOKER COMMITS GRISLY TRIPLE HOMICIDE
...she's a fan of murder.

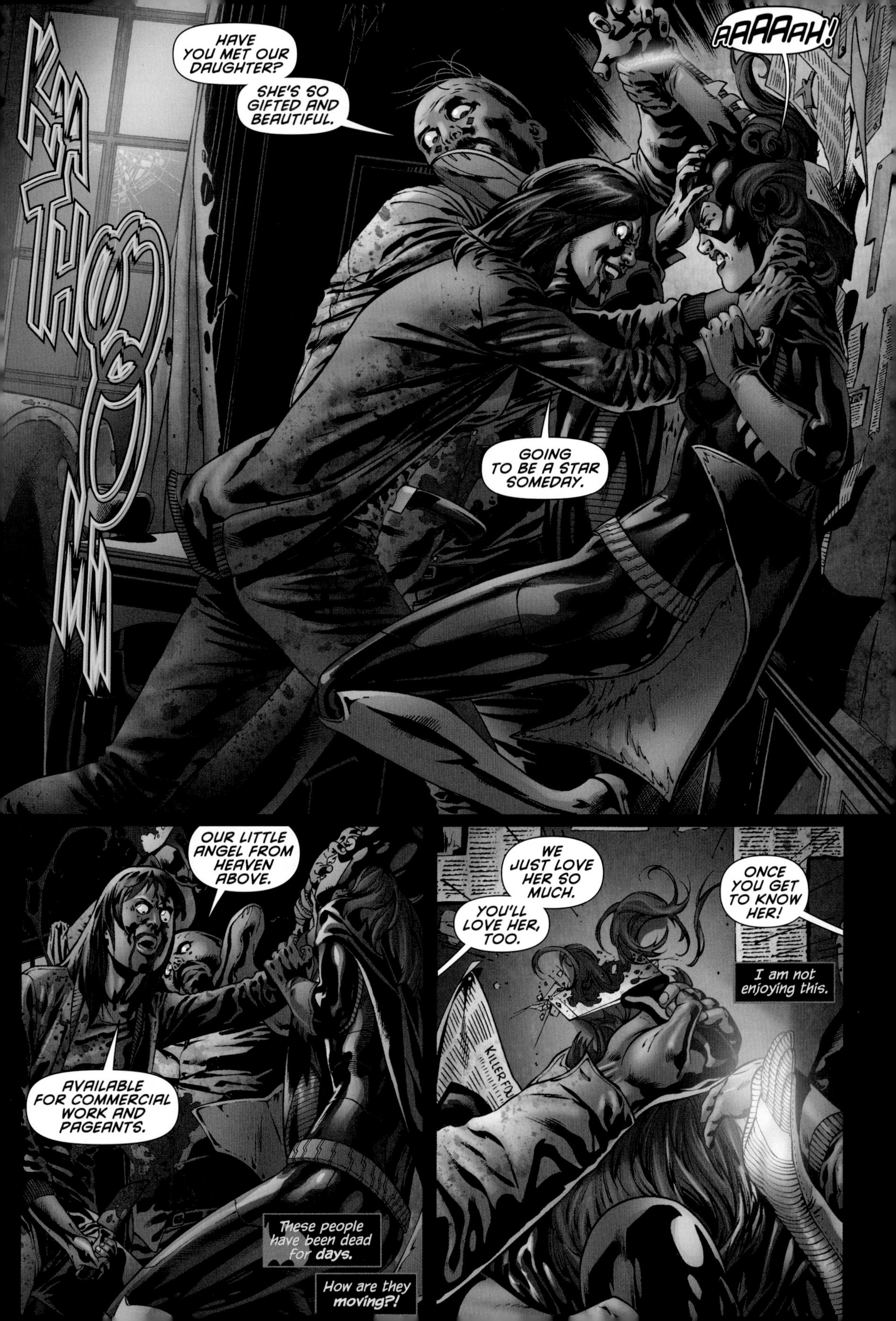

KA-THOOM
HAVE YOU MET OUR DAUGHTER?
SHE'S SO GIFTED AND BEAUTIFUL.
AAAAAH!
GOING TO BE A STAR SOMEDAY.
OUR LITTLE ANGEL FROM HEAVEN ABOVE.
AVAILABLE FOR COMMERCIAL WORK AND PAGEANTS.
These people have been dead for **days.**
How are they **moving?!**
WE JUST LOVE HER SO MUCH.
YOU'LL LOVE HER, TOO.
ONCE YOU GET TO KNOW HER!
I am not enjoying this.
KILLER

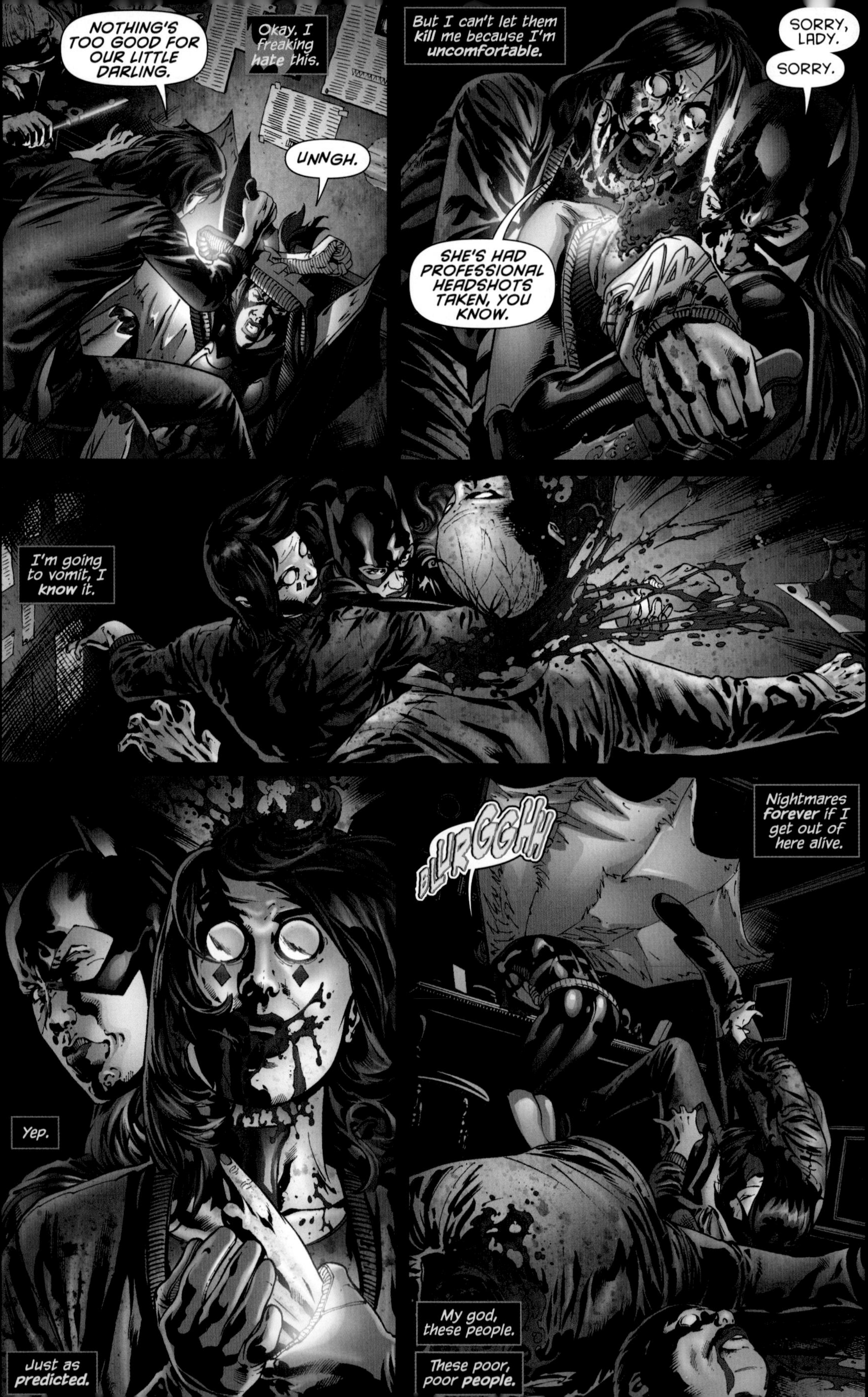
NOTHING'S TOO GOOD FOR OUR LITTLE DARLING.
Okay. I freaking hate this.
UNNGH.
But I can't let them kill me because I'm uncomfortable.
SORRY, LADY.
SORRY.
SHE'S HAD PROFESSIONAL HEADSHOTS TAKEN, YOU KNOW.
I'm going to vomit, I know it.
Nightmares forever if I get out of here alive.
BLURGGHH
Yep.
Just as predicted.
My god, these people.
These poor, poor people.

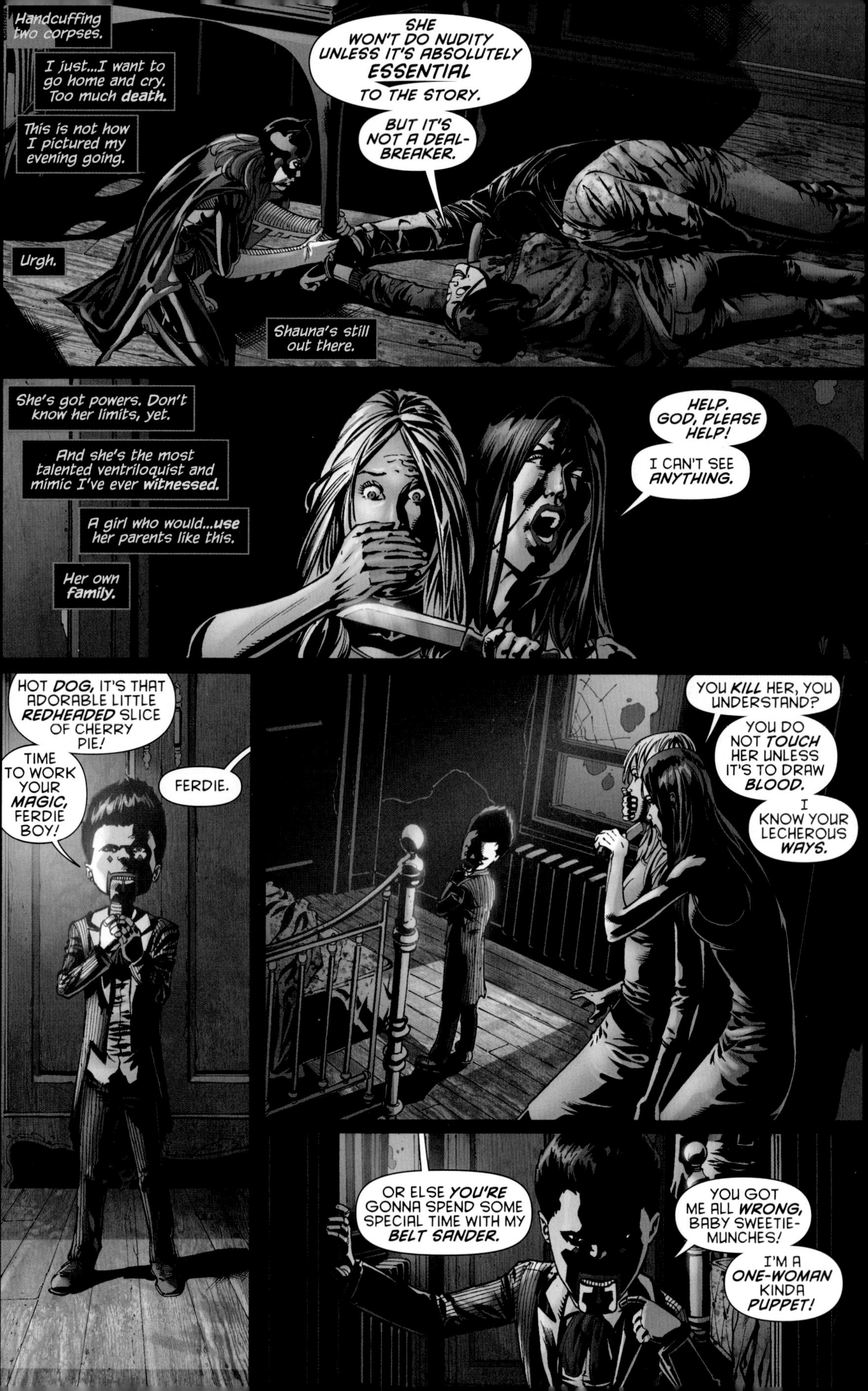

Handcuffing two corpses.
SHE WON'T DO NUDITY UNLESS IT'S ABSOLUTELY ESSENTIAL TO THE STORY.
I just...I want to go home and cry. Too much death.
This is not how I pictured my evening going.
BUT IT'S NOT A DEAL-BREAKER.
Urgh.
Shauna's still out there.
She's got powers. Don't know her limits, yet.
And she's the most talented ventriloquist and mimic I've ever witnessed.
A girl who would...use her parents like this.
Her own family.
HELP. GOD, PLEASE HELP!
I CAN'T SEE ANYTHING.
HOT DOG, IT'S THAT ADORABLE LITTLE REDHEADED SLICE OF CHERRY PIE!
TIME TO WORK YOUR MAGIC, FERDIE BOY!
FERDIE.
YOU KILL HER, YOU UNDERSTAND?
YOU DO NOT TOUCH HER UNLESS IT'S TO DRAW BLOOD.
I KNOW YOUR LECHEROUS WAYS.
OR ELSE YOU'RE GONNA SPEND SOME SPECIAL TIME WITH MY BELT SANDER.
YOU GOT ME ALL WRONG, BABY SWEETIE-MUNCHES!
I'M A ONE-WOMAN KINDA PUPPET!

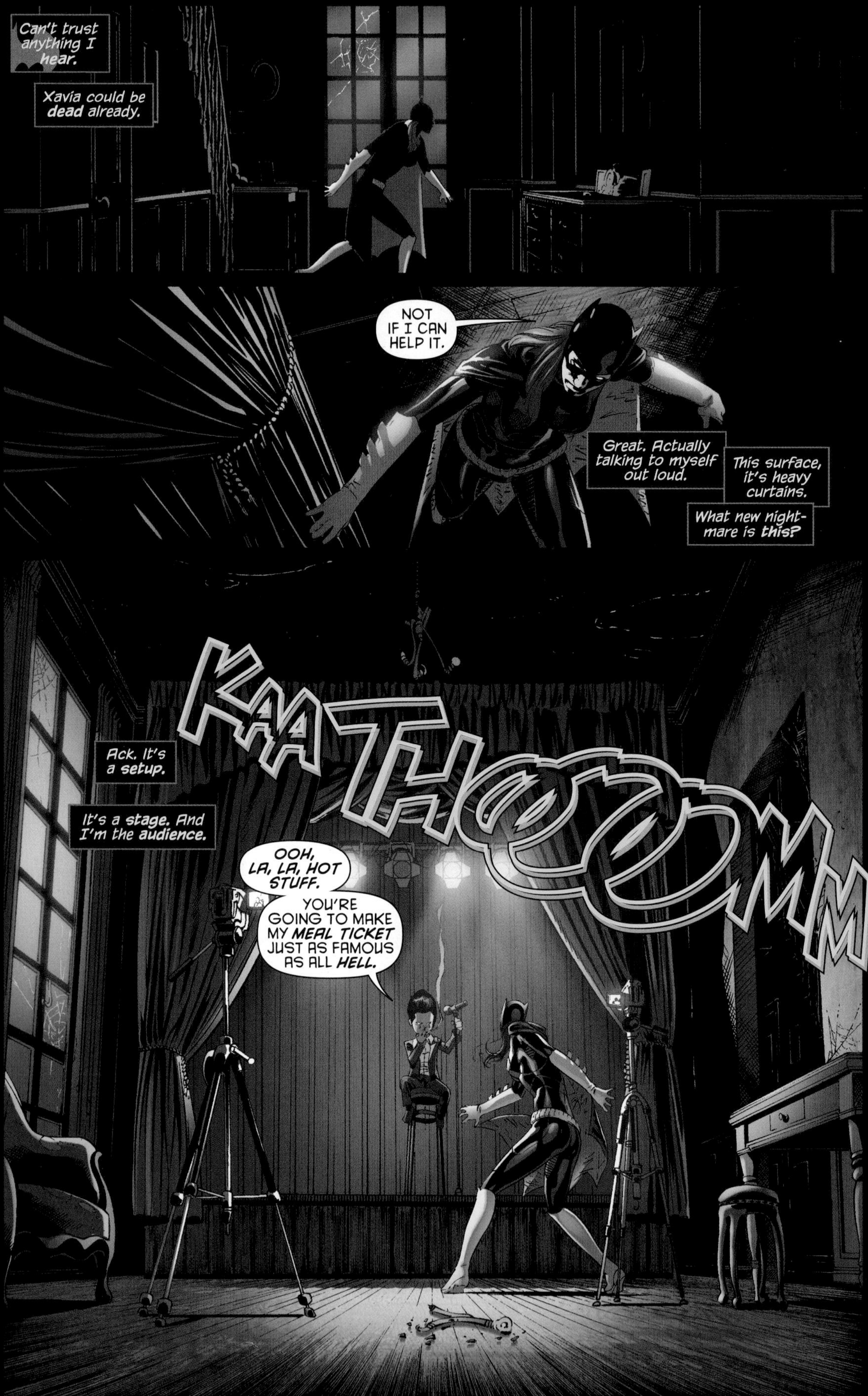
Can't trust anything I hear.
Xavia could be dead already.
NOT IF I CAN HELP IT.
Great. Actually talking to myself out loud.
This surface, it's heavy curtains.
What new night-mare is this?
KATHOOMM
Ack. It's a setup.
It's a stage. And I'm the audience.
OOH, LA, LA, HOT STUFF.
YOU'RE GOING TO MAKE MY MEAL TICKET JUST AS FAMOUS AS ALL HELL.

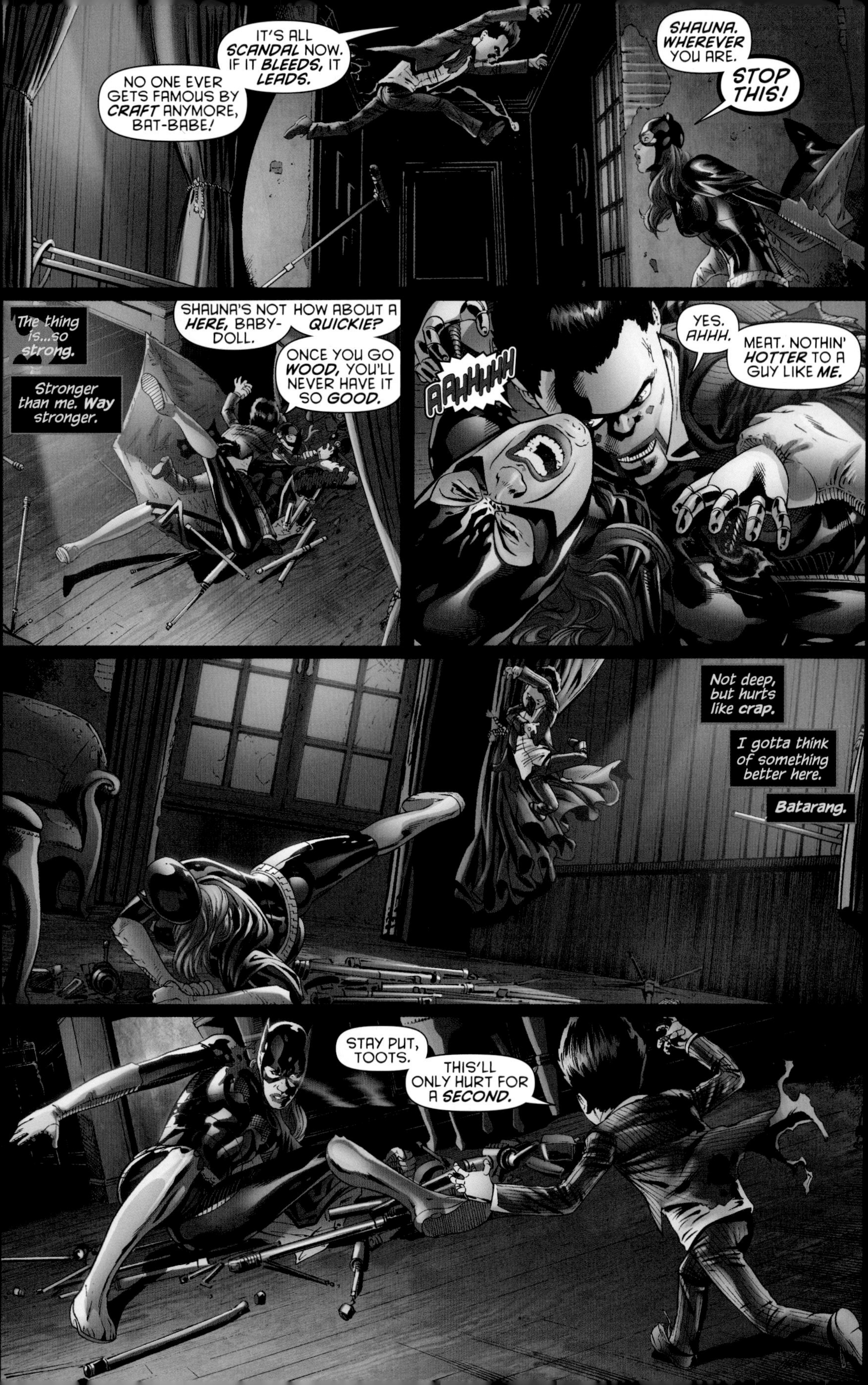

NO ONE EVER GETS FAMOUS BY CRAFT ANYMORE, BAT-BABE!
IT'S ALL SCANDAL NOW. IF IT BLEEDS, IT LEADS.
SHAUNA. WHEREVER YOU ARE. STOP THIS!
The thing is...so strong.
Stronger than me. Way stronger.
SHAUNA'S NOT HERE, BABY-DOLL.
HOW ABOUT A QUICKIE?
ONCE YOU GO WOOD, YOU'LL NEVER HAVE IT SO GOOD.
AAHHHHH
YES. AHHH.
MEAT. NOTHIN' HOTTER TO A GUY LIKE ME.
Not deep, but hurts like crap.
I gotta think of something better here.
Batarang.
STAY PUT, TOOTS.
THIS'LL ONLY HURT FOR A SECOND.

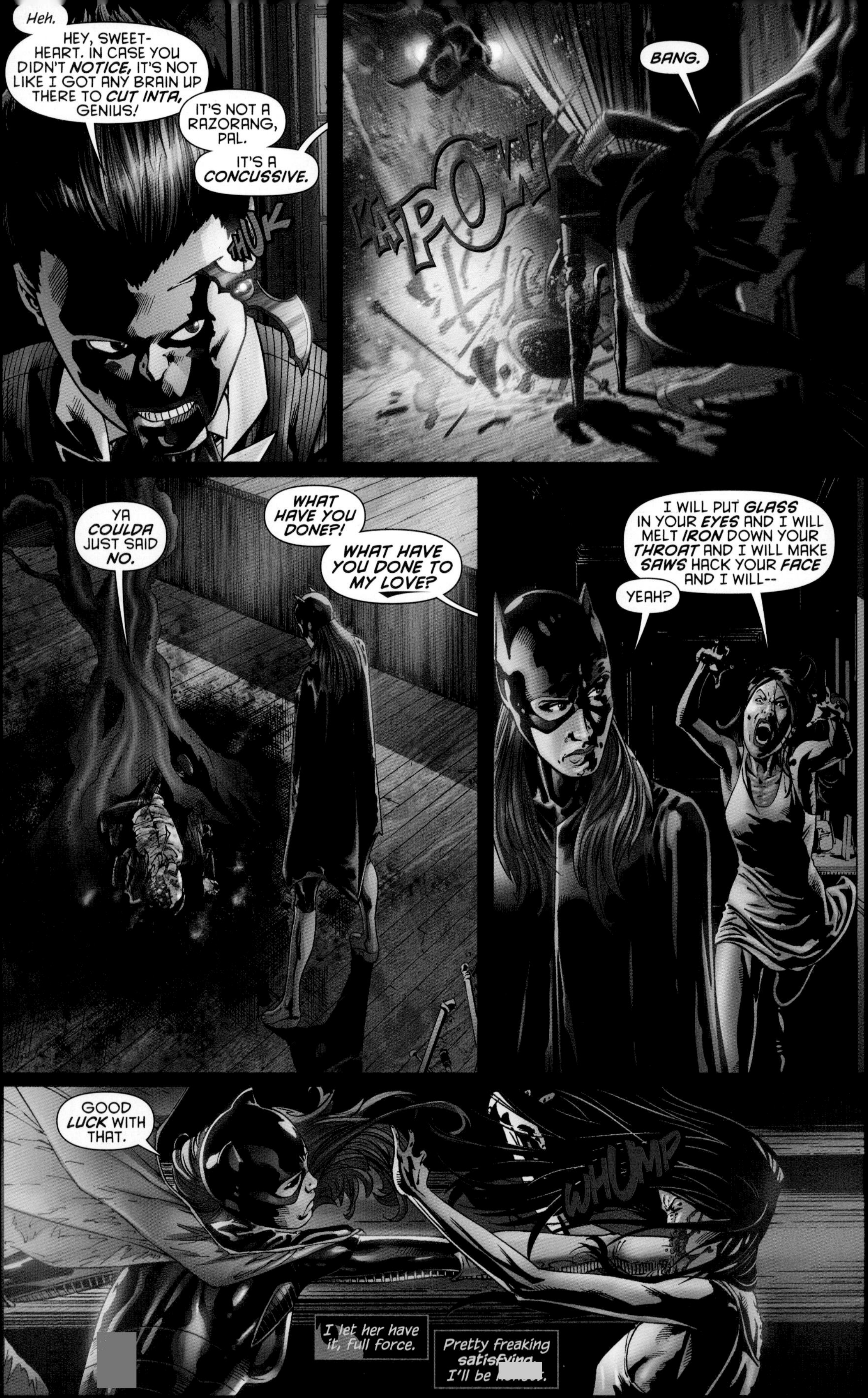
Heh.
HEY, SWEET-HEART. IN CASE YOU DIDN'T NOTICE, IT'S NOT LIKE I GOT ANY BRAIN UP THERE TO CUT INTA, GENIUS!
IT'S NOT A RAZORANG, PAL.
IT'S A CONCUSSIVE.
THUK
BANG.
KA-POW
YA COULDA JUST SAID NO.
WHAT HAVE YOU DONE?!
WHAT HAVE YOU DONE TO MY LOVE?
I WILL PUT GLASS IN YOUR EYES AND I WILL MELT IRON DOWN YOUR THROAT AND I WILL MAKE SAWS HACK YOUR FACE AND I WILL--
YEAH?
GOOD LUCK WITH THAT.
WHUMP
I let her have it, full force.
Pretty freaking satisfying. I'll be

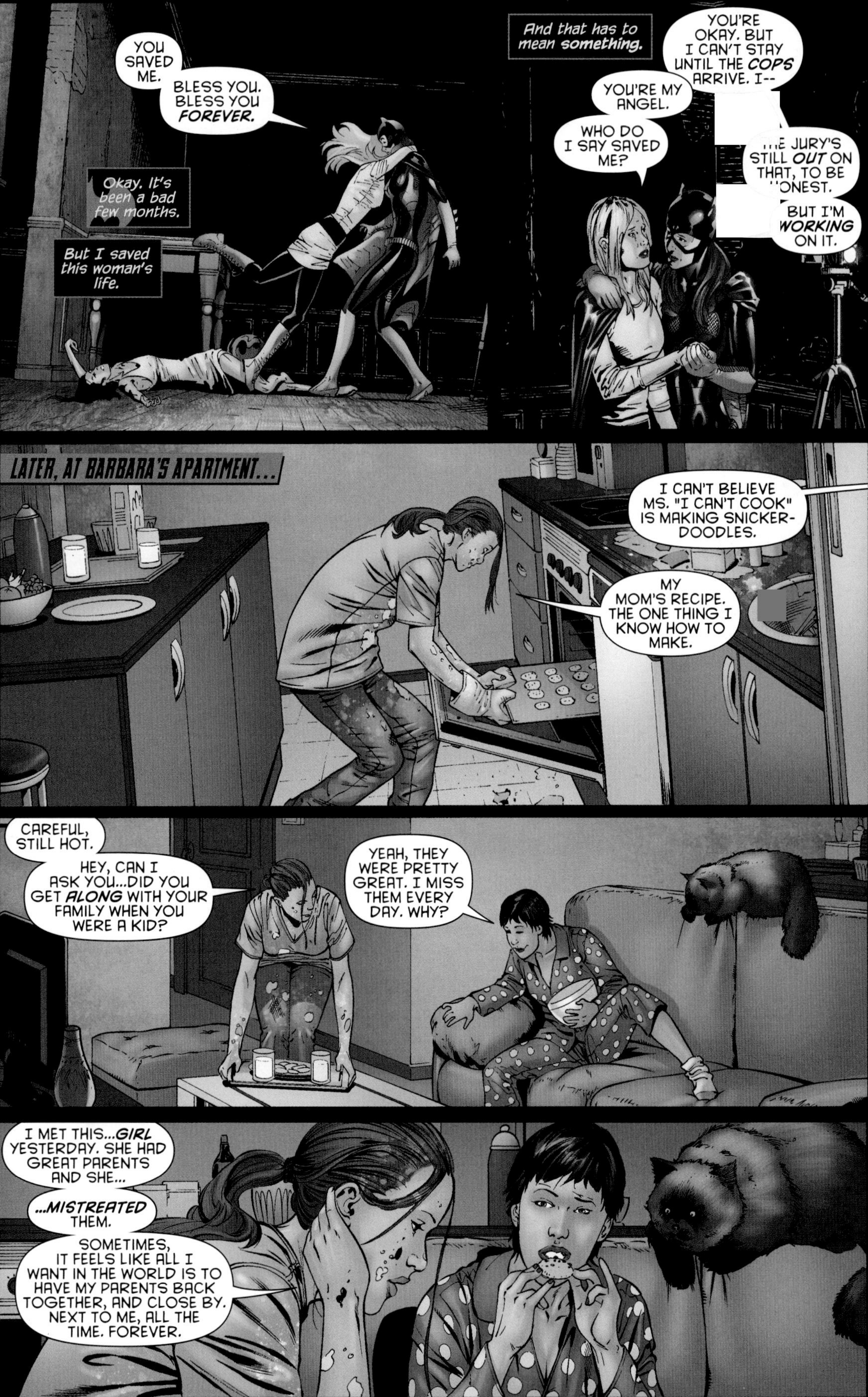

YOU SAVED ME.
BLESS YOU. BLESS YOU *FOREVER.*
Okay. It's been a bad few months.
But I saved this woman's life.
And that has to mean *something.*
YOU'RE MY ANGEL.
WHO DO I SAY SAVED ME?
YOU'RE OKAY. BUT I CAN'T STAY UNTIL THE *COPS* ARRIVE. I--
JURY'S STILL *OUT* ON THAT, TO BE
BUT I'M *WORKING* ON IT.
LATER, AT BARBARA'S APARTMENT...
I CAN'T BELIEVE MS. "I CAN'T COOK" IS MAKING SNICKER-DOODLES.
MY MOM'S RECIPE. THE ONE THING I KNOW HOW TO MAKE.
CAREFUL, STILL HOT.
HEY, CAN I ASK YOU...DID YOU GET *ALONG* WITH YOUR FAMILY WHEN YOU WERE A KID?
YEAH, THEY WERE PRETTY GREAT. I MISS THEM EVERY DAY. WHY?
I MET THIS...*GIRL* YESTERDAY. SHE HAD GREAT PARENTS AND SHE...
...*MISTREATED* THEM.
SOMETIMES, IT FEELS LIKE ALL I WANT IN THE WORLD IS TO HAVE MY PARENTS BACK TOGETHER, AND CLOSE BY. NEXT TO ME, ALL THE TIME. FOREVER.

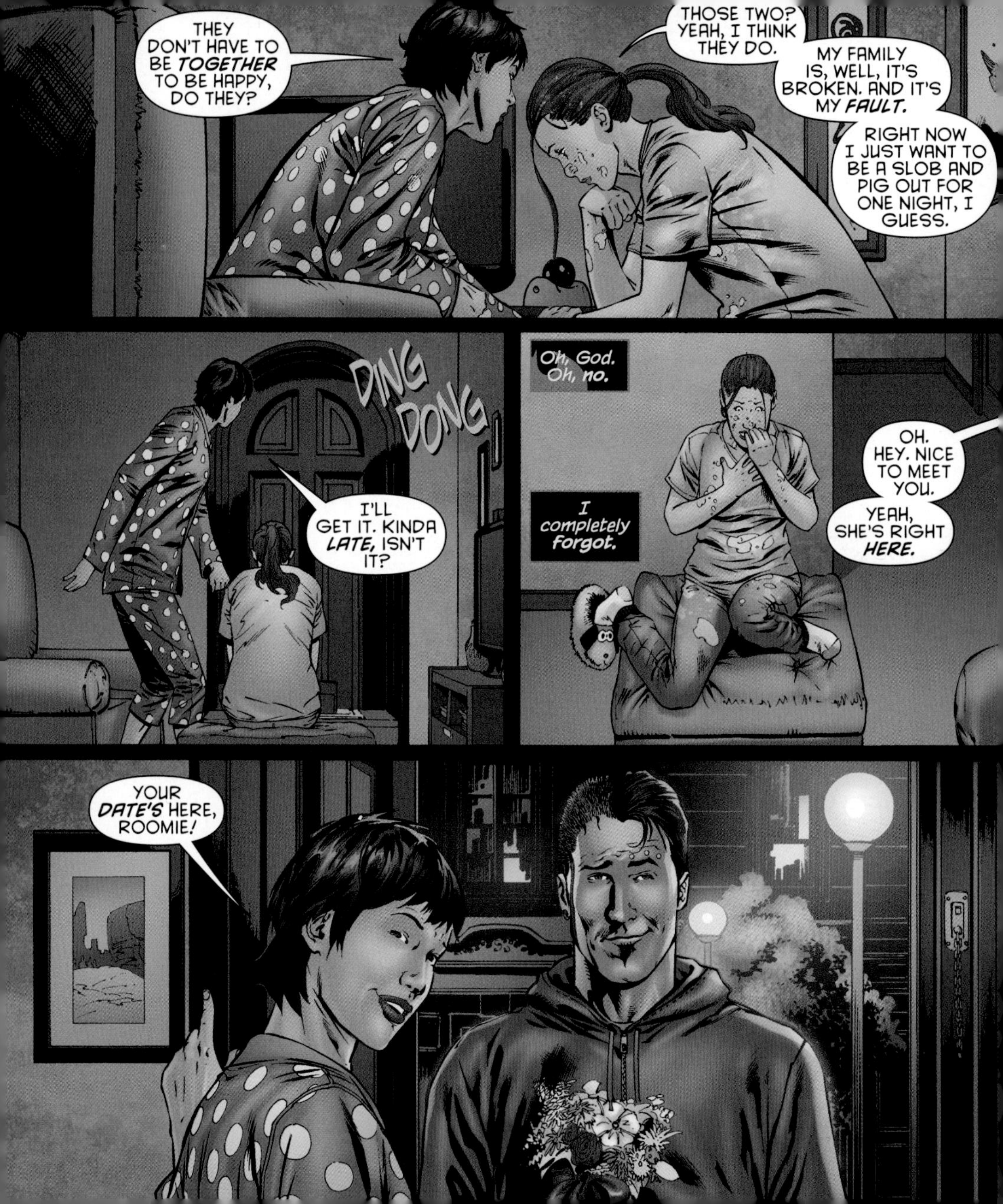
THEY DON'T HAVE TO BE *TOGETHER* TO BE HAPPY, DO THEY?
THOSE TWO? YEAH, I THINK THEY DO.
MY FAMILY IS, WELL, IT'S BROKEN. AND IT'S MY *FAULT.*
RIGHT NOW I JUST WANT TO BE A SLOB AND PIG OUT FOR ONE NIGHT, I GUESS.
DING DONG
I'LL GET IT. KINDA *LATE,* ISN'T IT?
*Oh, God. Oh, **no.***
I completely forgot.
OH. HEY. NICE TO MEET YOU.
YEAH, SHE'S RIGHT *HERE.*
YOUR *DATE'S* HERE, ROOMIE!

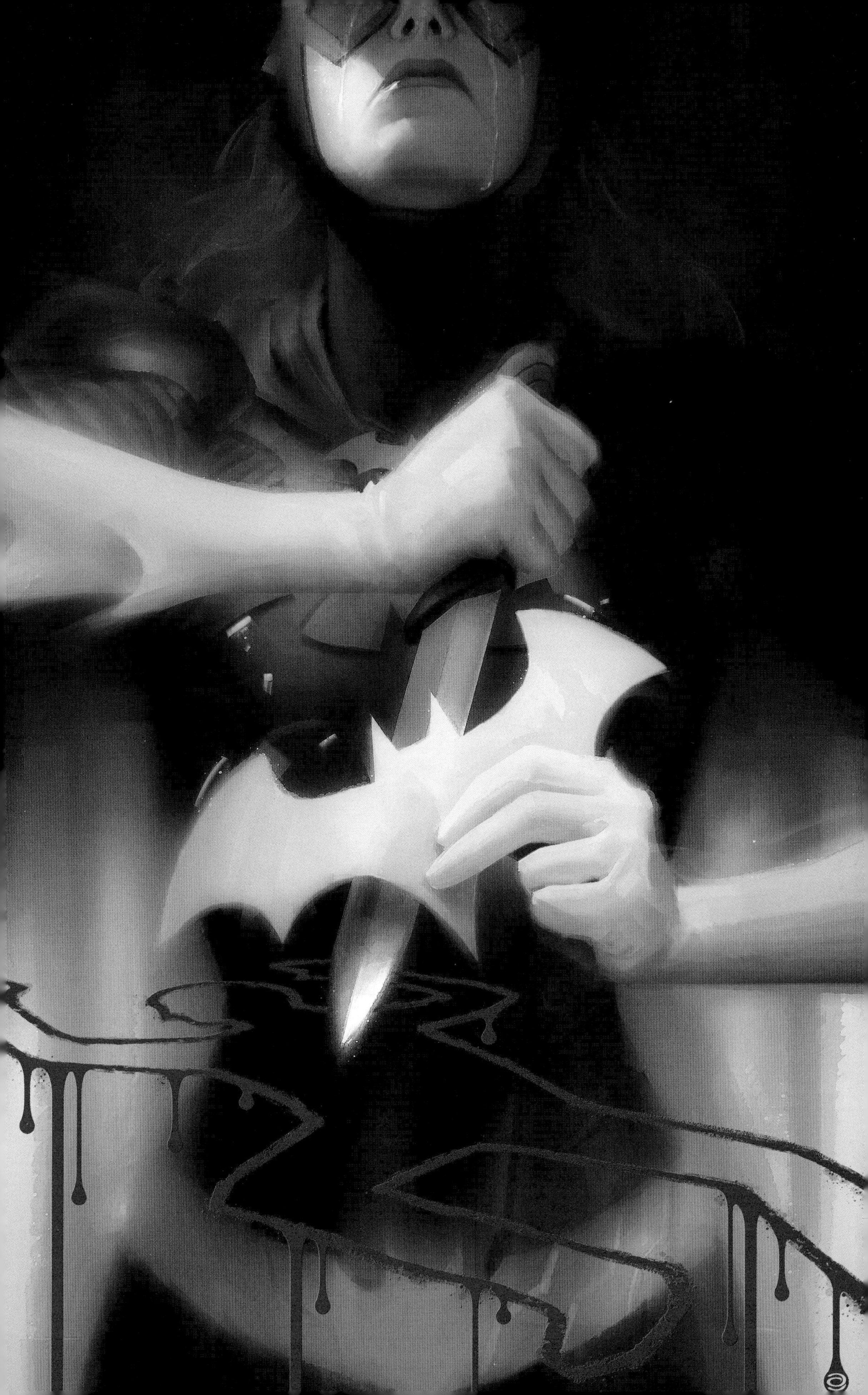

A DAY IN A LIFE OF ENDLESS VELOCITY

GAIL SIMONE writer FERNANDO PASARIN penciller JONATHAN GLAPION inker BLOND colorist

cover by ALEX GARNER

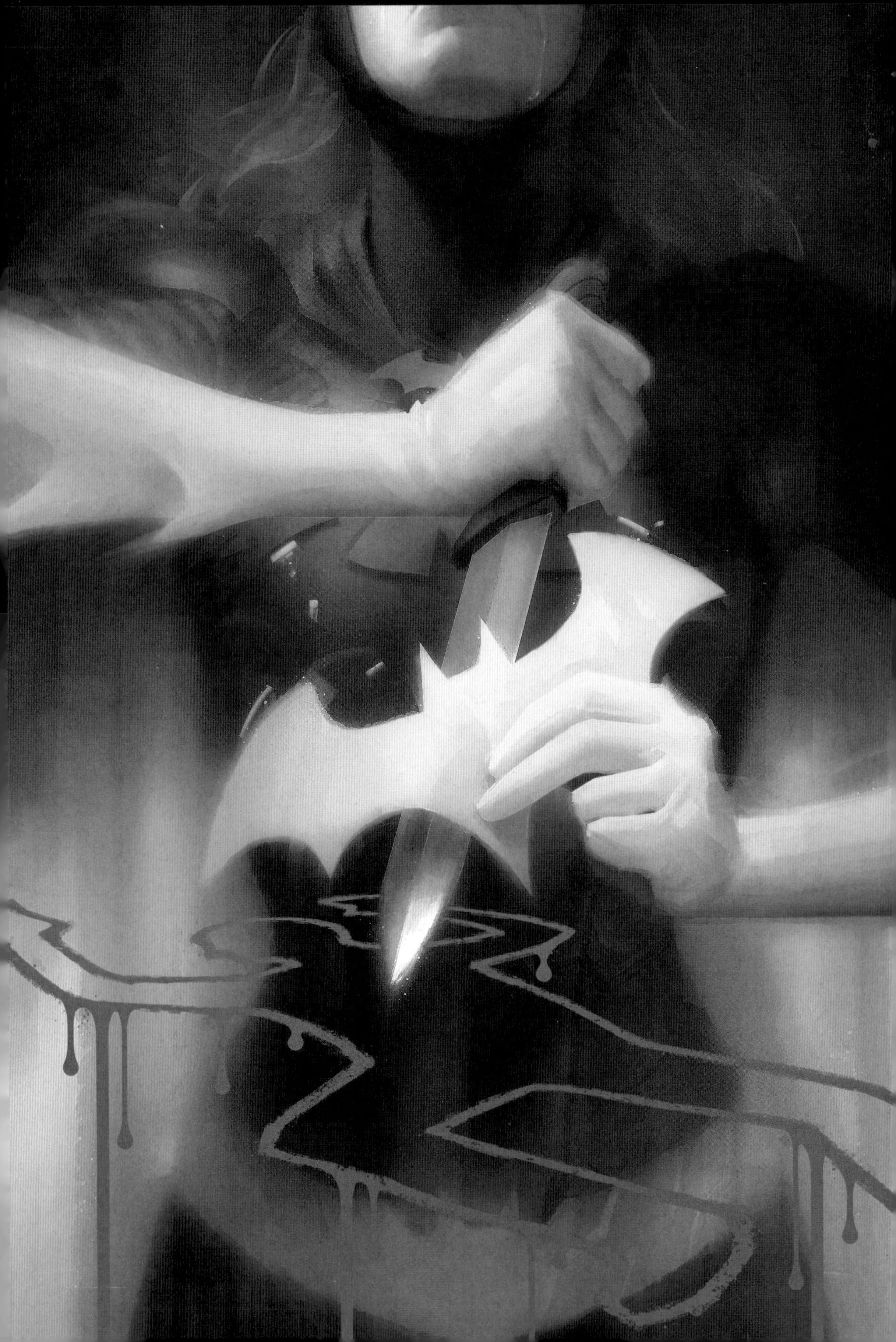

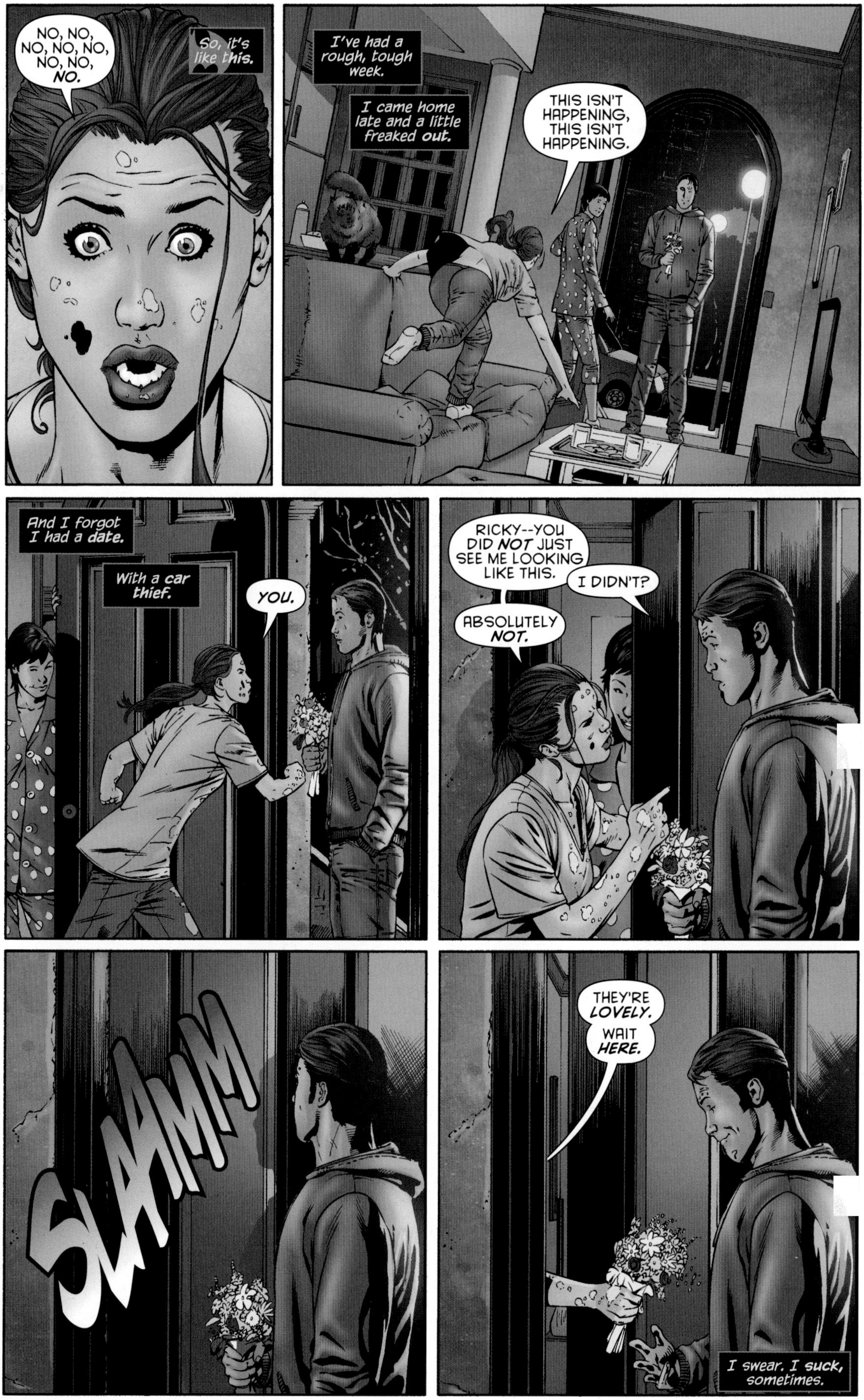
NO, NO, NO, NO, NO, NO, NO, NO.
So, it's like this.
I've had a rough, tough week.
I came home late and a little freaked out.
THIS ISN'T HAPPENING, THIS ISN'T HAPPENING.
And I forgot I had a date.
With a car thief.
YOU.
RICKY--YOU DID NOT JUST SEE ME LOOKING LIKE THIS.
I DIDN'T?
ABSOLUTELY NOT.
SLAMM
THEY'RE LOVELY.
WAIT HERE.
I swear. I suck, sometimes.

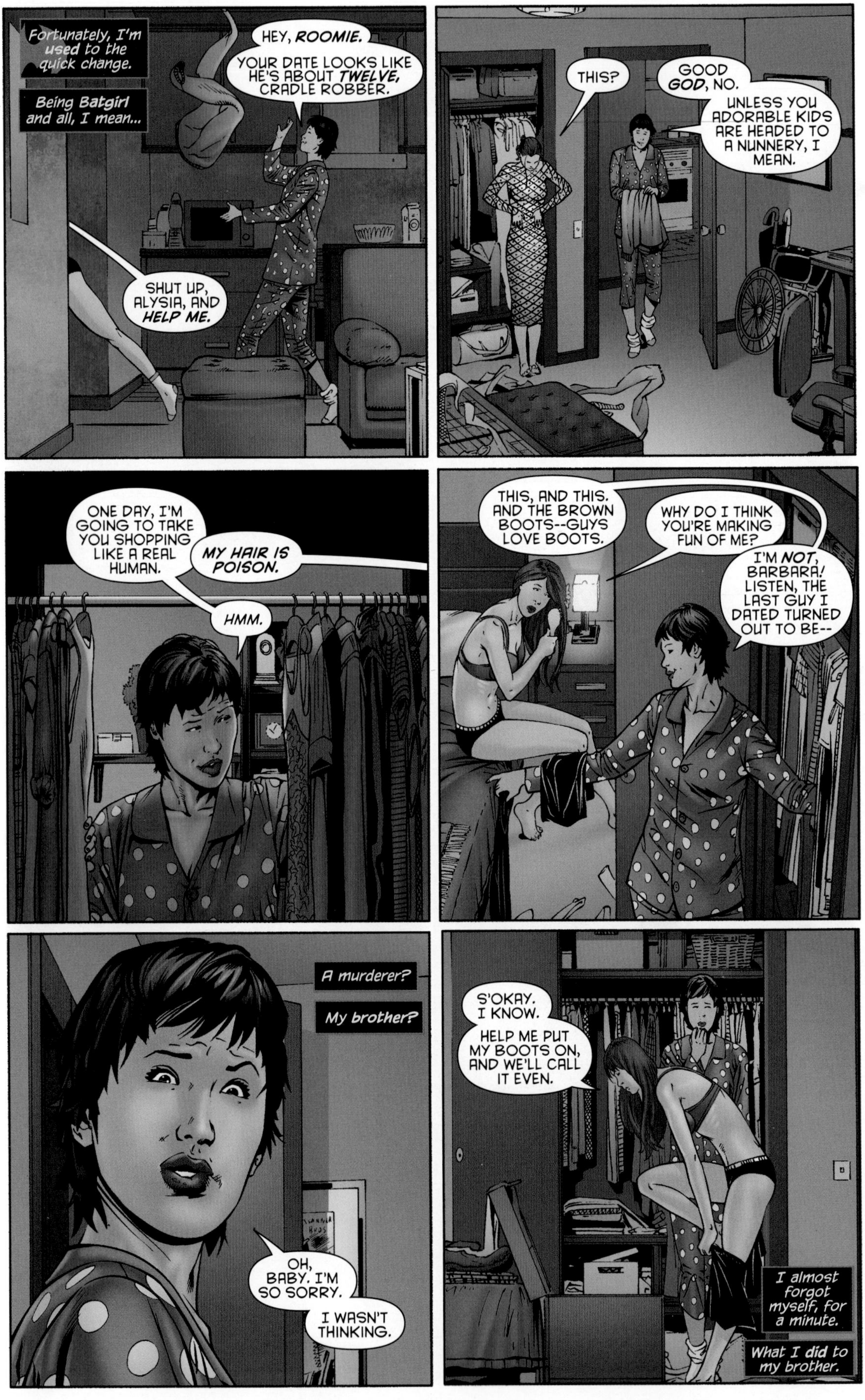
Fortunately, I'm used to the quick change.
Being Batgirl and all, I mean...
HEY, ROOMIE.
YOUR DATE LOOKS LIKE HE'S ABOUT TWELVE, CRADLE ROBBER.
SHUT UP, ALYSIA, AND HELP ME.
THIS?
GOOD GOD, NO.
UNLESS YOU ADORABLE KIDS ARE HEADED TO A NUNNERY, I MEAN.
ONE DAY, I'M GOING TO TAKE YOU SHOPPING LIKE A REAL HUMAN.
MY HAIR IS POISON.
HMM.
THIS, AND THIS. AND THE BROWN BOOTS--GUYS LOVE BOOTS.
WHY DO I THINK YOU'RE MAKING FUN OF ME?
I'M NOT, BARBARA! LISTEN, THE LAST GUY I DATED TURNED OUT TO BE--
A murderer?
My brother?
OH, BABY. I'M SO SORRY.
I WASN'T THINKING.
S'OKAY. I KNOW.
HELP ME PUT MY BOOTS ON, AND WE'LL CALL IT EVEN.
I almost forgot myself, for a minute.
What I did to my brother.

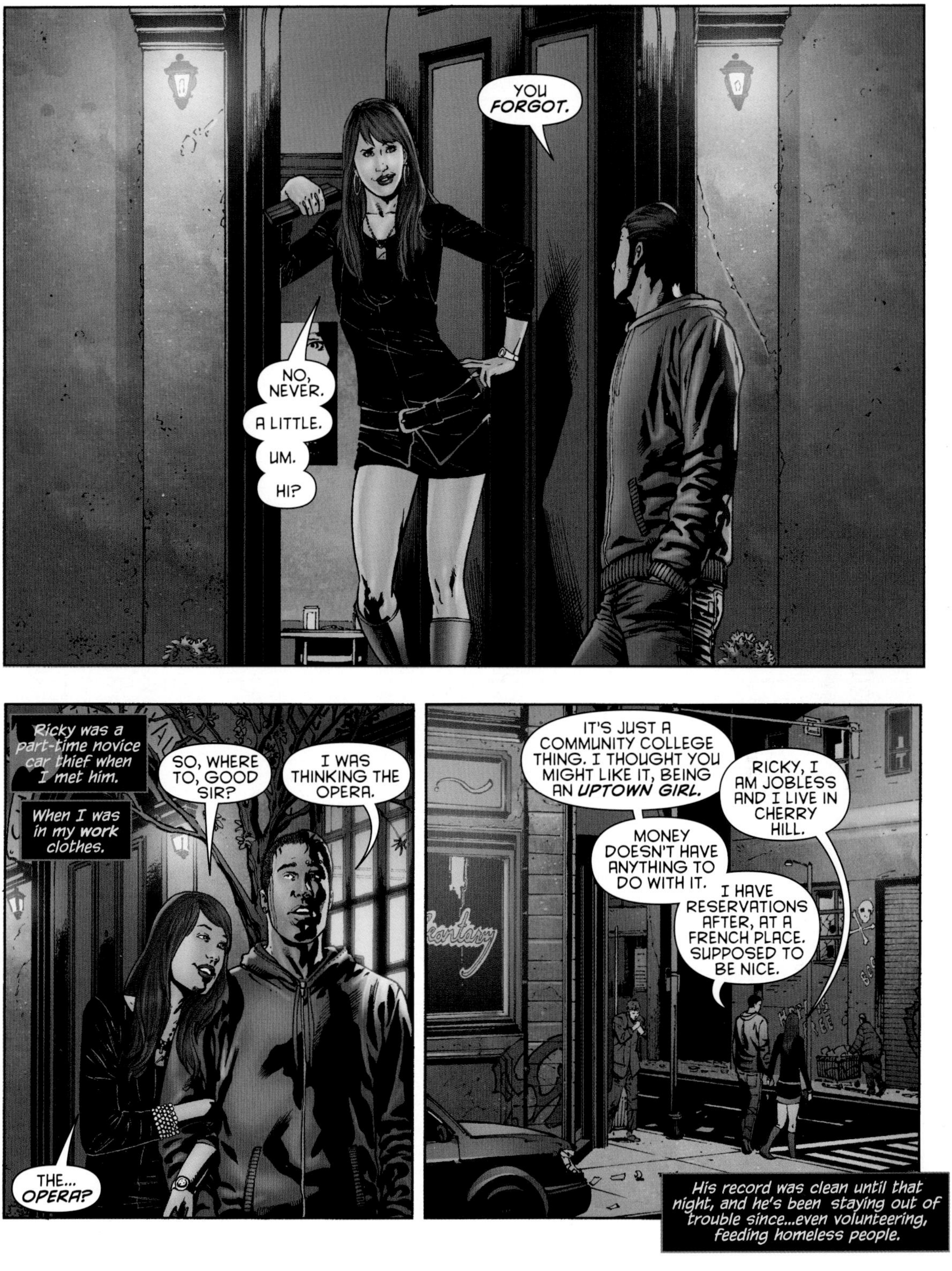
YOU FORGOT.
NO, NEVER.
A LITTLE.
UM.
HI?
Ricky was a part-time novice car thief when I met him.
When I was in my work clothes.
SO, WHERE TO, GOOD SIR?
I WAS THINKING THE OPERA.
THE... OPERA?
IT'S JUST A COMMUNITY COLLEGE THING. I THOUGHT YOU MIGHT LIKE IT, BEING AN UPTOWN GIRL.
RICKY, I AM JOBLESS AND I LIVE IN CHERRY HILL.
MONEY DOESN'T HAVE ANYTHING TO DO WITH IT.
I HAVE RESERVATIONS AFTER, AT A FRENCH PLACE. SUPPOSED TO BE NICE.
His record was clean until that night, and he's been staying out of trouble since...even volunteering, feeding homeless people.

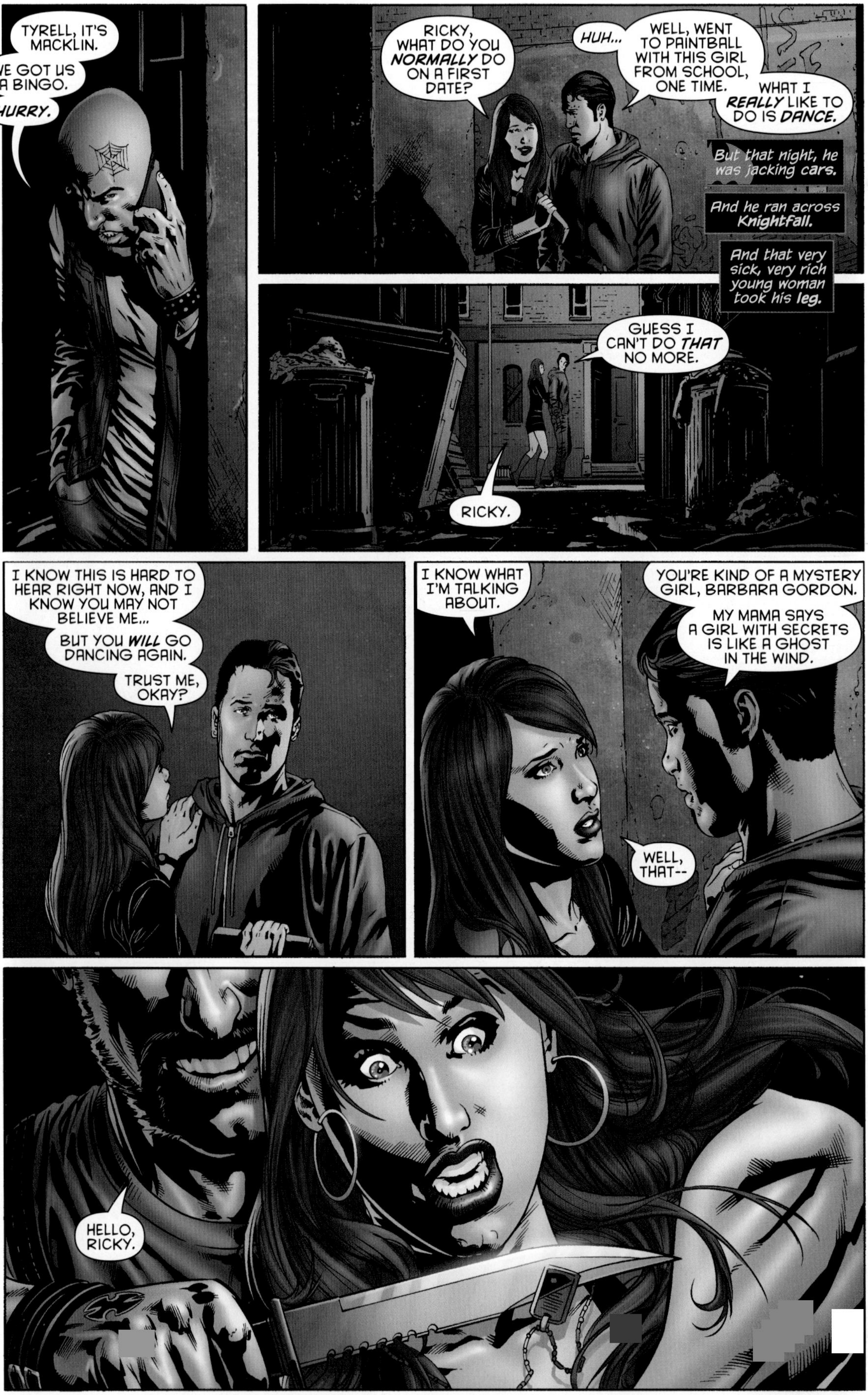

TYRELL, IT'S MACKLIN.
WE GOT US A BINGO.
HURRY.
RICKY, WHAT DO YOU NORMALLY DO ON A FIRST DATE?
HUH...
WELL, WENT TO PAINTBALL WITH THIS GIRL FROM SCHOOL, ONE TIME.
WHAT I REALLY LIKE TO DO IS DANCE.
But that night, he was jacking cars.
And he ran across Knightfall.
And that very sick, very rich young woman took his leg.
GUESS I CAN'T DO THAT NO MORE.
RICKY.
I KNOW THIS IS HARD TO HEAR RIGHT NOW, AND I KNOW YOU MAY NOT BELIEVE ME...
BUT YOU WILL GO DANCING AGAIN.
TRUST ME, OKAY?
I KNOW WHAT I'M TALKING ABOUT.
YOU'RE KIND OF A MYSTERY GIRL, BARBARA GORDON.
MY MAMA SAYS A GIRL WITH SECRETS IS LIKE A GHOST IN THE WIND.
WELL, THAT--
HELLO, RICKY.

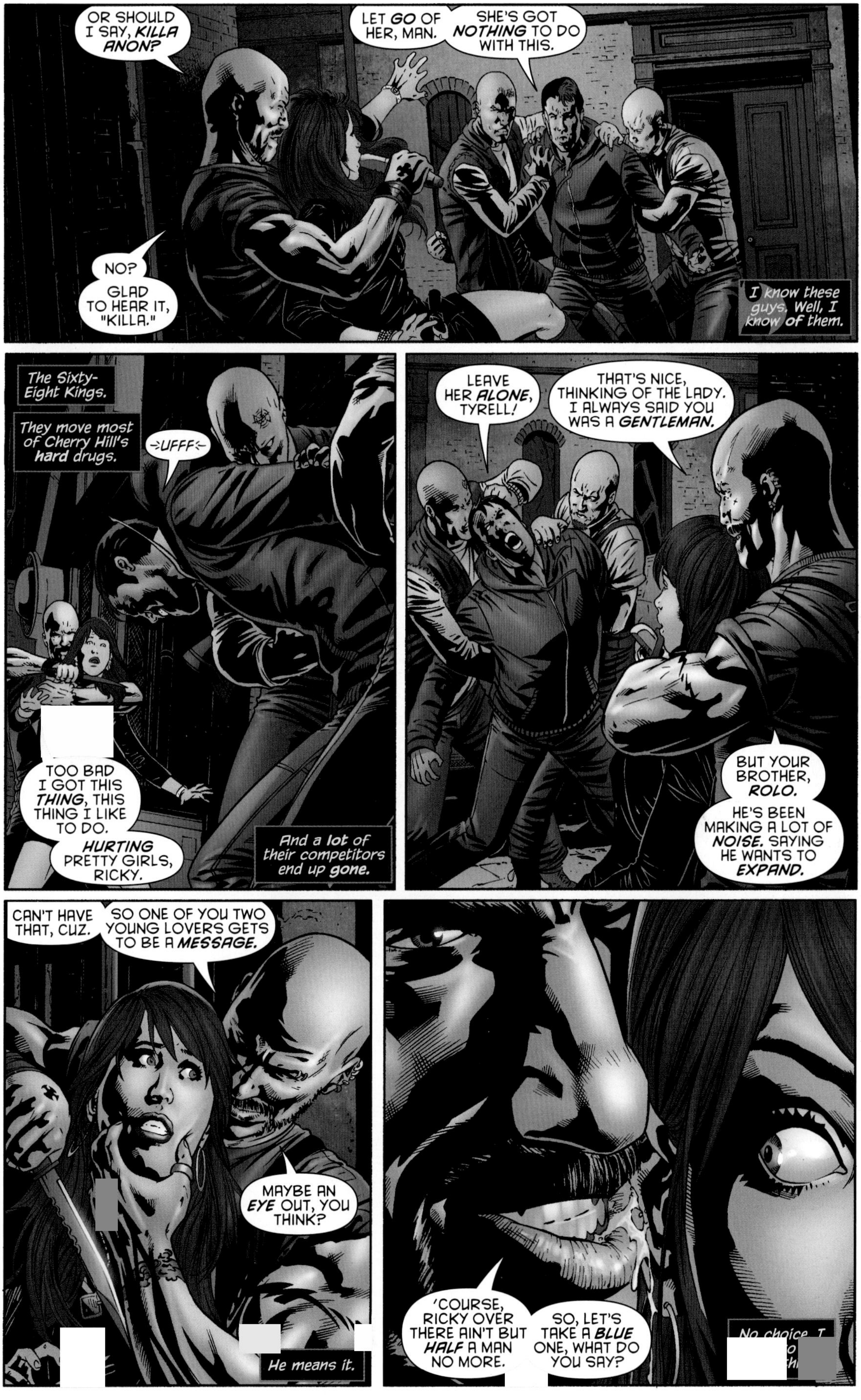

OR SHOULD I SAY, KILLA ANON?
LET GO OF HER, MAN.
SHE'S GOT NOTHING TO DO WITH THIS.
NO?
GLAD TO HEAR IT, "KILLA."
I know these guys. Well, I know of them.
The Sixty-Eight Kings.
They move most of Cherry Hill's hard drugs.
-UFFF-
TOO BAD I GOT THIS THING, THIS THING I LIKE TO DO.
HURTING PRETTY GIRLS, RICKY.
And a lot of their competitors end up gone.
LEAVE HER ALONE, TYRELL!
THAT'S NICE, THINKING OF THE LADY. I ALWAYS SAID YOU WAS A GENTLEMAN.
BUT YOUR BROTHER, ROLO.
HE'S BEEN MAKING A LOT OF NOISE. SAYING HE WANTS TO EXPAND.
CAN'T HAVE THAT, CUZ.
SO ONE OF YOU TWO YOUNG LOVERS GETS TO BE A MESSAGE.
MAYBE AN EYE OUT, YOU THINK?
He means it.
'COURSE, RICKY OVER THERE AIN'T BUT HALF A MAN NO MORE.
SO, LET'S TAKE A BLUE ONE, WHAT DO YOU SAY?
No choice. I

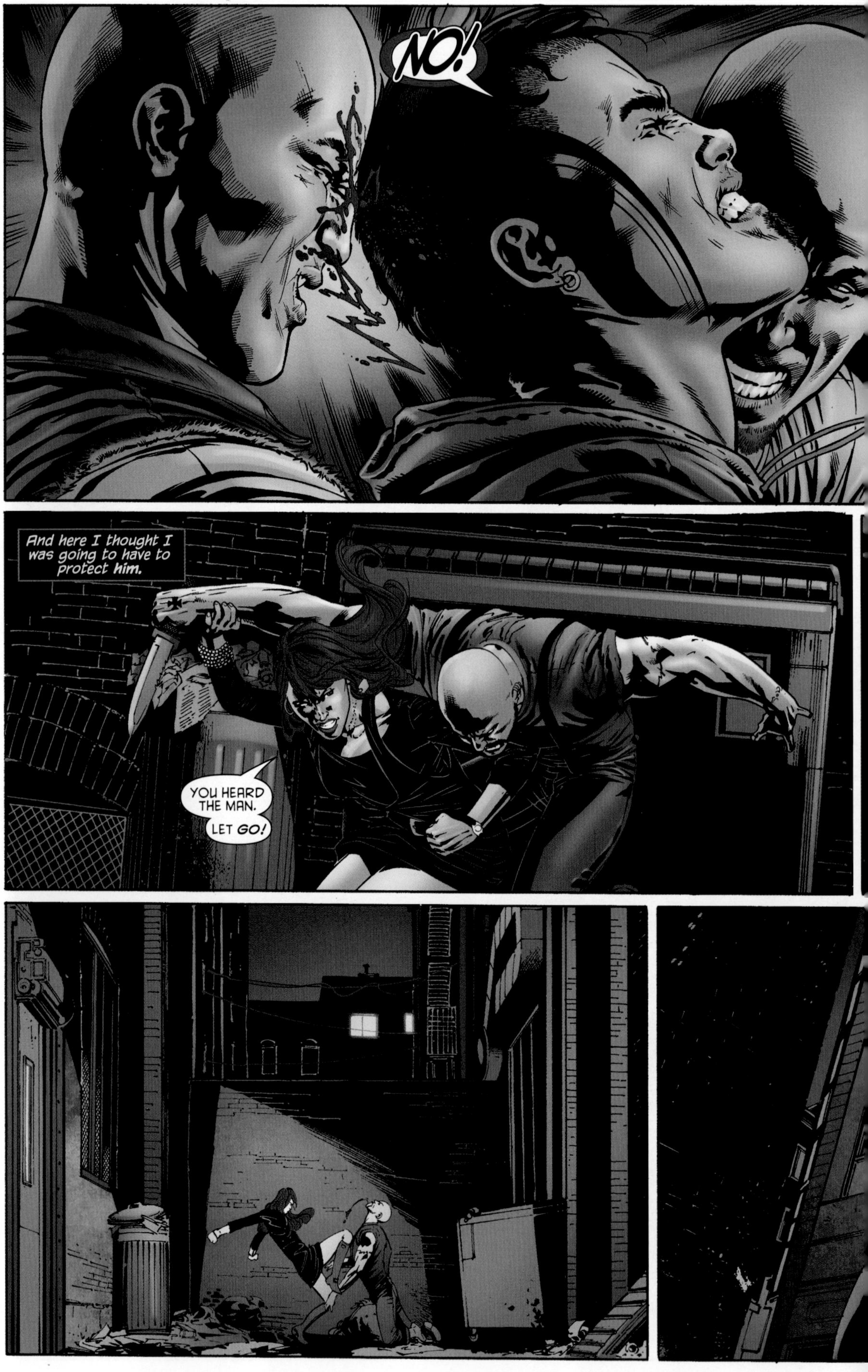
NO!
And here I thought I was going to have to protect him.
YOU HEARD THE MAN.
LET GO!

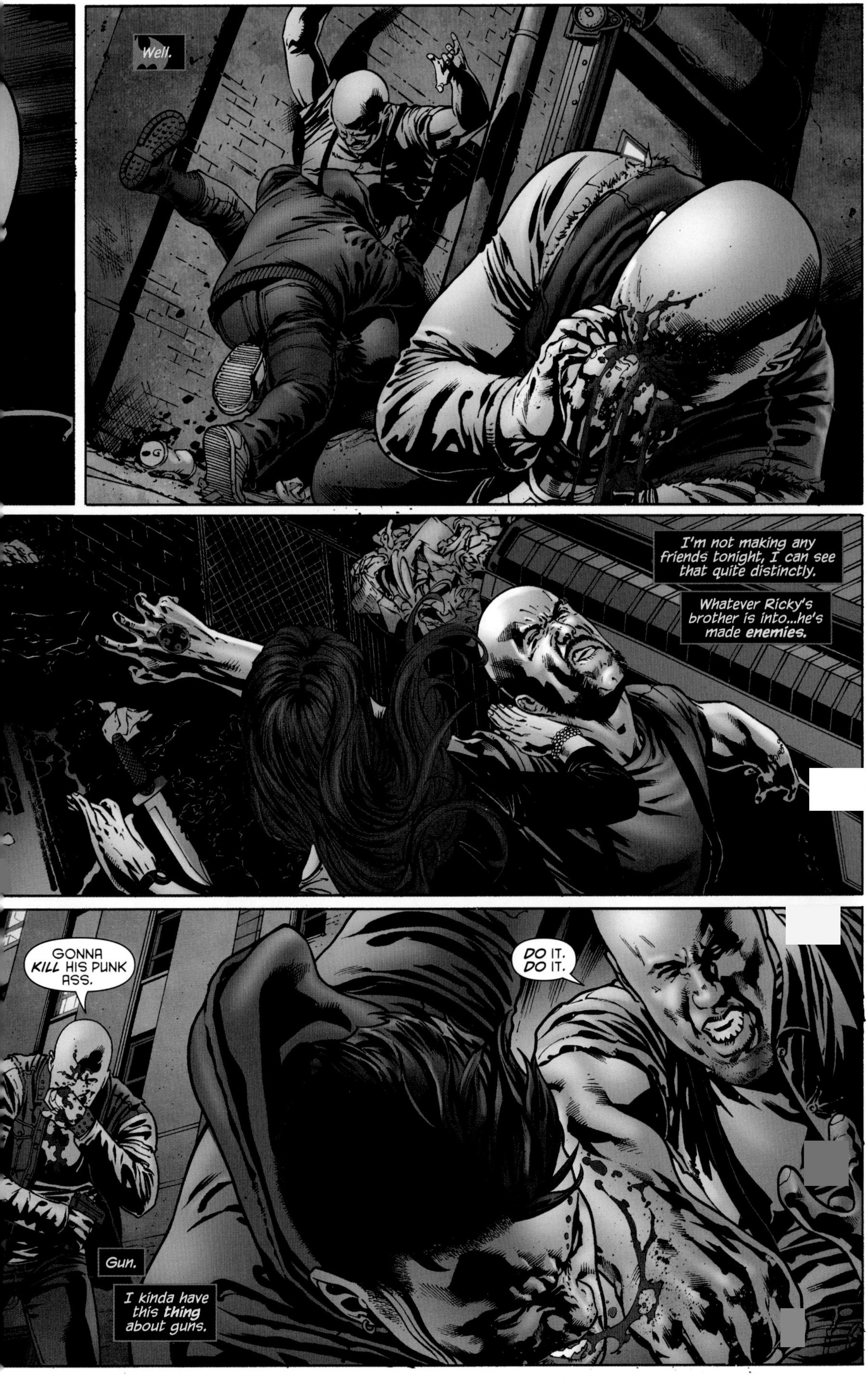
Well.
I'm not making any friends tonight, I can see that quite distinctly.
Whatever Ricky's brother is into...he's made enemies.
GONNA KILL HIS PUNK ASS.
DO IT. DO IT.
Gun.
I kinda have this thing about guns.

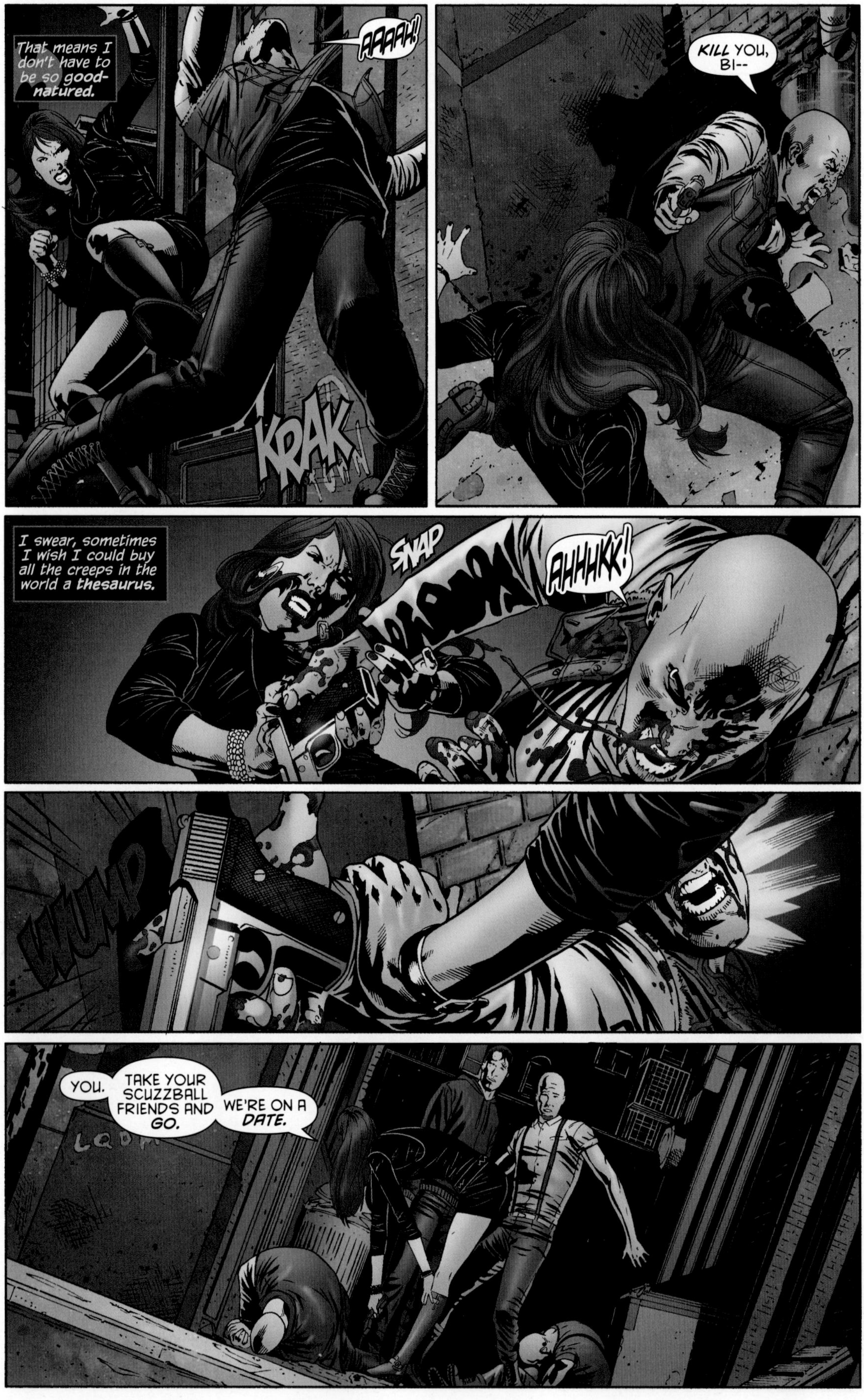
That means I don't have to be so good-natured.
AAAAH!
KRAK
KILL YOU, BI--
I swear, sometimes I wish I could buy all the creeps in the world a thesaurus.
SNAP
AHHHKK!
WUMP
YOU.
TAKE YOUR SCUZZBALL FRIENDS AND GO.
WE'RE ON A DATE.

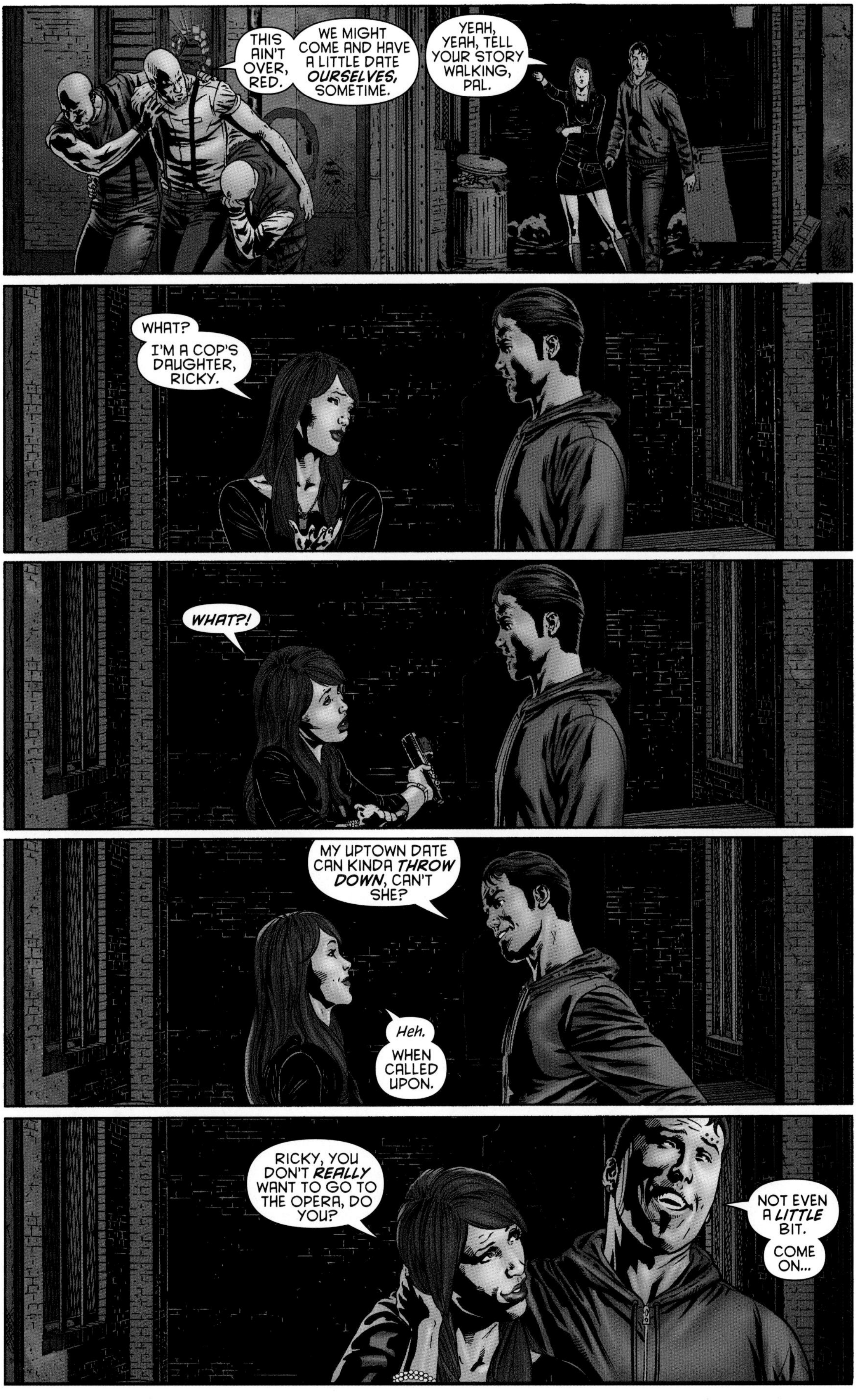
THIS AIN'T OVER, RED.
WE MIGHT COME AND HAVE A LITTLE DATE *OURSELVES,* SOMETIME.
YEAH, YEAH, TELL YOUR STORY WALKING, PAL.
WHAT?
I'M A COP'S DAUGHTER, RICKY.
WHAT?!
MY UPTOWN DATE CAN KINDA *THROW DOWN*, CAN'T SHE?
Heh.
WHEN CALLED UPON.
RICKY, YOU DON'T *REALLY* WANT TO GO TO THE OPERA, DO YOU?
NOT EVEN A *LITTLE* BIT.
COME ON...

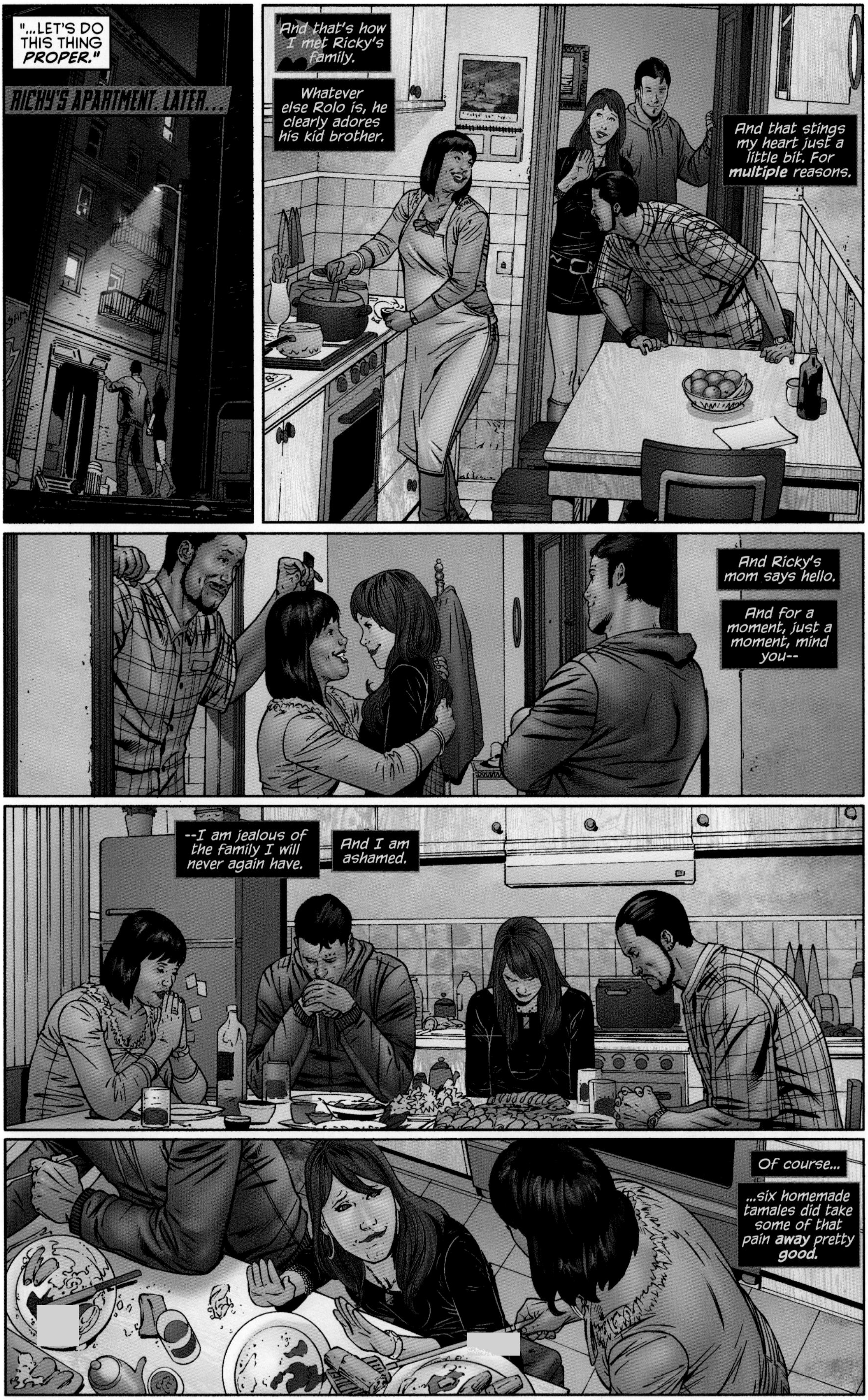
"...LET'S DO THIS THING PROPER."
RICKY'S APARTMENT. LATER...
And that's how I met Ricky's family.
Whatever else Rolo is, he clearly adores his kid brother.
And that stings my heart just a little bit. For multiple reasons.
And Ricky's mom says hello.
And for a moment, just a moment, mind you--
--I am jealous of the family I will never again have.
And I am ashamed.
Of course...
...six homemade tamales did take some of that pain away pretty good.

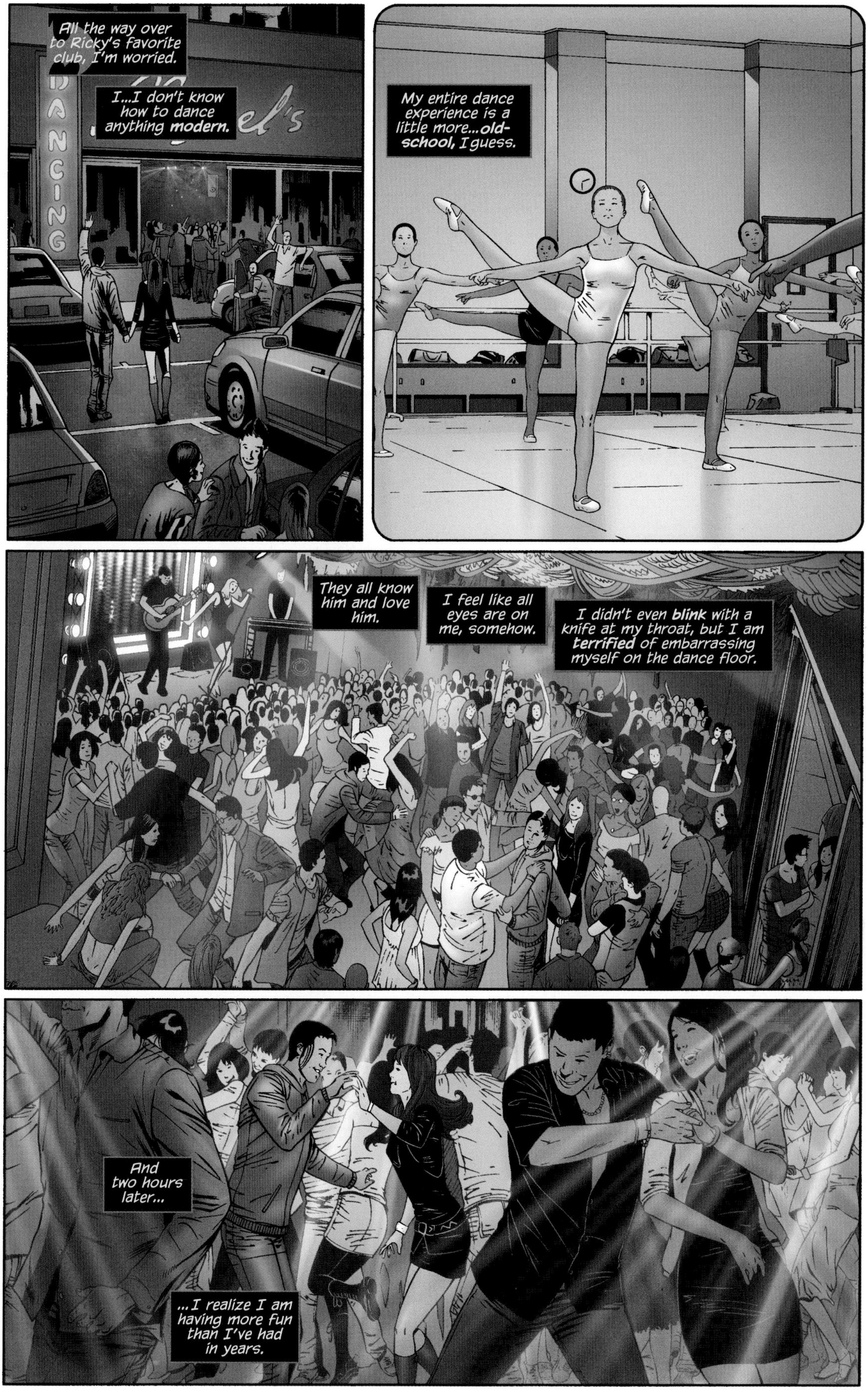
All the way over to Ricky's favorite club, I'm worried.
I...I don't know how to dance anything **modern.**
DANCING
My entire dance experience is a little more...**old-school,** I guess.
They all know him and love him.
I feel like all eyes are on me, somehow.
I didn't even **blink** with a knife at my throat, but I am **terrified** of embarrassing myself on the dance floor.
And two hours later...
...I realize I am having more fun than I've had in years.

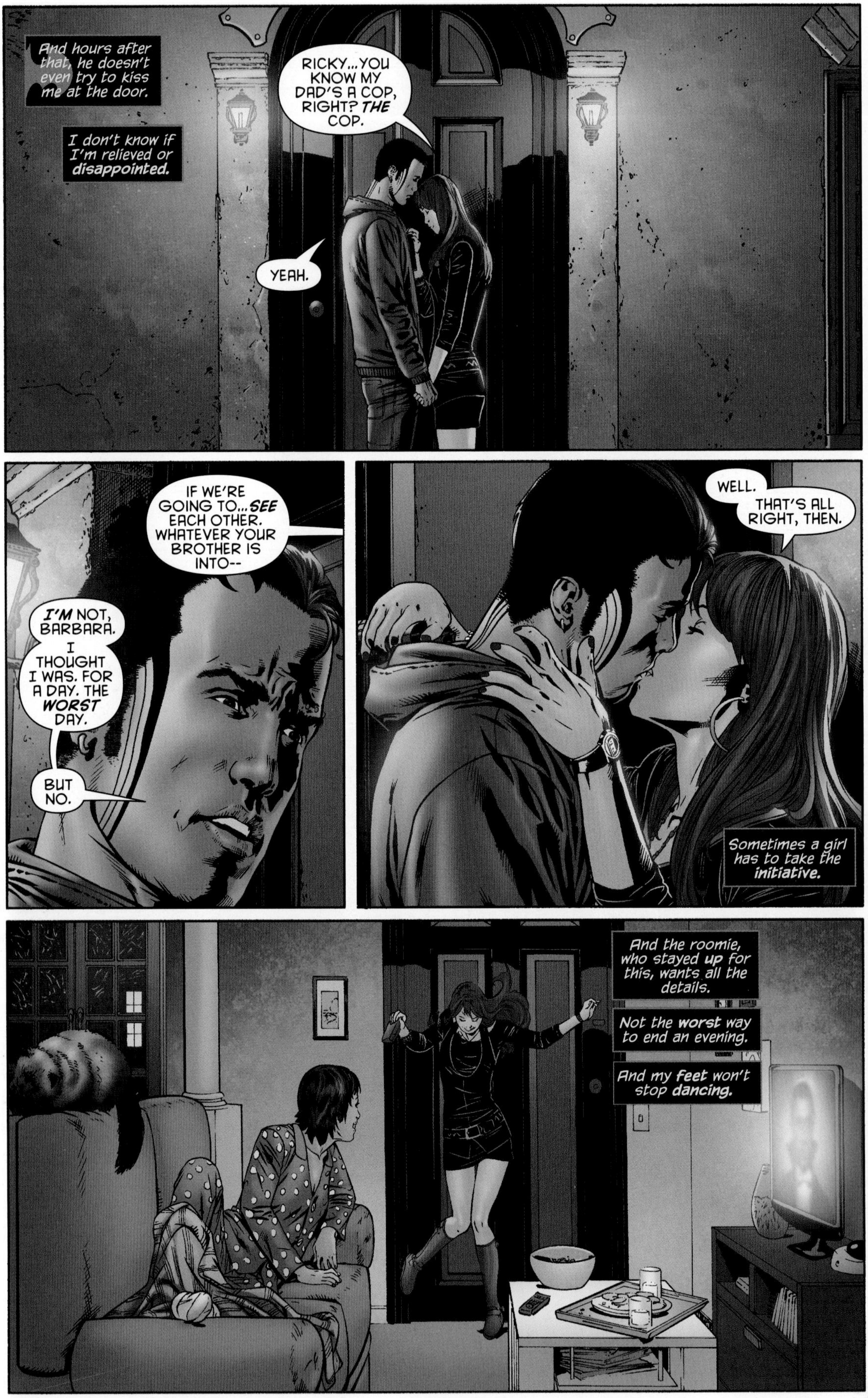

And hours after that, he doesn't even try to kiss me at the door.
I don't know if I'm relieved or *disappointed.*
RICKY...YOU KNOW MY DAD'S A COP, RIGHT? *THE* COP.
YEAH.
IF WE'RE GOING TO...*SEE* EACH OTHER. WHATEVER YOUR BROTHER IS INTO--
I'M NOT, BARBARA. I THOUGHT I WAS. FOR A DAY. THE *WORST* DAY.
BUT NO.
WELL.
THAT'S ALL RIGHT, THEN.
Sometimes a girl has to take the *initiative.*
And the roomie, who stayed *up* for this, wants all the details.
Not the *worst* way to end an evening.
And my *feet* won't stop *dancing.*

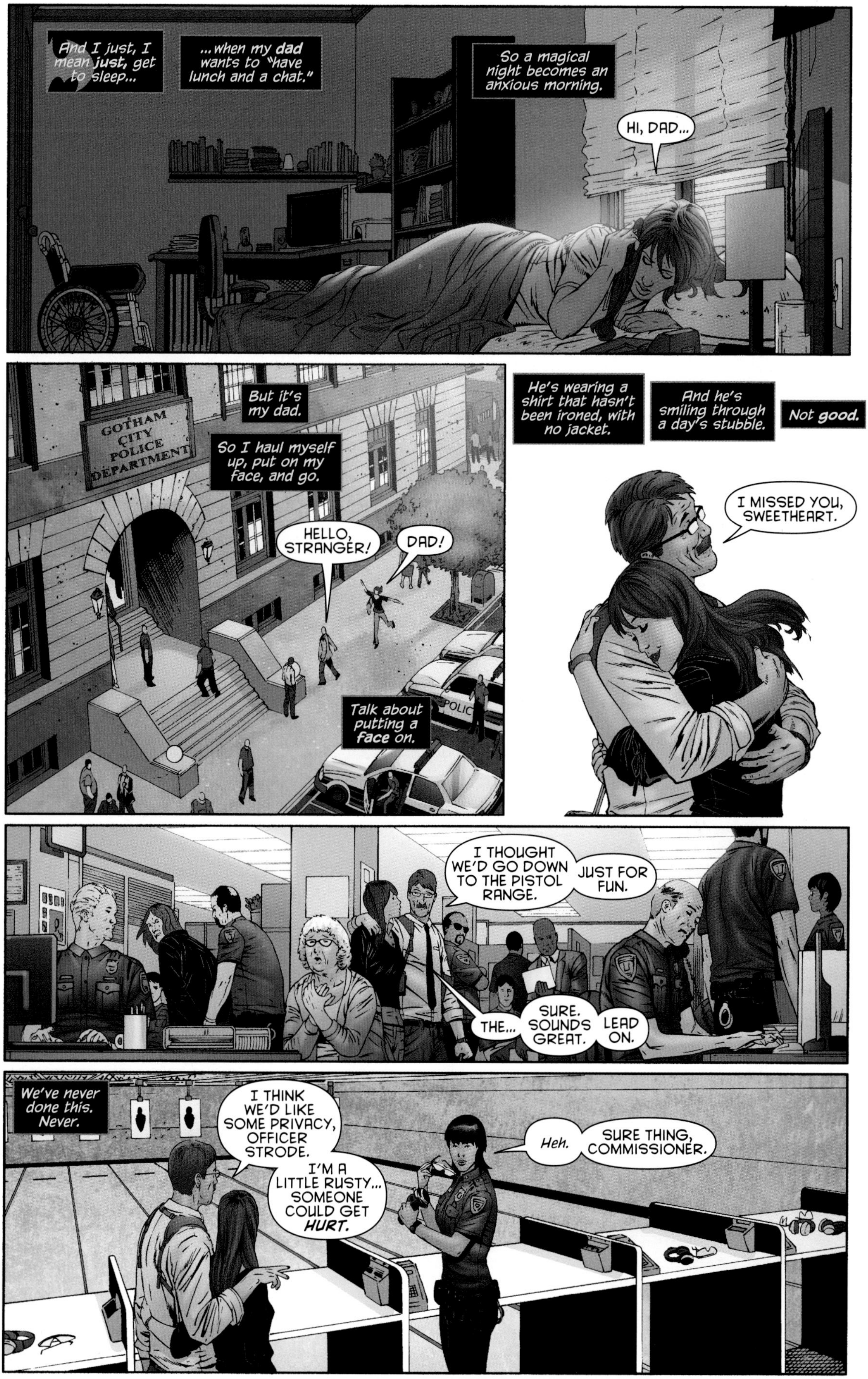
And I just, I mean just, get to sleep...
...when my dad wants to "have lunch and a chat."
So a magical night becomes an anxious morning.
HI, DAD...
But it's my dad.
GOTHAM CITY POLICE DEPARTMENT
So I haul myself up, put on my face, and go.
HELLO, STRANGER!
DAD!
Talk about putting a face on.
He's wearing a shirt that hasn't been ironed, with no jacket.
And he's smiling through a day's stubble.
Not good.
I MISSED YOU, SWEETHEART.
I THOUGHT WE'D GO DOWN TO THE PISTOL RANGE.
JUST FOR FUN.
THE...
SURE. SOUNDS GREAT.
LEAD ON.
We've never done this. Never.
I THINK WE'D LIKE SOME PRIVACY, OFFICER STRODE.
I'M A LITTLE RUSTY... SOMEONE COULD GET HURT.
Heh.
SURE THING, COMMISSIONER.

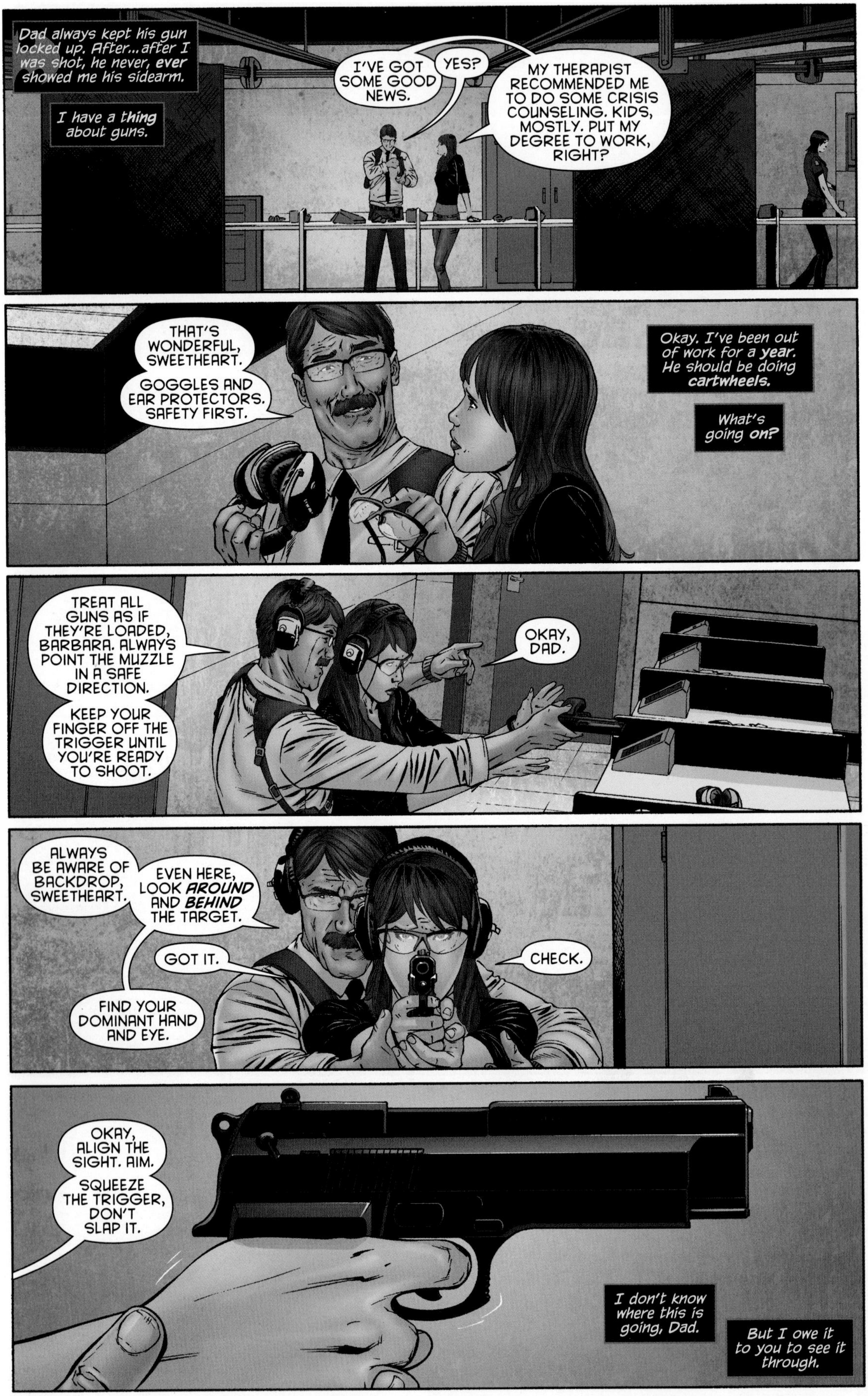
Dad always kept his gun locked up. After...after I was shot, he never, ever showed me his sidearm.
I have a thing about guns.
I'VE GOT SOME GOOD NEWS.
YES?
MY THERAPIST RECOMMENDED ME TO DO SOME CRISIS COUNSELING. KIDS, MOSTLY. PUT MY DEGREE TO WORK, RIGHT?
THAT'S WONDERFUL, SWEETHEART.
GOGGLES AND EAR PROTECTORS. SAFETY FIRST.
Okay. I've been out of work for a year. He should be doing cartwheels.
What's going on?
TREAT ALL GUNS AS IF THEY'RE LOADED, BARBARA. ALWAYS POINT THE MUZZLE IN A SAFE DIRECTION.
KEEP YOUR FINGER OFF THE TRIGGER UNTIL YOU'RE READY TO SHOOT.
OKAY, DAD.
ALWAYS BE AWARE OF BACKDROP, SWEETHEART.
EVEN HERE, LOOK AROUND AND BEHIND THE TARGET.
GOT IT.
CHECK.
FIND YOUR DOMINANT HAND AND EYE.
OKAY, ALIGN THE SIGHT. AIM.
SQUEEZE THE TRIGGER, DON'T SLAP IT.
I don't know where this is going, Dad.
But I owe it to you to see it through.

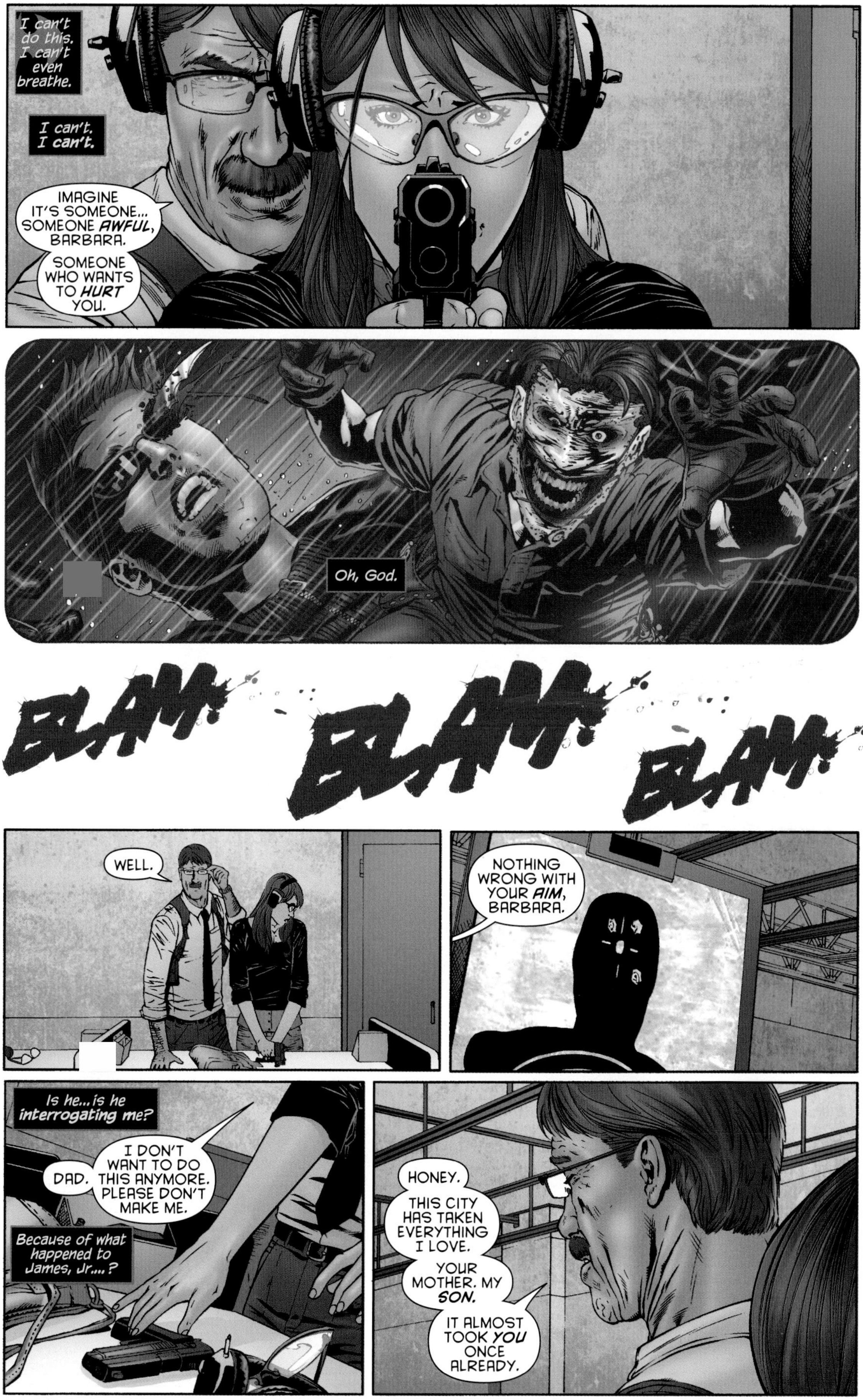
I can't do this. I can't even breathe.
I can't. I can't.
IMAGINE IT'S SOMEONE... SOMEONE AWFUL, BARBARA.
SOMEONE WHO WANTS TO HURT YOU.
Oh, God.
BLAM BLAM BLAM
WELL.
NOTHING WRONG WITH YOUR AIM, BARBARA.
Is he...is he interrogating me?
DAD.
I DON'T WANT TO DO THIS ANYMORE. PLEASE DON'T MAKE ME.
Because of what happened to James, Jr....?
HONEY.
THIS CITY HAS TAKEN EVERYTHING I LOVE.
YOUR MOTHER. MY SON.
IT ALMOST TOOK YOU ONCE ALREADY.

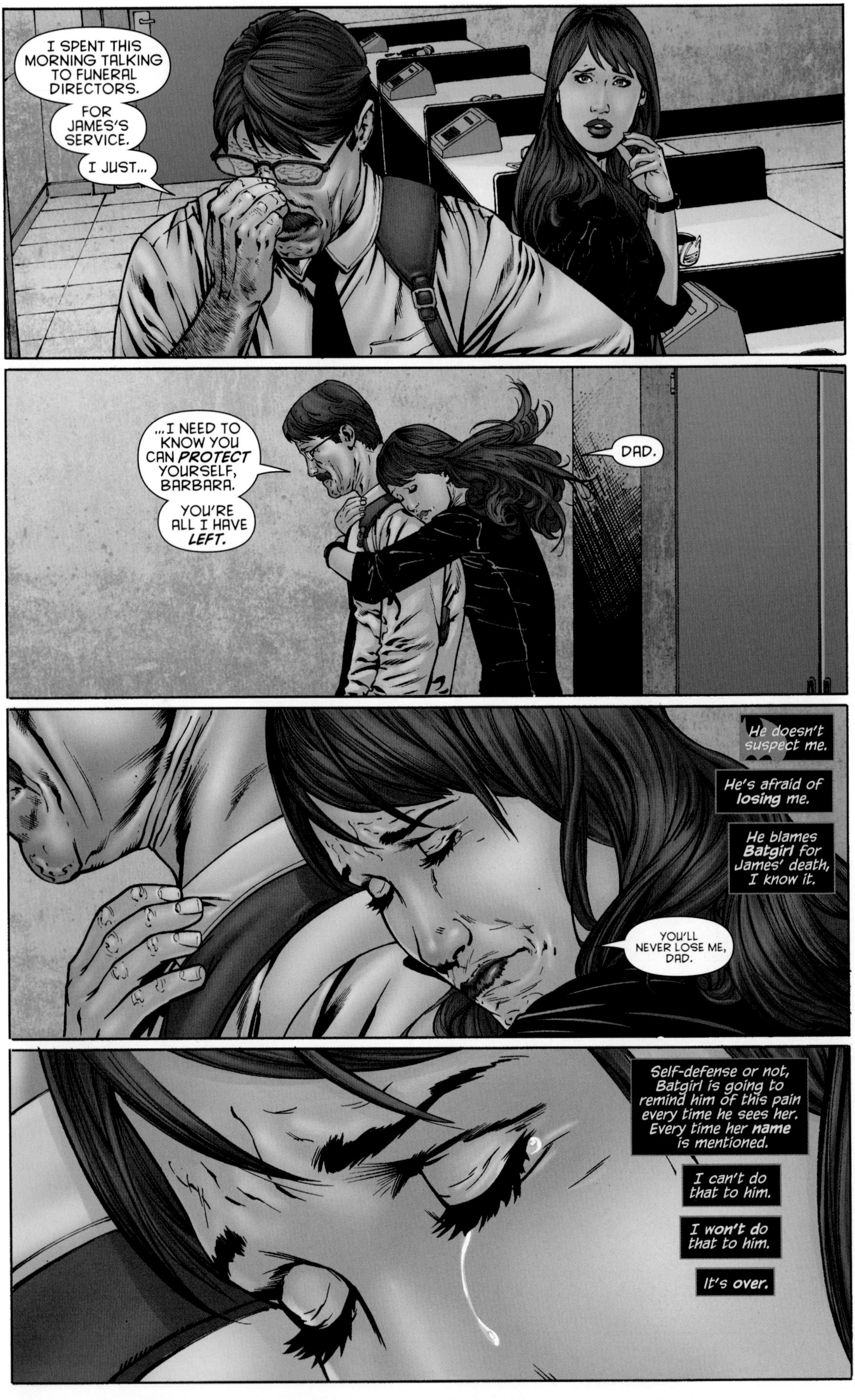

I SPENT THIS MORNING TALKING TO FUNERAL DIRECTORS.
FOR JAMES'S SERVICE.
I JUST...
...I NEED TO KNOW YOU CAN PROTECT YOURSELF, BARBARA.
YOU'RE ALL I HAVE LEFT.
DAD.
He doesn't suspect me.
He's afraid of losing me.
He blames Batgirl for James' death, I know it.
YOU'LL NEVER LOSE ME, DAD.
Self-defense or not, Batgirl is going to remind him of this pain every time he sees her. Every time her name is mentioned.
I can't do that to him.
I won't do that to him.
It's over.

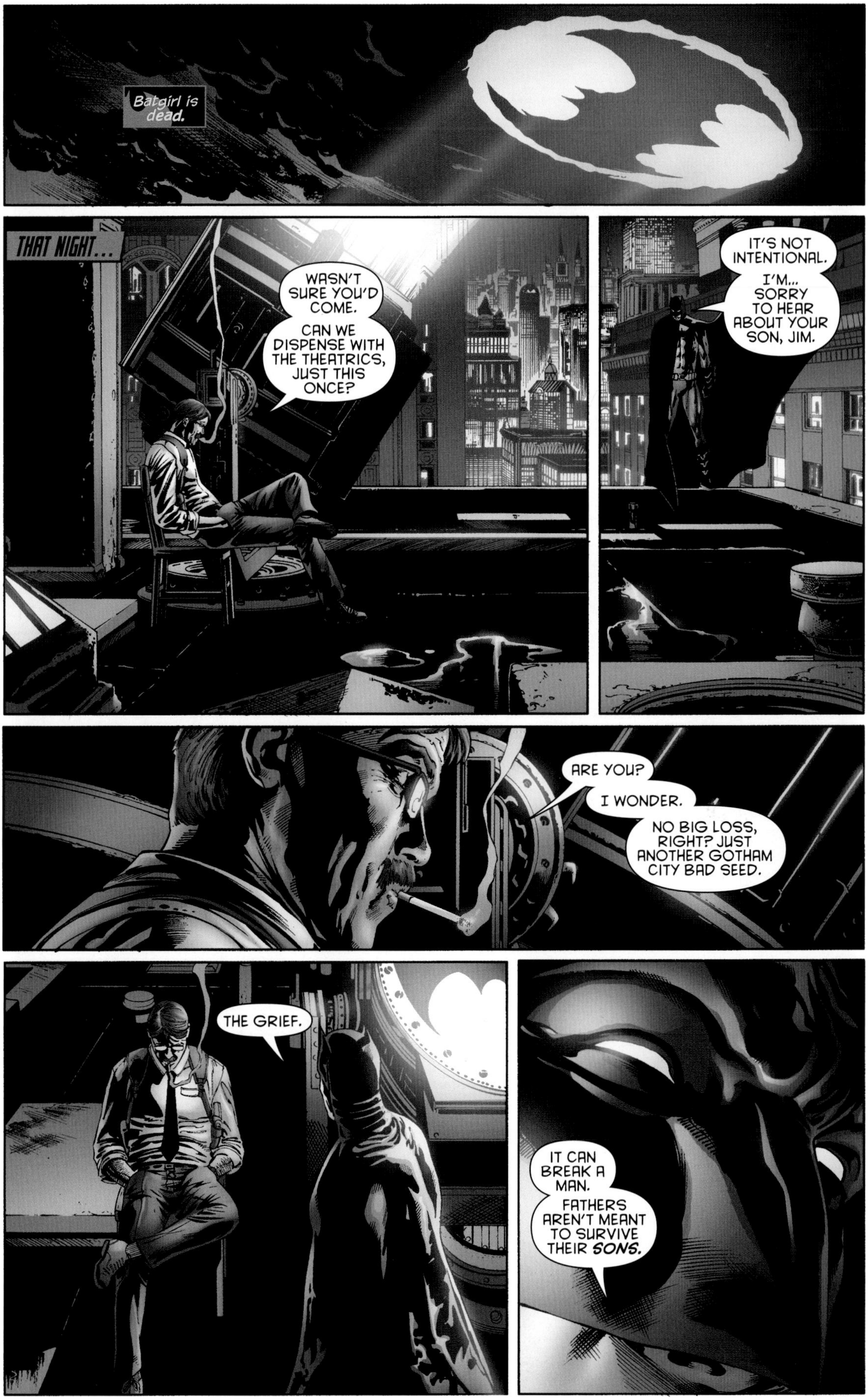

Batgirl is dead.
THAT NIGHT...
WASN'T SURE YOU'D COME.
CAN WE DISPENSE WITH THE THEATRICS, JUST THIS ONCE?
IT'S NOT INTENTIONAL.
I'M... SORRY TO HEAR ABOUT YOUR SON, JIM.
ARE YOU?
I WONDER.
NO BIG LOSS, RIGHT? JUST ANOTHER GOTHAM CITY BAD SEED.
THE GRIEF.
IT CAN BREAK A MAN.
FATHERS AREN'T MEANT TO SURVIVE THEIR SONS.

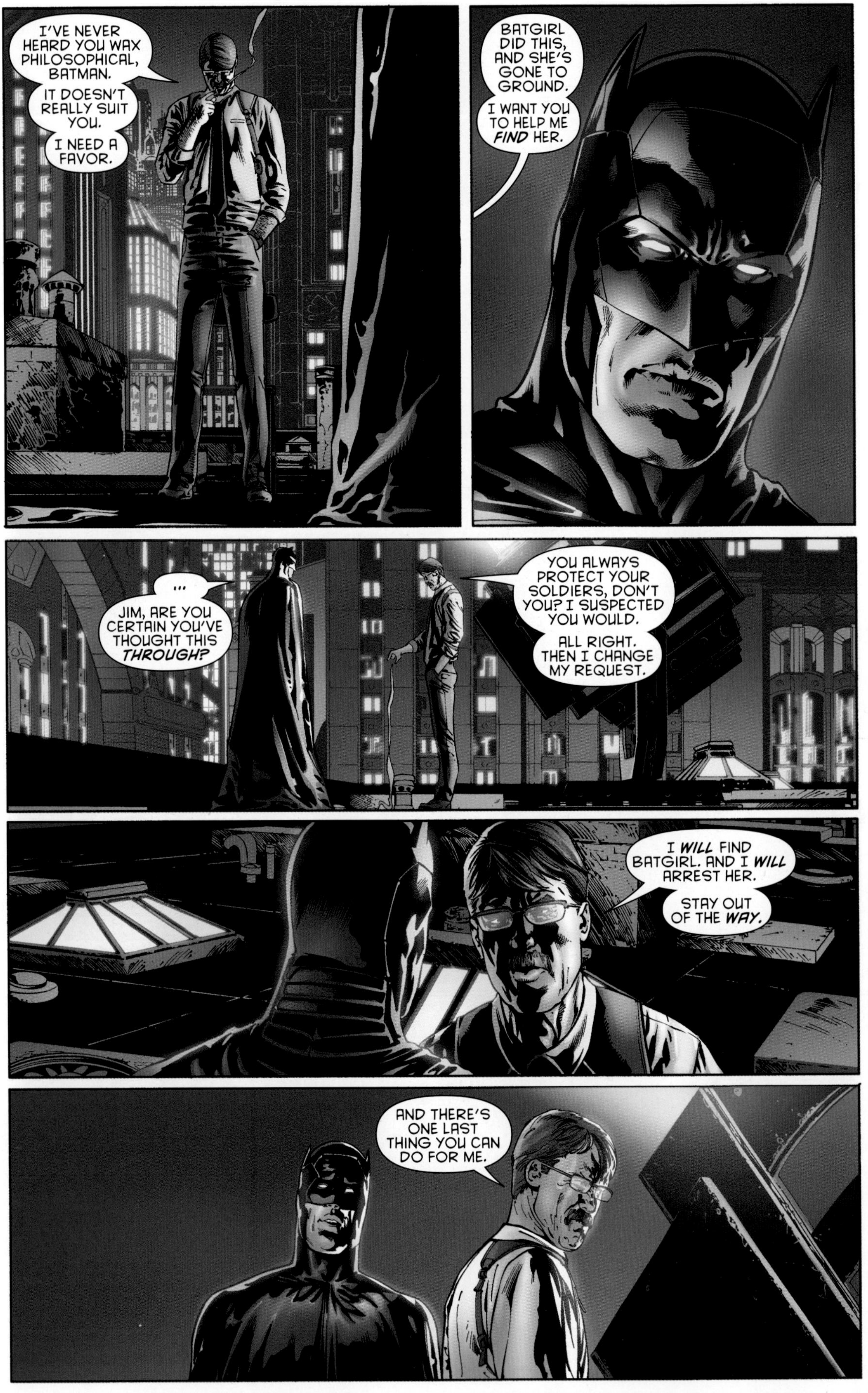
I'VE NEVER HEARD YOU WAX PHILOSOPHICAL, BATMAN.
IT DOESN'T REALLY SUIT YOU.
I NEED A FAVOR.
BATGIRL DID THIS, AND SHE'S GONE TO GROUND.
I WANT YOU TO HELP ME FIND HER.
...
JIM, ARE YOU CERTAIN YOU'VE THOUGHT THIS THROUGH?
YOU ALWAYS PROTECT YOUR SOLDIERS, DON'T YOU? I SUSPECTED YOU WOULD.
ALL RIGHT. THEN I CHANGE MY REQUEST.
I WILL FIND BATGIRL. AND I WILL ARREST HER.
STAY OUT OF THE WAY.
AND THERE'S ONE LAST THING YOU CAN DO FOR ME.

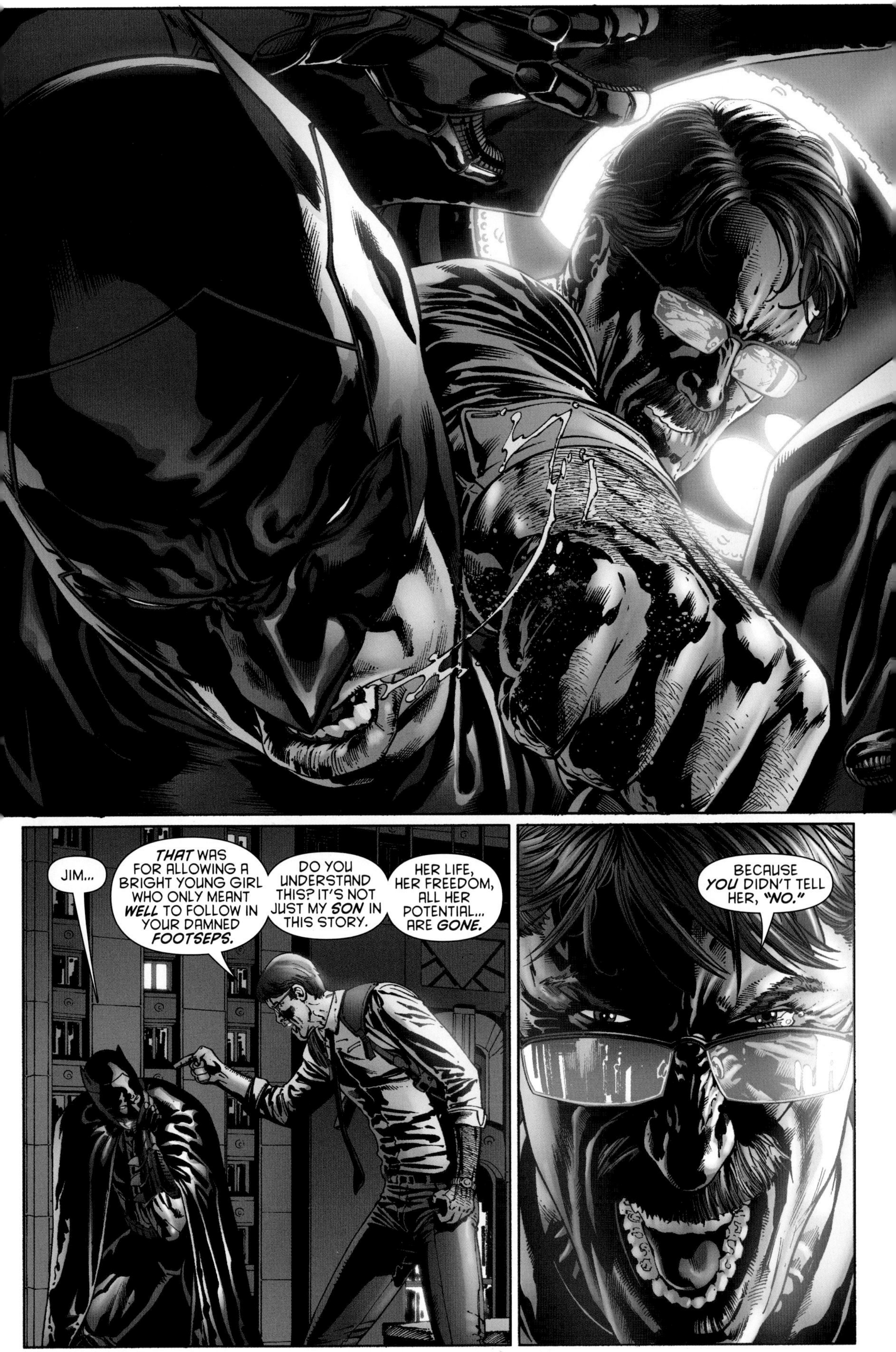
JIM...
THAT WAS FOR ALLOWING A BRIGHT YOUNG GIRL WHO ONLY MEANT ***WELL*** TO FOLLOW IN YOUR DAMNED ***FOOTSEPS.***
DO YOU UNDERSTAND THIS? IT'S NOT JUST MY ***SON*** IN THIS STORY.
HER LIFE, HER FREEDOM, ALL HER POTENTIAL... ARE ***GONE.***
BECAUSE ***YOU*** DIDN'T TELL HER, ***"NO."***

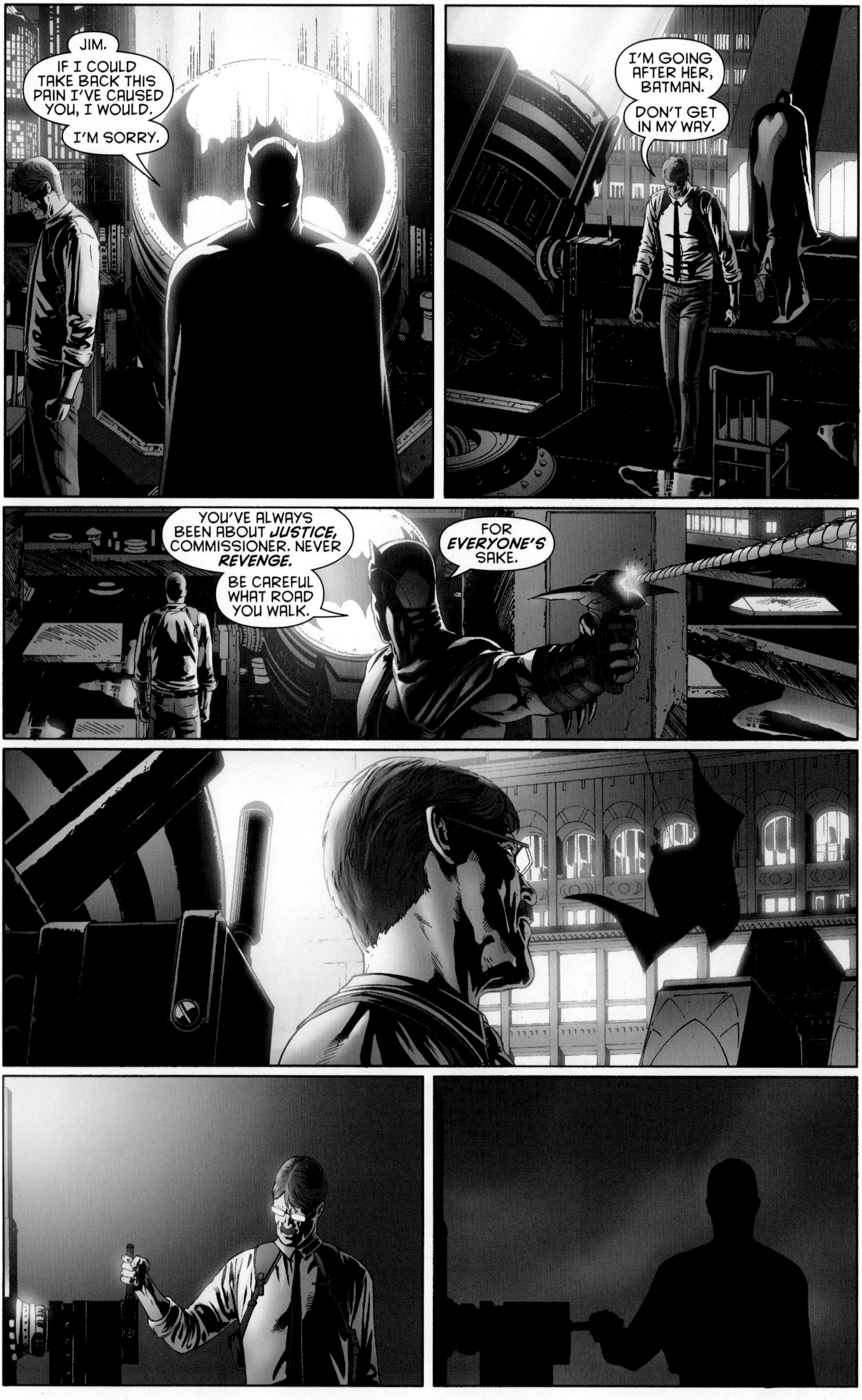
JIM.
IF I COULD TAKE BACK THIS PAIN I'VE CAUSED YOU, I WOULD.
I'M SORRY.
I'M GOING AFTER HER, BATMAN.
DON'T GET IN MY WAY.
YOU'VE ALWAYS BEEN ABOUT JUSTICE, COMMISSIONER. NEVER REVENGE.
BE CAREFUL WHAT ROAD YOU WALK.
FOR EVERYONE'S SAKE.

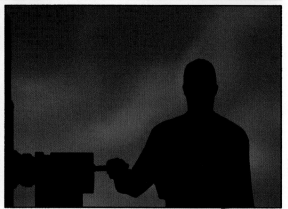

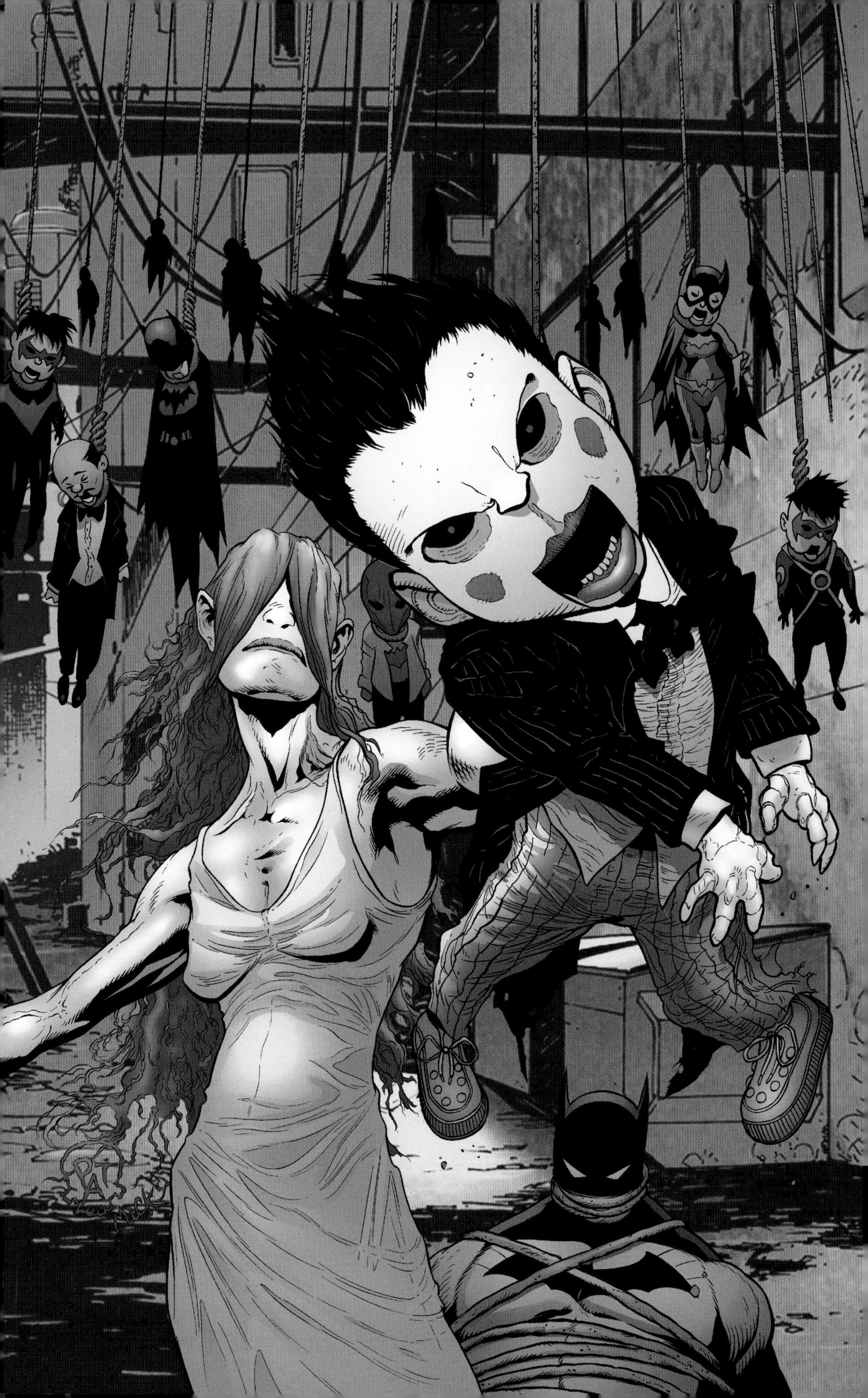

A RISING STAR OF RED

GAIL SIMONE writer **DERLIS SANTACRUZ** penciller **KARL KESEL** inker **BRETT SMITH** colorist
cover by **PAT GLEASON, MICK GRAY** and **JOHN KALISZ**

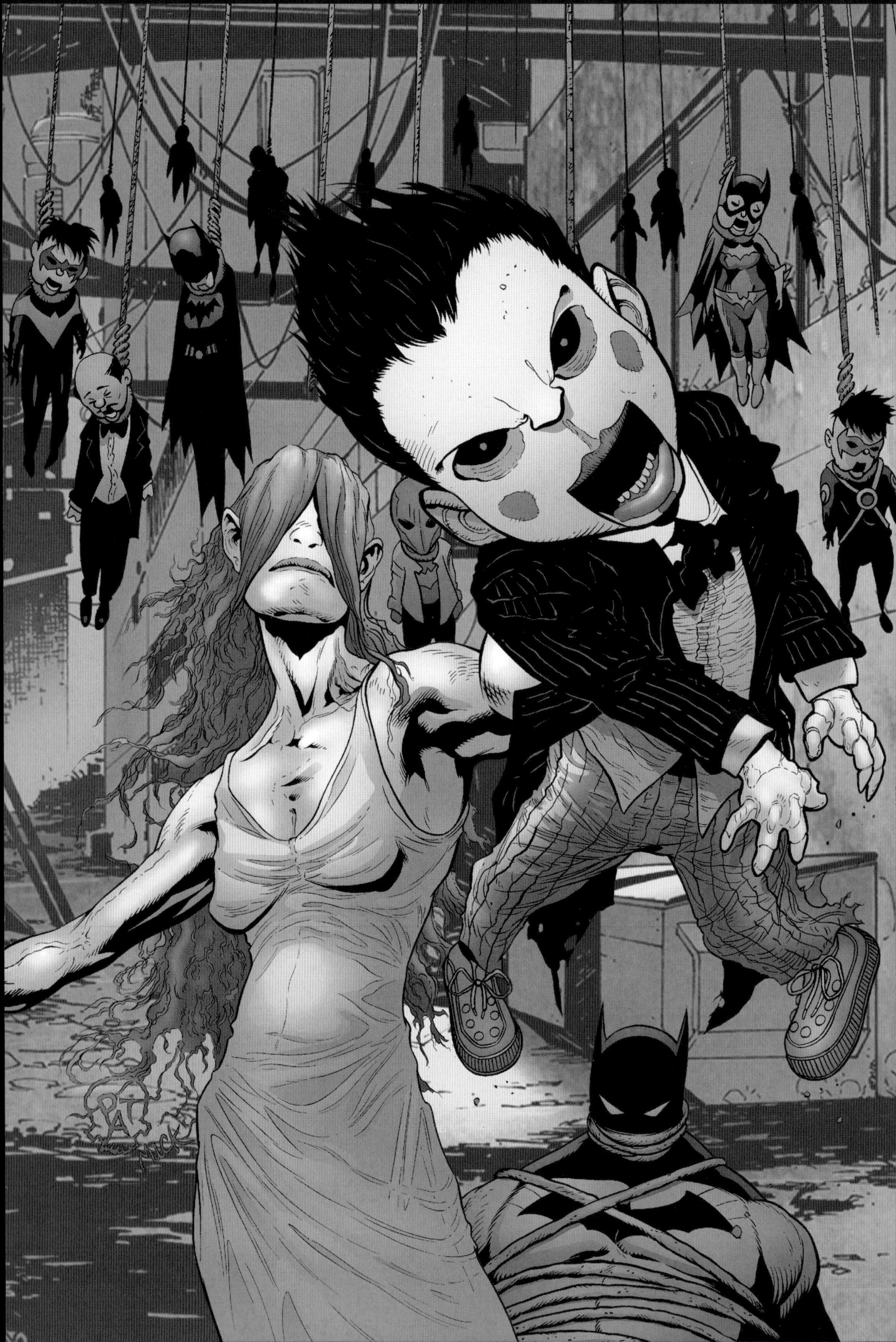
PAT
MICK

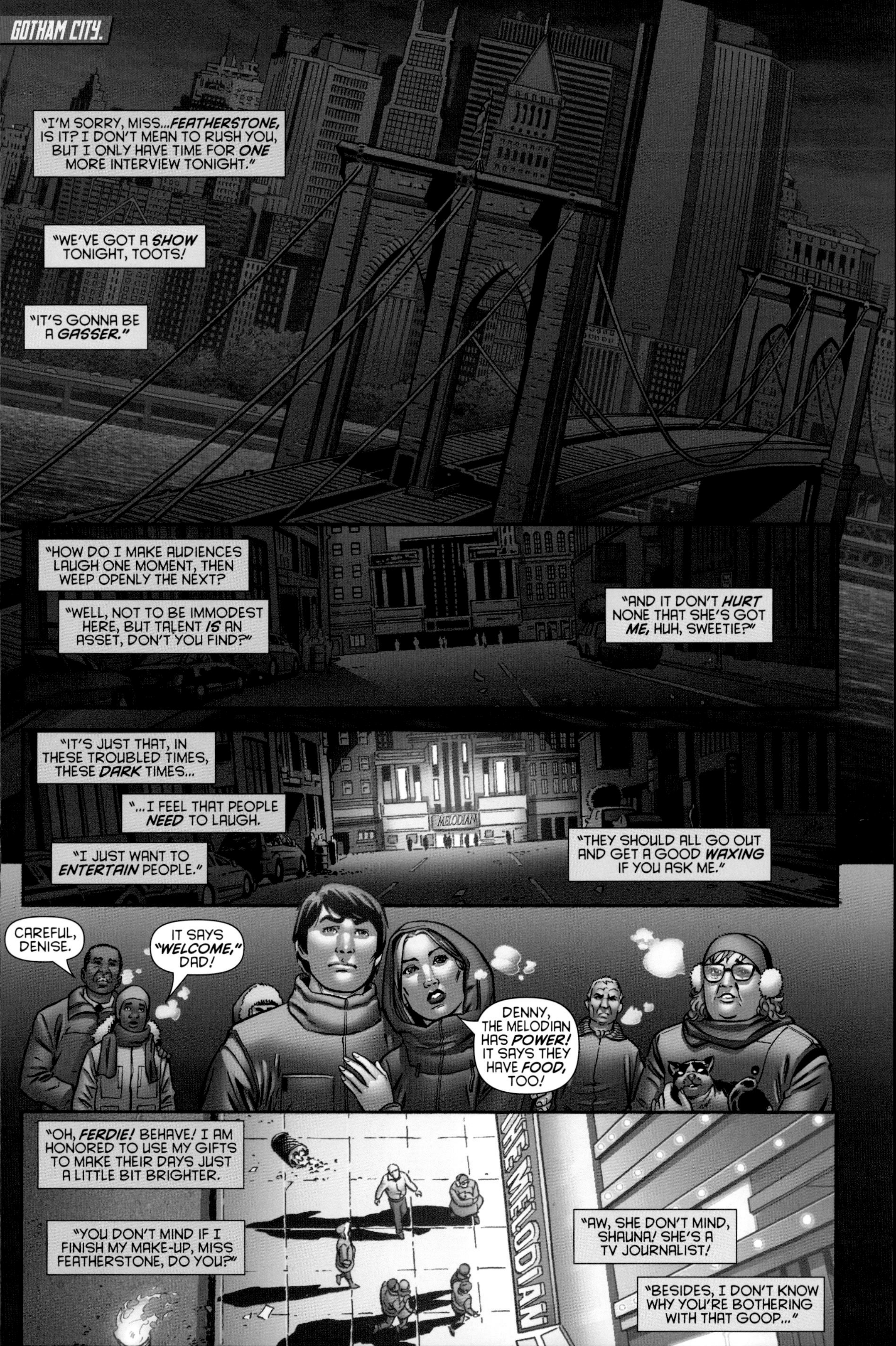
GOTHAM CITY.
"I'M SORRY, MISS...FEATHERSTONE, IS IT? I DON'T MEAN TO RUSH YOU, BUT I ONLY HAVE TIME FOR ONE MORE INTERVIEW TONIGHT."
"WE'VE GOT A SHOW TONIGHT, TOOTS!
"IT'S GONNA BE A GASSER."
"HOW DO I MAKE AUDIENCES LAUGH ONE MOMENT, THEN WEEP OPENLY THE NEXT?
"WELL, NOT TO BE IMMODEST HERE, BUT TALENT IS AN ASSET, DON'T YOU FIND?"
"AND IT DON'T HURT NONE THAT SHE'S GOT ME, HUH, SWEETIE?"
"IT'S JUST THAT, IN THESE TROUBLED TIMES, THESE DARK TIMES...
"...I FEEL THAT PEOPLE NEED TO LAUGH.
"I JUST WANT TO ENTERTAIN PEOPLE."
"THEY SHOULD ALL GO OUT AND GET A GOOD WAXING IF YOU ASK ME."
MELODIAN
CAREFUL, DENISE.
IT SAYS "WELCOME," DAD!
DENNY, THE MELODIAN HAS POWER! IT SAYS THEY HAVE FOOD, TOO!
"OH, FERDIE! BEHAVE! I AM HONORED TO USE MY GIFTS TO MAKE THEIR DAYS JUST A LITTLE BIT BRIGHTER.
"YOU DON'T MIND IF I FINISH MY MAKE-UP, MISS FEATHERSTONE, DO YOU?"
"AW, SHE DON'T MIND, SHAUNA! SHE'S A TV JOURNALIST!
"BESIDES, I DON'T KNOW WHY YOU'RE BOTHERING WITH THAT GOOP..."
THE MELODIAN

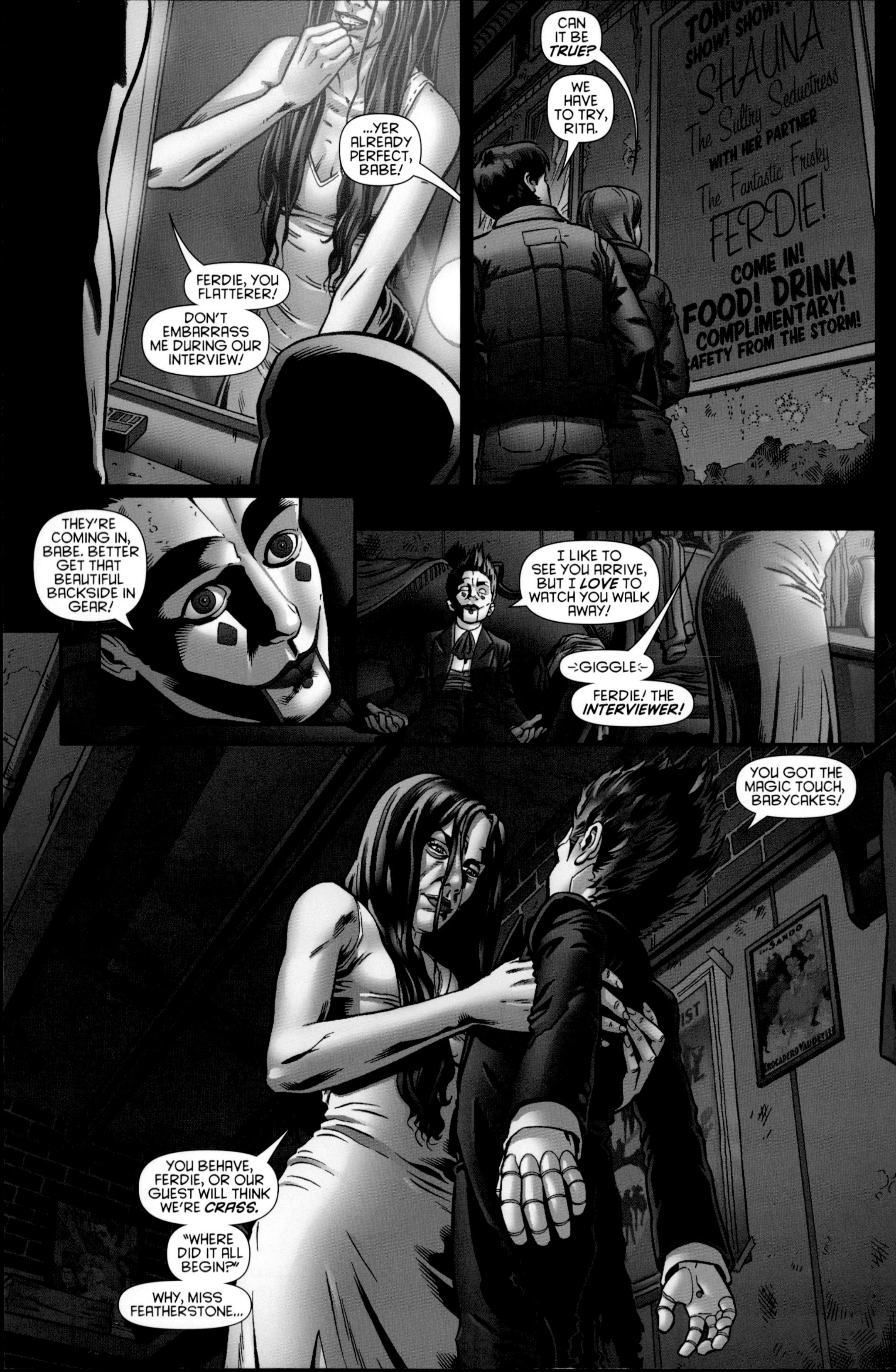

...YER ALREADY PERFECT, BABE!
FERDIE, YOU FLATTERER!
DON'T EMBARRASS ME DURING OUR INTERVIEW!
CAN IT BE TRUE?
WE HAVE TO TRY, RITA.
SHOW! SHOW!
SHAUNA
The Sultry Seductress
WITH HER PARTNER
The Fantastic Frisky
FERDIE!
COME IN!
FOOD! DRINK!
COMPLIMENTARY!
SAFETY FROM THE STORM!
THEY'RE COMING IN, BABE. BETTER GET THAT BEAUTIFUL BACKSIDE IN GEAR!
I LIKE TO SEE YOU ARRIVE, BUT I LOVE TO WATCH YOU WALK AWAY!
GIGGLE
FERDIE! THE INTERVIEWER!
YOU GOT THE MAGIC TOUCH, BABYCAKES!
YOU BEHAVE, FERDIE, OR OUR GUEST WILL THINK WE'RE CRASS.
"WHERE DID IT ALL BEGIN?"
WHY, MISS FEATHERSTONE...

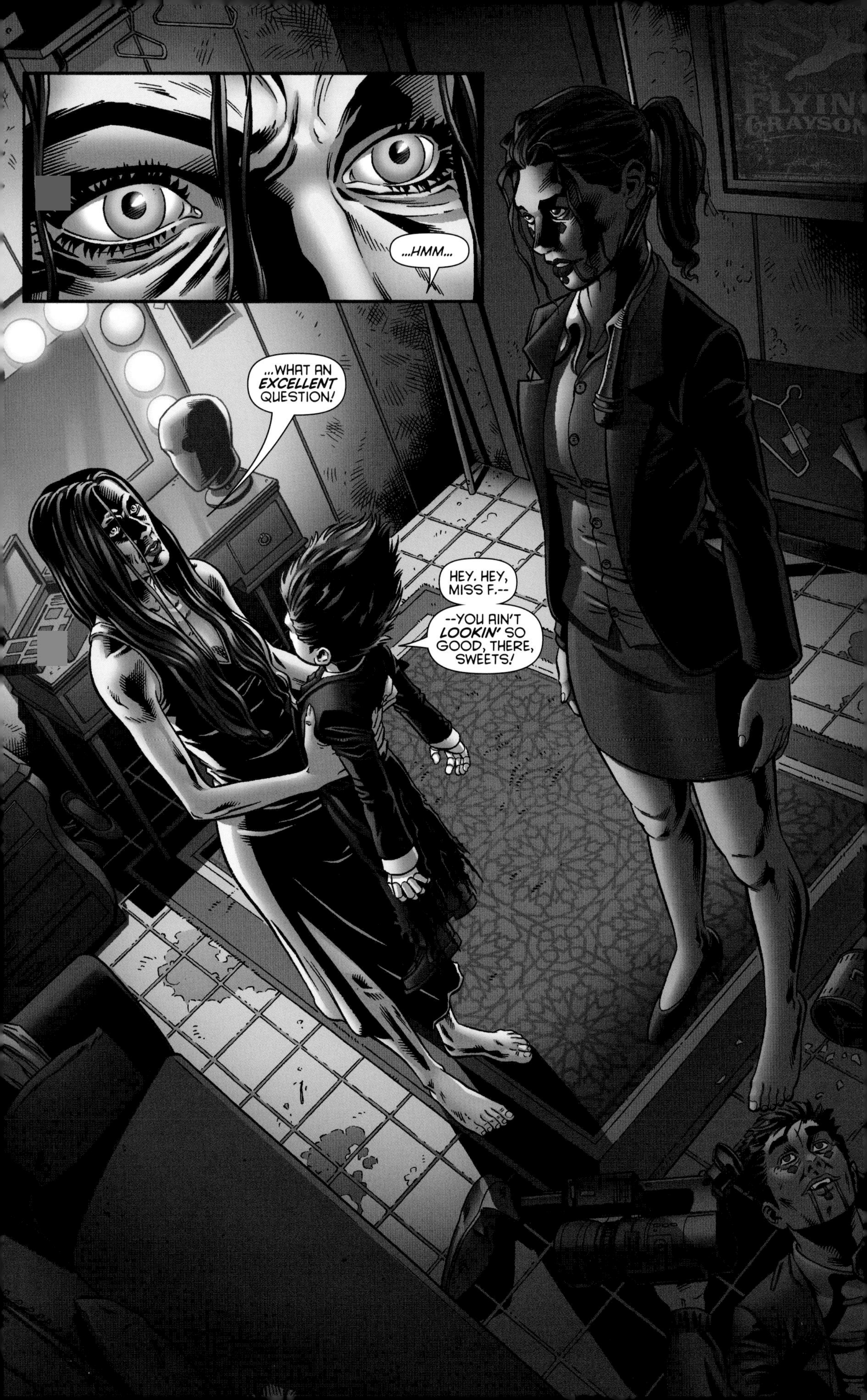
...HMM...
...WHAT AN EXCELLENT QUESTION!
HEY. HEY, MISS F.--
--YOU AIN'T LOOKIN' SO GOOD, THERE, SWEETS!
FLYING GRAYSON

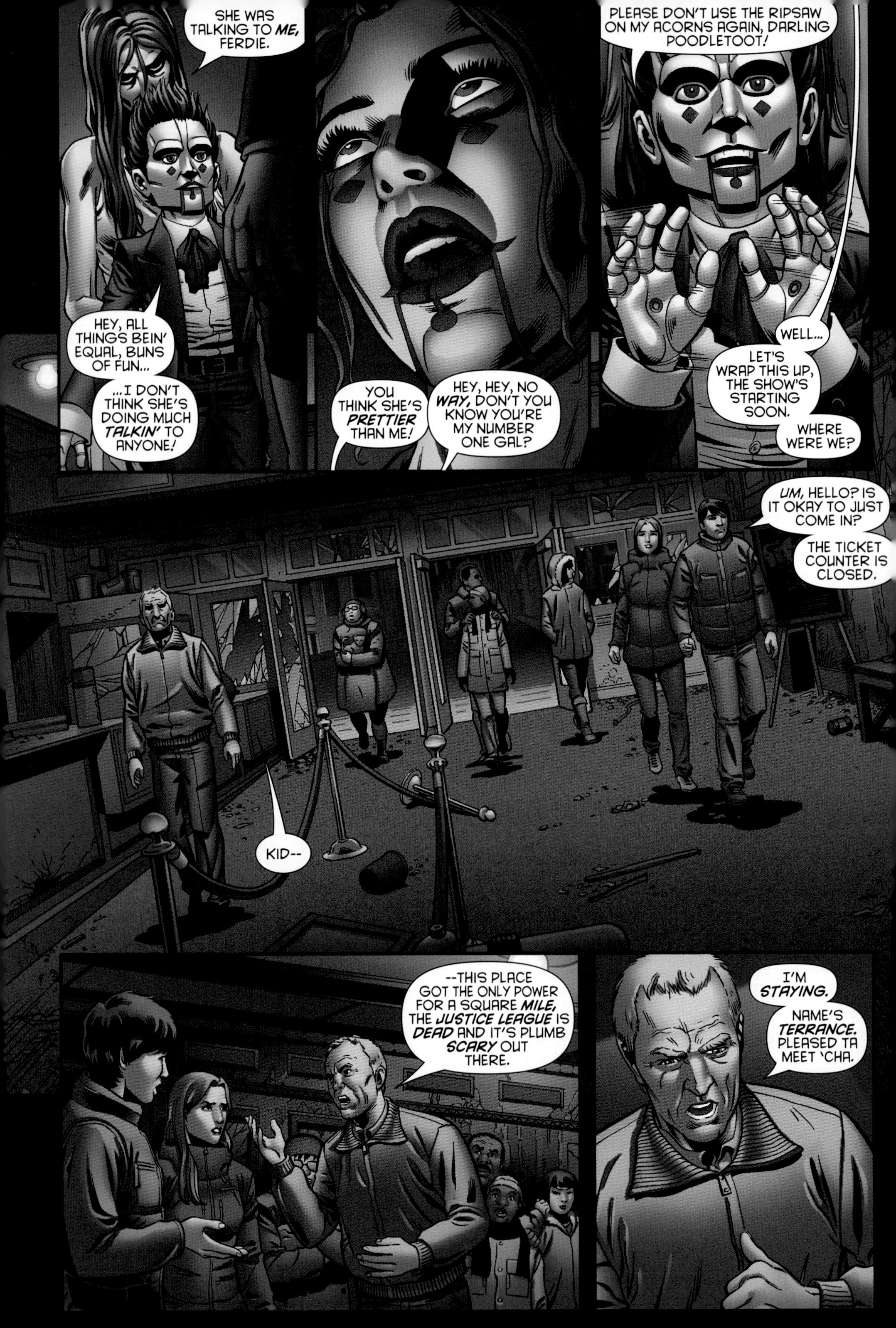
SHE WAS TALKING TO ME, FERDIE.
HEY, ALL THINGS BEIN' EQUAL, BUNS OF FUN...
...I DON'T THINK SHE'S DOING MUCH TALKIN' TO ANYONE!
YOU THINK SHE'S PRETTIER THAN ME!
HEY, HEY, NO WAY, DON'T YOU KNOW YOU'RE MY NUMBER ONE GAL?
PLEASE DON'T USE THE RIPSAW ON MY ACORNS AGAIN, DARLING POODLETOOT!
WELL...
LET'S WRAP THIS UP, THE SHOW'S STARTING SOON.
WHERE WERE WE?
UM, HELLO? IS IT OKAY TO JUST COME IN?
THE TICKET COUNTER IS CLOSED.
KID--
--THIS PLACE GOT THE ONLY POWER FOR A SQUARE MILE, THE JUSTICE LEAGUE IS DEAD AND IT'S PLUMB SCARY OUT THERE.
I'M STAYING.
NAME'S TERRANCE. PLEASED TA MEET 'CHA.

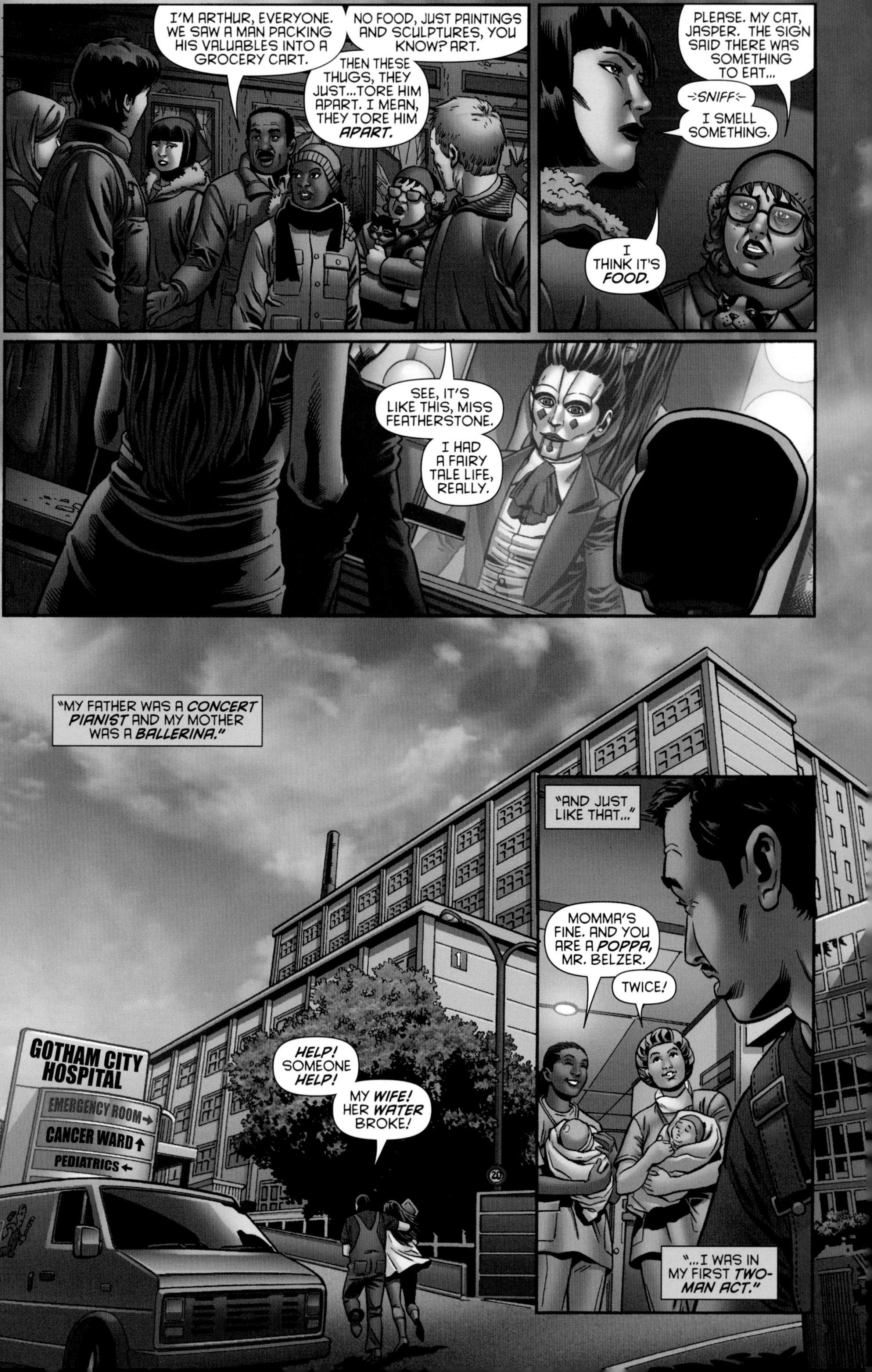
I'M ARTHUR, EVERYONE. WE SAW A MAN PACKING HIS VALUABLES INTO A GROCERY CART.
NO FOOD, JUST PAINTINGS AND SCULPTURES, YOU KNOW? ART.
THEN THESE THUGS, THEY JUST...TORE HIM APART. I MEAN, THEY TORE HIM APART.
PLEASE. MY CAT, JASPER. THE SIGN SAID THERE WAS SOMETHING TO EAT...
SNIFF
I SMELL SOMETHING.
I THINK IT'S FOOD.
SEE, IT'S LIKE THIS, MISS FEATHERSTONE.
I HAD A FAIRY TALE LIFE, REALLY.
"MY FATHER WAS A CONCERT PIANIST AND MY MOTHER WAS A BALLERINA."
GOTHAM CITY HOSPITAL
EMERGENCY ROOM
CANCER WARD
PEDIATRICS
HELP! SOMEONE HELP!
MY WIFE! HER WATER BROKE!
"AND JUST LIKE THAT..."
MOMMA'S FINE. AND YOU ARE A POPPA, MR. BELZER.
TWICE!
"...I WAS IN MY FIRST TWO-MAN ACT."

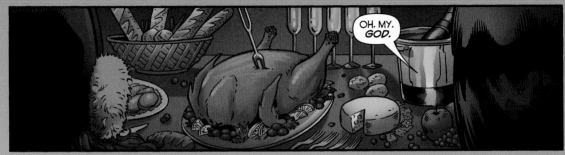

OH. MY. *GOD.*

PLEASE, MISS. MY CAT IS *STARVING.*

IS IT OKAY, DAD?

MY NAME IS *TRACY,* NOT "MISS."

I'M...I'M *SANDY.* THIS IS *JASPER.*

GO AHEAD, DENISE.

DIG IN.

AND BLESS THE *ANGEL* WHO BROUGHT US HERE.

"MY BROTHER AND I, WELL, WE WERE *IMMEDIATE* HITS EVERYWHERE WE WENT.

"I MAY HAVE GOTTEN A BIT MORE OF THE SPOTLIGHT, BEING A GIRL, AND VERY BEAUTIFUL, IF I SAY SO MYSELF."

MRS. BELZER, YOUR *SON*... HE'S THE MOST PERFECTLY BEAUTIFUL BABY I'VE EVER SEEN. I JUST HAD TO TELL YOU!

AND MY *DAUGHTER?*

WHO?

"I'M SURE IT WAS HARD FOR MY BROTHER. HE WAS VERY *PLAIN.*

"HE HAD TO LIVE IN MY SHADOW."

WELL, AREN'T *YOU* THE MOST *HANDSOME* LITTLE BOY I'VE EVER SEEN?

DON'T WORRY, LITTLE GIRL, I'M SURE YOU'LL BLOSSOM INTO A PRETTY THING, TOO...

...ONE DAY.

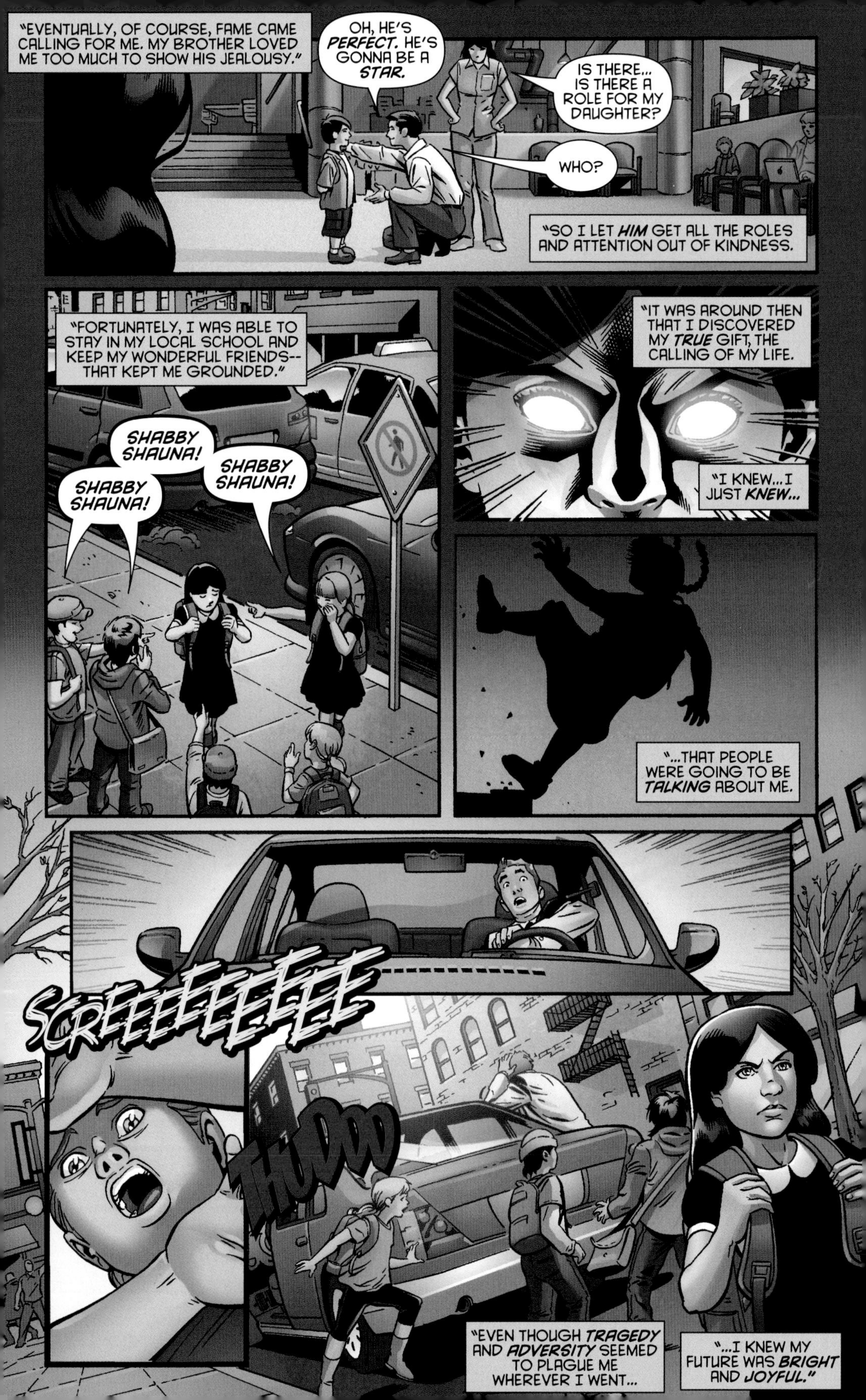
"EVENTUALLY, OF COURSE, FAME CAME CALLING FOR ME. MY BROTHER LOVED ME TOO MUCH TO SHOW HIS JEALOUSY."
OH, HE'S PERFECT. HE'S GONNA BE A STAR.
IS THERE... IS THERE A ROLE FOR MY DAUGHTER?
WHO?
"SO I LET HIM GET ALL THE ROLES AND ATTENTION OUT OF KINDNESS.
"FORTUNATELY, I WAS ABLE TO STAY IN MY LOCAL SCHOOL AND KEEP MY WONDERFUL FRIENDS-- THAT KEPT ME GROUNDED."
SHABBY SHAUNA!
SHABBY SHAUNA!
SHABBY SHAUNA!
"IT WAS AROUND THEN THAT I DISCOVERED MY TRUE GIFT, THE CALLING OF MY LIFE.
"I KNEW...I JUST KNEW...
"...THAT PEOPLE WERE GOING TO BE TALKING ABOUT ME.
SCREEEEEEEEEE
THUDD
"EVEN THOUGH TRAGEDY AND ADVERSITY SEEMED TO PLAGUE ME WHEREVER I WENT...
"...I KNEW MY FUTURE WAS BRIGHT AND JOYFUL."

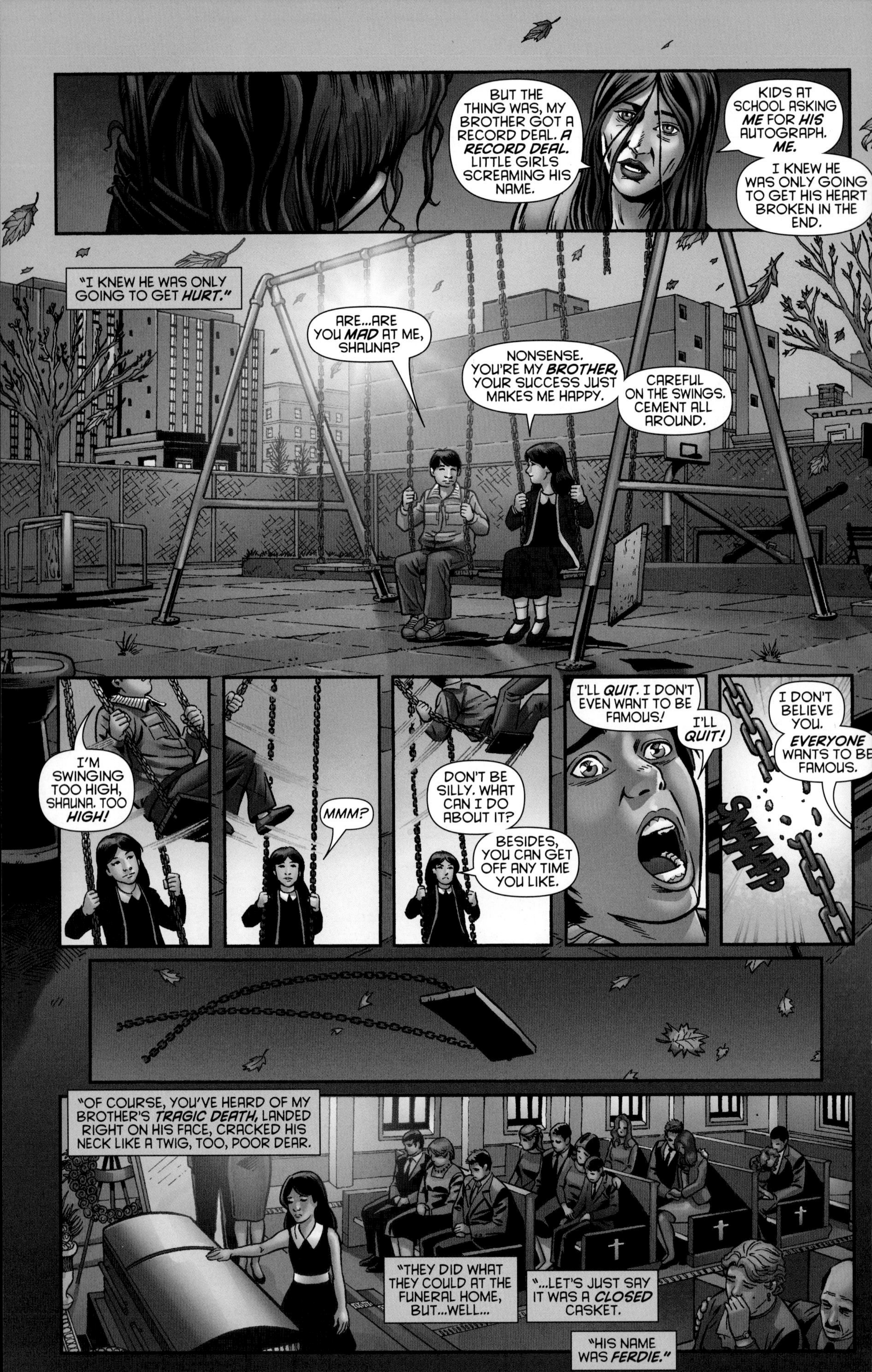
BUT THE THING WAS, MY BROTHER GOT A RECORD DEAL. A RECORD DEAL. LITTLE GIRLS SCREAMING HIS NAME.
KIDS AT SCHOOL ASKING ME FOR HIS AUTOGRAPH. ME.
I KNEW HE WAS ONLY GOING TO GET HIS HEART BROKEN IN THE END.
"I KNEW HE WAS ONLY GOING TO GET HURT."
ARE...ARE YOU MAD AT ME, SHAUNA?
NONSENSE. YOU'RE MY BROTHER, YOUR SUCCESS JUST MAKES ME HAPPY.
CAREFUL ON THE SWINGS. CEMENT ALL AROUND.
I'M SWINGING TOO HIGH, SHAUNA. TOO HIGH!
MMM?
DON'T BE SILLY. WHAT CAN I DO ABOUT IT?
BESIDES, YOU CAN GET OFF ANY TIME YOU LIKE.
I'LL QUIT. I DON'T EVEN WANT TO BE FAMOUS!
I'LL QUIT!
I DON'T BELIEVE YOU. EVERYONE WANTS TO BE FAMOUS.
SNAP
"OF COURSE, YOU'VE HEARD OF MY BROTHER'S TRAGIC DEATH, LANDED RIGHT ON HIS FACE, CRACKED HIS NECK LIKE A TWIG, TOO, POOR DEAR.
"THEY DID WHAT THEY COULD AT THE FUNERAL HOME, BUT...WELL...
"...LET'S JUST SAY IT WAS A CLOSED CASKET.
"HIS NAME WAS FERDIE."

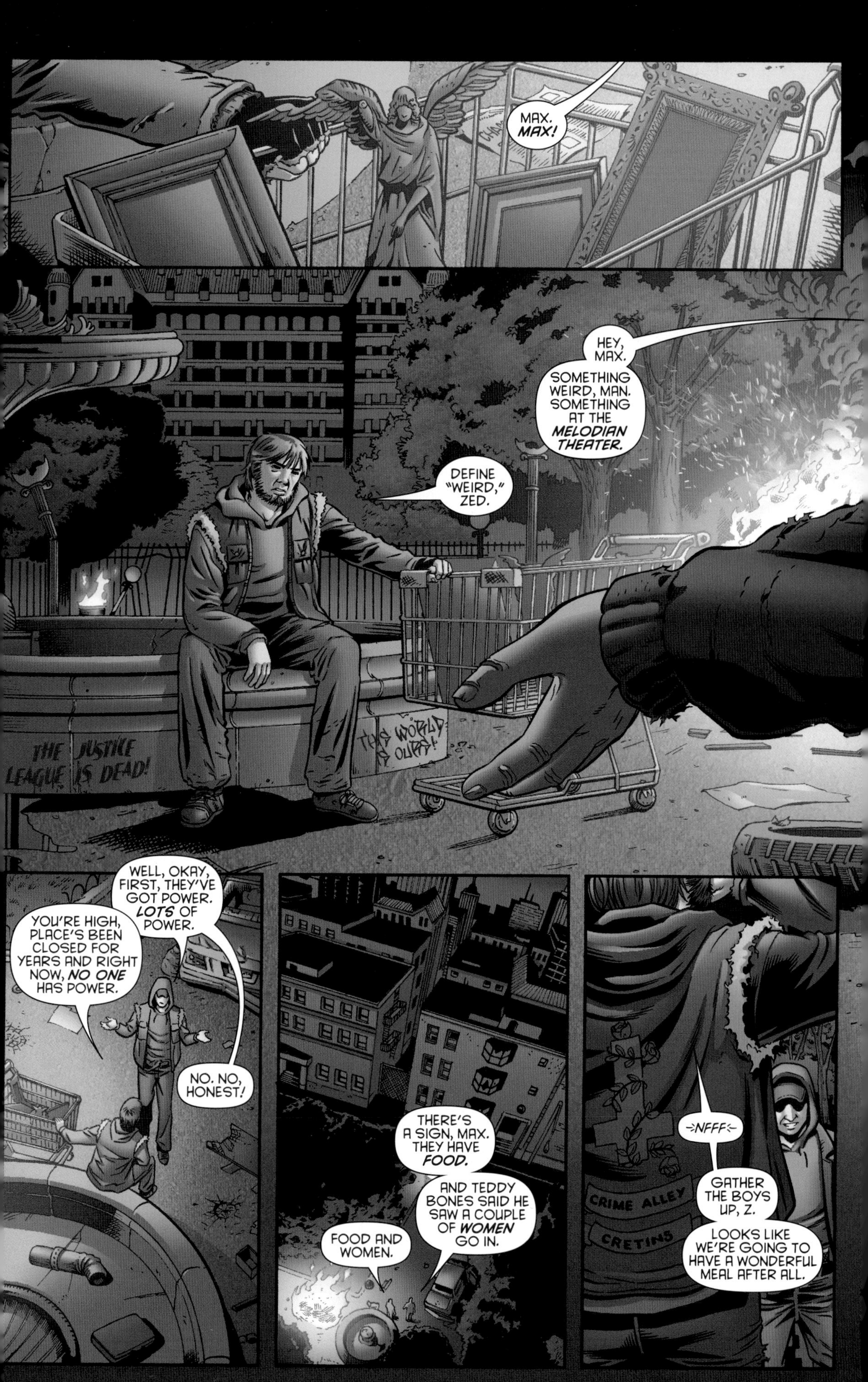
MAX. MAX!
HEY, MAX.
SOMETHING WEIRD, MAN. SOMETHING AT THE MELODIAN THEATER.
DEFINE "WEIRD," ZED.
THE JUSTICE LEAGUE IS DEAD!
THE WORLD IS OURS!
WELL, OKAY, FIRST, THEY'VE GOT POWER. LOTS OF POWER.
YOU'RE HIGH, PLACE'S BEEN CLOSED FOR YEARS AND RIGHT NOW, NO ONE HAS POWER.
NO. NO, HONEST!
THERE'S A SIGN, MAX. THEY HAVE FOOD.
AND TEDDY BONES SAID HE SAW A COUPLE OF WOMEN GO IN.
FOOD AND WOMEN.
-NFFF-
GATHER THE BOYS UP, Z.
LOOKS LIKE WE'RE GOING TO HAVE A WONDERFUL MEAL AFTER ALL.
CRIME ALLEY
CRETINS

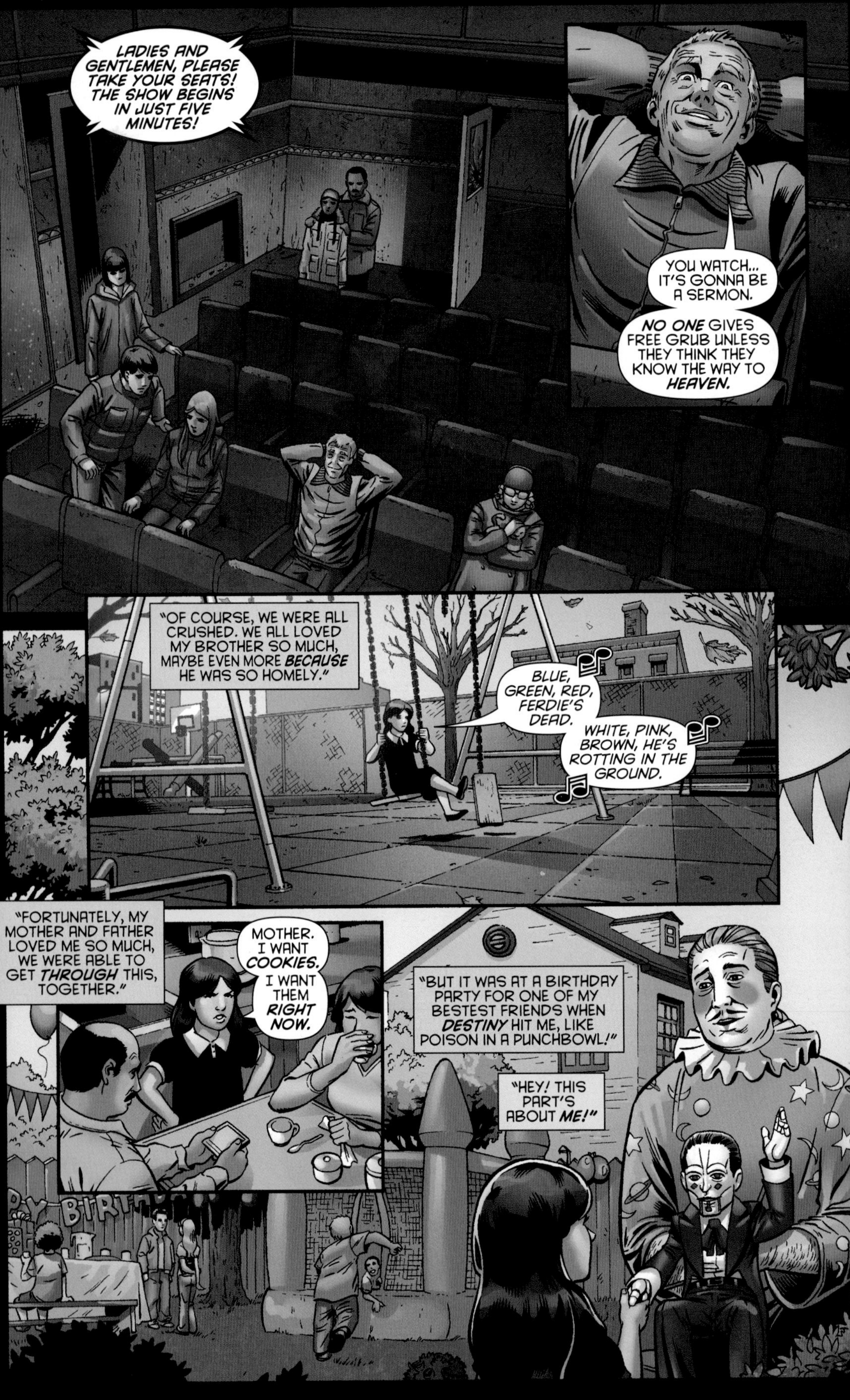
LADIES AND GENTLEMEN, PLEASE TAKE YOUR SEATS! THE SHOW BEGINS IN JUST FIVE MINUTES!
YOU WATCH... IT'S GONNA BE A SERMON.
NO ONE GIVES FREE GRUB UNLESS THEY THINK THEY KNOW THE WAY TO HEAVEN.
"OF COURSE, WE WERE ALL CRUSHED. WE ALL LOVED MY BROTHER SO MUCH, MAYBE EVEN MORE BECAUSE HE WAS SO HOMELY."
BLUE, GREEN, RED, FERDIE'S DEAD.
WHITE, PINK, BROWN, HE'S ROTTING IN THE GROUND.
"FORTUNATELY, MY MOTHER AND FATHER LOVED ME SO MUCH, WE WERE ABLE TO GET THROUGH THIS, TOGETHER."
MOTHER. I WANT COOKIES. I WANT THEM RIGHT NOW.
"BUT IT WAS AT A BIRTHDAY PARTY FOR ONE OF MY BESTEST FRIENDS WHEN DESTINY HIT ME, LIKE POISON IN A PUNCHBOWL!"
"HEY! THIS PART'S ABOUT ME!"

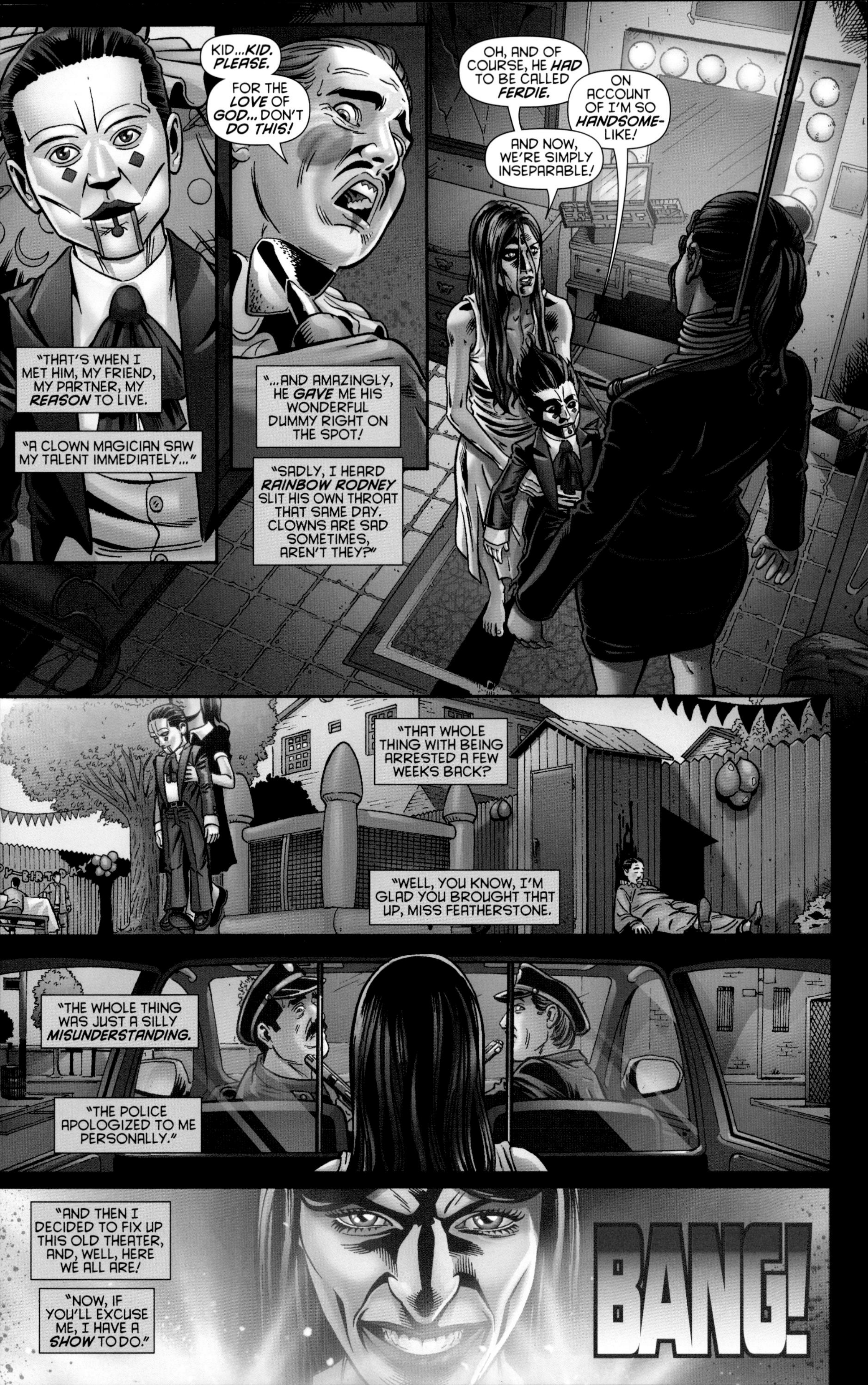

"THAT'S WHEN I MET HIM, MY FRIEND, MY PARTNER, MY REASON TO LIVE.
"A CLOWN MAGICIAN SAW MY TALENT IMMEDIATELY..."
KID...KID. PLEASE.
FOR THE LOVE OF GOD... DON'T DO THIS!
"...AND AMAZINGLY, HE GAVE ME HIS WONDERFUL DUMMY RIGHT ON THE SPOT!
"SADLY, I HEARD RAINBOW RODNEY SLIT HIS OWN THROAT THAT SAME DAY. CLOWNS ARE SAD SOMETIMES, AREN'T THEY?"
OH, AND OF COURSE, HE HAD TO BE CALLED FERDIE.
ON ACCOUNT OF I'M SO HANDSOME-LIKE!
AND NOW, WE'RE SIMPLY INSEPARABLE!
"THAT WHOLE THING WITH BEING ARRESTED A FEW WEEKS BACK?
"WELL, YOU KNOW, I'M GLAD YOU BROUGHT THAT UP, MISS FEATHERSTONE.
"THE WHOLE THING WAS JUST A SILLY MISUNDERSTANDING.
"THE POLICE APOLOGIZED TO ME PERSONALLY."
"AND THEN I DECIDED TO FIX UP THIS OLD THEATER, AND, WELL, HERE WE ALL ARE!
"NOW, IF YOU'LL EXCUSE ME, I HAVE A SHOW TO DO."
BANG!

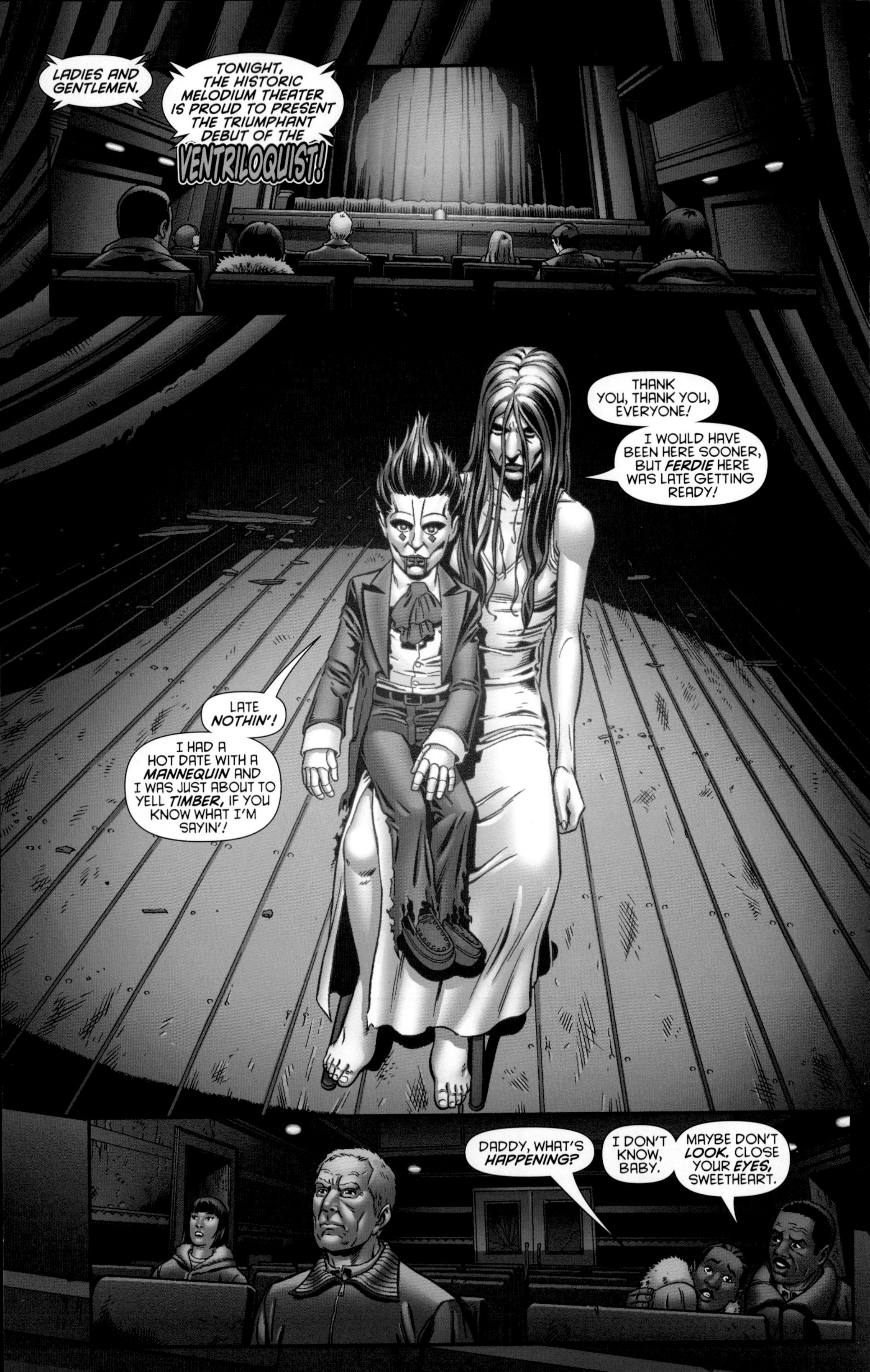
LADIES AND GENTLEMEN.
TONIGHT, THE HISTORIC MELODIUM THEATER IS PROUD TO PRESENT THE TRIUMPHANT DEBUT OF THE VENTRILOQUIST!
THANK YOU, THANK YOU, EVERYONE!
I WOULD HAVE BEEN HERE SOONER, BUT FERDIE HERE WAS LATE GETTING READY!
LATE NOTHIN'!
I HAD A HOT DATE WITH A MANNEQUIN AND I WAS JUST ABOUT TO YELL TIMBER, IF YOU KNOW WHAT I'M SAYIN'!
DADDY, WHAT'S HAPPENING?
I DON'T KNOW, BABY.
MAYBE DON'T LOOK. CLOSE YOUR EYES, SWEETHEART.

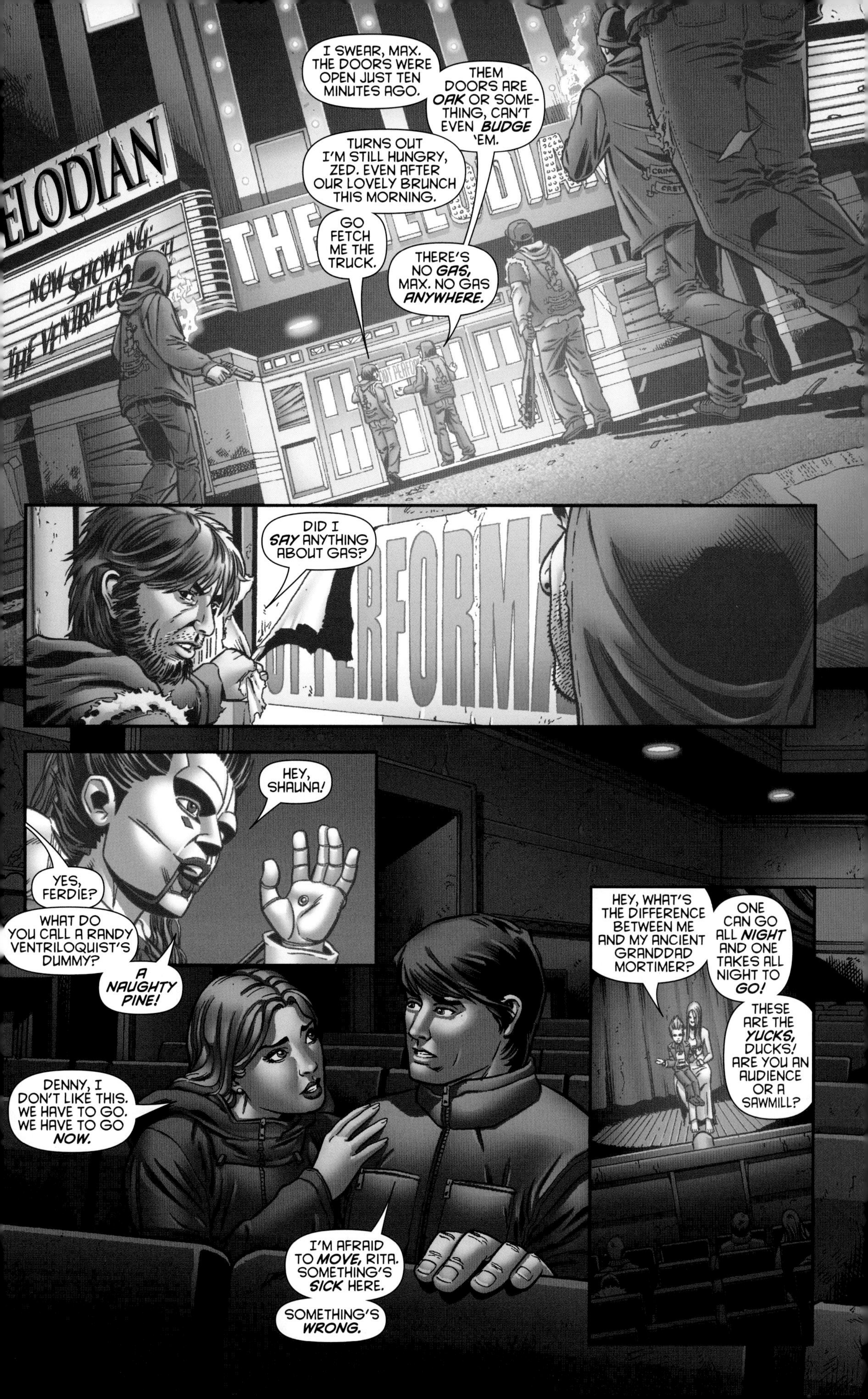
ELODIAN
NOW SHOWING: THE VENTRILOQ
THE MELODIAN
I SWEAR, MAX. THE DOORS WERE OPEN JUST TEN MINUTES AGO.
THEM DOORS ARE *OAK* OR SOMETHING, CAN'T EVEN *BUDGE* 'EM.
TURNS OUT I'M STILL HUNGRY, ZED. EVEN AFTER OUR LOVELY BRUNCH THIS MORNING.
GO FETCH ME THE TRUCK.
THERE'S NO *GAS*, MAX. NO GAS *ANYWHERE.*
DID I *SAY* ANYTHING ABOUT GAS?
RFORMA
HEY, SHAUNA!
YES, FERDIE?
WHAT DO YOU CALL A RANDY VENTRILOQUIST'S DUMMY?
A NAUGHTY PINE!
HEY, WHAT'S THE DIFFERENCE BETWEEN ME AND MY ANCIENT GRANDDAD MORTIMER?
ONE CAN GO ALL *NIGHT* AND ONE TAKES ALL NIGHT TO *GO!*
THESE ARE THE *YUCKS,* DUCKS! ARE YOU AN AUDIENCE OR A SAWMILL?
DENNY, I DON'T LIKE THIS. WE HAVE TO GO. WE HAVE TO GO *NOW.*
I'M AFRAID TO *MOVE,* RITA. SOMETHING'S *SICK* HERE.
SOMETHING'S *WRONG.*

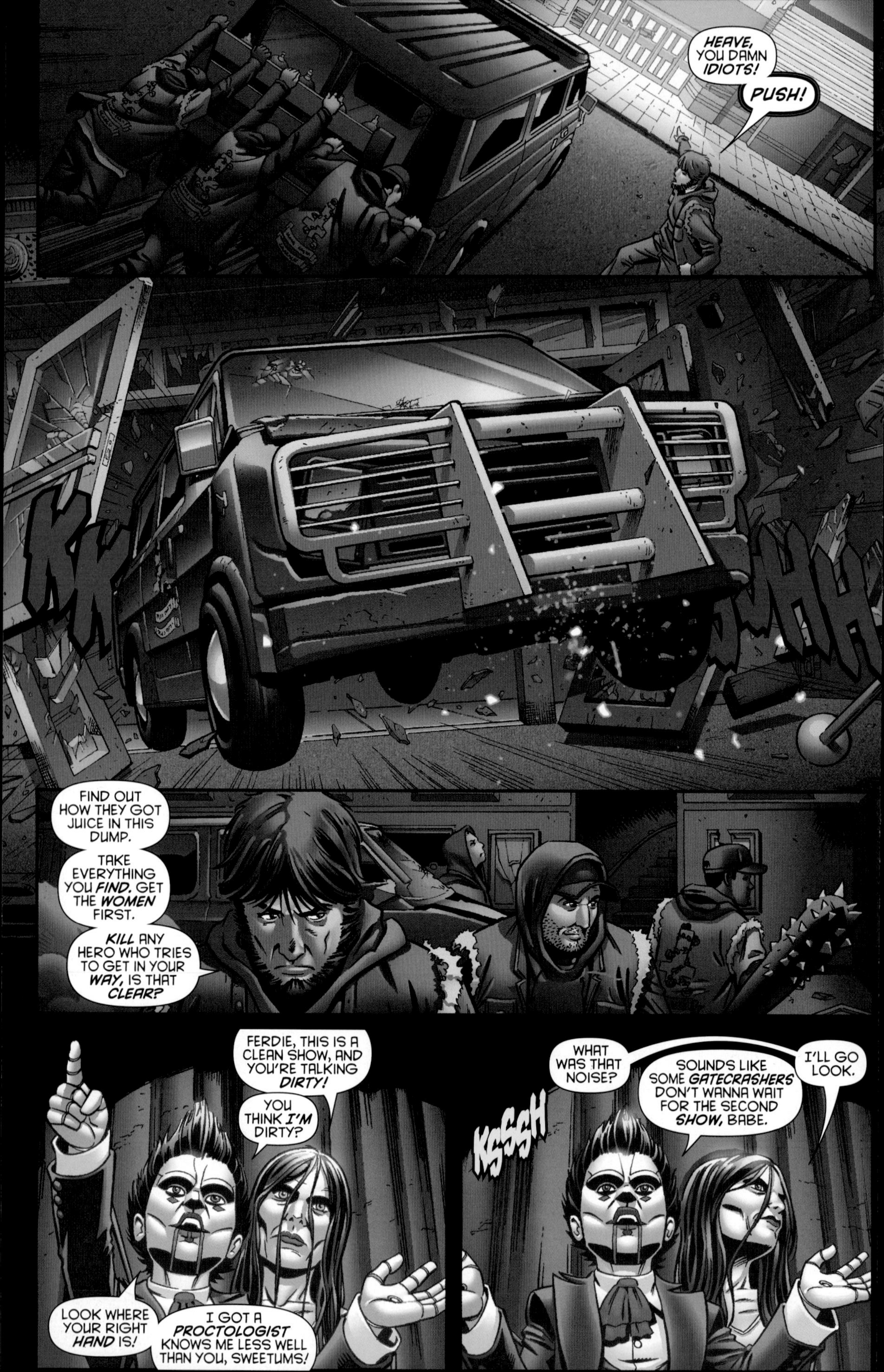

HEAVE, YOU DAMN IDIOTS!
PUSH!
FIND OUT HOW THEY GOT JUICE IN THIS DUMP.
TAKE EVERYTHING YOU FIND. GET THE WOMEN FIRST.
KILL ANY HERO WHO TRIES TO GET IN YOUR WAY, IS THAT CLEAR?
FERDIE, THIS IS A CLEAN SHOW, AND YOU'RE TALKING DIRTY!
YOU THINK I'M DIRTY?
LOOK WHERE YOUR RIGHT HAND IS!
I GOT A PROCTOLOGIST KNOWS ME LESS WELL THAN YOU, SWEETUMS!
KSSSH
WHAT WAS THAT NOISE?
SOUNDS LIKE SOME GATECRASHERS DON'T WANNA WAIT FOR THE SECOND SHOW, BABE.
I'LL GO LOOK.

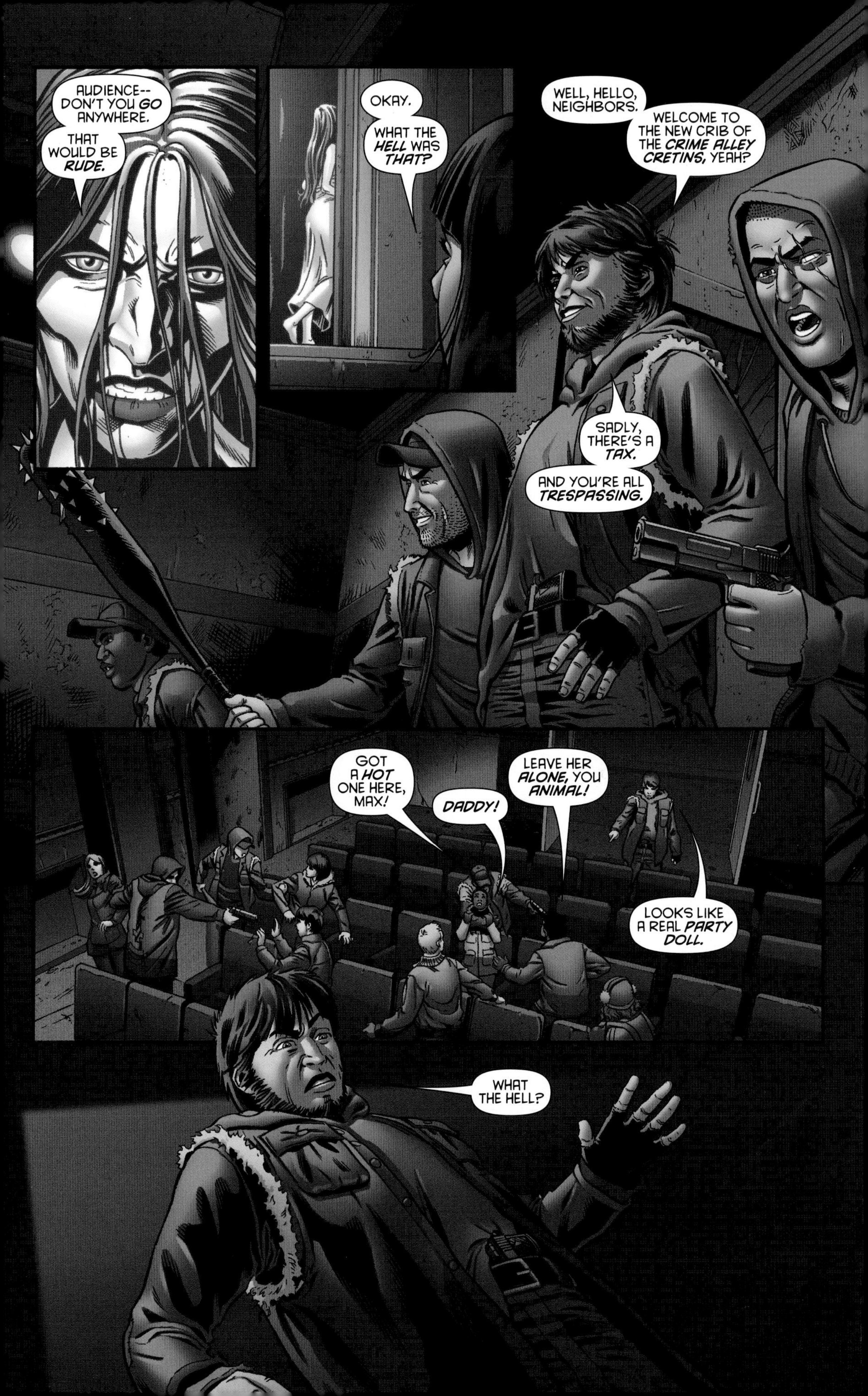
AUDIENCE-- DON'T YOU GO ANYWHERE.
THAT WOULD BE RUDE.
OKAY.
WHAT THE HELL WAS THAT?
WELL, HELLO, NEIGHBORS.
WELCOME TO THE NEW CRIB OF THE CRIME ALLEY CRETINS, YEAH?
SADLY, THERE'S A TAX.
AND YOU'RE ALL TRESPASSING.
GOT A HOT ONE HERE, MAX!
DADDY!
LEAVE HER ALONE, YOU ANIMAL!
LOOKS LIKE A REAL PARTY DOLL.
WHAT THE HELL?

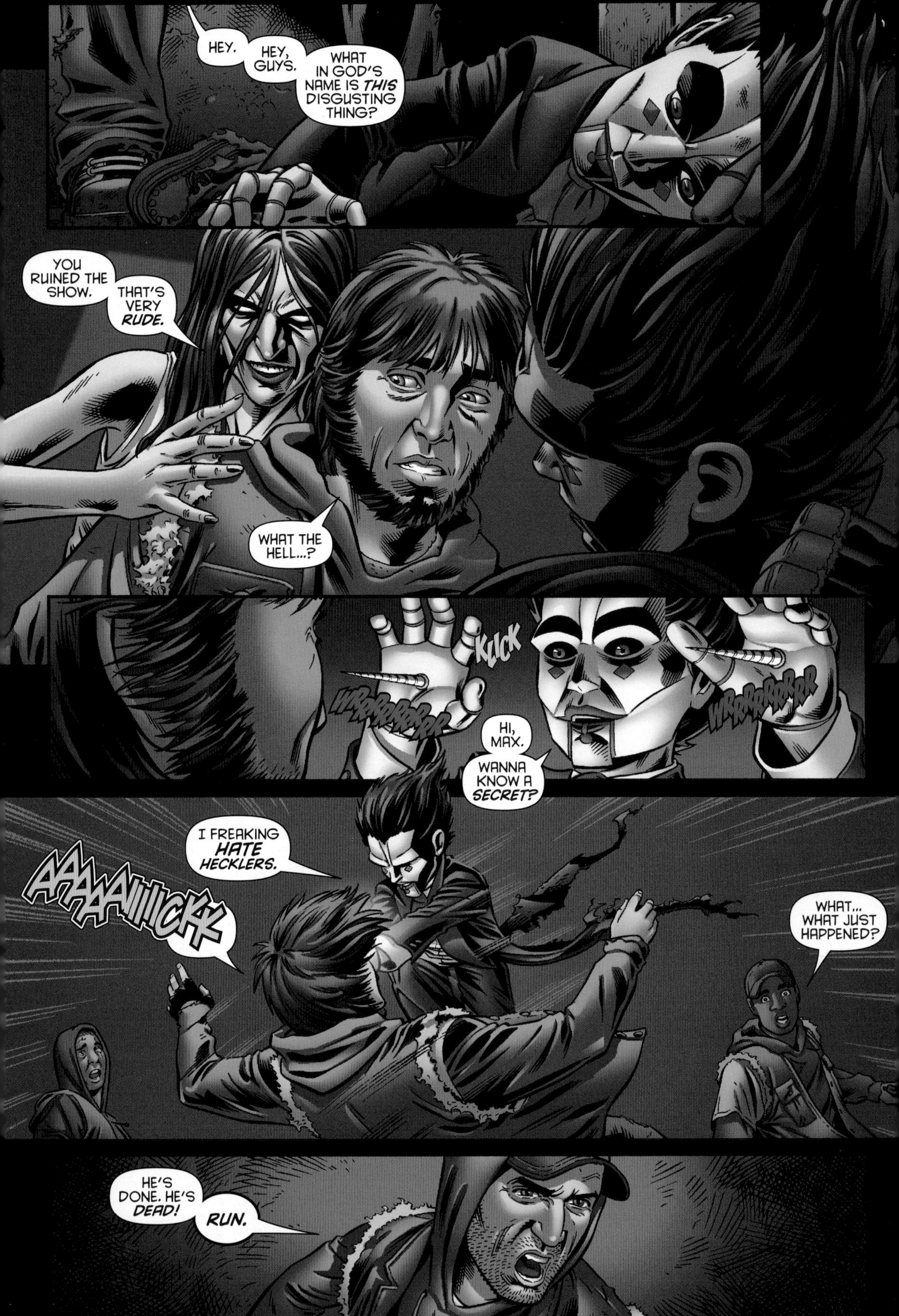
HEY.
HEY, GUYS.
WHAT IN GOD'S NAME IS *THIS* DISGUSTING THING?
YOU RUINED THE SHOW.
THAT'S VERY *RUDE.*
WHAT THE HELL...?
KLICK
WRRRRRRRR
WRRRRRRRR
HI, MAX.
WANNA KNOW A *SECRET?*
I FREAKING *HATE* HECKLERS.
AAAAAIIIICKK
WHAT... WHAT JUST HAPPENED?
HE'S DONE. HE'S *DEAD!*
RUN.

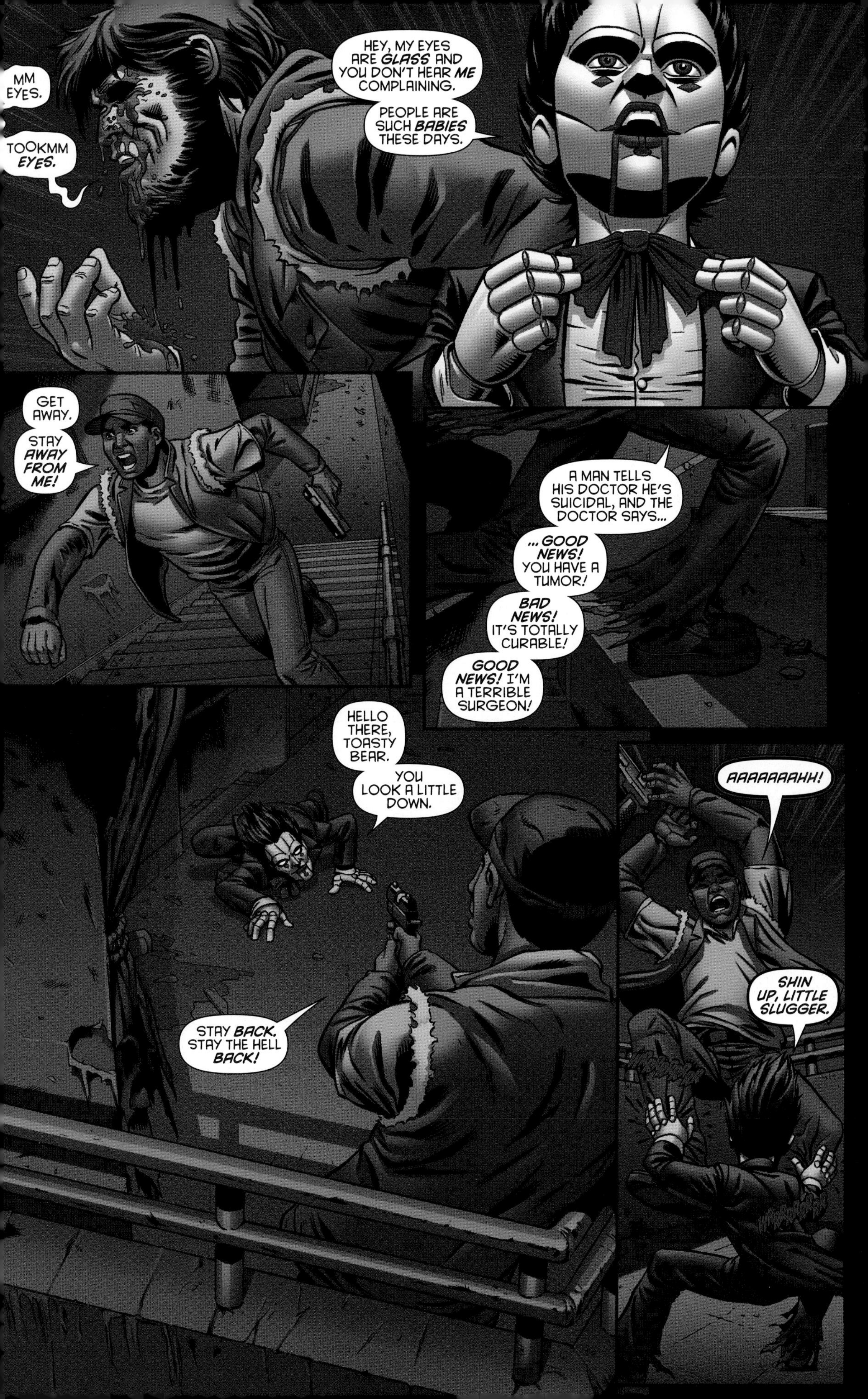
MM EYES.
TOOKMM EYES.
HEY, MY EYES ARE GLASS AND YOU DON'T HEAR ME COMPLAINING.
PEOPLE ARE SUCH BABIES THESE DAYS.
GET AWAY.
STAY AWAY FROM ME!
A MAN TELLS HIS DOCTOR HE'S SUICIDAL, AND THE DOCTOR SAYS...
...GOOD NEWS! YOU HAVE A TUMOR!
BAD NEWS! IT'S TOTALLY CURABLE!
GOOD NEWS! I'M A TERRIBLE SURGEON!
HELLO THERE, TOASTY BEAR.
YOU LOOK A LITTLE DOWN.
STAY BACK. STAY THE HELL BACK!
AAAAAAAHH!
SHIN UP, LITTLE SLUGGER.

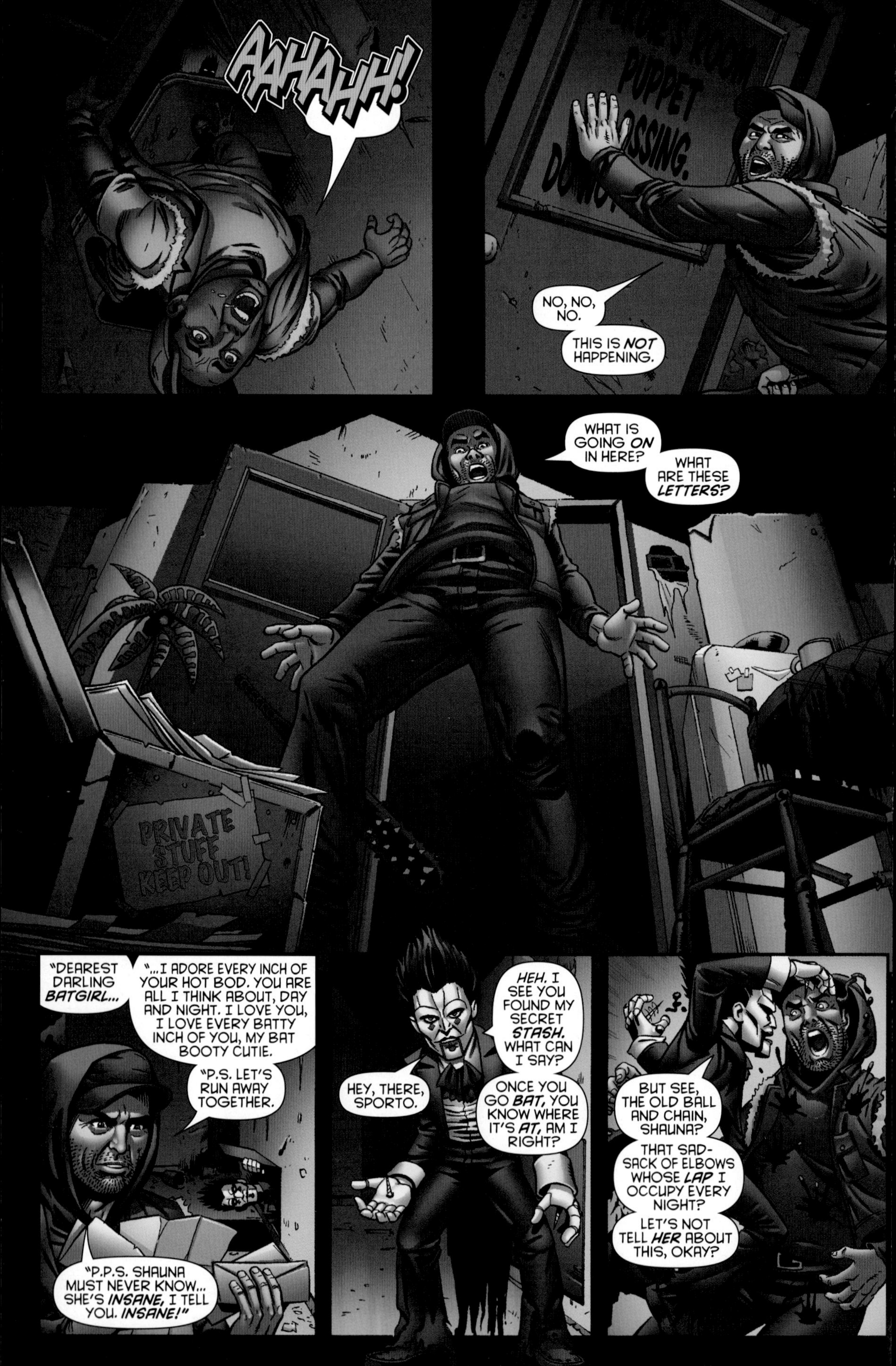
AAHAHH!
NO, NO, NO.
THIS IS NOT HAPPENING.
WHAT IS GOING ON IN HERE?
WHAT ARE THESE LETTERS?
PRIVATE STUFF KEEP OUT!
"DEAREST DARLING BATGIRL...
"...I ADORE EVERY INCH OF YOUR HOT BOD. YOU ARE ALL I THINK ABOUT, DAY AND NIGHT. I LOVE YOU, I LOVE EVERY BATTY INCH OF YOU, MY BAT BOOTY CUTIE.
"P.S. LET'S RUN AWAY TOGETHER.
"P.P.S. SHAUNA MUST NEVER KNOW... SHE'S INSANE, I TELL YOU. INSANE!"
HEY, THERE, SPORTO.
HEH. I SEE YOU FOUND MY SECRET STASH. WHAT CAN I SAY?
ONCE YOU GO BAT, YOU KNOW WHERE IT'S AT, AM I RIGHT?
BUT SEE, THE OLD BALL AND CHAIN, SHAUNA?
THAT SAD-SACK OF ELBOWS WHOSE LAP I OCCUPY EVERY NIGHT?
LET'S NOT TELL HER ABOUT THIS, OKAY?

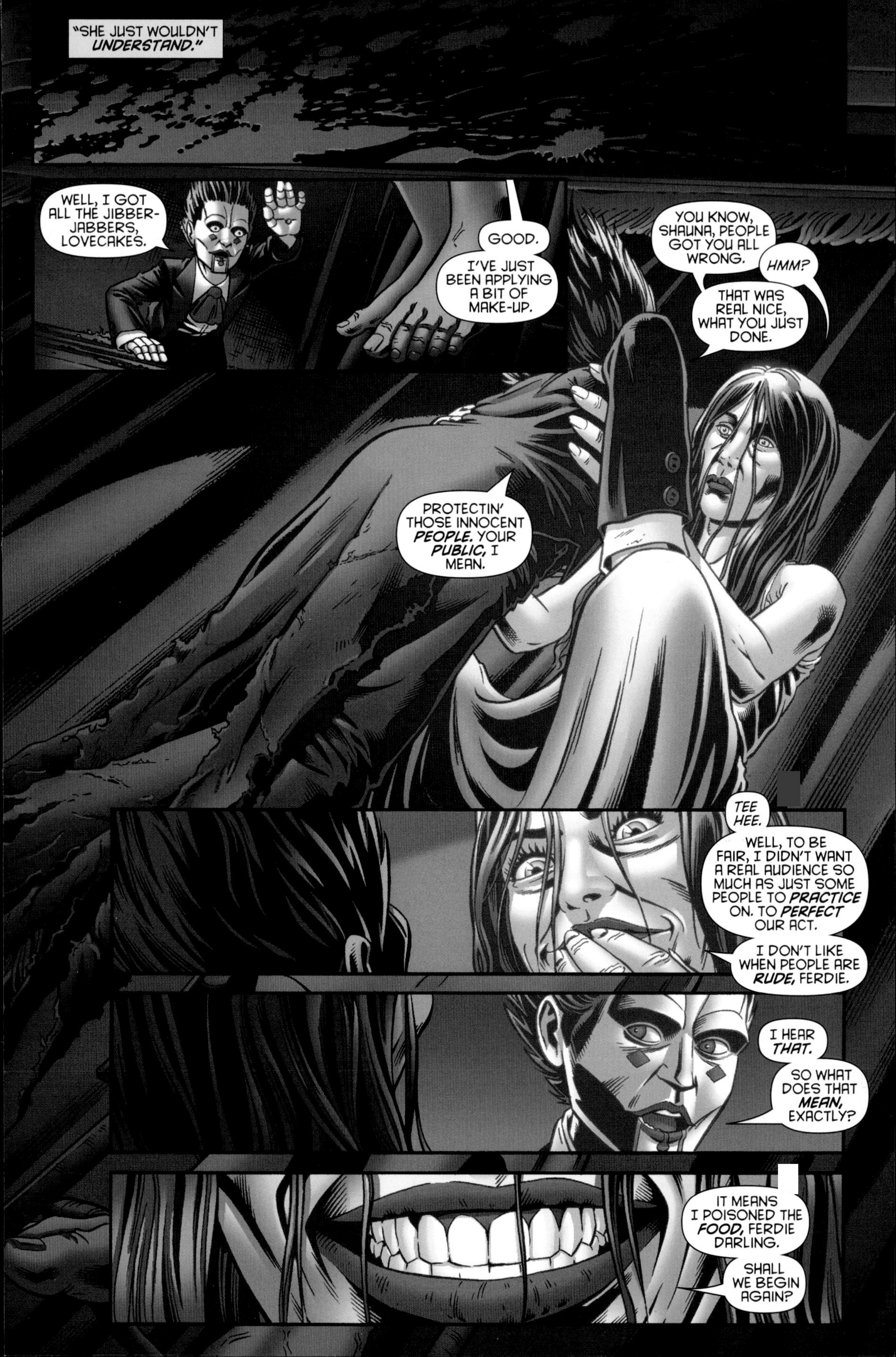

"SHE JUST WOULDN'T UNDERSTAND."
WELL, I GOT ALL THE JIBBER-JABBERS, LOVECAKES.
GOOD.
I'VE JUST BEEN APPLYING A BIT OF MAKE-UP.
YOU KNOW, SHAUNA, PEOPLE GOT YOU ALL WRONG.
HMM?
THAT WAS REAL NICE, WHAT YOU JUST DONE.
PROTECTIN' THOSE INNOCENT PEOPLE. YOUR PUBLIC, I MEAN.
TEE HEE.
WELL, TO BE FAIR, I DIDN'T WANT A REAL AUDIENCE SO MUCH AS JUST SOME PEOPLE TO PRACTICE ON. TO PERFECT OUR ACT.
I DON'T LIKE WHEN PEOPLE ARE RUDE, FERDIE.
I HEAR THAT.
SO WHAT DOES THAT MEAN, EXACTLY?
IT MEANS I POISONED THE FOOD, FERDIE DARLING.
SHALL WE BEGIN AGAIN?

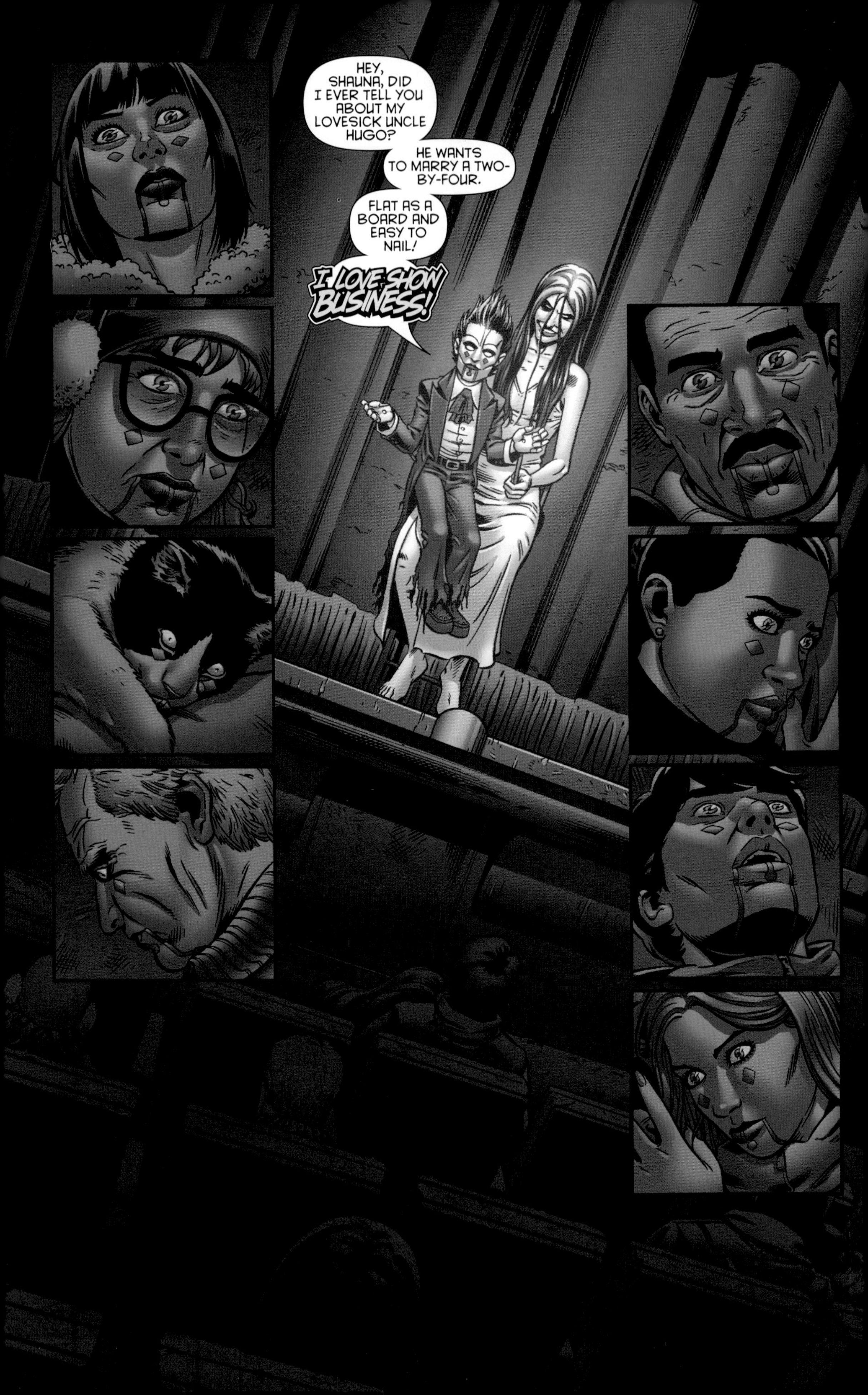
HEY, SHAUNA, DID I EVER TELL YOU ABOUT MY LOVESICK UNCLE HUGO?
HE WANTS TO MARRY A TWO-BY-FOUR.
FLAT AS A BOARD AND EASY TO NAIL!
I LOVE SHOW BUSINESS!

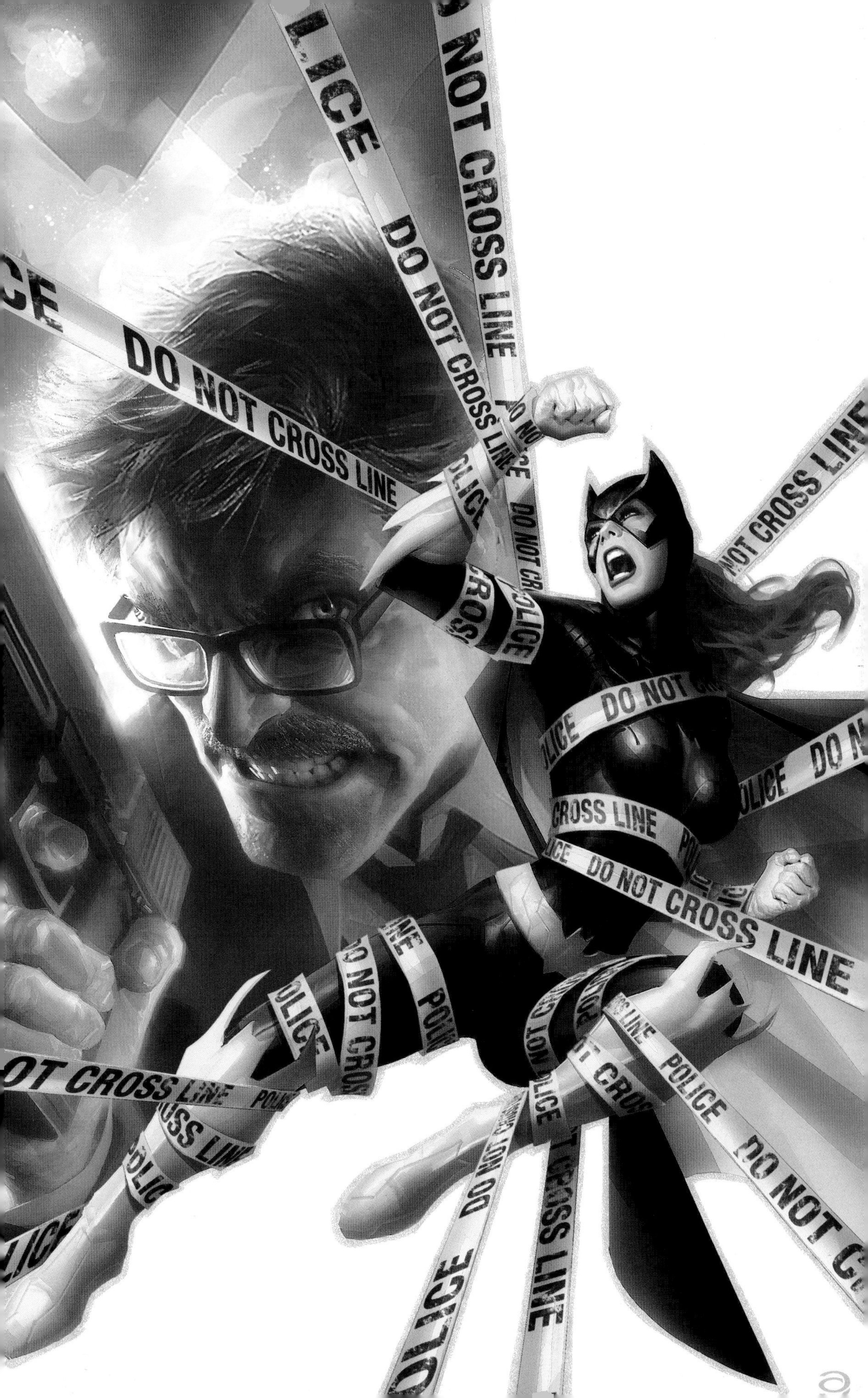
DO NOT CROSS LINE
DO NOT CROSS LINE
DO NOT CROSS LINE
DO NOT CROSS LINE
POLICE
POLICE

BATGIRL WANTED part one: MANHUNT

GAIL SIMONE writer **FERNANDO PASARIN** penciller **JONATHAN GLAPION** inker **BLOND** colorist

cover by **ALEX GARNER**

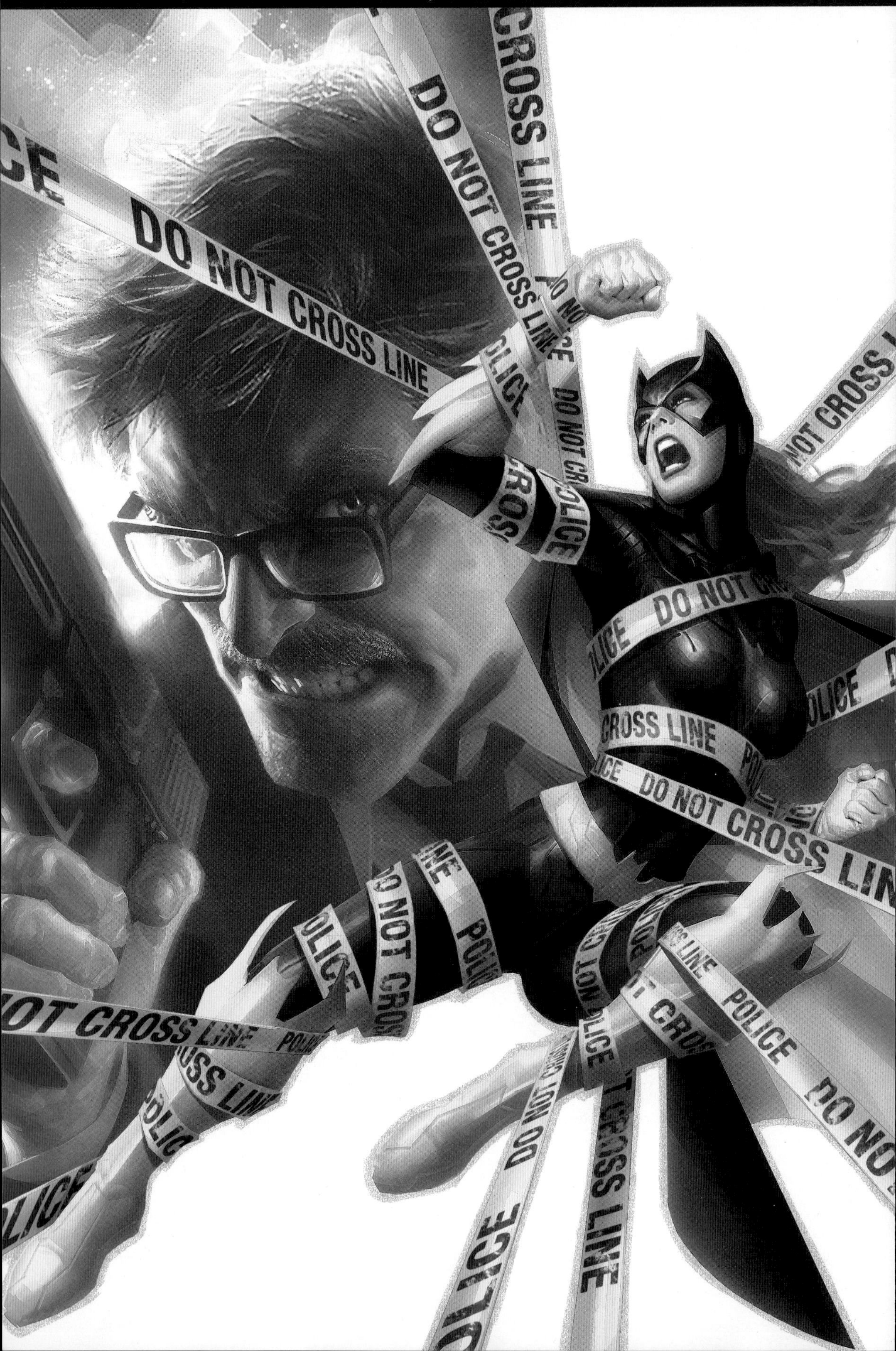

DO NOT CROSS LINE
CROSS LINE
DO NOT CROSS LINE
POLICE
DO NOT CROSS LINE
CROSS LINE
POLICE

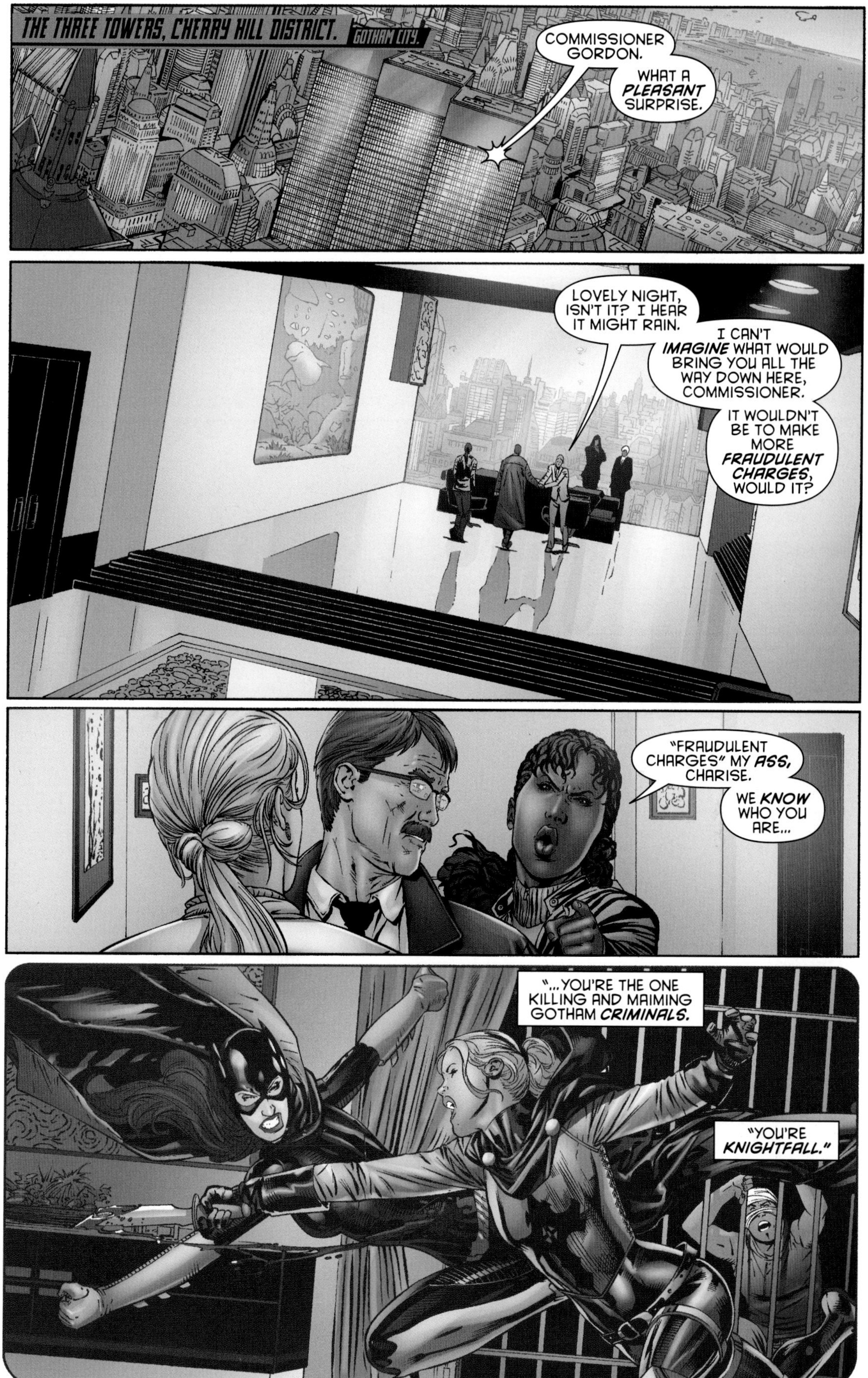
THE THREE TOWERS, CHERRY HILL DISTRICT.
GOTHAM CITY.
COMMISSIONER GORDON.
WHAT A PLEASANT SURPRISE.
LOVELY NIGHT, ISN'T IT? I HEAR IT MIGHT RAIN.
I CAN'T IMAGINE WHAT WOULD BRING YOU ALL THE WAY DOWN HERE, COMMISSIONER.
IT WOULDN'T BE TO MAKE MORE FRAUDULENT CHARGES, WOULD IT?
"FRAUDULENT CHARGES" MY ASS, CHARISE.
WE KNOW WHO YOU ARE...
"...YOU'RE THE ONE KILLING AND MAIMING GOTHAM CRIMINALS.
"YOU'RE KNIGHTFALL."

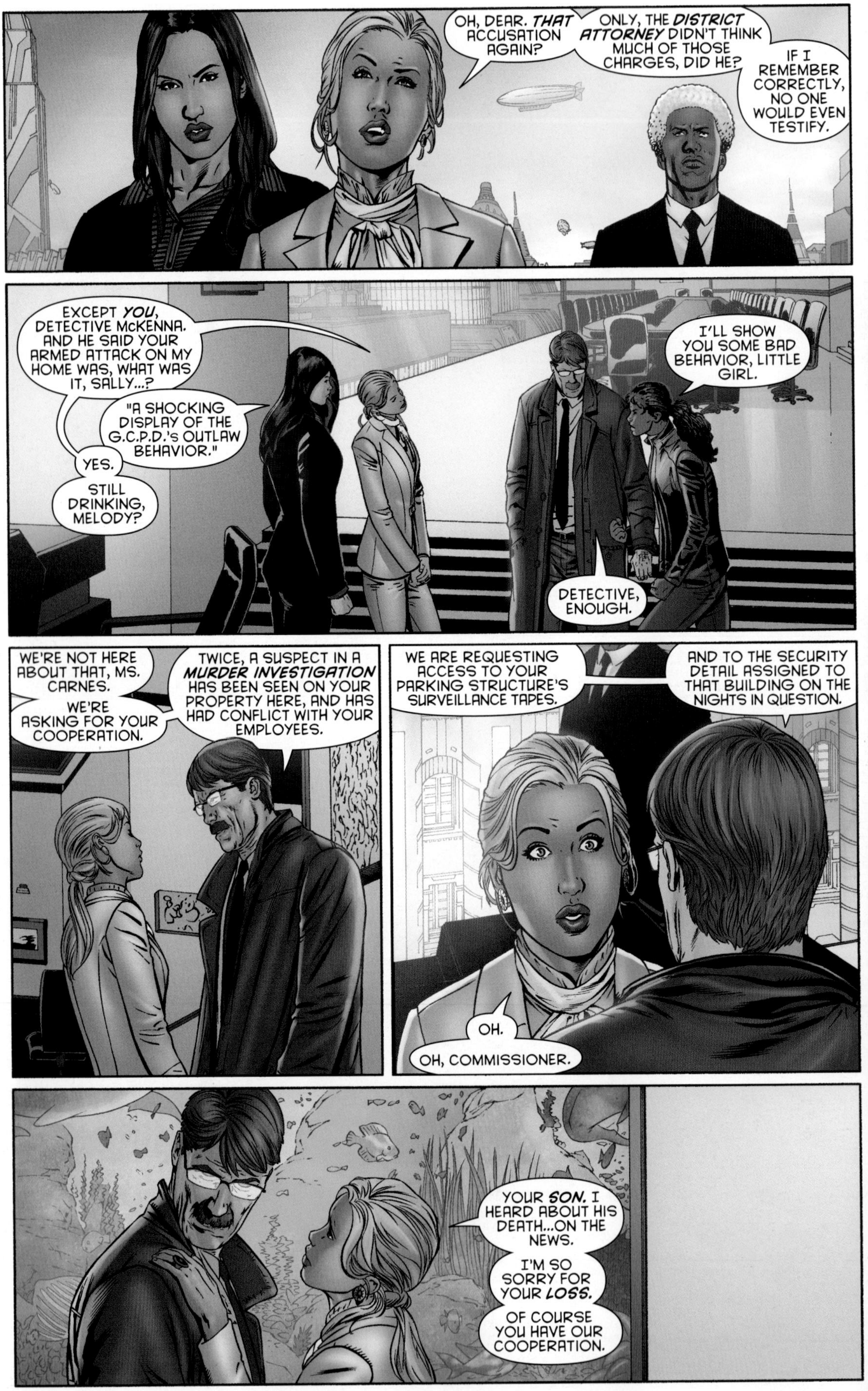
OH, DEAR. *THAT* ACCUSATION AGAIN?
ONLY, THE *DISTRICT ATTORNEY* DIDN'T THINK MUCH OF THOSE CHARGES, DID HE?
IF I REMEMBER CORRECTLY, NO ONE WOULD EVEN TESTIFY.
EXCEPT *YOU*, DETECTIVE McKENNA. AND HE SAID YOUR ARMED ATTACK ON MY HOME WAS, WHAT WAS IT, SALLY...?
"A SHOCKING DISPLAY OF THE G.C.P.D.'s OUTLAW BEHAVIOR."
YES.
STILL DRINKING, MELODY?
I'LL SHOW YOU SOME BAD BEHAVIOR, LITTLE GIRL.
DETECTIVE, ENOUGH.
WE'RE NOT HERE ABOUT THAT, MS. CARNES.
WE'RE ASKING FOR YOUR COOPERATION.
TWICE, A SUSPECT IN A *MURDER INVESTIGATION* HAS BEEN SEEN ON YOUR PROPERTY HERE, AND HAS HAD CONFLICT WITH YOUR EMPLOYEES.
WE ARE REQUESTING ACCESS TO YOUR PARKING STRUCTURE'S SURVEILLANCE TAPES.
AND TO THE SECURITY DETAIL ASSIGNED TO THAT BUILDING ON THE NIGHTS IN QUESTION.
OH.
OH, COMMISSIONER.
YOUR *SON.* I HEARD ABOUT HIS DEATH...ON THE NEWS.
I'M SO SORRY FOR YOUR *LOSS.*
OF COURSE YOU HAVE OUR COOPERATION.

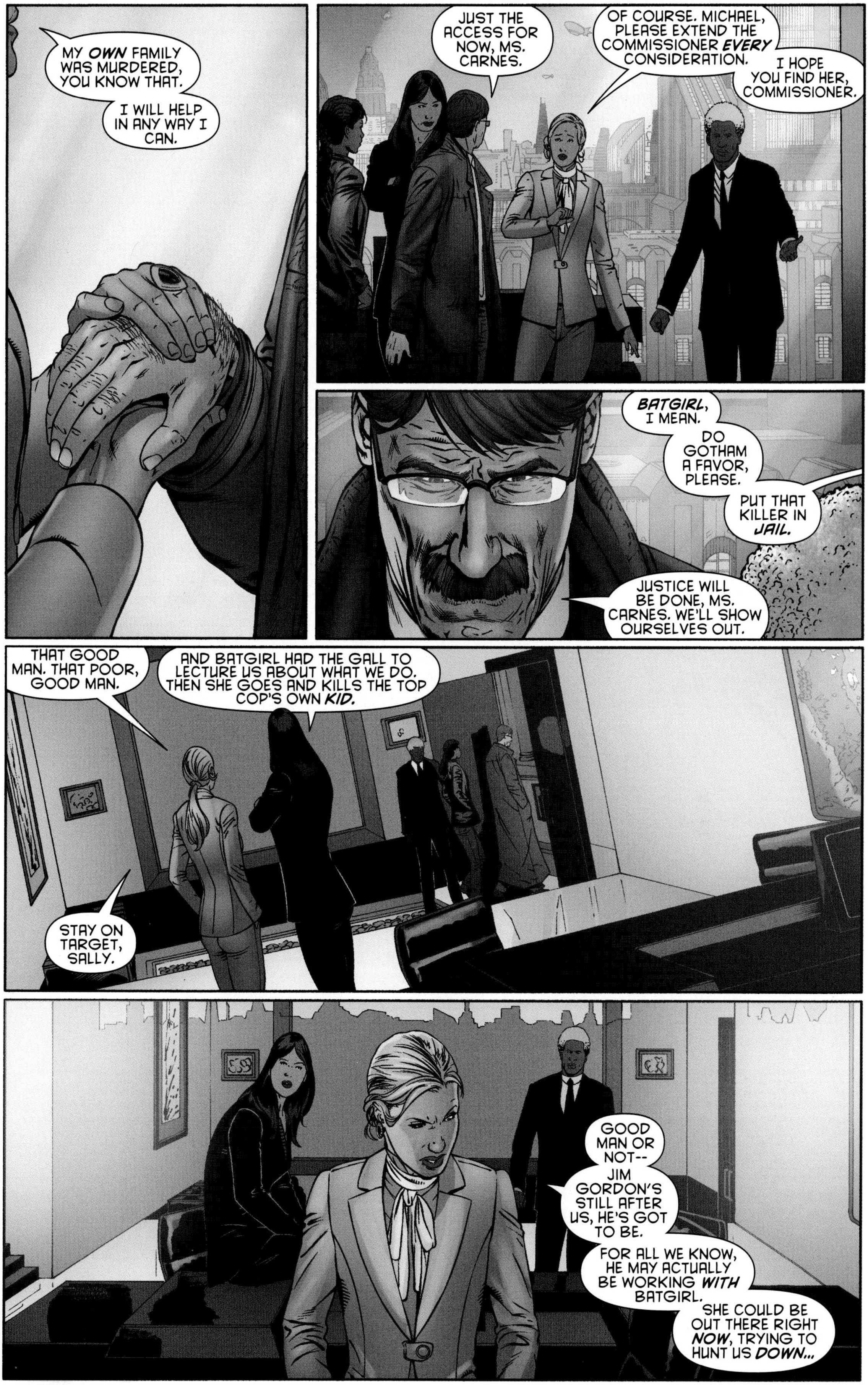
MY OWN FAMILY WAS MURDERED, YOU KNOW THAT.
I WILL HELP IN ANY WAY I CAN.
JUST THE ACCESS FOR NOW, MS. CARNES.
OF COURSE. MICHAEL, PLEASE EXTEND THE COMMISSIONER EVERY CONSIDERATION.
I HOPE YOU FIND HER, COMMISSIONER.
BATGIRL, I MEAN.
DO GOTHAM A FAVOR, PLEASE.
PUT THAT KILLER IN JAIL.
JUSTICE WILL BE DONE, MS. CARNES. WE'LL SHOW OURSELVES OUT.
THAT GOOD MAN. THAT POOR, GOOD MAN.
AND BATGIRL HAD THE GALL TO LECTURE US ABOUT WHAT WE DO. THEN SHE GOES AND KILLS THE TOP COP'S OWN KID.
STAY ON TARGET, SALLY.
GOOD MAN OR NOT--
JIM GORDON'S STILL AFTER US, HE'S GOT TO BE.
FOR ALL WE KNOW, HE MAY ACTUALLY BE WORKING WITH BATGIRL.
SHE COULD BE OUT THERE RIGHT NOW, TRYING TO HUNT US DOWN...

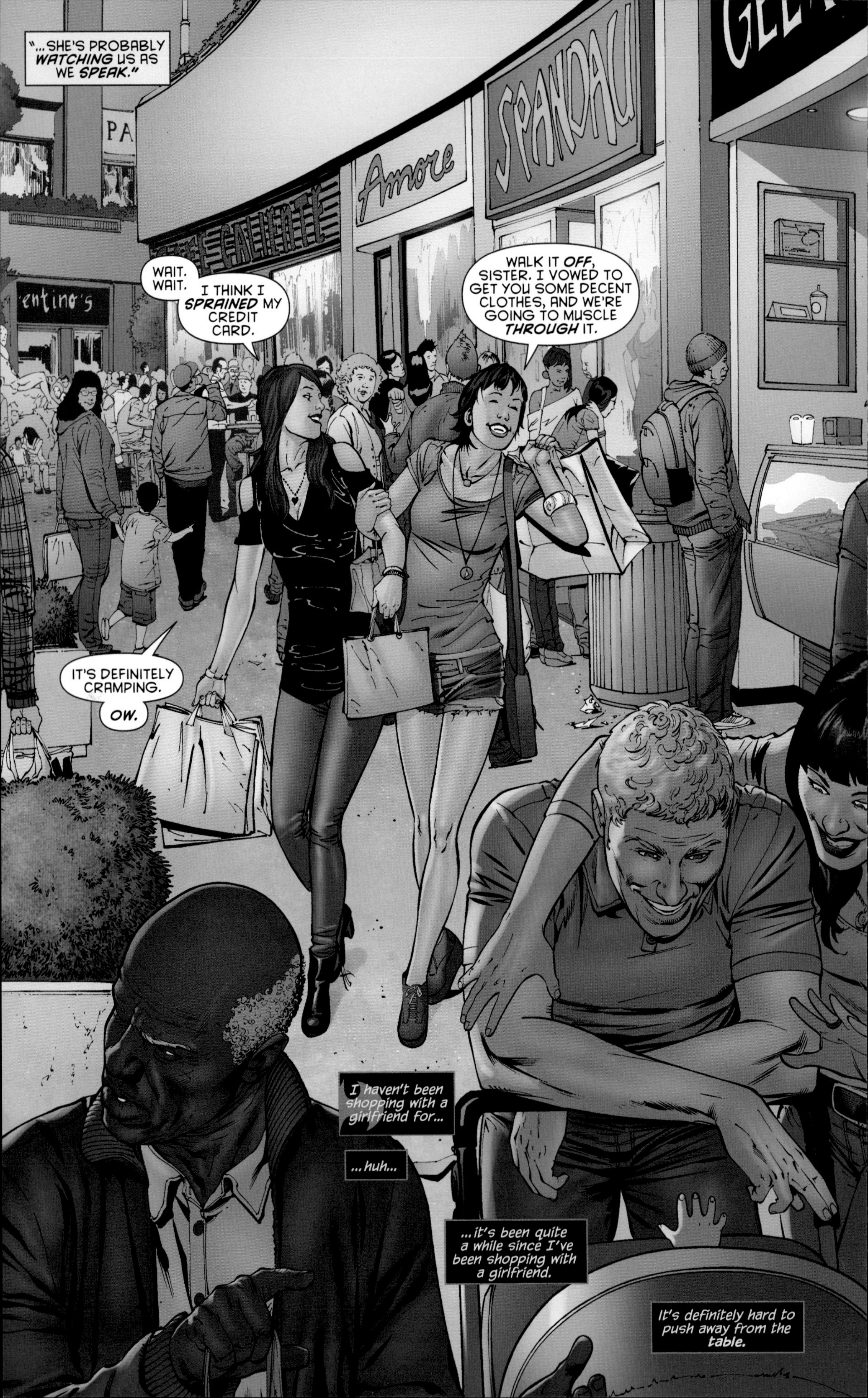
"...SHE'S PROBABLY WATCHING US AS WE SPEAK."
PA
CAFE CALIENTE
Amore
SPANDAU
entino's
WAIT. WAIT.
I THINK I SPRAINED MY CREDIT CARD.
WALK IT OFF, SISTER. I VOWED TO GET YOU SOME DECENT CLOTHES, AND WE'RE GOING TO MUSCLE THROUGH IT.
IT'S DEFINITELY CRAMPING.
OW.
I haven't been shopping with a girlfriend for...
...huh...
...it's been quite a while since I've been shopping with a girlfriend.
It's definitely hard to push away from the table.

SHOES.

WE *DID* SHOES!

WE DIDN'T DO *THESE* SHOES.

I pushed so many people away the past few years.

It's nice to have someone who chooses to stick.

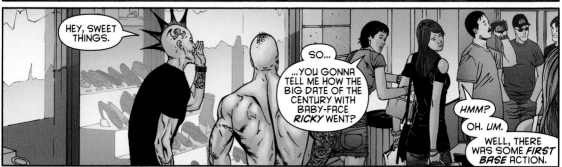

HEY, SWEET THINGS.

SO... ...YOU GONNA TELL ME HOW THE BIG DATE OF THE CENTURY WITH BABY-FACE *RICKY* WENT?

HMM?

OH. UM.

WELL, THERE WAS SOME *FIRST BASE* ACTION.

HOW ABOUT WE MAKE IT A FOURSOME? THAT SOUND GOOD?

OH, MY GOD, FIRST BASE.

IN BARBARA YEARS, THAT'S LIKE HAVING *OCTUPLETS* TOGETHER.

THOSE GUYS...

IGNORE THEM, THEY GO AWAY. USUALLY.

I don't like the way she said that.

Like she's gotten used to it.

HEY, MAYBE THEY'RE TOGETHER.

THAT WHY YOU'RE SO *FRIGID,* SWEETCHEEKS?

YOU TWO A COUPLE OF LOVEBIRDS?

I GOT SOMETHIN' THAT'LL *FIX* THAT RIGHT UP.

LET'S GO. THERE'S GOT TO BE SOME *SECURITY* HERE.

I don't like it.

The bit of panic in her voice.

I don't like it.

We were just *shopping.*

SOUND GOOD, SWEETCHEEKS?

YOU *KNOW* YOU LIKE IT.

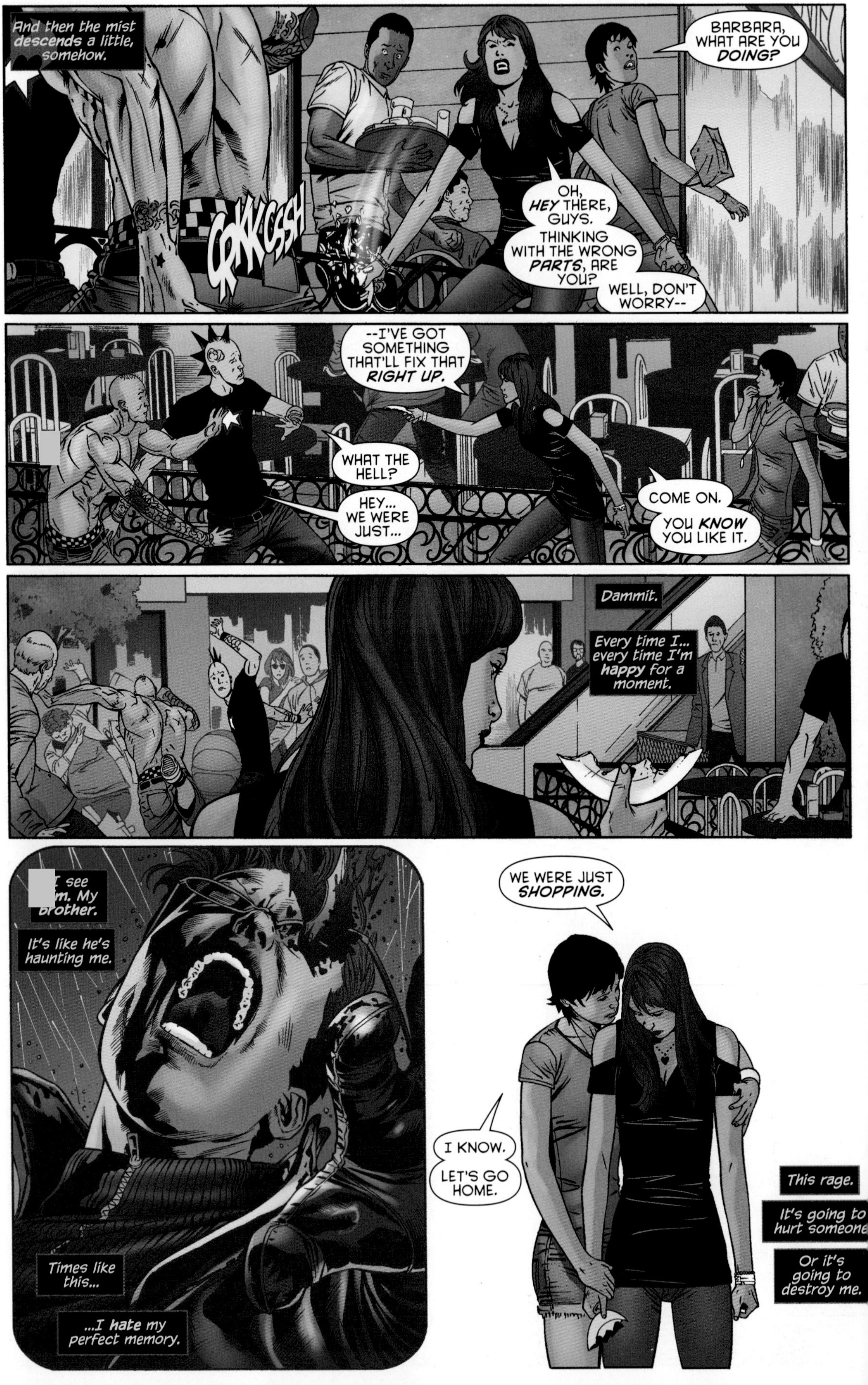

And then the mist descends a little, somehow.
BARBARA, WHAT ARE YOU DOING?
CRKKCSSH
OH, HEY THERE, GUYS.
THINKING WITH THE WRONG PARTS, ARE YOU?
WELL, DON'T WORRY--
--I'VE GOT SOMETHING THAT'LL FIX THAT RIGHT UP.
WHAT THE HELL?
HEY... WE WERE JUST...
COME ON.
YOU KNOW YOU LIKE IT.
Dammit.
Every time I... every time I'm happy for a moment.
see m. My brother.
It's like he's haunting me.
Times like this...
...I hate my perfect memory.
WE WERE JUST SHOPPING.
I KNOW.
LET'S GO HOME.
This rage.
It's going to hurt someone
Or it's going to destroy me.

CHERRY HILL, LATER.

COMMISSIONER, YOU DON'T HAVE TO DO THIS.

WHAT WOULD YOU DO, MELODY? JAMES WAS MY *SON*.

NO, I GET THAT. I DO. BUT LET YOUR *COPS* DO THIS LEGWORK STUFF. LET'S GET SOME BACKUP, AT LEAST. THIS *IS* CHERRY HILL.

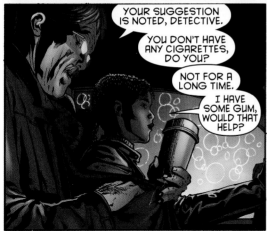

YOUR SUGGESTION IS NOTED, DETECTIVE.

YOU DON'T HAVE ANY CIGARETTES, DO YOU?

NOT FOR A LONG TIME. I HAVE SOME GUM, WOULD THAT HELP?

NO. GOT IT. JIM--OFF THE RECORD.

IS IT...IS IT JUST BARELY *POSSIBLE* THAT BATGIRL HAD NO CHOICE TRYING TO *STOP* JAMES, JR.?

I JUST...OF ALL OF THEM, I CAN'T *BELIEVE* THAT *SHE* WOULD KILL, ON PURPOSE. MY GUT SAYS--

I WITNESSED IT, MELODY. I'D SAY THAT TRUMPS YOUR LITTLE HUNCH. PULL OVER.

WHO'S OUR NEXT INTERVIEW, COMMISSIONER?

SOME LOCAL WITH A RECORD BATGIRL WAS SEEN IN CONTACT WITH.

RICKY GUTIERREZ.

Officer

☑ YES ☐ NO

15-01-1981292856
VAL II-P 7C
33098

...AGAIN SO YOU *UNDERSTAND*, RICKY.

YOU AND YOUR BROTHER, YOU SCREWED WITH THE *SIXTY-EIGHT KINGS.*

WE HAVE *FRIENDS* IN THIS TOWN, RICK.

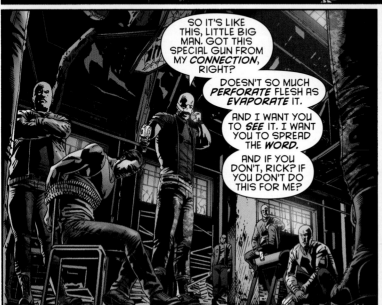

SO IT'S LIKE THIS, LITTLE BIG MAN. GOT THIS SPECIAL GUN FROM MY *CONNECTION*, RIGHT?

DOESN'T SO MUCH *PERFORATE* FLESH AS *EVAPORATE* IT.

AND I WANT YOU TO *SEE* IT. I WANT YOU TO SPREAD THE *WORD.*

AND IF YOU DON'T, RICK? IF YOU DON'T DO THIS FOR ME?

I'M A COME VISIT YOUR *MOMS*, SON. AND THAT LITTLE *REDHEAD* TWIST OF YOURS.

BEST *BELIEVE* THAT.

YOU GOT FIFTEEN MINUTES, KISS MOMMY GOODBYE AND COME DOWN TO OUR ALMA MATER, MAN. WHERE WE ALL FIRST *MET.*

OR *I'LL* COME UP AND KISS HER GOODBYE, YOU HEAR ME?

I EVEN *SMELL* A COP AND EVERY ONE OF YOU *BURNS.*

I HAVE TO GO, MOMMA. YOU NEED TO GO STAY AT AUNT CYNTHIA'S.

RICKY, *NO.*

DO IT FOR ME, MOM. *PLEASE.*

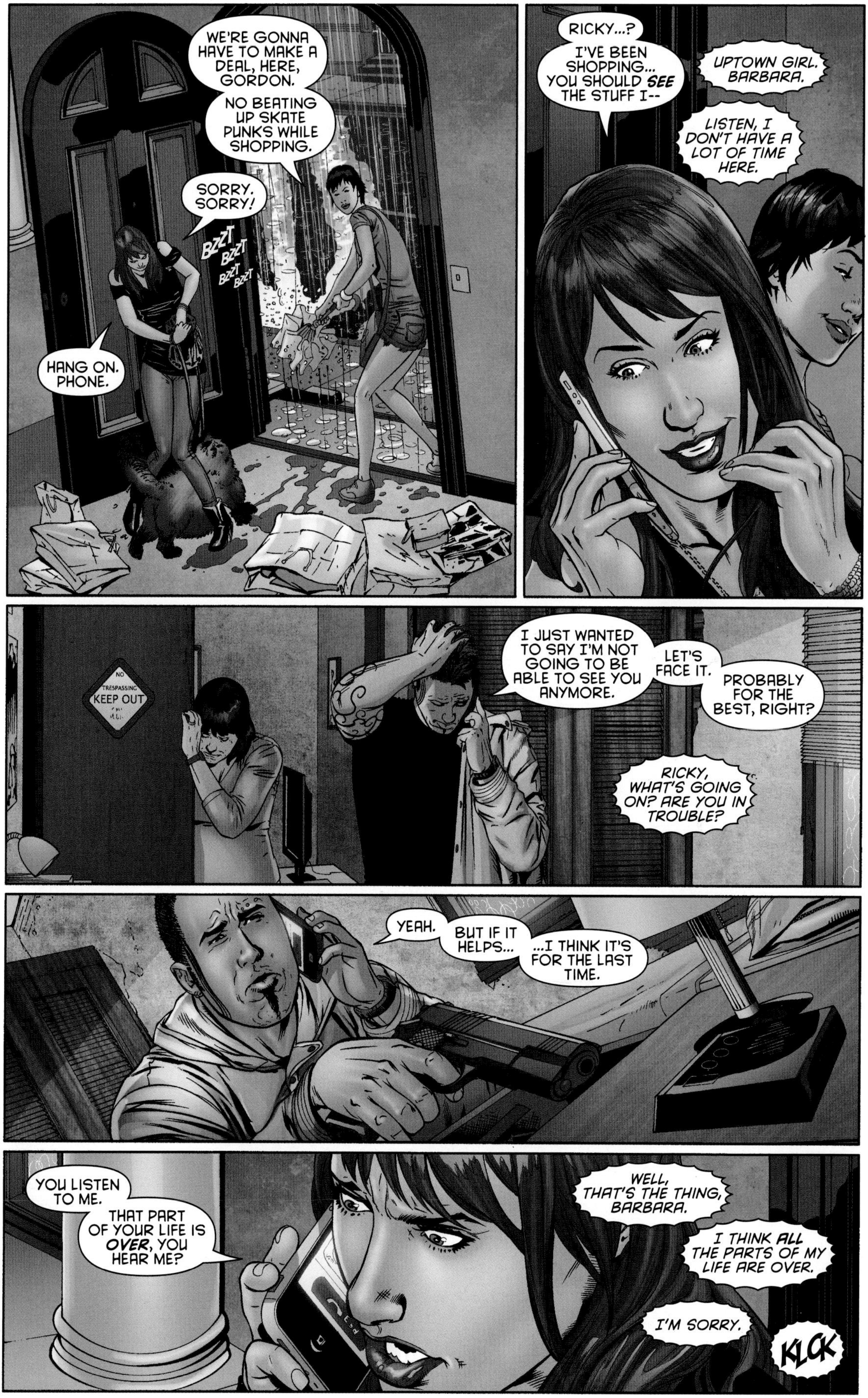

WE'RE GONNA HAVE TO MAKE A DEAL, HERE, GORDON.
NO BEATING UP SKATE PUNKS WHILE SHOPPING.
SORRY. SORRY!
BZZZT BZZT BZZT BZZT
HANG ON. PHONE.
RICKY...?
I'VE BEEN SHOPPING... YOU SHOULD ***SEE*** THE STUFF I--
UPTOWN GIRL. BARBARA.
LISTEN, I DON'T HAVE A LOT OF TIME HERE.
NO TRESPASSING KEEP OUT
I JUST WANTED TO SAY I'M NOT GOING TO BE ABLE TO SEE YOU ANYMORE.
LET'S FACE IT.
PROBABLY FOR THE BEST, RIGHT?
RICKY, WHAT'S GOING ON? ARE YOU IN TROUBLE?
YEAH.
BUT IF IT HELPS...
...I THINK IT'S FOR THE LAST TIME.
YOU LISTEN TO ME.
THAT PART OF YOUR LIFE IS ***OVER***, YOU HEAR ME?
WELL, THAT'S THE THING, BARBARA.
*I THINK **ALL** THE PARTS OF MY LIFE ARE OVER.*
I'M SORRY.
KLCK

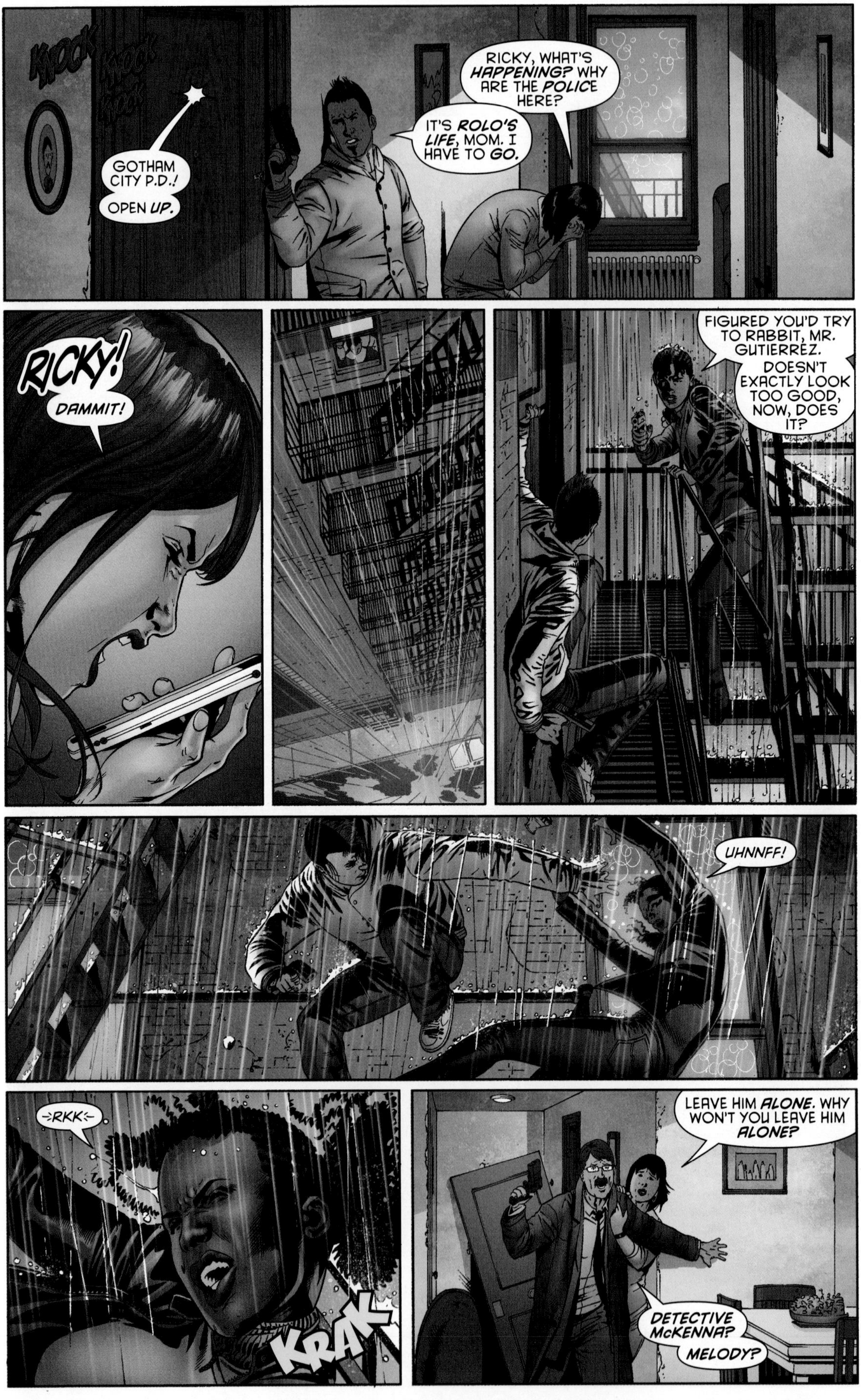
KNOCK KNOCK
GOTHAM CITY P.D.!
OPEN UP.
IT'S ROLO'S LIFE, MOM. I HAVE TO GO.
RICKY, WHAT'S HAPPENING? WHY ARE THE POLICE HERE?
RICKY!
DAMMIT!
FIGURED YOU'D TRY TO RABBIT, MR. GUTIERREZ.
DOESN'T EXACTLY LOOK TOO GOOD, NOW, DOES IT?
UHNNFF!
RKK
KRAK
LEAVE HIM ALONE. WHY WON'T YOU LEAVE HIM ALONE?
DETECTIVE McKENNA?
MELODY?

MELODY!

DAMMIT. *DAMMIT.*

STOP!
POLICE!

DAMN.

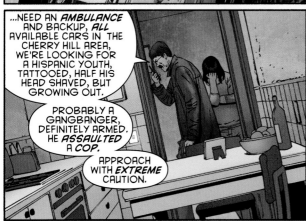

...NEED AN *AMBULANCE* AND BACKUP, *ALL* AVAILABLE CARS IN THE CHERRY HILL AREA, WE'RE LOOKING FOR A HISPANIC YOUTH, TATTOOED, HALF HIS HEAD SHAVED, BUT GROWING OUT.

PROBABLY A GANGBANGER, DEFINITELY ARMED. HE *ASSAULTED* A COP.

APPROACH WITH *EXTREME* CAUTION.

EH? JUST A SECOND, DISPATCH.

OH, BARBARA.

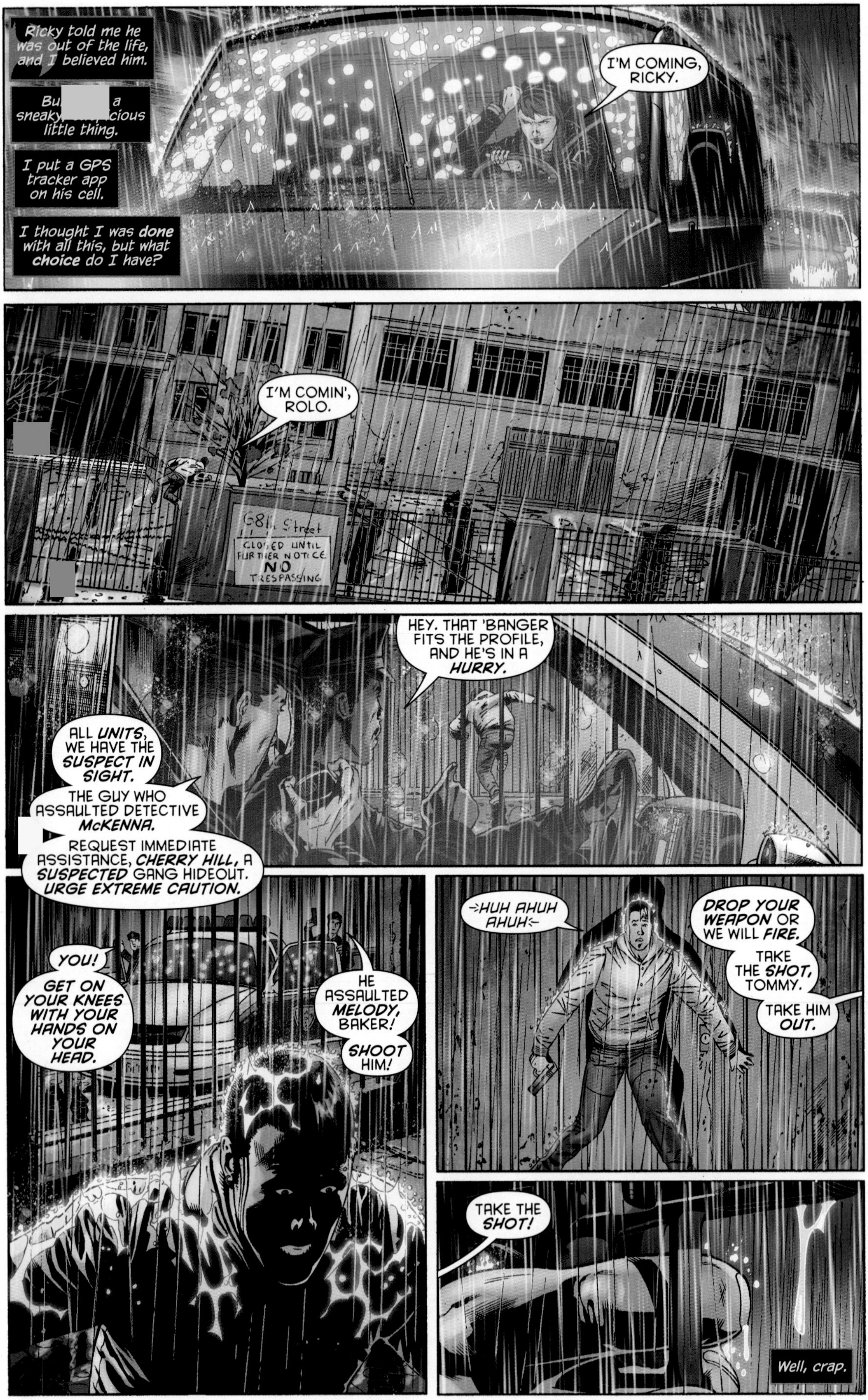
Ricky told me he was out of the life, and I believed him.
Bu a sneaky cious little thing.
I put a GPS tracker app on his cell.
I thought I was done with all this, but what choice do I have?
I'M COMING, RICKY.
I'M COMIN', ROLO.
68th Street
CLOSED UNTIL FURTHER NOTICE
NO TRESPASSING
HEY. THAT 'BANGER FITS THE PROFILE, AND HE'S IN A HURRY.
ALL UNITS, WE HAVE THE SUSPECT IN SIGHT.
THE GUY WHO ASSAULTED DETECTIVE McKENNA.
REQUEST IMMEDIATE ASSISTANCE, CHERRY HILL, A SUSPECTED GANG HIDEOUT. URGE EXTREME CAUTION.
YOU!
GET ON YOUR KNEES WITH YOUR HANDS ON YOUR HEAD.
HE ASSAULTED MELODY, BAKER!
SHOOT HIM!
HUH AHUH AHUH
DROP YOUR WEAPON OR WE WILL FIRE.
TAKE THE SHOT, TOMMY.
TAKE HIM OUT.
TAKE THE SHOT!
Well, crap.

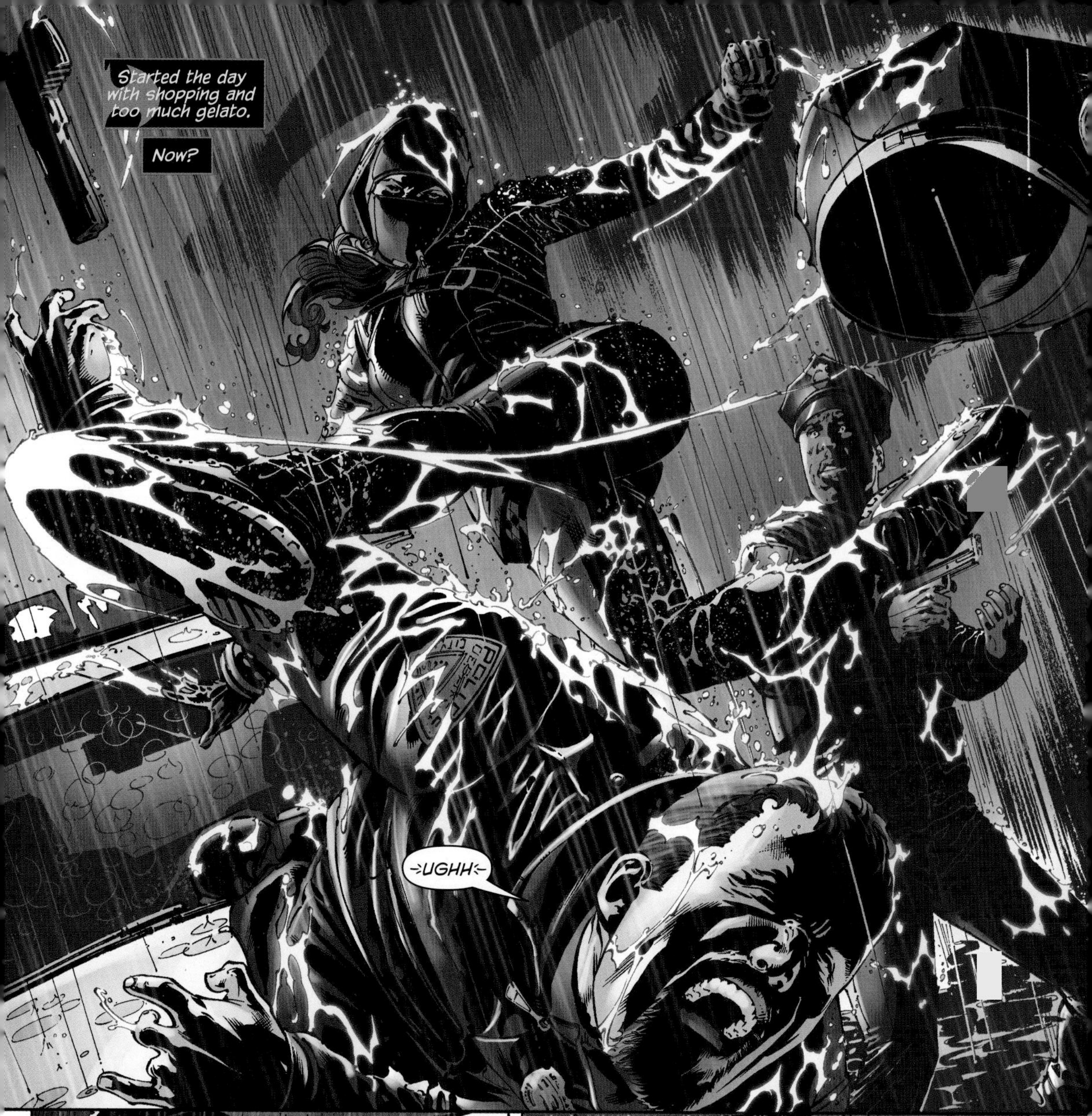
Started the day with shopping and too much gelato.
Now?
UGHH

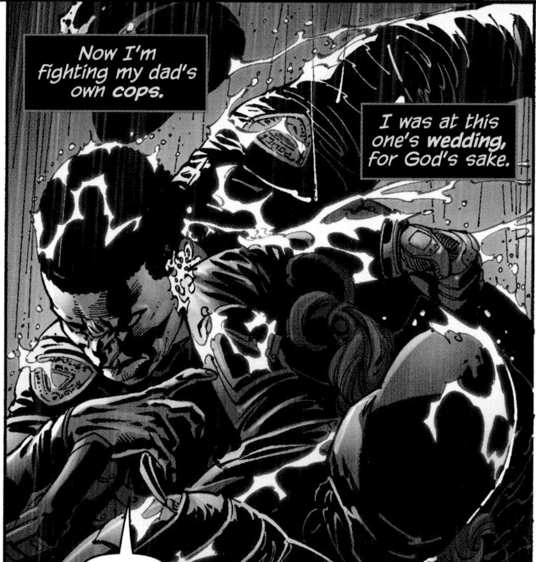
Now I'm fighting my dad's own cops.
I was at this one's wedding, for God's sake.
GNN

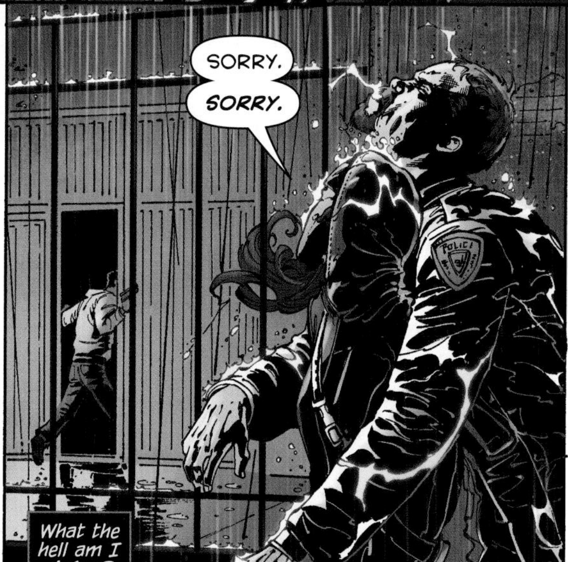
SORRY.
SORRY.
What the hell am I doing?
Oh, Ricky...

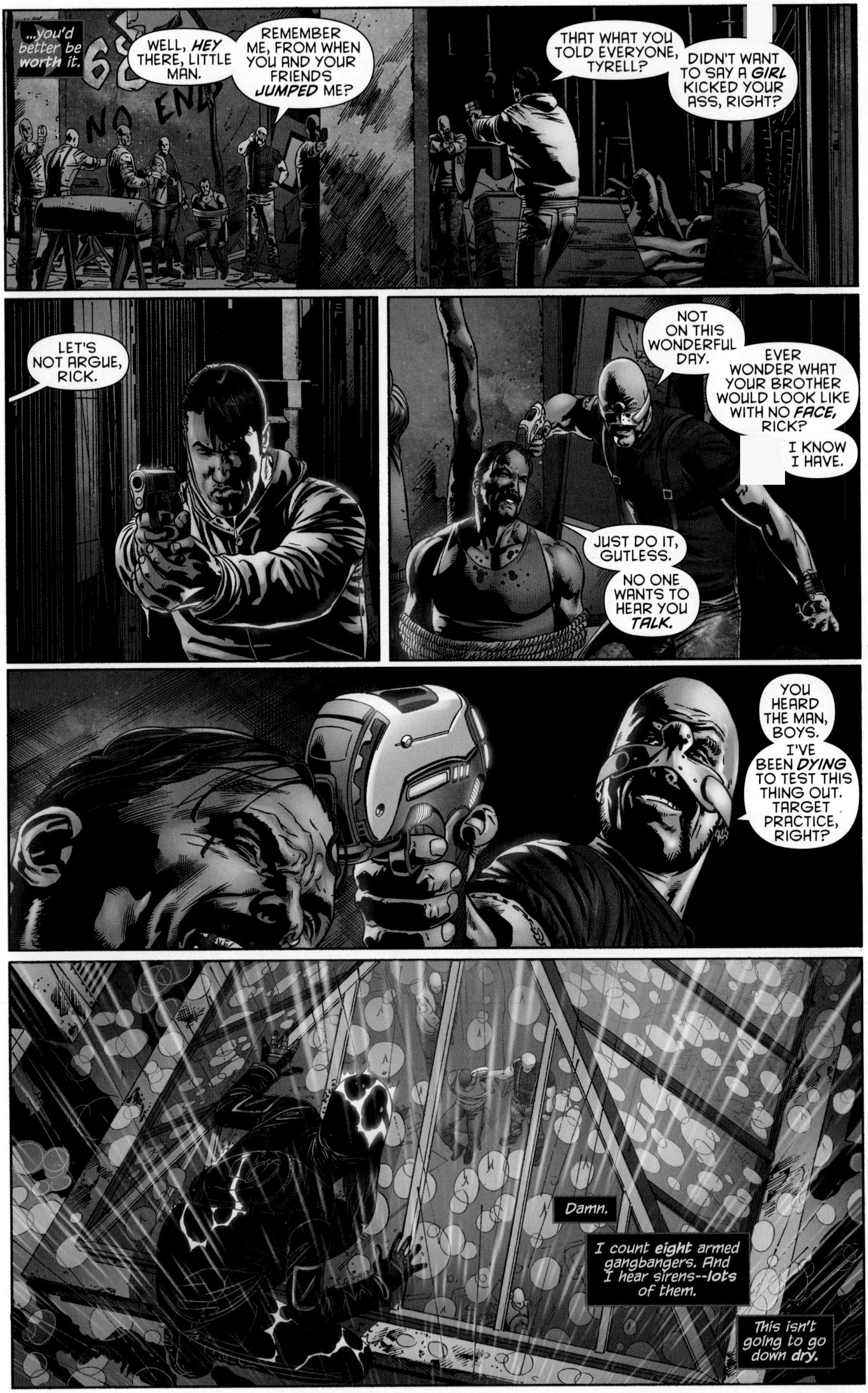
...you'd better be worth it.
WELL, HEY THERE, LITTLE MAN.
REMEMBER ME, FROM WHEN YOU AND YOUR FRIENDS JUMPED ME?
THAT WHAT YOU TOLD EVERYONE, TYRELL?
DIDN'T WANT TO SAY A GIRL KICKED YOUR ASS, RIGHT?
LET'S NOT ARGUE, RICK.
NOT ON THIS WONDERFUL DAY.
EVER WONDER WHAT YOUR BROTHER WOULD LOOK LIKE WITH NO FACE, RICK?
I KNOW I HAVE.
JUST DO IT, GUTLESS.
NO ONE WANTS TO HEAR YOU TALK.
YOU HEARD THE MAN, BOYS.
I'VE BEEN DYING TO TEST THIS THING OUT. TARGET PRACTICE, RIGHT?
Damn.
I count eight armed gangbangers. And I hear sirens--lots of them.
This isn't going to go down dry.

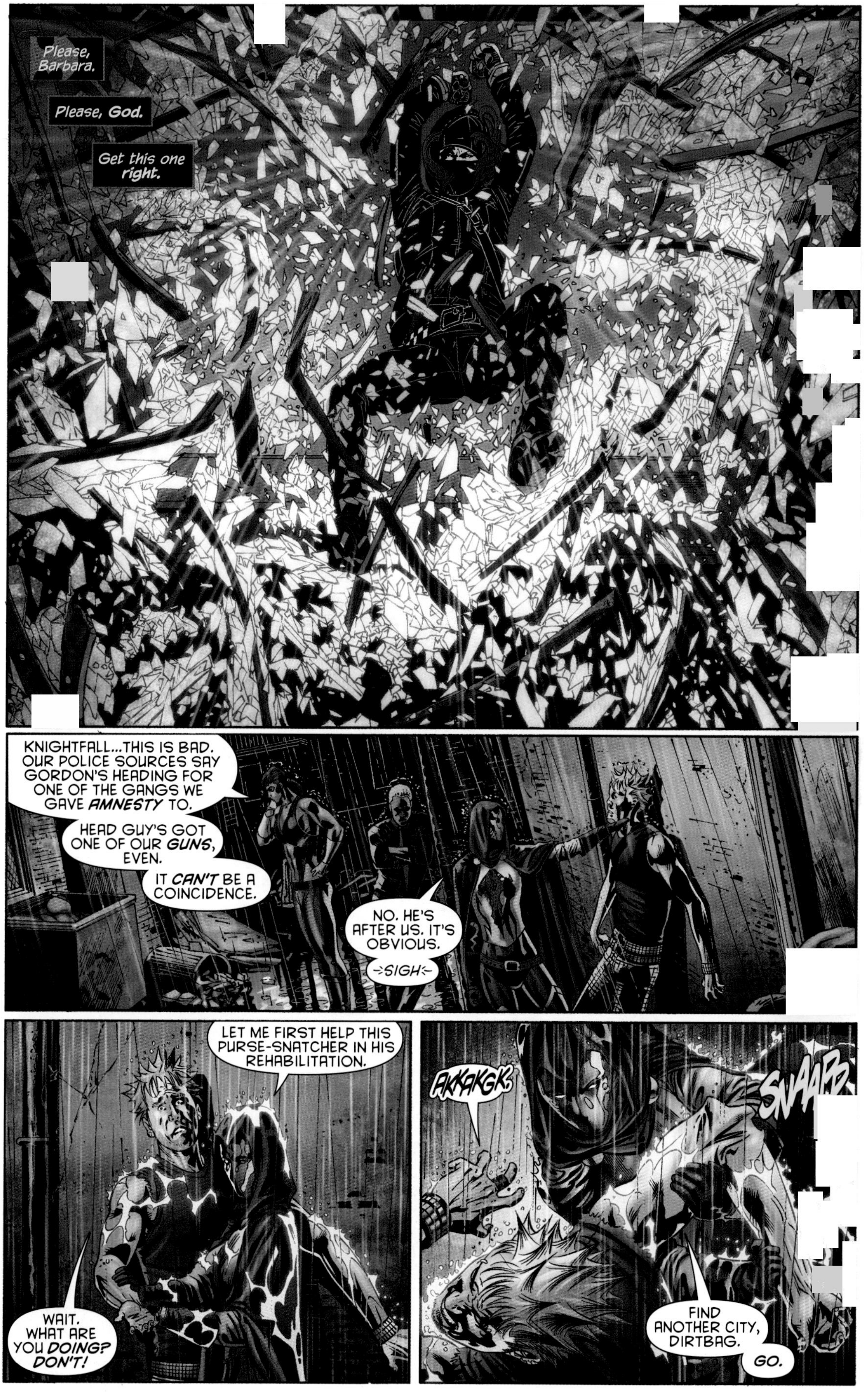
Please, Barbara.
Please, God.
Get this one right.
KNIGHTFALL...THIS IS BAD. OUR POLICE SOURCES SAY GORDON'S HEADING FOR ONE OF THE GANGS WE GAVE AMNESTY TO.
HEAD GUY'S GOT ONE OF OUR GUNS, EVEN.
IT CAN'T BE A COINCIDENCE.
NO. HE'S AFTER US. IT'S OBVIOUS.
SIGH
LET ME FIRST HELP THIS PURSE-SNATCHER IN HIS REHABILITATION.
WAIT. WHAT ARE YOU DOING? DON'T!
AKKAKGK.
SNAARB
FIND ANOTHER CITY, DIRTBAG.
GO.

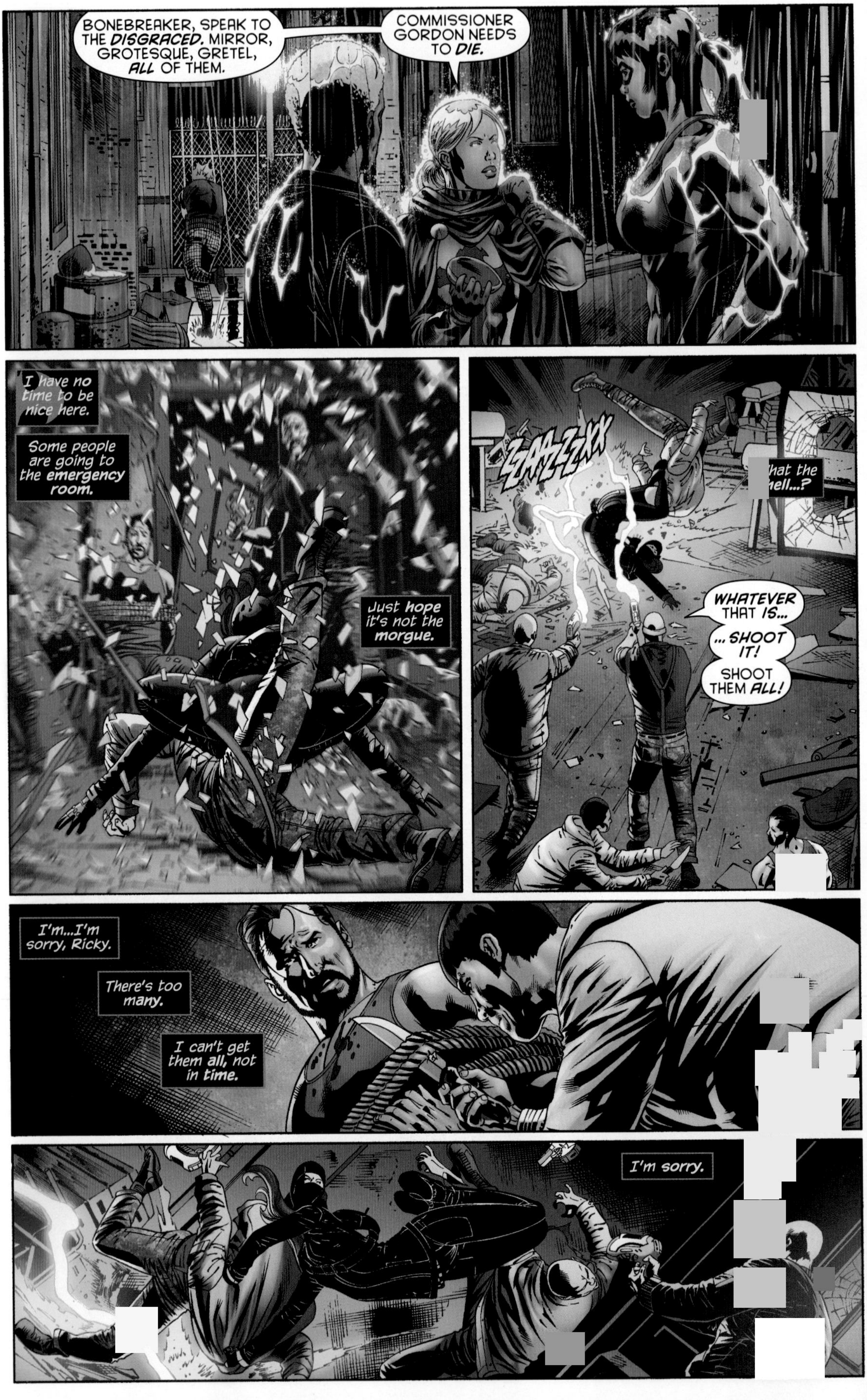
BONEBREAKER, SPEAK TO THE DISGRACED. MIRROR, GROTESQUE, GRETEL, ALL OF THEM.
COMMISSIONER GORDON NEEDS TO DIE.
I have no time to be nice here.
Some people are going to the emergency room.
Just hope it's not the morgue.
ZZAAZZZXX
hat the hell...?
WHATEVER THAT IS...
...SHOOT IT!
SHOOT THEM ALL!
I'm...I'm sorry, Ricky.
There's too many.
I can't get them all, not in time.
I'm sorry.

WE CAN'T WAIT FOR *SWAT*.

THIS MAN HAS ASSAULTED AND INJURED *THREE* POLICE OFFICERS. YOU GET THE SHOT, TAKE HIM *DOWN*.

I chose not to wear the bat.

RRAHUGH'KK!

KRACKK

When killed my brother--

--I lost that privilege.

Ricky here is willing to throw his life away.

To save his brother.

OH, WELL. YOU WANT SOMEONE DONE *RIGHT*-- --I GUESS YOU HAVE TO DO THEM *YOURSELF*.

ZZZAAZXXX

Which one of us is the hero, I wonder?

UHGNNG.

IT'S *OVER*, TYRELL. YOU'RE *DONE*.

SIRENS. *COPS*.

HELL WITH *THIS*.

I'M ON *PAROLE*. I'M *OUT*.

Or maybe...

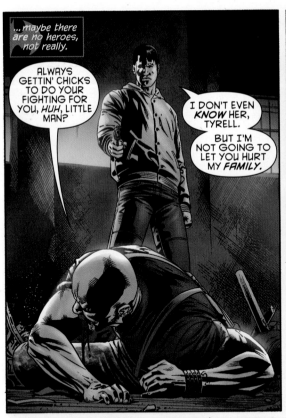

...maybe there are no heroes, not really.

ALWAYS GETTIN' CHICKS TO DO YOUR FIGHTING FOR YOU, *HUH*, LITTLE MAN?

I DON'T EVEN *KNOW* HER, TYRELL.

BUT I'M NOT GOING TO LET YOU HURT MY *FAMILY*.

Ricky.

HEY. DON'T *DO* THIS.

YEAH, LITTLE MAN. DON'T *DO* THIS.

STAY A *WUSSY*, LIKE YOU *ALWAYS* BEEN.

I HEAR YOUR MOM CAN *COOK*, RICKY.

MAYBE I MAKE HER *COOK* ME SOMETHING, 'FORE SHE DIES, *HUH*?

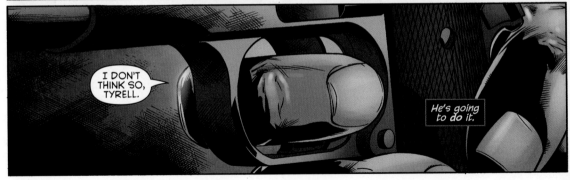

I DON'T THINK SO, TYRELL.

He's going to do it.

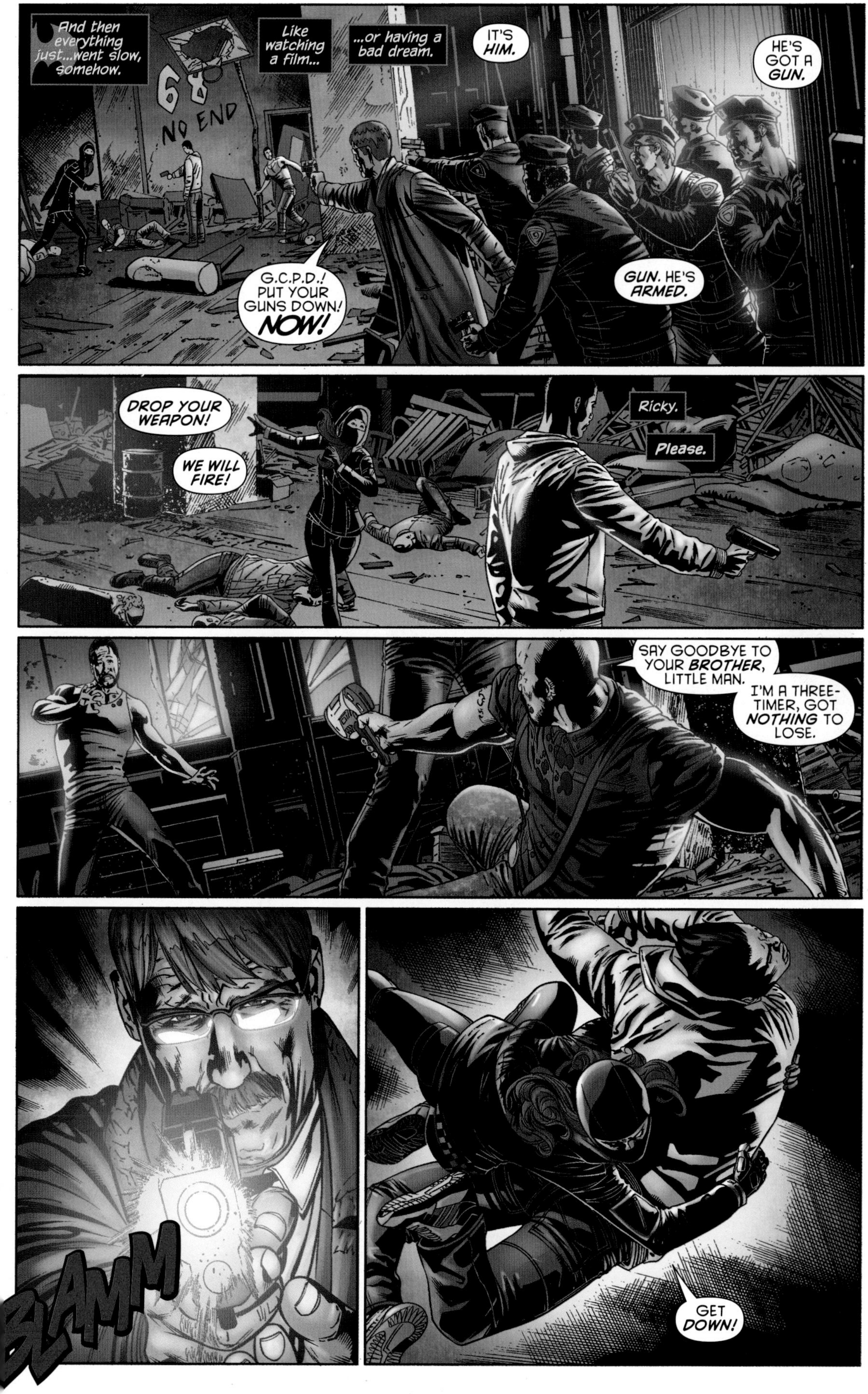
And then everything just...went slow, somehow.
Like watching a film...
...or having a bad dream.
IT'S HIM.
HE'S GOT A GUN.
68 NO END
G.C.P.D.! PUT YOUR GUNS DOWN! NOW!
GUN. HE'S ARMED.
DROP YOUR WEAPON!
WE WILL FIRE!
Ricky.
Please.
SAY GOODBYE TO YOUR BROTHER, LITTLE MAN.
I'M A THREE-TIMER, GOT NOTHING TO LOSE.
BLAMM
GET DOWN!

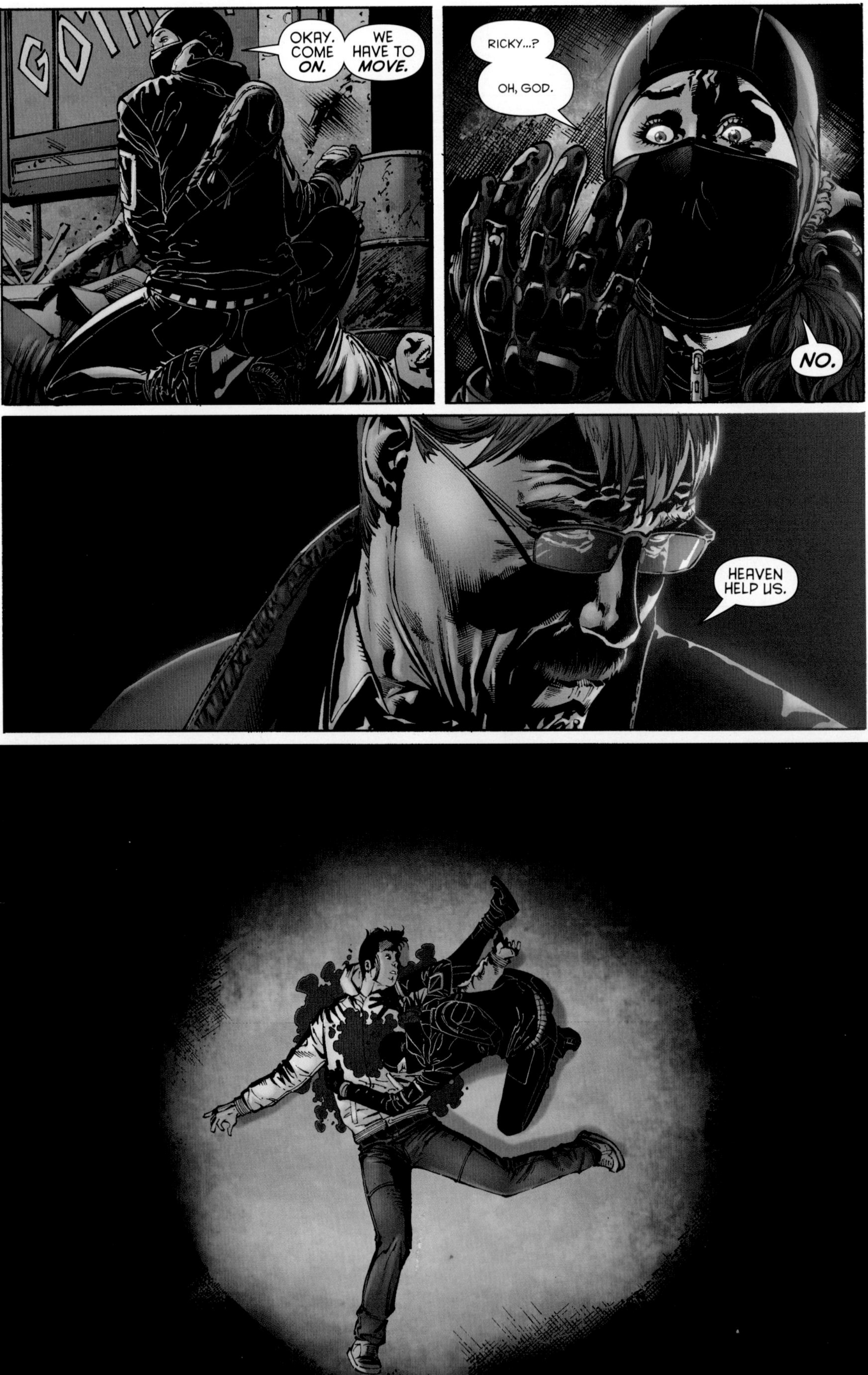
OKAY. COME *ON.*
WE HAVE TO *MOVE.*
RICKY...?
OH, GOD.
NO.
HEAVEN HELP US.

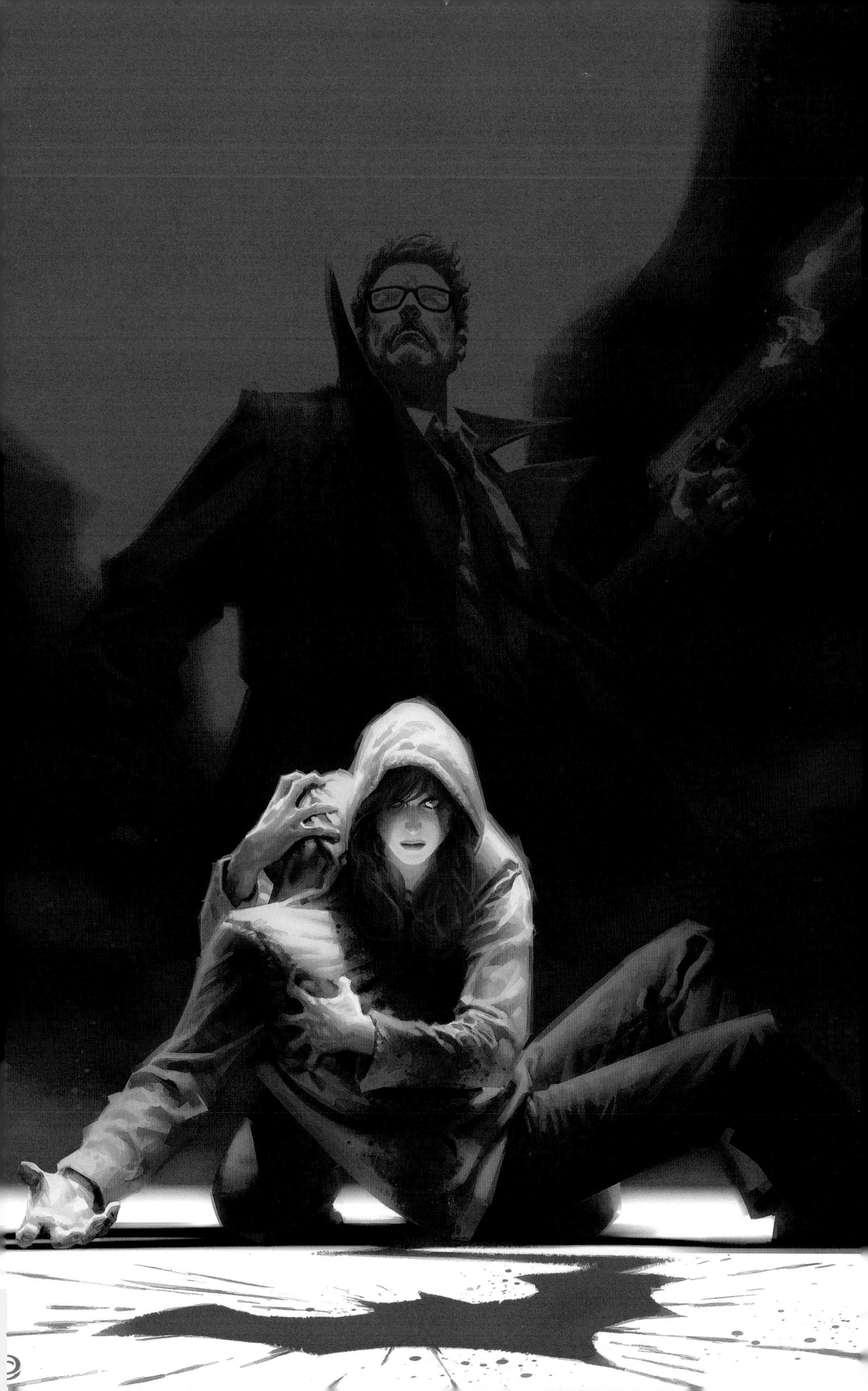

BATGIRL WANTED part two: DRAGNET

GAIL SIMONE writer **FERNANDO PASARIN** penciller **JONATHAN GLAPION** inker **BLOND** colorist
cover by **ALEX GARNER**

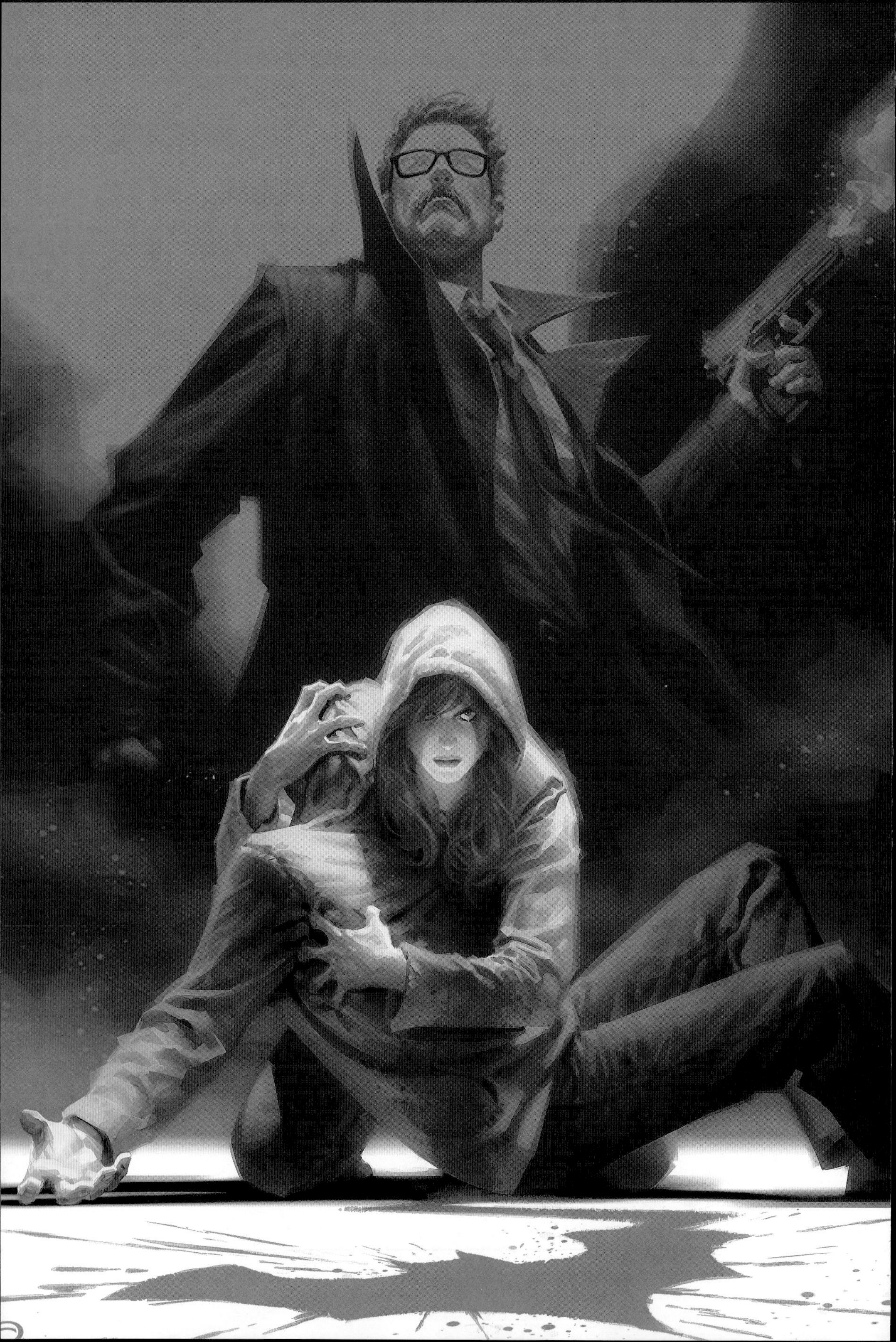

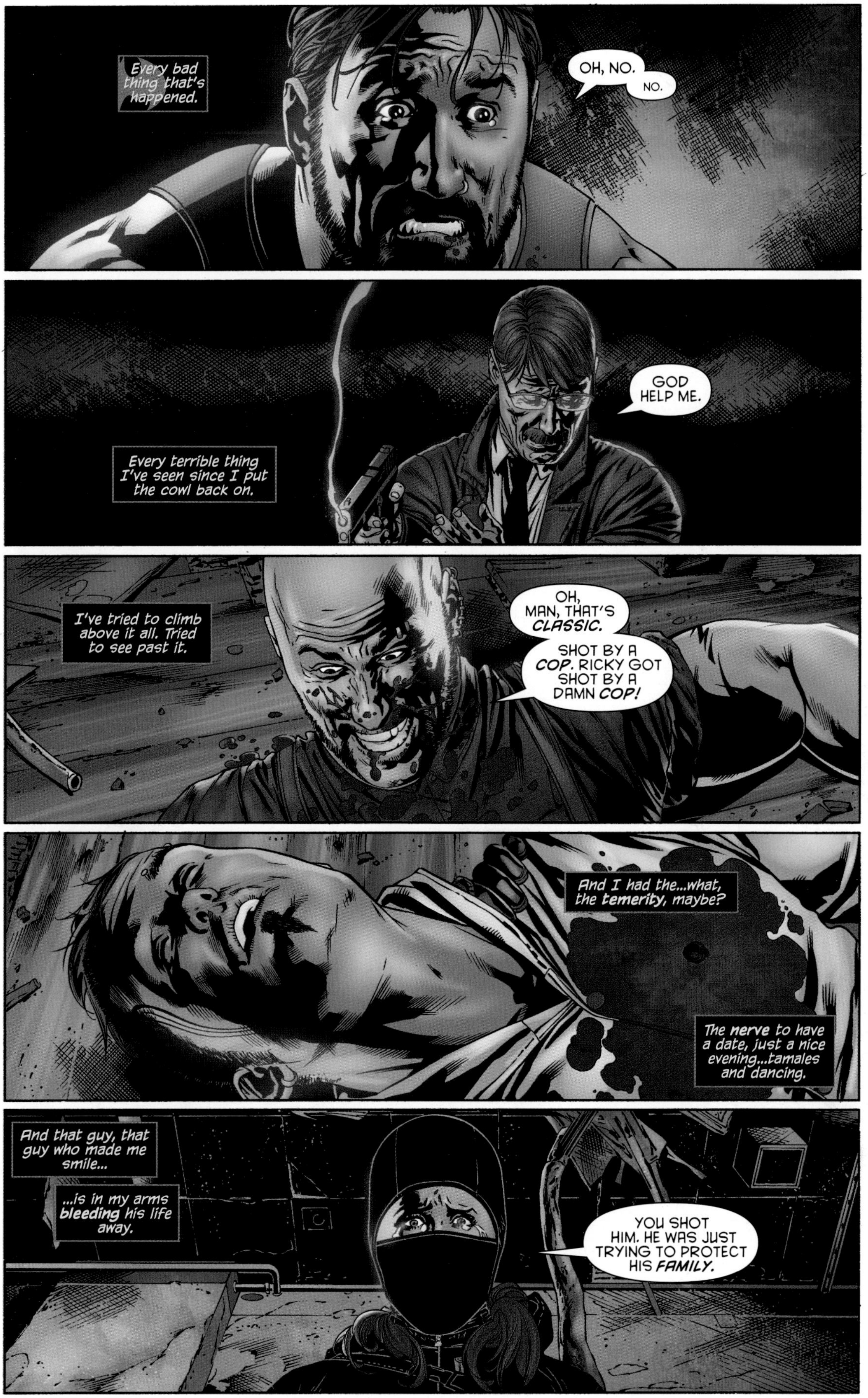

Every bad thing that's happened.
OH, NO.
NO.
Every terrible thing I've seen since I put the cowl back on.
GOD HELP ME.
I've tried to climb above it all. Tried to see past it.
OH, MAN, THAT'S CLASSIC.
SHOT BY A COP. RICKY GOT SHOT BY A DAMN COP!
And I had the...what, the temerity, maybe?
The nerve to have a date, just a nice evening...tamales and dancing.
And that guy, that guy who made me smile...
...is in my arms bleeding his life away.
YOU SHOT HIM. HE WAS JUST TRYING TO PROTECT HIS FAMILY.

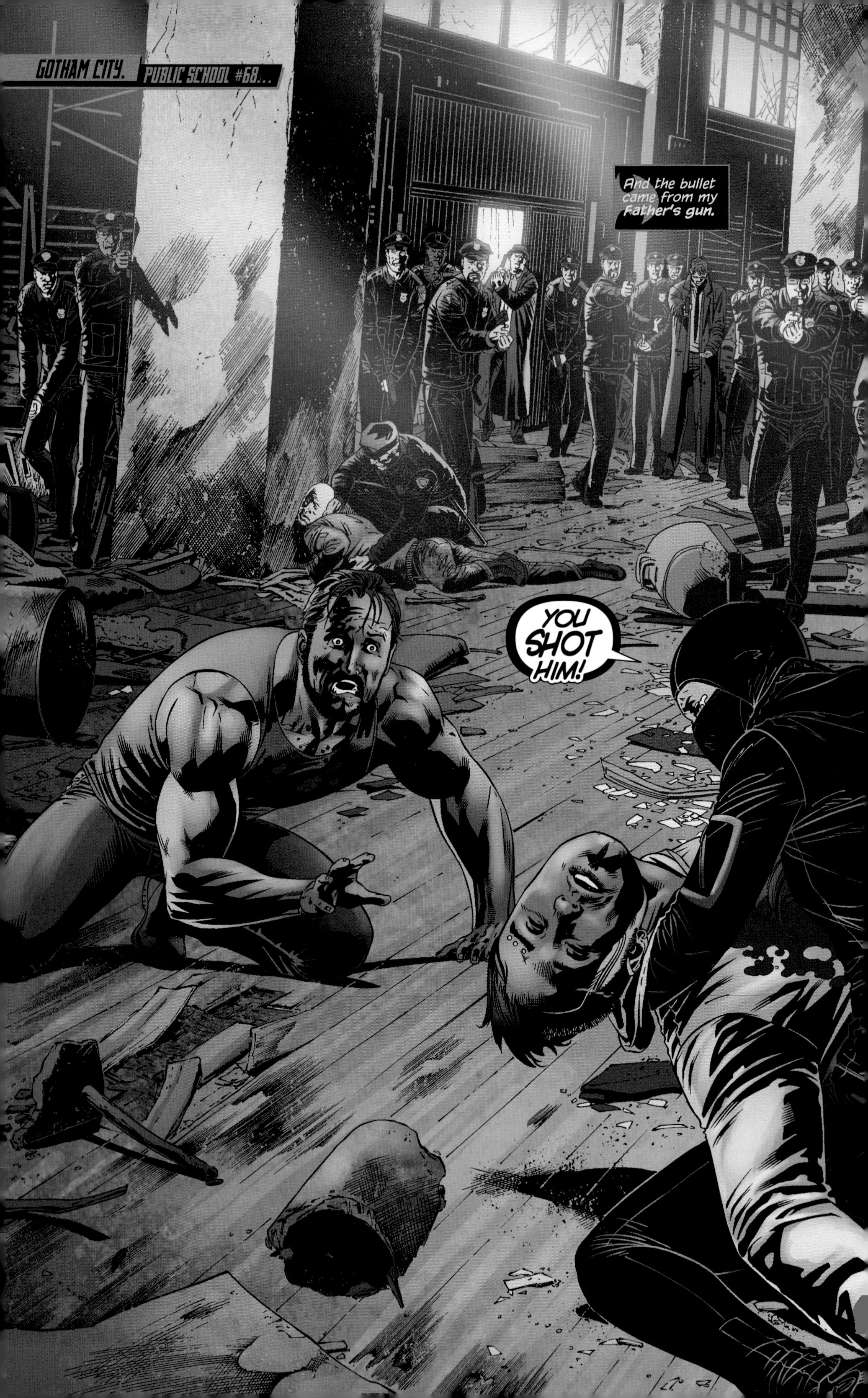
GOTHAM CITY.
PUBLIC SCHOOL #68...
And the bullet came from my Father's gun.
YOU SHOT HIM!

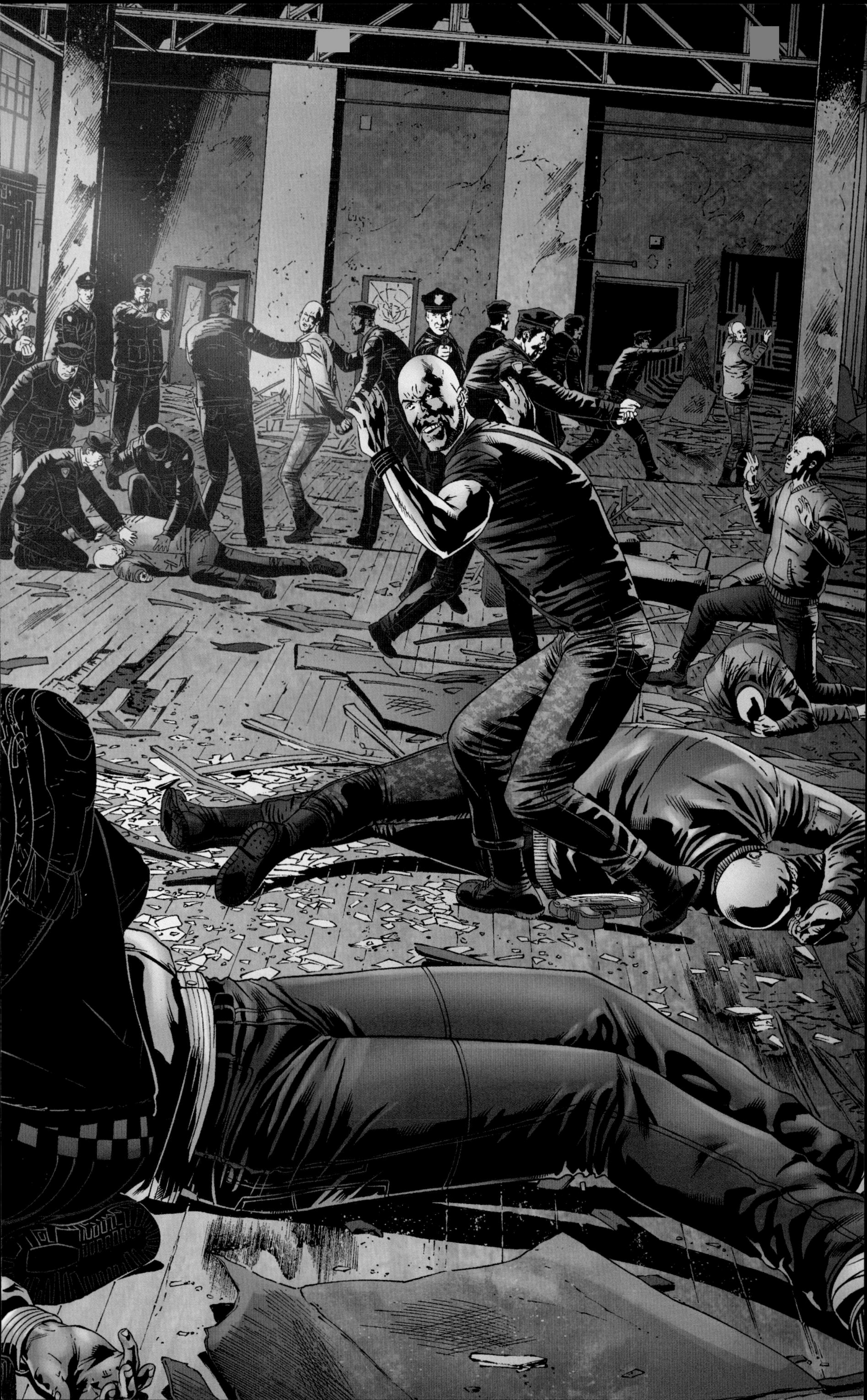

HARVEY, I...

THAT WAS A RIGHTEOUS SHOOTING, COMMISSIONER GORDON.

KID WOULDN'T PUT HIS *WEAPON* DOWN. NO CHOICE AT *ALL*.

EVERYONE TAKE *TWO STEPS* BACK!

GET ON YOUR *KNEES* WITH BOTH *HANDS* ON YOUR *HEADS!*

Is this how it ends?

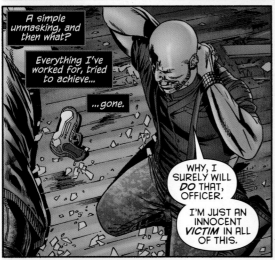

A simple unmasking, and then what?

Everything I've worked for, tried to achieve...

...gone.

WHY, I SURELY WILL *DO* THAT, OFFICER.

I'M JUST AN INNOCENT *VICTIM* IN ALL OF THIS.

I SAID GET *DOWN*, MR. GUTIERREZ.

MY BROTHER RICKY. *PLEASE.*

YOU GOTTA *HELP* HIM.

And Ricky... *...I couldn't protect you, Ricky.*

HANDS ON YOUR *HEAD*, LADY. NOW.

Is this how it ends?

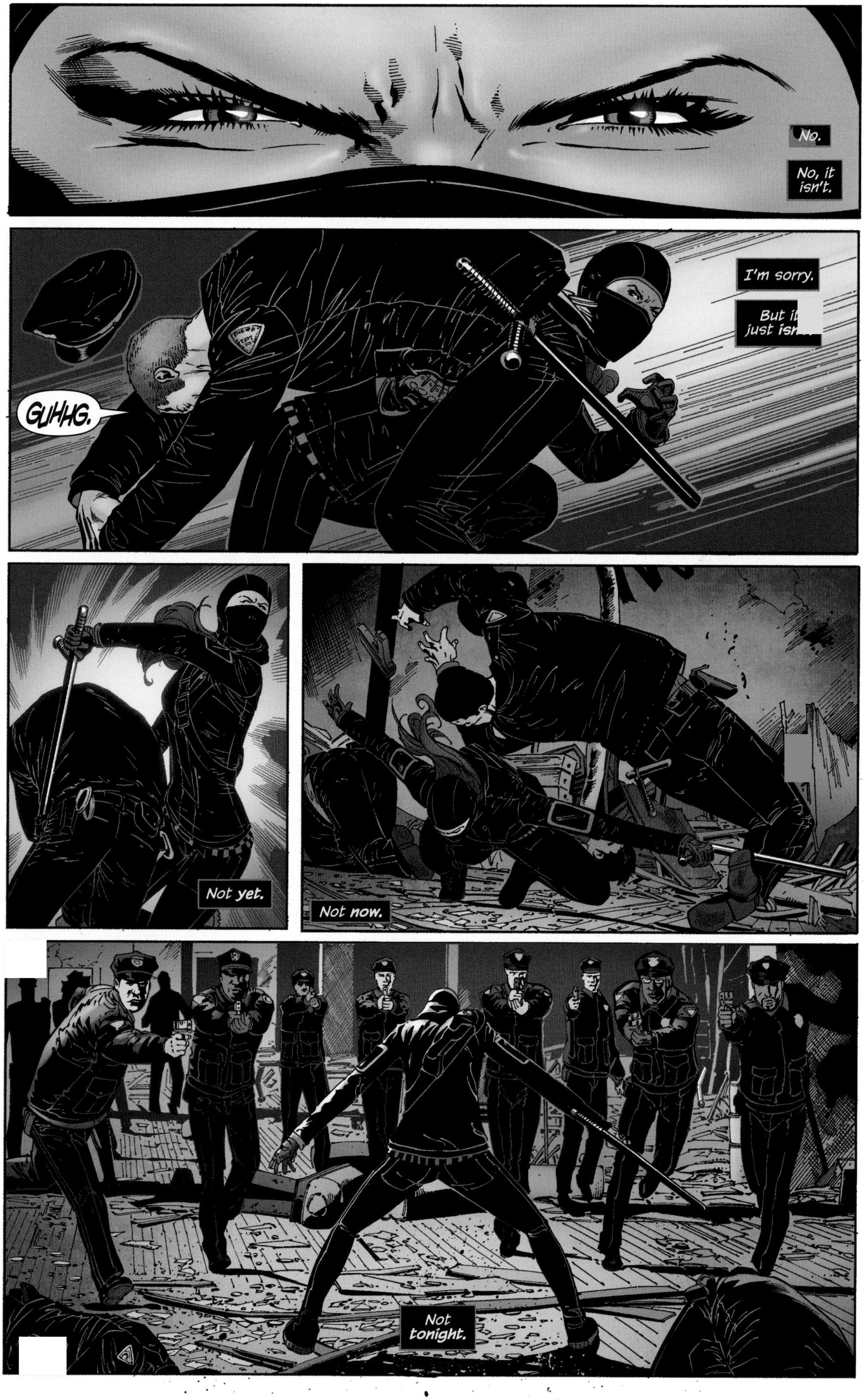
No.
No, it isn't.
I'm sorry.
But i
just isn
GUHHG.
Not yet.
Not now.
Not tonight.

That's right. Come *at* me. *Surround* me.

Make it impossible to draw a *bead* on me.

GET *CLEAR,* YOU DOPES! GET *CLEAR.*

Someone set this night up.

Someone gave a street punk like *Tyrell* a gun that costs as much as a small *airplane.*

Only *one* person in Cherry Hill has that kind of disposable income and influence.

Charise Carnes.

A.K.A. Knightfall.

So here's the plan.

HUH. EVERYONE'S ALL DISTRACTED, RIGHT?

NO ONE PAYING *ANY* ATTENTION TO TYRELL.

COME TO DADDY, SWEET THING. I'VE DECIDED TO GET *OUT.*

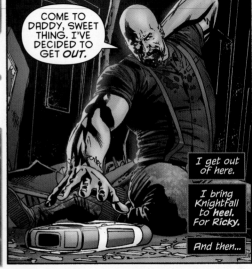

I get out of here.

I bring Knightfall to *heel.* For Ricky.

And then...

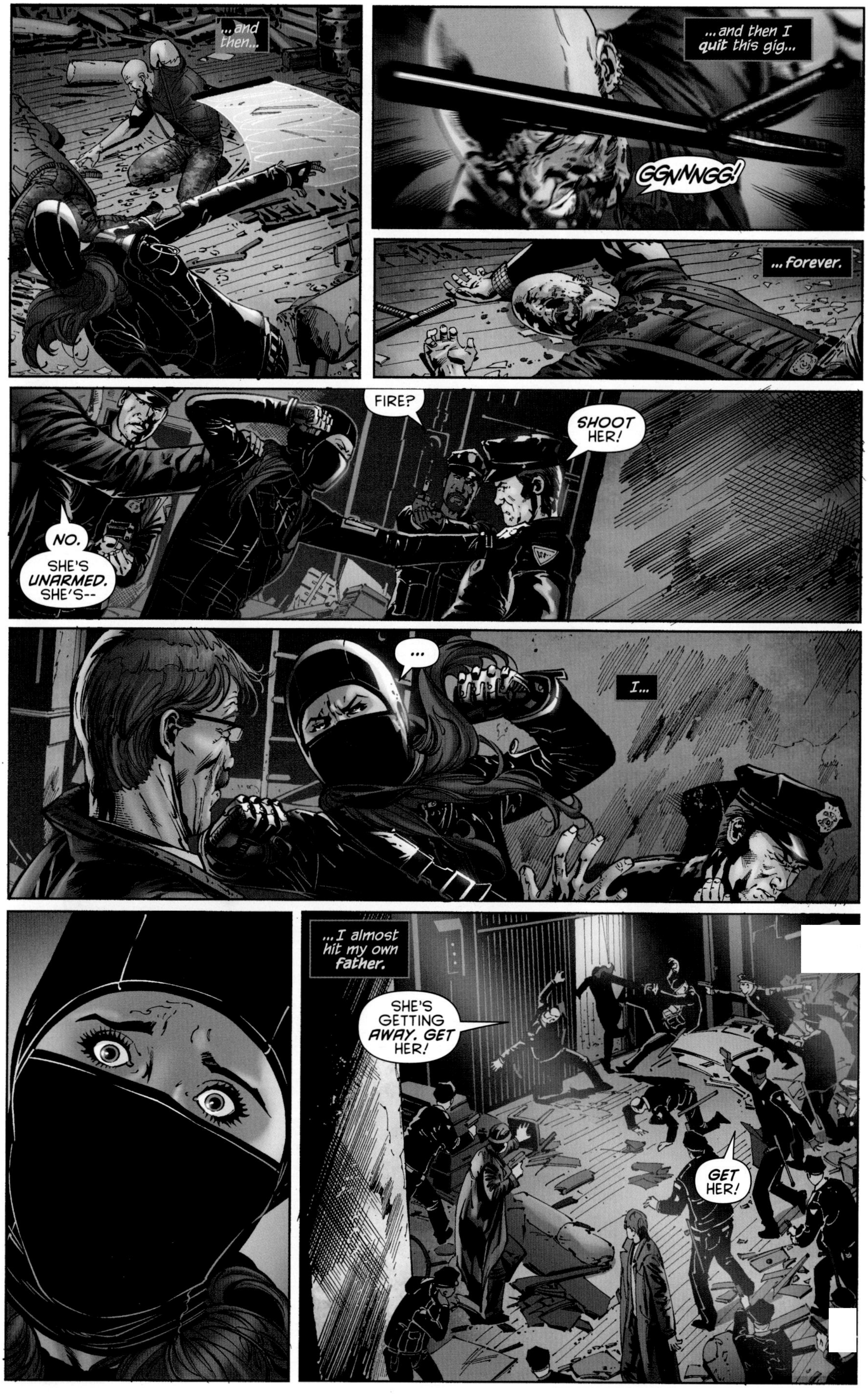
...and then...
...and then I quit this gig...
GGNNNGG!
...forever.
FIRE?
SHOOT HER!
NO. SHE'S UNARMED. SHE'S--
...
I...
...I almost hit my own father.
SHE'S GETTING AWAY. GET HER!
GET HER!

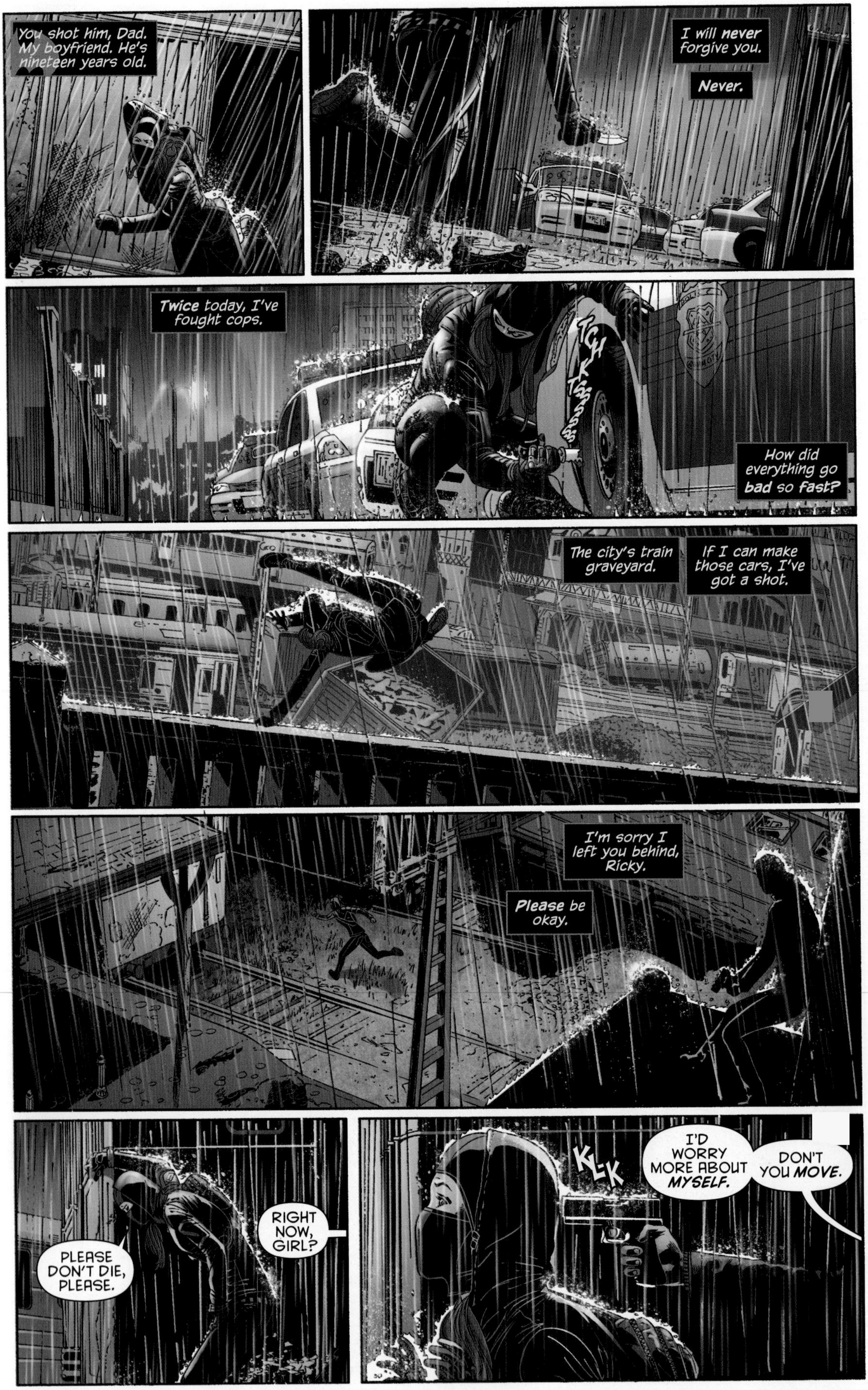

You shot him, Dad. My boyfriend. He's nineteen years old.
I will never forgive you.
Never.
Twice today, I've fought cops.
TCH KSSSSSSS
How did everything go bad so fast?
The city's train graveyard.
If I can make those cars, I've got a shot.
I'm sorry I left you behind, Ricky.
Please be okay.
PLEASE DON'T DIE, PLEASE.
RIGHT NOW, GIRL?
KLIK
I'D WORRY MORE ABOUT MYSELF.
DON'T YOU MOVE.

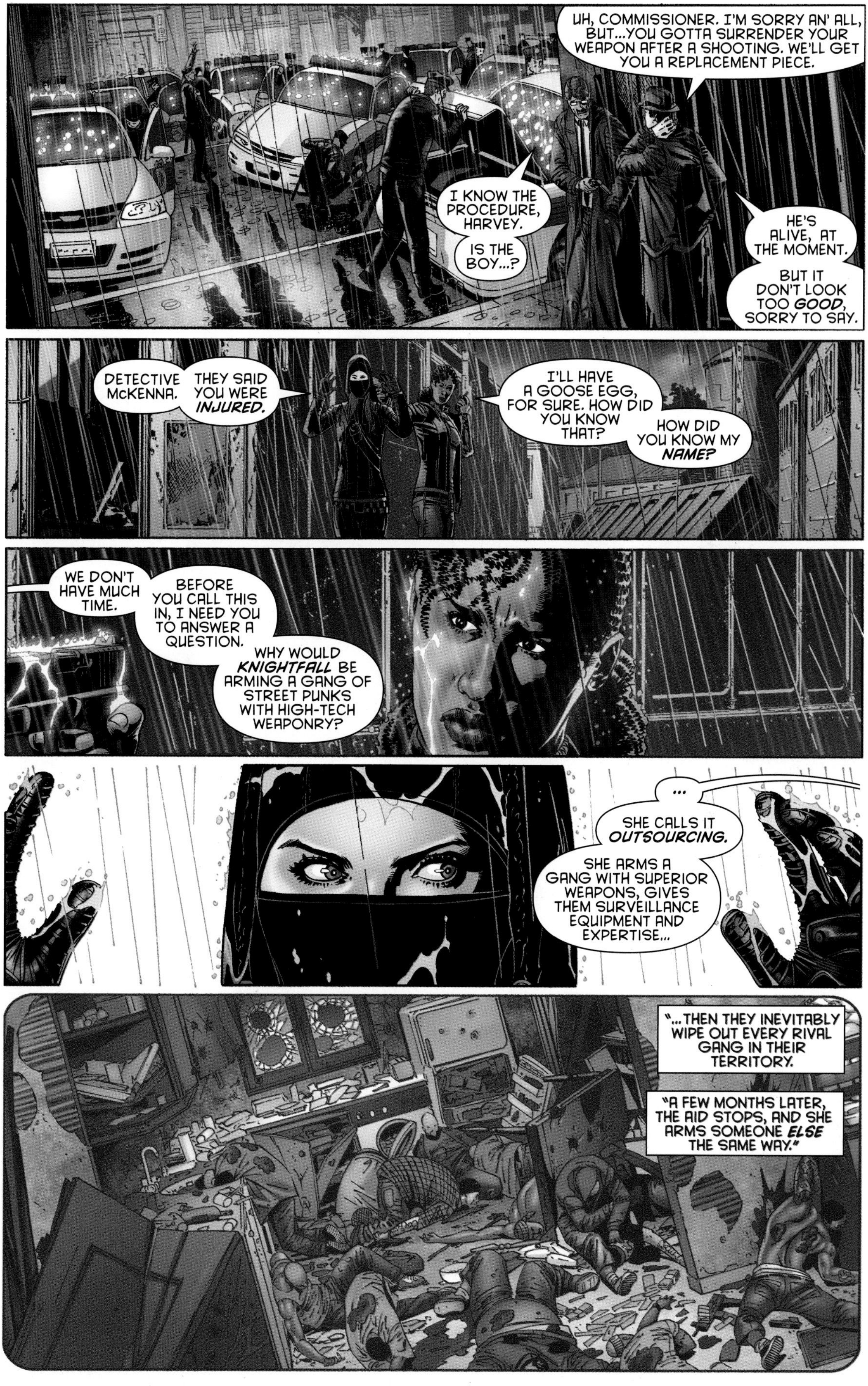
UH, COMMISSIONER. I'M SORRY AN' ALL, BUT...YOU GOTTA SURRENDER YOUR WEAPON AFTER A SHOOTING. WE'LL GET YOU A REPLACEMENT PIECE.
I KNOW THE PROCEDURE, HARVEY.
IS THE BOY...?
HE'S ALIVE, AT THE MOMENT.
BUT IT DON'T LOOK TOO GOOD, SORRY TO SAY.
DETECTIVE McKENNA.
THEY SAID YOU WERE INJURED.
I'LL HAVE A GOOSE EGG, FOR SURE. HOW DID YOU KNOW THAT?
HOW DID YOU KNOW MY NAME?
WE DON'T HAVE MUCH TIME.
BEFORE YOU CALL THIS IN, I NEED YOU TO ANSWER A QUESTION.
WHY WOULD KNIGHTFALL BE ARMING A GANG OF STREET PUNKS WITH HIGH-TECH WEAPONRY?
...
SHE CALLS IT OUTSOURCING.
SHE ARMS A GANG WITH SUPERIOR WEAPONS, GIVES THEM SURVEILLANCE EQUIPMENT AND EXPERTISE...
"...THEN THEY INEVITABLY WIPE OUT EVERY RIVAL GANG IN THEIR TERRITORY.
"A FEW MONTHS LATER, THE AID STOPS, AND SHE ARMS SOMEONE ELSE THE SAME WAY."

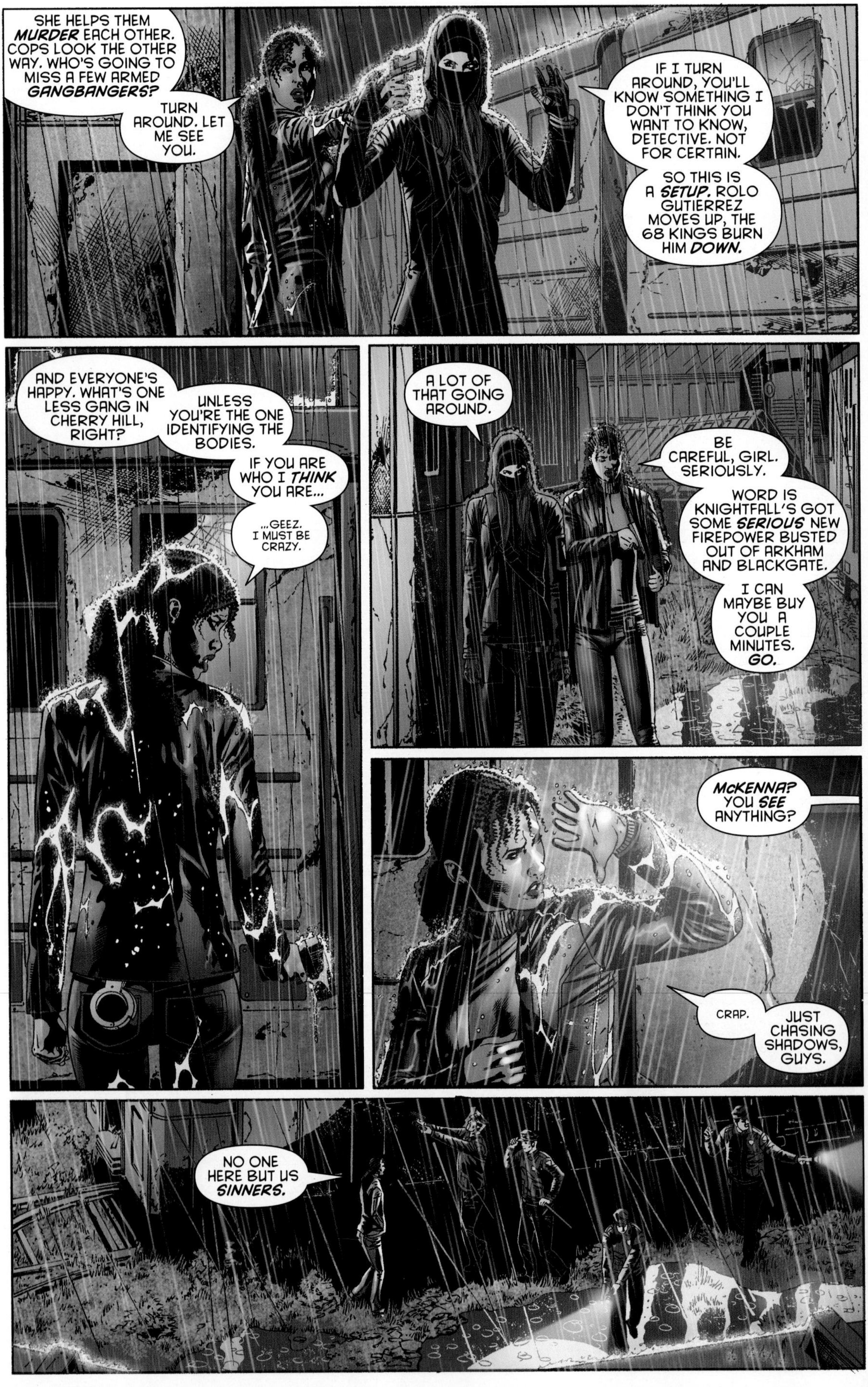

SHE HELPS THEM MURDER EACH OTHER. COPS LOOK THE OTHER WAY. WHO'S GOING TO MISS A FEW ARMED GANGBANGERS?
TURN AROUND. LET ME SEE YOU.
IF I TURN AROUND, YOU'LL KNOW SOMETHING I DON'T THINK YOU WANT TO KNOW, DETECTIVE. NOT FOR CERTAIN.
SO THIS IS A SETUP. ROLO GUTIERREZ MOVES UP, THE 68 KINGS BURN HIM DOWN.
AND EVERYONE'S HAPPY. WHAT'S ONE LESS GANG IN CHERRY HILL, RIGHT?
UNLESS YOU'RE THE ONE IDENTIFYING THE BODIES.
IF YOU ARE WHO I THINK YOU ARE...
...GEEZ. I MUST BE CRAZY.
A LOT OF THAT GOING AROUND.
BE CAREFUL, GIRL. SERIOUSLY.
WORD IS KNIGHTFALL'S GOT SOME SERIOUS NEW FIREPOWER BUSTED OUT OF ARKHAM AND BLACKGATE.
I CAN MAYBE BUY YOU A COUPLE MINUTES. GO.
McKENNA? YOU SEE ANYTHING?
CRAP.
JUST CHASING SHADOWS, GUYS.
NO ONE HERE BUT US SINNERS.

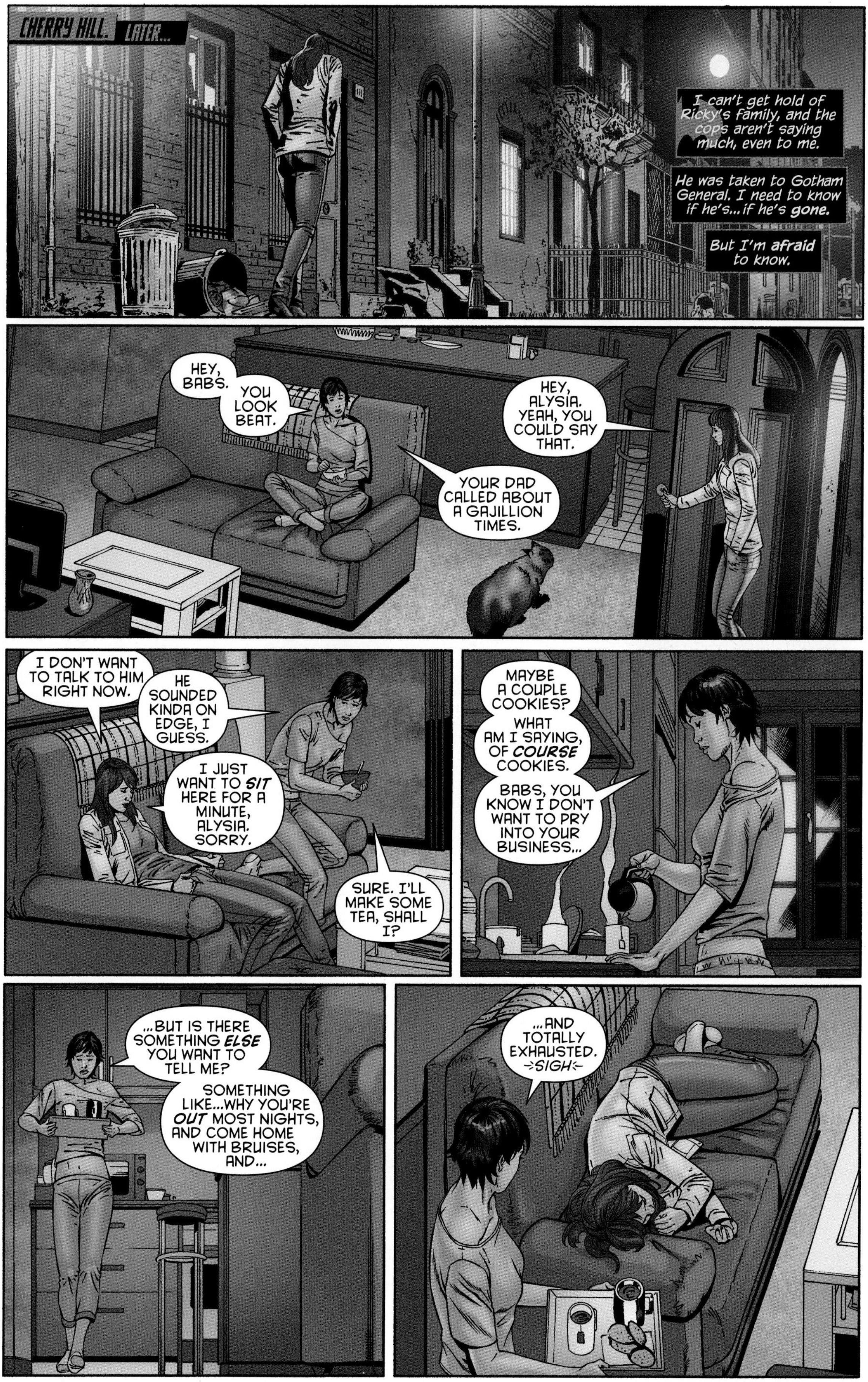
CHERRY HILL. LATER...
I can't get hold of Ricky's family, and the cops aren't saying much, even to me.
He was taken to Gotham General. I need to know if he's...if he's gone.
But I'm afraid to know.
HEY, BABS.
YOU LOOK BEAT.
HEY, ALYSIA. YEAH, YOU COULD SAY THAT.
YOUR DAD CALLED ABOUT A GAJILLION TIMES.
I DON'T WANT TO TALK TO HIM RIGHT NOW.
HE SOUNDED KINDA ON EDGE, I GUESS.
I JUST WANT TO SIT HERE FOR A MINUTE, ALYSIA. SORRY.
SURE. I'LL MAKE SOME TEA, SHALL I?
MAYBE A COUPLE COOKIES?
WHAT AM I SAYING, OF COURSE COOKIES.
BABS, YOU KNOW I DON'T WANT TO PRY INTO YOUR BUSINESS...
...BUT IS THERE SOMETHING ELSE YOU WANT TO TELL ME?
SOMETHING LIKE...WHY YOU'RE OUT MOST NIGHTS, AND COME HOME WITH BRUISES, AND...
...AND TOTALLY EXHAUSTED.
-SIGH-

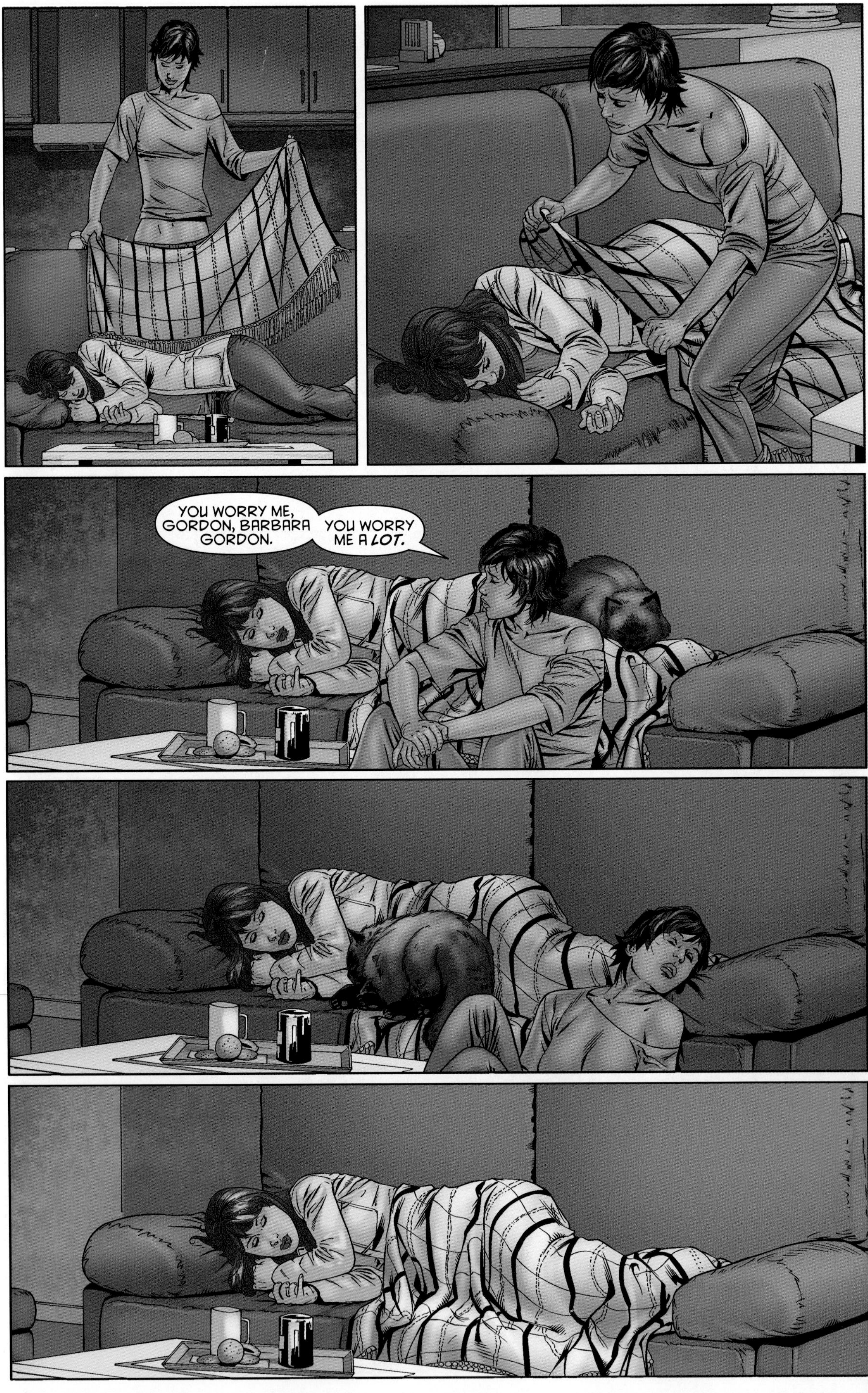
YOU WORRY ME, GORDON, BARBARA GORDON.
YOU WORRY ME A LOT.

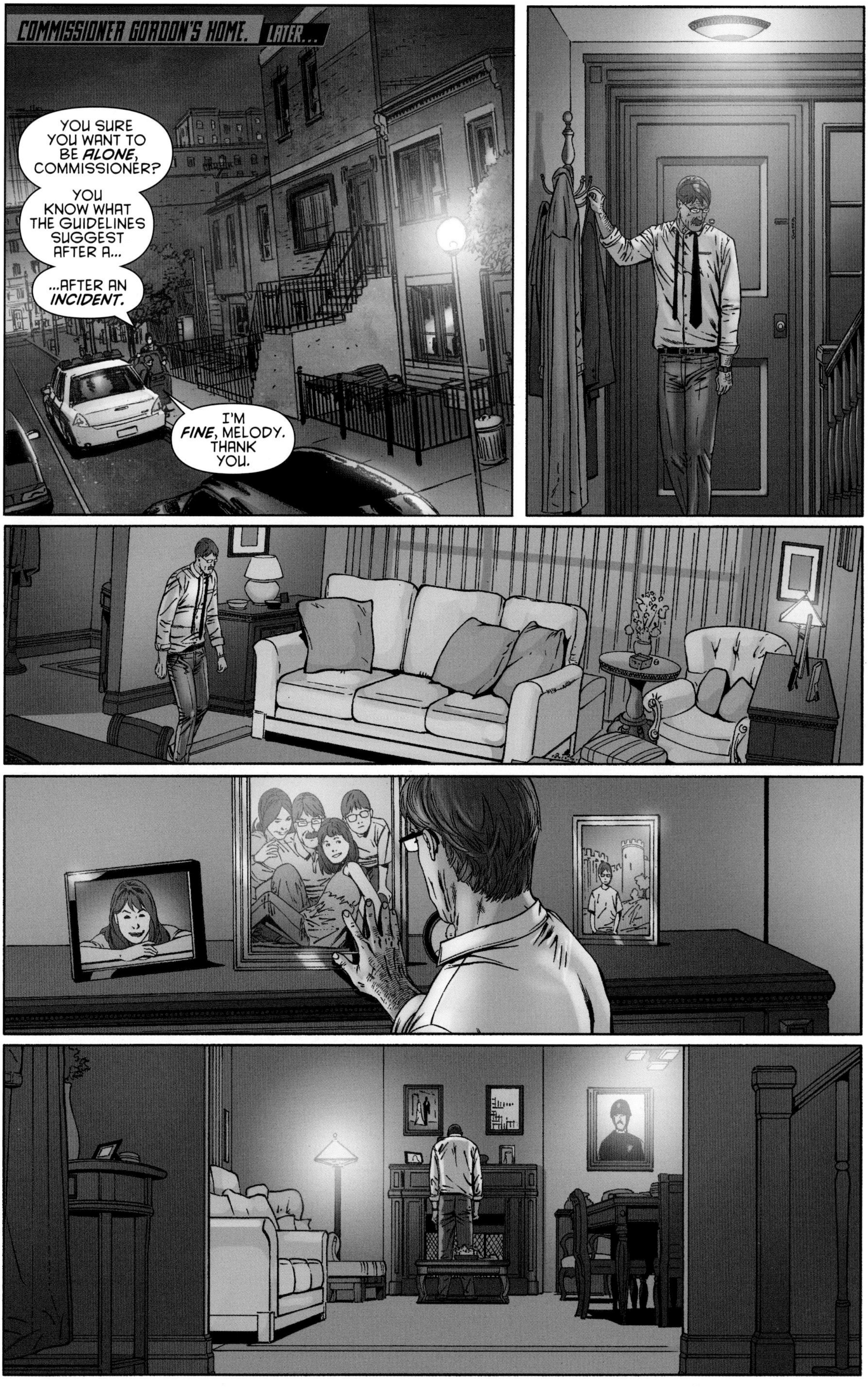
COMMISSIONER GORDON'S HOME.
LATER...
YOU SURE YOU WANT TO BE ALONE, COMMISSIONER?
YOU KNOW WHAT THE GUIDELINES SUGGEST AFTER A...
...AFTER AN INCIDENT.
I'M FINE, MELODY. THANK YOU.

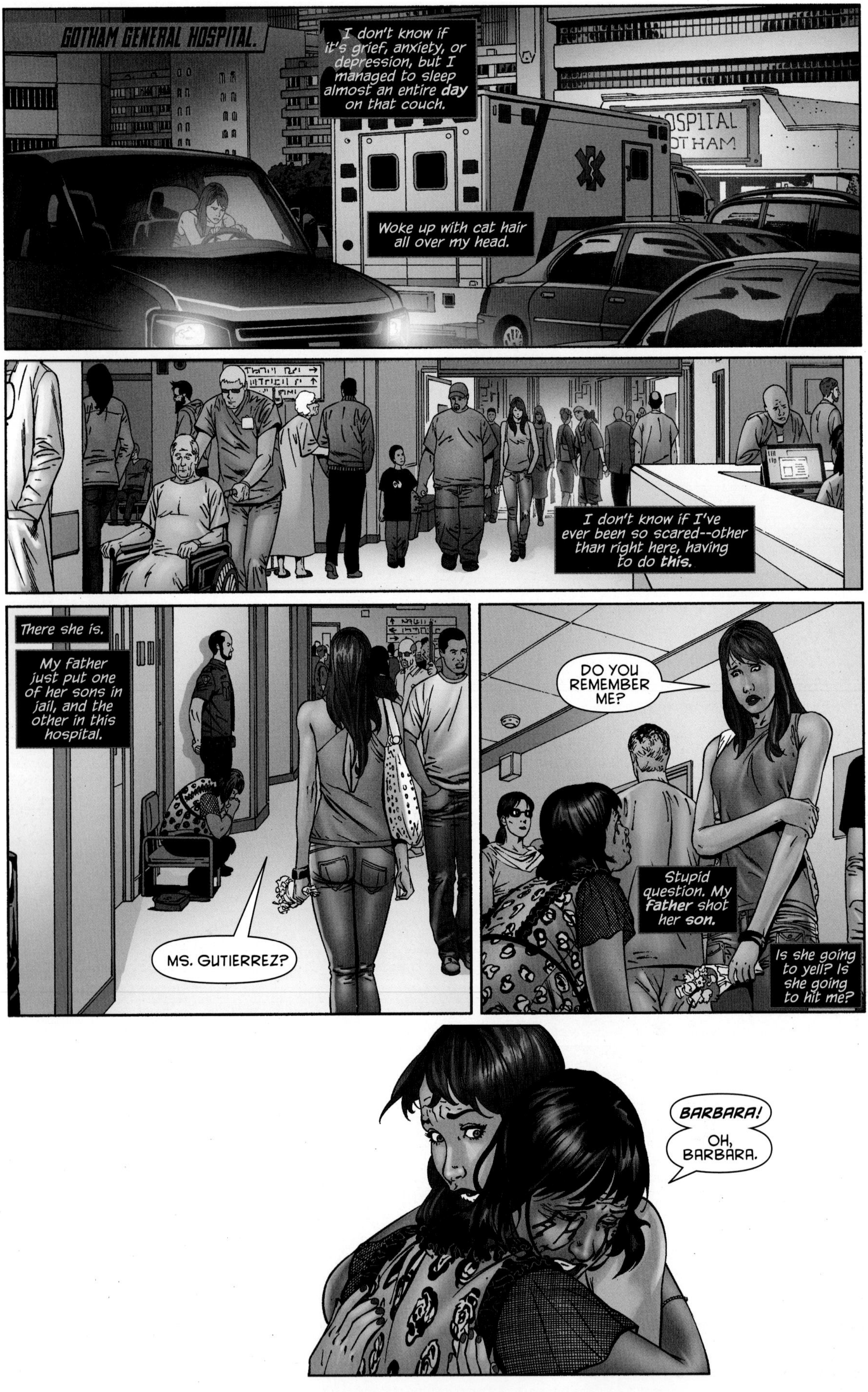
GOTHAM GENERAL HOSPITAL.
I don't know if it's grief, anxiety, or depression, but I managed to sleep almost an entire day on that couch.
HOSPITAL GOTHAM
Woke up with cat hair all over my head.
I don't know if I've ever been so scared--other than right here, having to do this.
There she is.
My father just put one of her sons in jail, and the other in this hospital.
MS. GUTIERREZ?
DO YOU REMEMBER ME?
Stupid question. My father shot her son.
Is she going to yell? Is she going to hit me?
BARBARA!
OH, BARBARA.

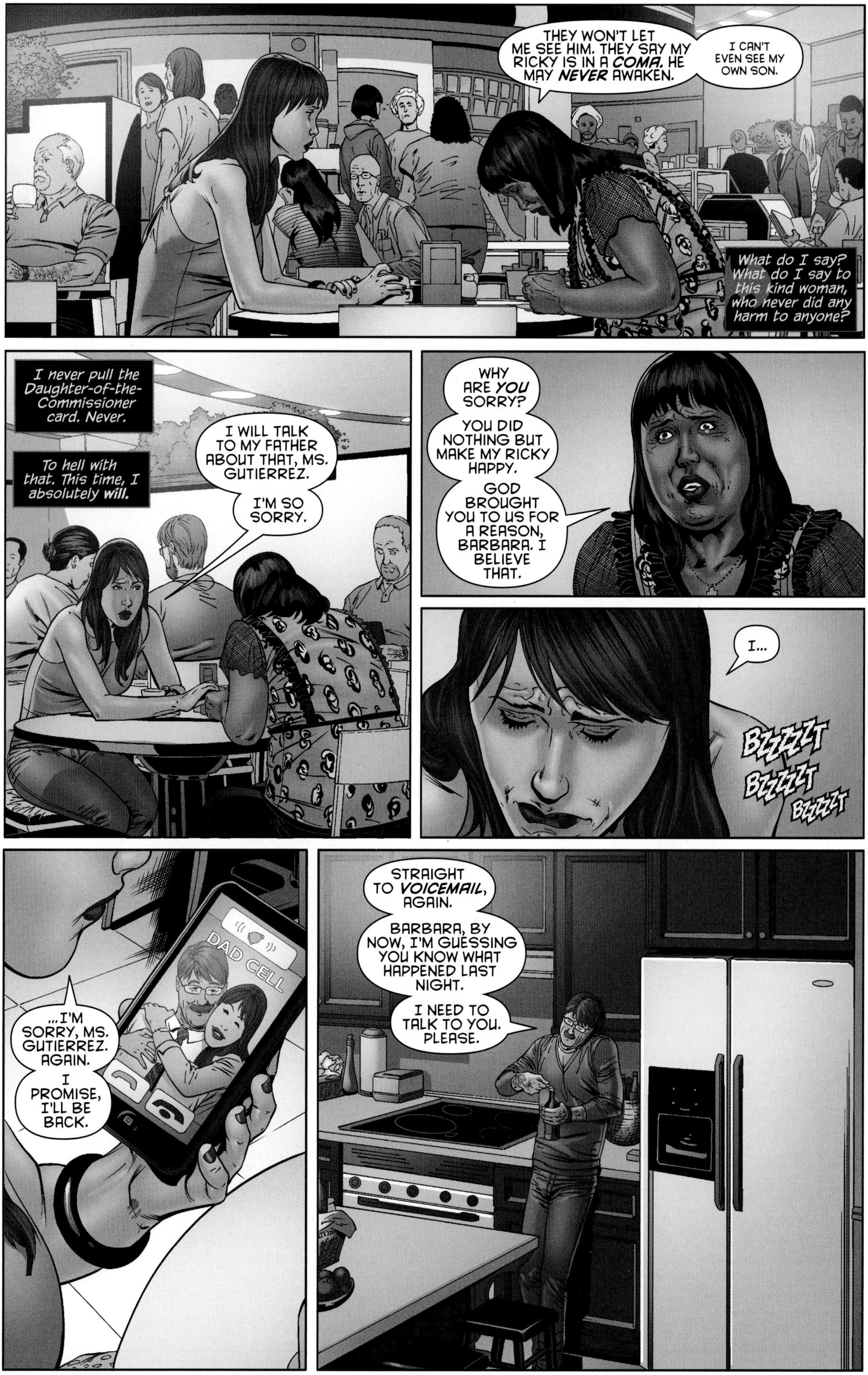
THEY WON'T LET ME SEE HIM. THEY SAY MY RICKY IS IN A COMA. HE MAY NEVER AWAKEN.
I CAN'T EVEN SEE MY OWN SON.
What do I say? What do I say to this kind woman, who never did any harm to anyone?
I never pull the Daughter-of-the-Commissioner card. Never.
To hell with that. This time, I absolutely will.
I WILL TALK TO MY FATHER ABOUT THAT, MS. GUTIERREZ.
I'M SO SORRY.
WHY ARE YOU SORRY?
YOU DID NOTHING BUT MAKE MY RICKY HAPPY.
GOD BROUGHT YOU TO US FOR A REASON, BARBARA. I BELIEVE THAT.
I...
BZZZZZT
BZZZZZT
BZZZZZT
DAD CELL
...I'M SORRY, MS. GUTIERREZ. AGAIN.
I PROMISE, I'LL BE BACK.
STRAIGHT TO VOICEMAIL, AGAIN.
BARBARA, BY NOW, I'M GUESSING YOU KNOW WHAT HAPPENED LAST NIGHT.
I NEED TO TALK TO YOU. PLEASE.

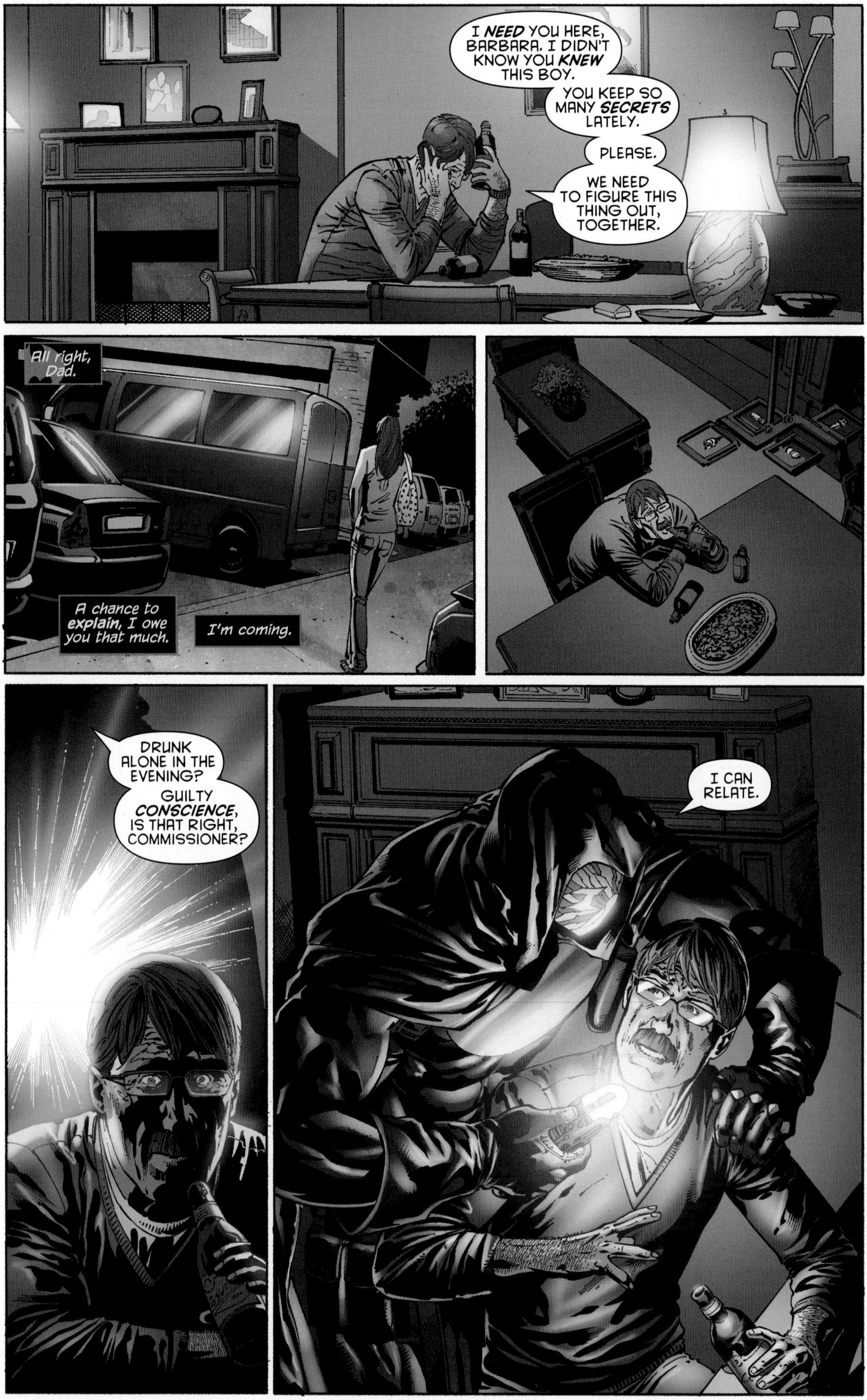

I NEED YOU HERE, BARBARA. I DIDN'T KNOW YOU KNEW THIS BOY.
YOU KEEP SO MANY SECRETS LATELY.
PLEASE.
WE NEED TO FIGURE THIS THING OUT, TOGETHER.
All right, Dad.
A chance to explain, I owe you that much.
I'm coming.
DRUNK ALONE IN THE EVENING?
GUILTY CONSCIENCE, IS THAT RIGHT, COMMISSIONER?
I CAN RELATE.

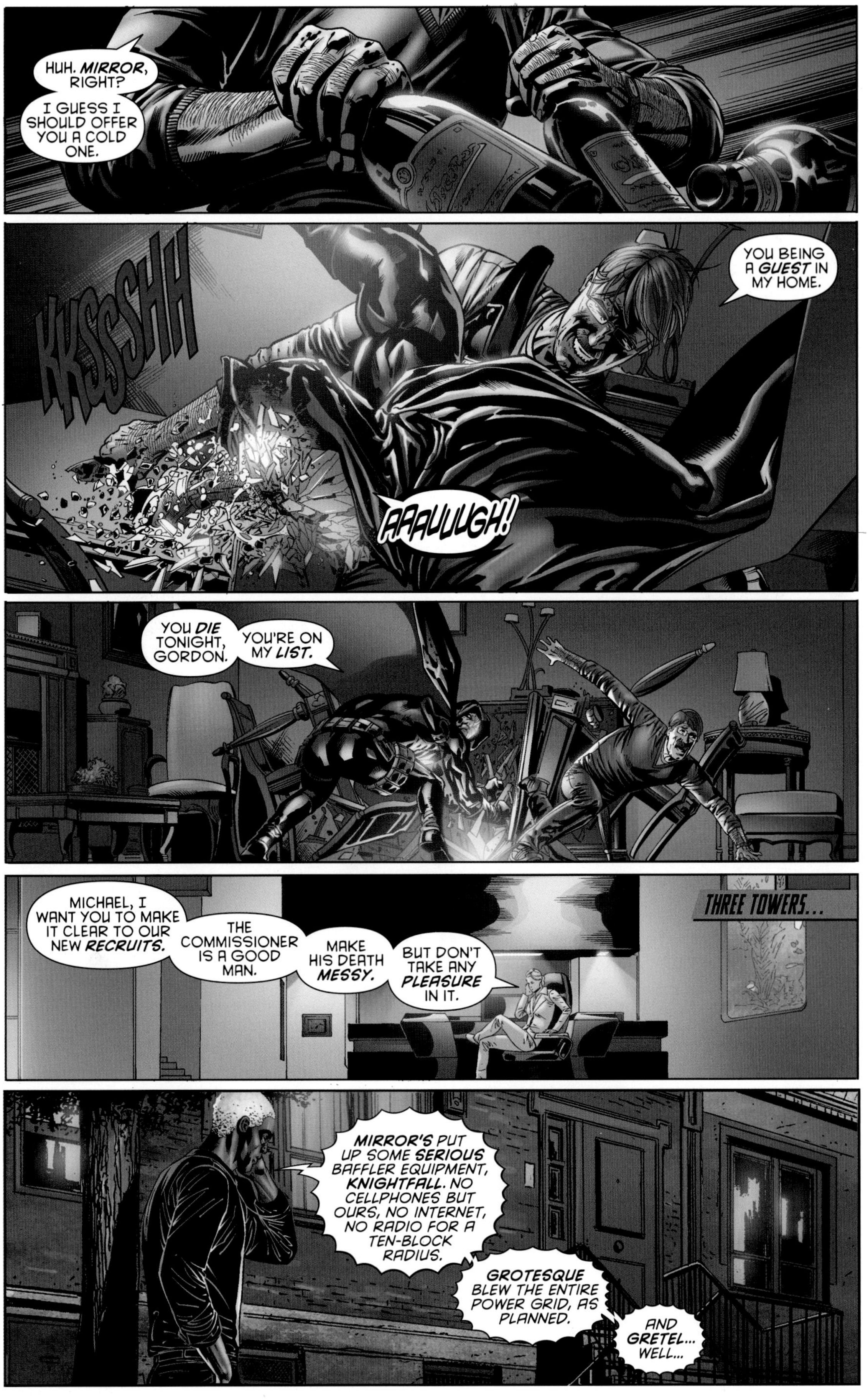
HUH. MIRROR, RIGHT?
I GUESS I SHOULD OFFER YOU A COLD ONE.
YOU BEING A GUEST IN MY HOME.
KKSSSHH
AAAUUUGH!
YOU DIE TONIGHT, GORDON.
YOU'RE ON MY LIST.
THREE TOWERS...
MICHAEL, I WANT YOU TO MAKE IT CLEAR TO OUR NEW RECRUITS.
THE COMMISSIONER IS A GOOD MAN.
MAKE HIS DEATH MESSY.
BUT DON'T TAKE ANY PLEASURE IN IT.
MIRROR'S PUT UP SOME SERIOUS BAFFLER EQUIPMENT, KNIGHTFALL. NO CELLPHONES BUT OURS, NO INTERNET, NO RADIO FOR A TEN-BLOCK RADIUS.
GROTESQUE BLEW THE ENTIRE POWER GRID, AS PLANNED.
AND GRETEL... WELL...

"...I THINK *GRETEL* JUST LIKES TO *HURT* PEOPLE."

HELLO, COMMISSIONER.

NICE *NIGHT*.

UHNNF!

"KNIGHTFALL... *CHARISE*, I HAVE TO ASK YOU..."

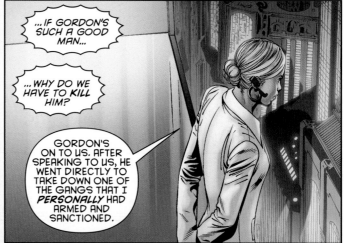

"...IF GORDON'S SUCH A GOOD MAN...

"...WHY DO WE HAVE TO *KILL* HIM?"

GORDON'S ON TO US. AFTER SPEAKING TO US, HE WENT DIRECTLY TO TAKE DOWN ONE OF THE GANGS THAT I *PERSONALLY* HAD ARMED AND SANCTIONED.

"HE HAS TO *DIE*. AND IT HAS TO LOOK LIKE *GANGBANGERS* DID IT.

"MAKE IT *UGLY* FOR ME, MICHAEL."

GUN.

MY *GUN*.

HUH.

The uber-expensive radio I just installed fizzed out...

...weird.

SORRY ABOUT THIS, MY GOOD FELLOW.

I'M AFRAID ORDERS ARE TO GIVE YOU QUITE AN *ORDEAL*!

AAAAHHHH.

ZZZZ
ZZZ
ZZ

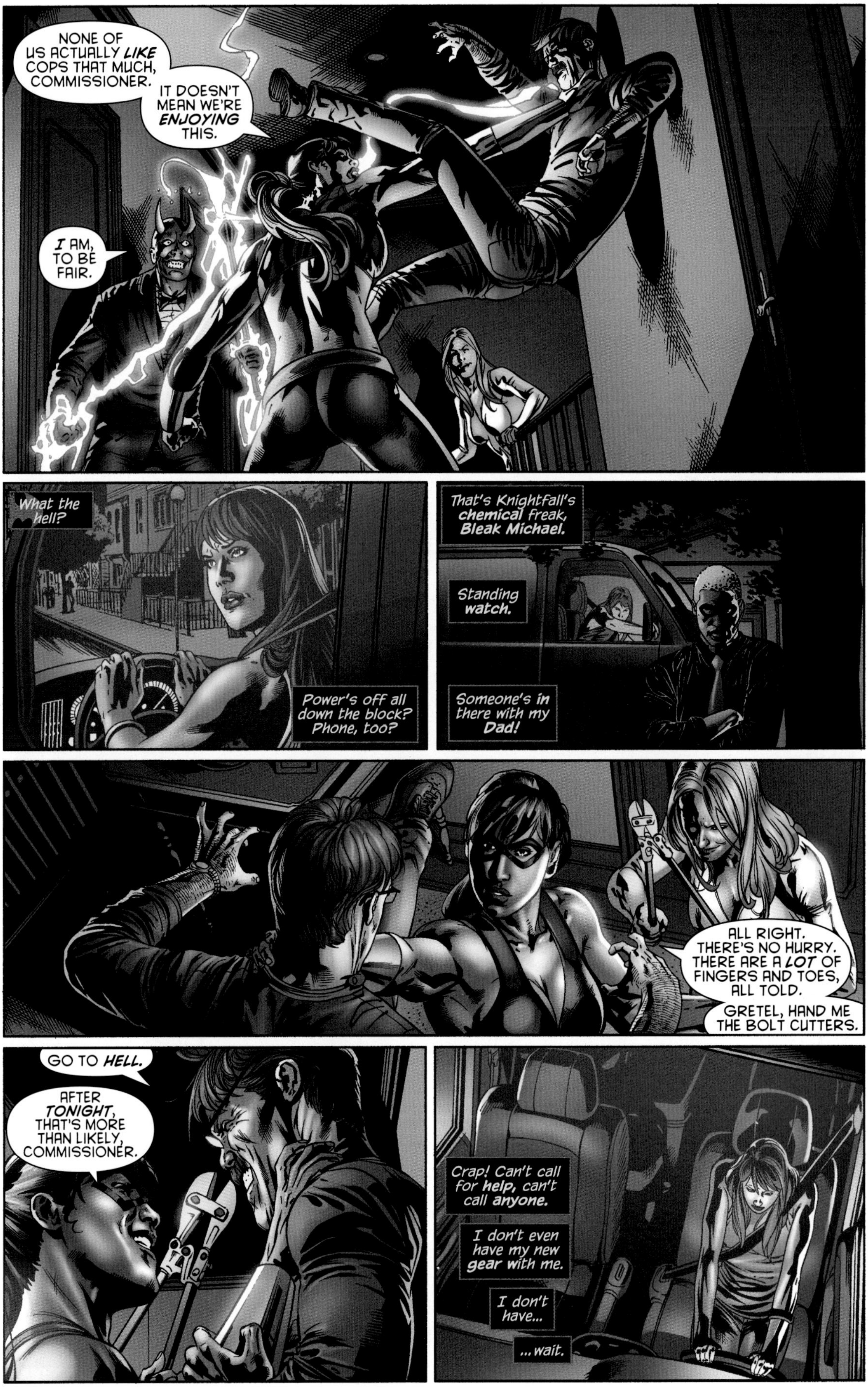
NONE OF US ACTUALLY *LIKE* COPS THAT MUCH, COMMISSIONER.
IT DOESN'T MEAN WE'RE *ENJOYING* THIS.
I AM, TO BE FAIR.
What the hell?
Power's off all down the block? Phone, too?
That's Knightfall's **chemical** freak, **Bleak Michael.**
Standing **watch.**
Someone's **in** there with my **Dad!**
ALL RIGHT. THERE'S NO HURRY. THERE ARE A *LOT* OF FINGERS AND TOES, ALL TOLD.
GRETEL, HAND ME THE BOLT CUTTERS.
GO TO *HELL.*
AFTER *TONIGHT*, THAT'S MORE THAN LIKELY, COMMISSIONER.
Crap! Can't call for **help,** can't call **anyone.**
I don't even have my new **gear with me.**
I don't have...
...wait.

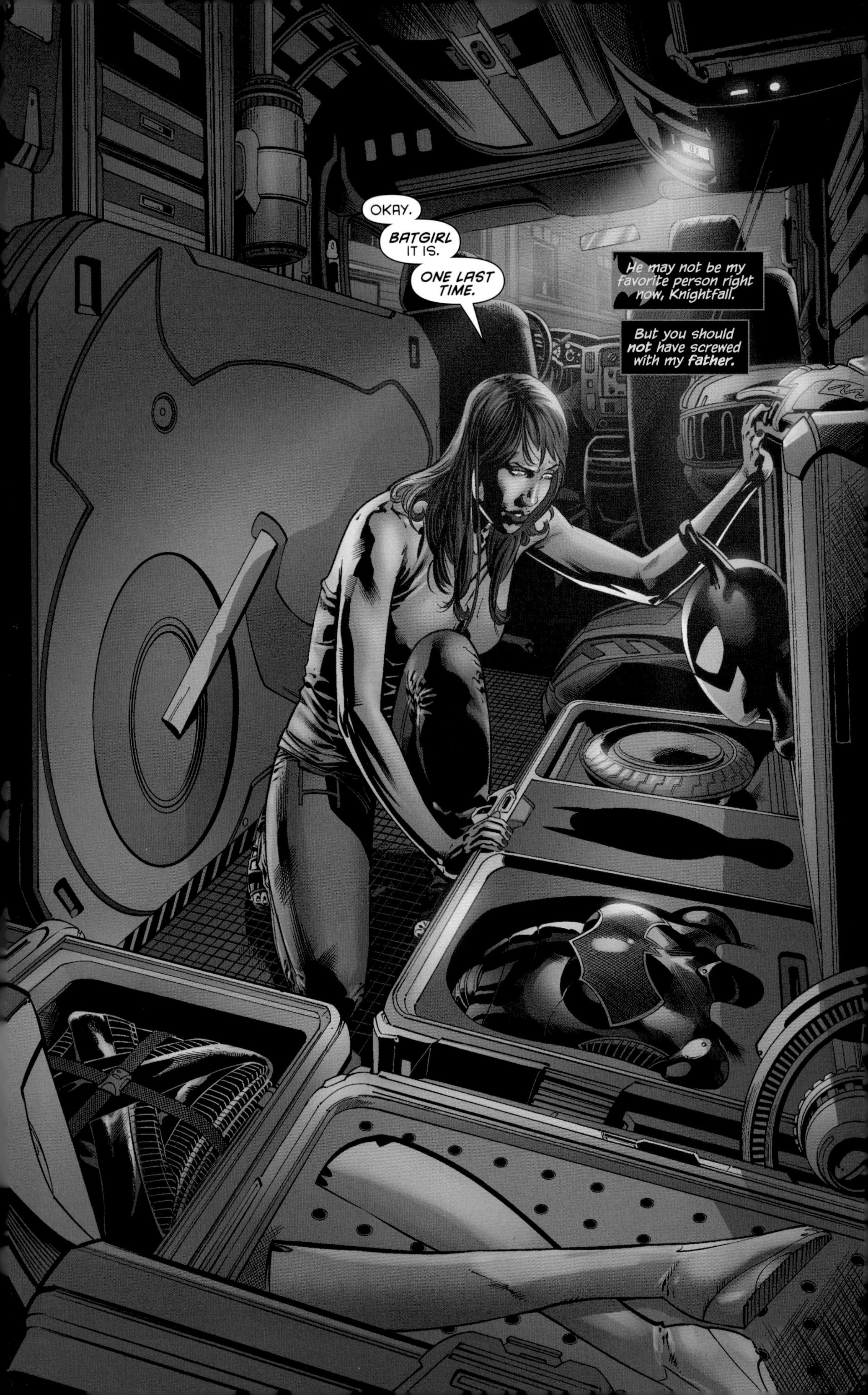
OKAY.
BATGIRL IT IS.
ONE LAST TIME.
He may not be my favorite person right now, Knightfall.
But you should **not** have screwed with my **father.**

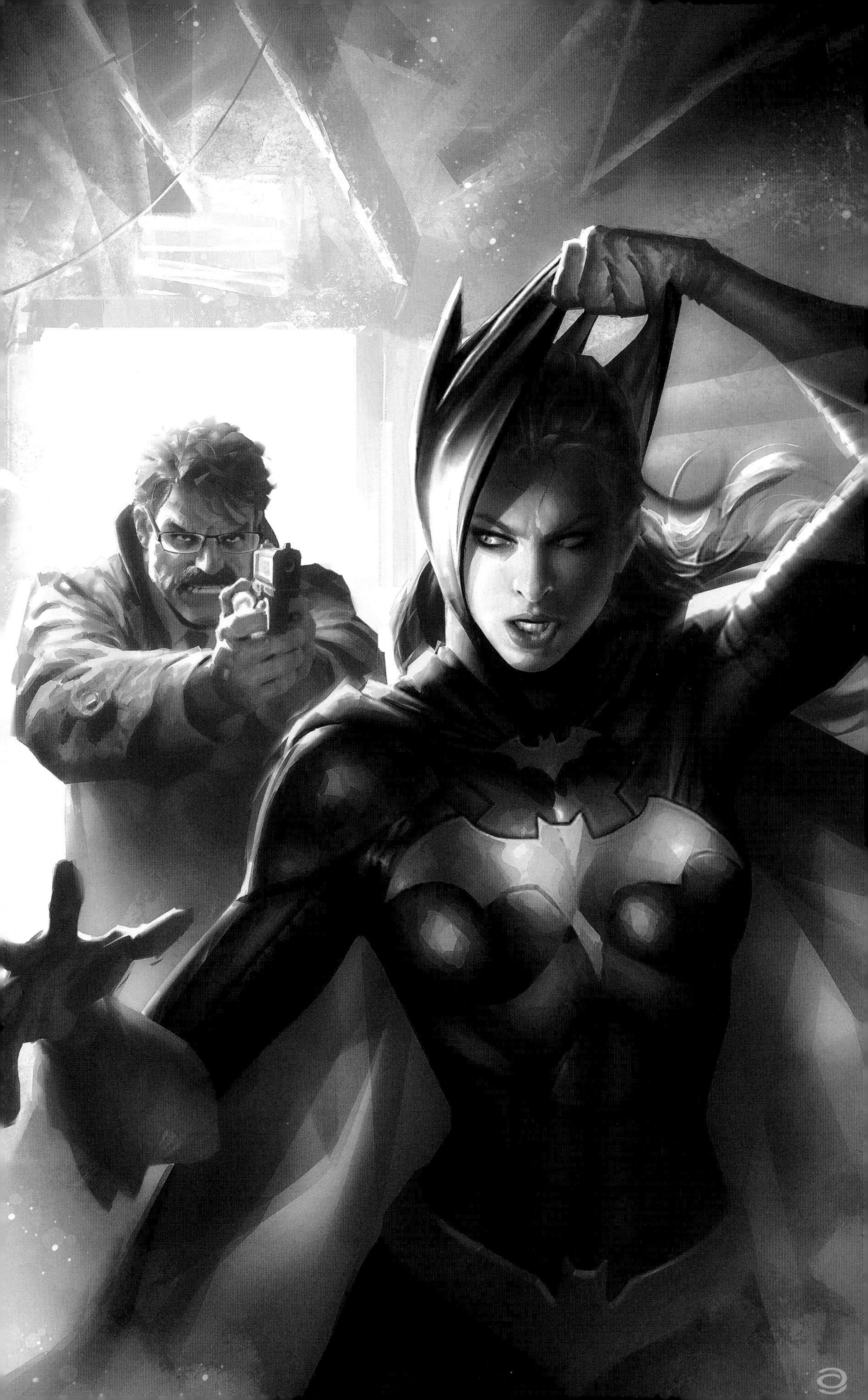

cover by **ALEX GARNER**

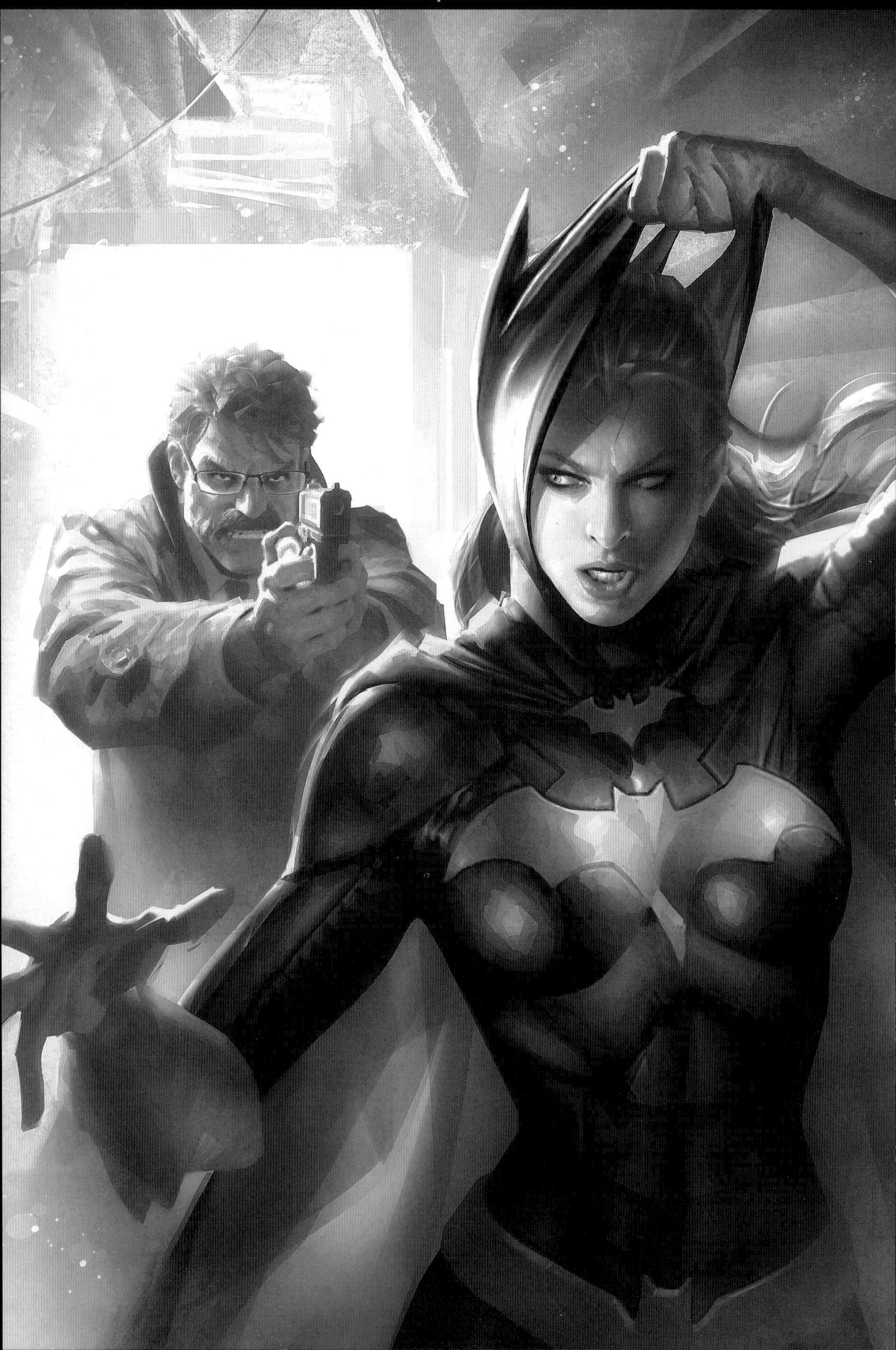

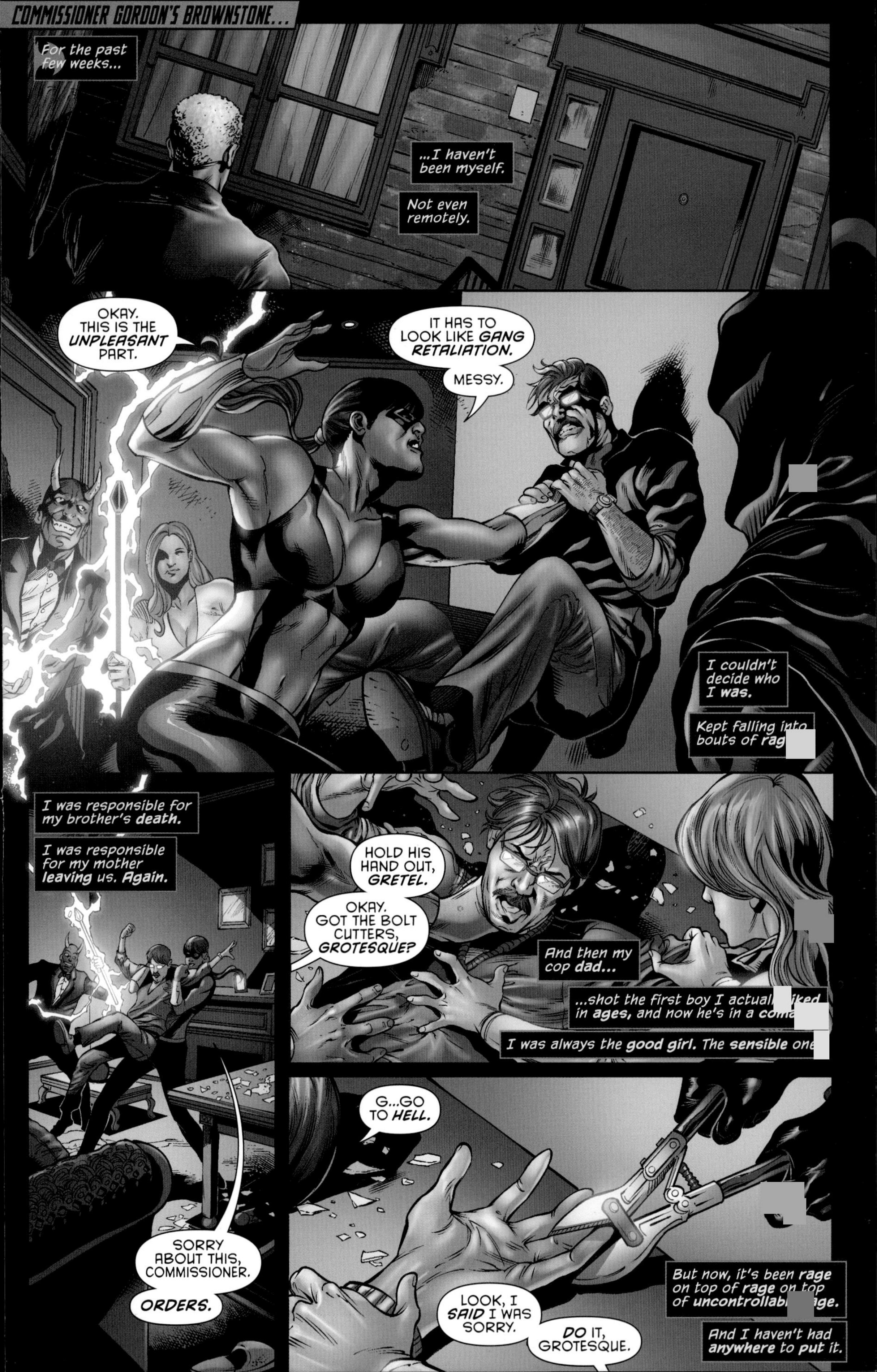
COMMISSIONER GORDON'S BROWNSTONE...
For the past few weeks...
...I haven't been myself.
Not even remotely.
OKAY. THIS IS THE UNPLEASANT PART.
IT HAS TO LOOK LIKE GANG RETALIATION.
MESSY.
I couldn't decide who I was.
Kept falling into bouts of rag
I was responsible for my brother's death.
I was responsible for my mother leaving us. Again.
HOLD HIS HAND OUT, GRETEL.
OKAY. GOT THE BOLT CUTTERS, GROTESQUE?
And then my cop dad...
...shot the first boy I actual iked in ages, and now he's in a com
I was always the good girl. The sensible one
SORRY ABOUT THIS, COMMISSIONER.
ORDERS.
G...GO TO HELL.
LOOK, I SAID I WAS SORRY.
DO IT, GROTESQUE.
But now, it's been rage on top of rage on top of uncontrollab age.
And I haven't had anywhere to put it.

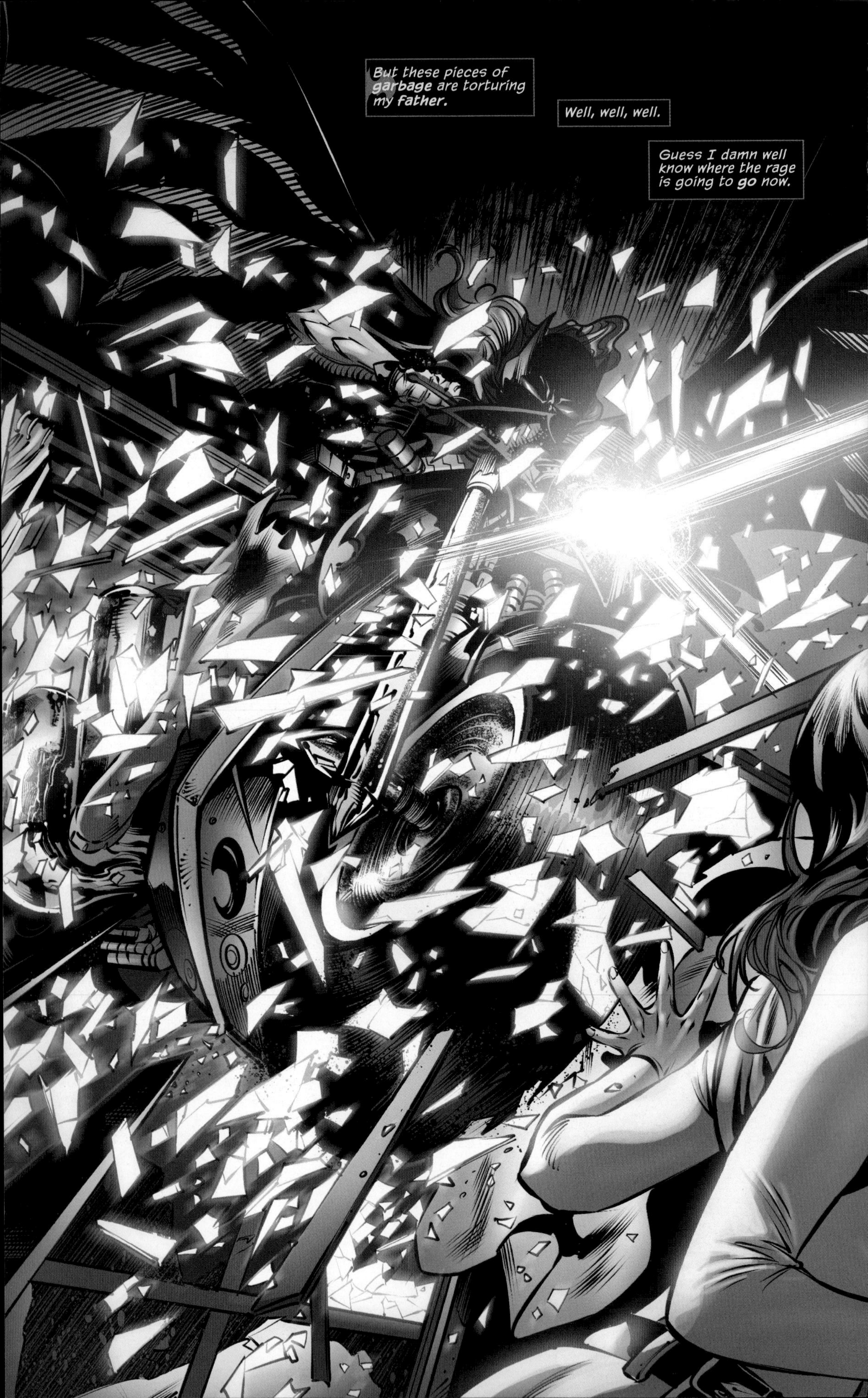
But these pieces of garbage are torturing my father.
Well, well, well.
Guess I damn well know where the rage is going to go now.

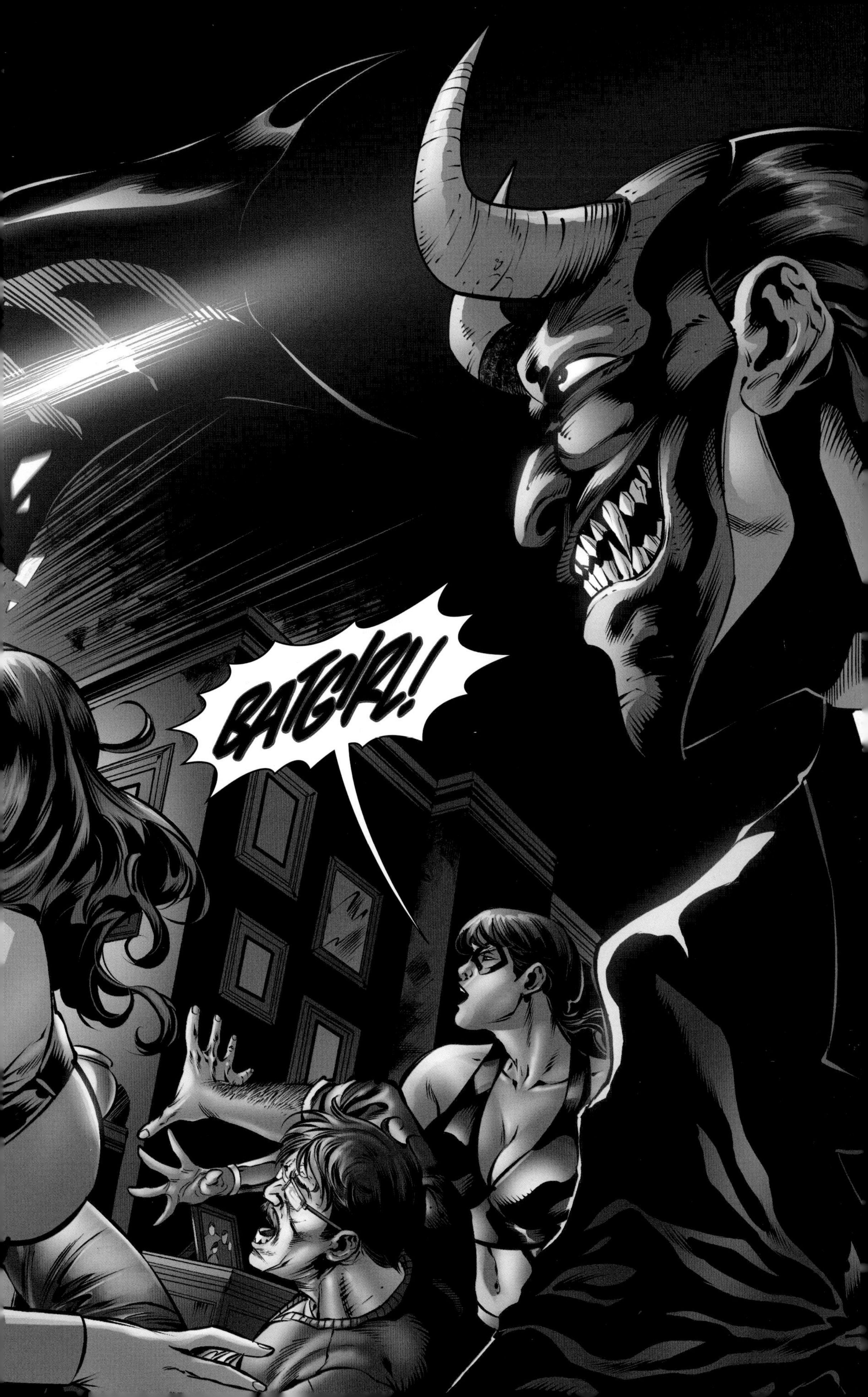
BATGIRL!

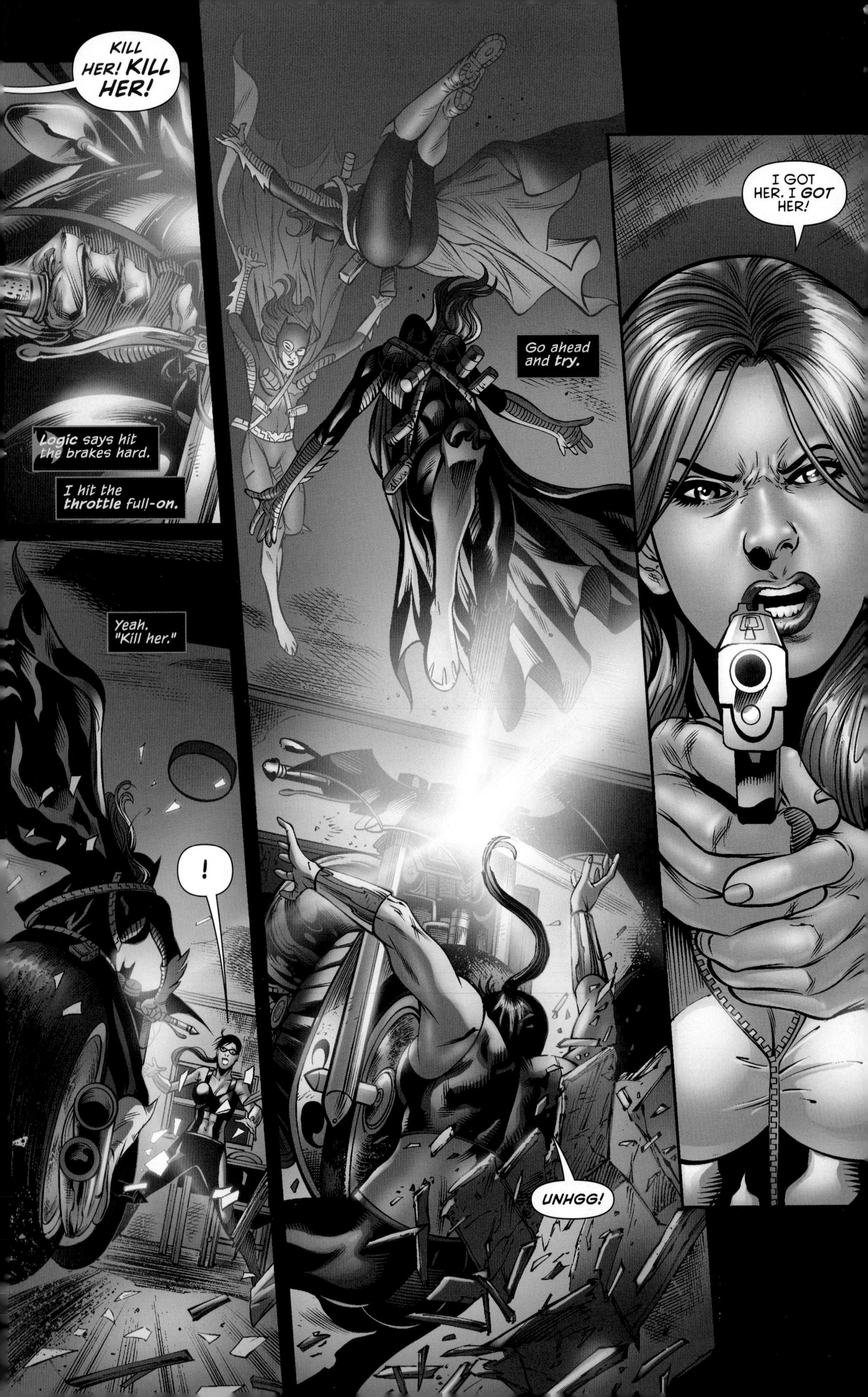
KILL HER! KILL HER!
Logic says hit the brakes hard.
I hit the throttle full-on.
Yeah. "Kill her."
!
Go ahead and try.
UNHGG!
I GOT HER. I GOT HER!

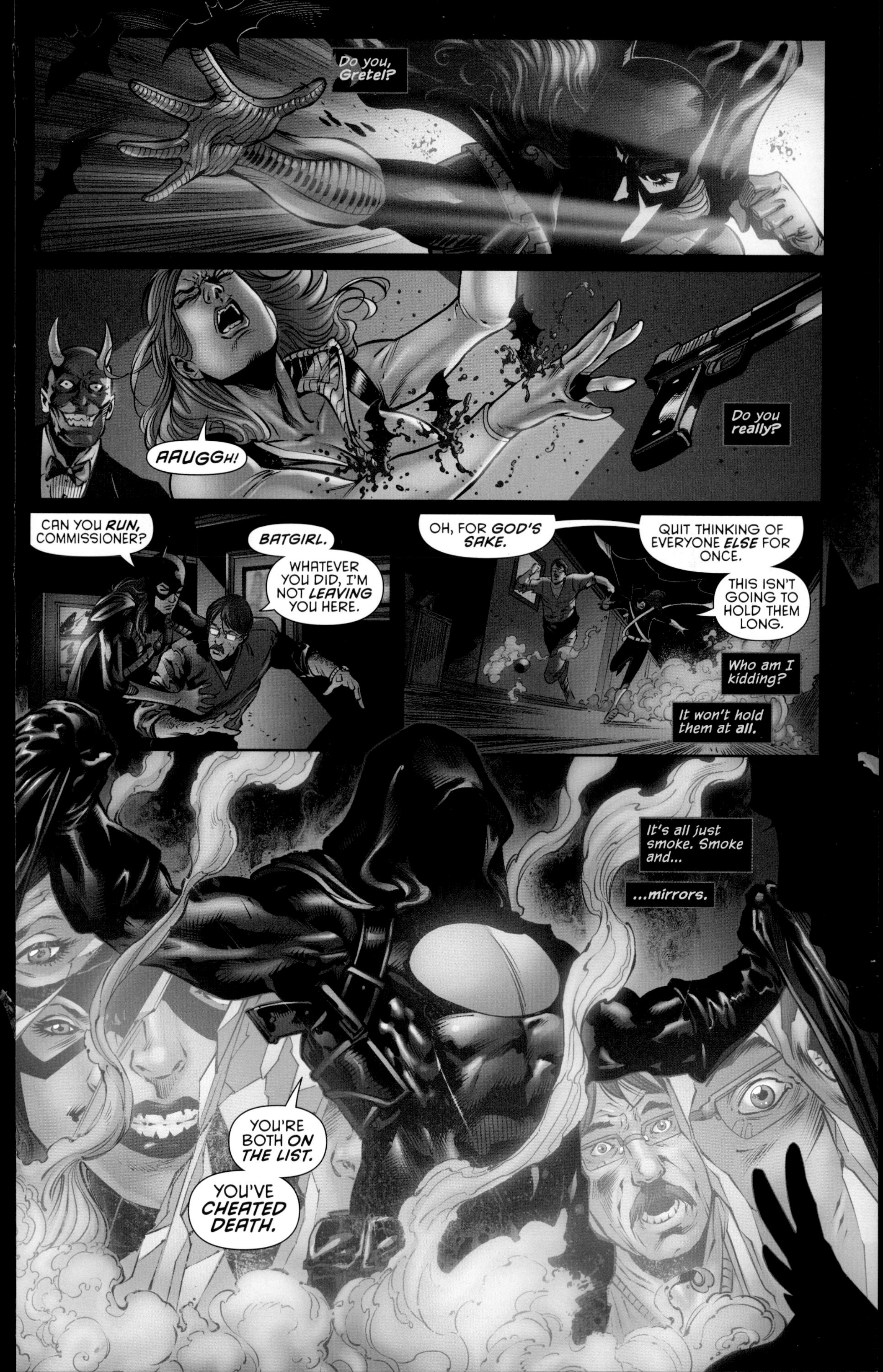

Do you, Gretel?
AAUGGH!
Do you really?
CAN YOU RUN, COMMISSIONER?
BATGIRL.
WHATEVER YOU DID, I'M NOT LEAVING YOU HERE.
OH, FOR GOD'S SAKE.
QUIT THINKING OF EVERYONE ELSE FOR ONCE.
THIS ISN'T GOING TO HOLD THEM LONG.
Who am I kidding?
It won't hold them at all.
It's all just smoke. Smoke and...
...mirrors.
YOU'RE BOTH ON THE LIST.
YOU'VE CHEATED DEATH.

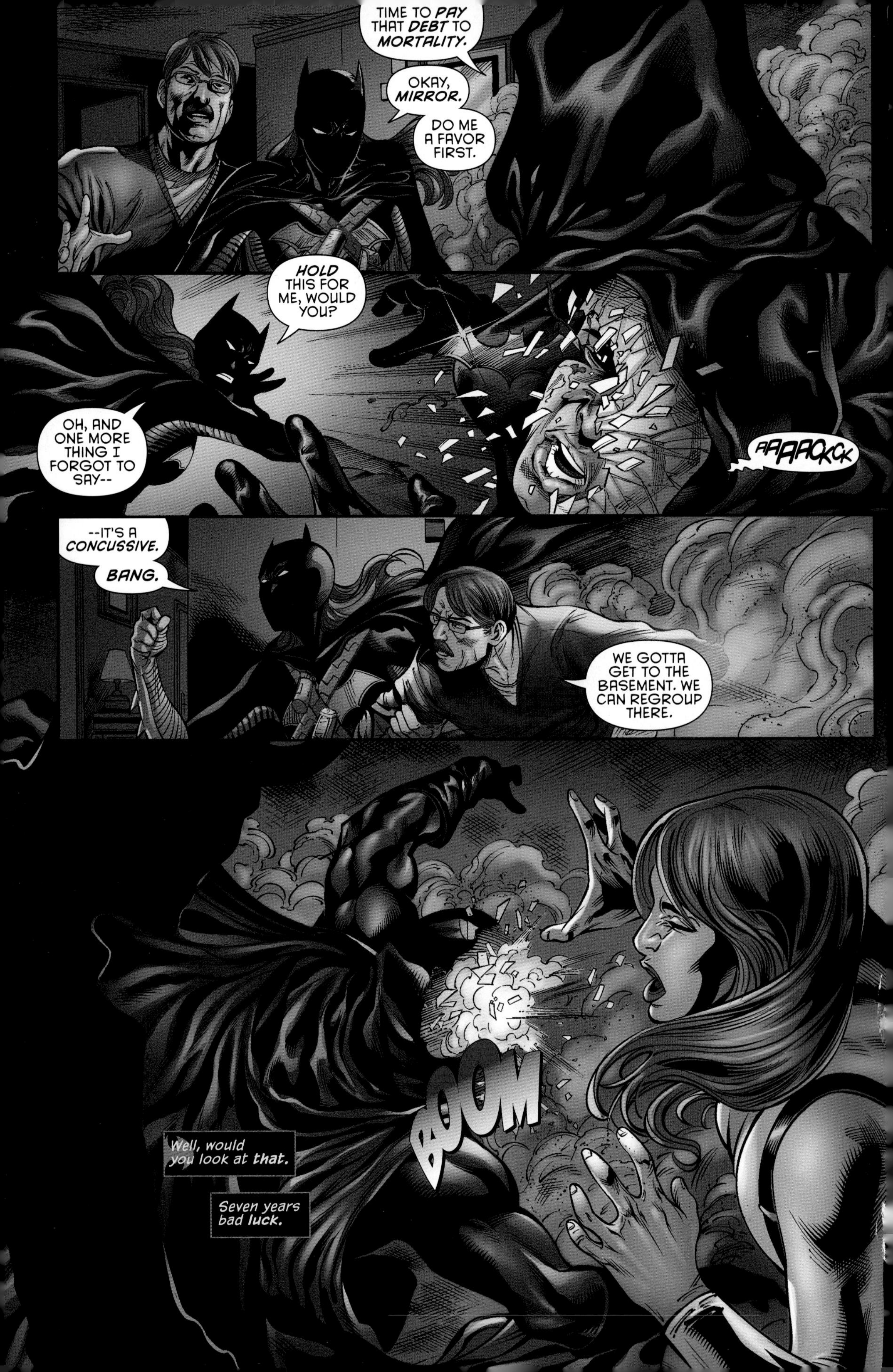
TIME TO PAY THAT DEBT TO MORTALITY.
OKAY, MIRROR.
DO ME A FAVOR FIRST.
HOLD THIS FOR ME, WOULD YOU?
OH, AND ONE MORE THING I FORGOT TO SAY--
AAAAACKCK
--IT'S A CONCUSSIVE.
BANG.
WE GOTTA GET TO THE BASEMENT. WE CAN REGROUP THERE.
BOOM
Well, would you look at that.
Seven years bad luck.

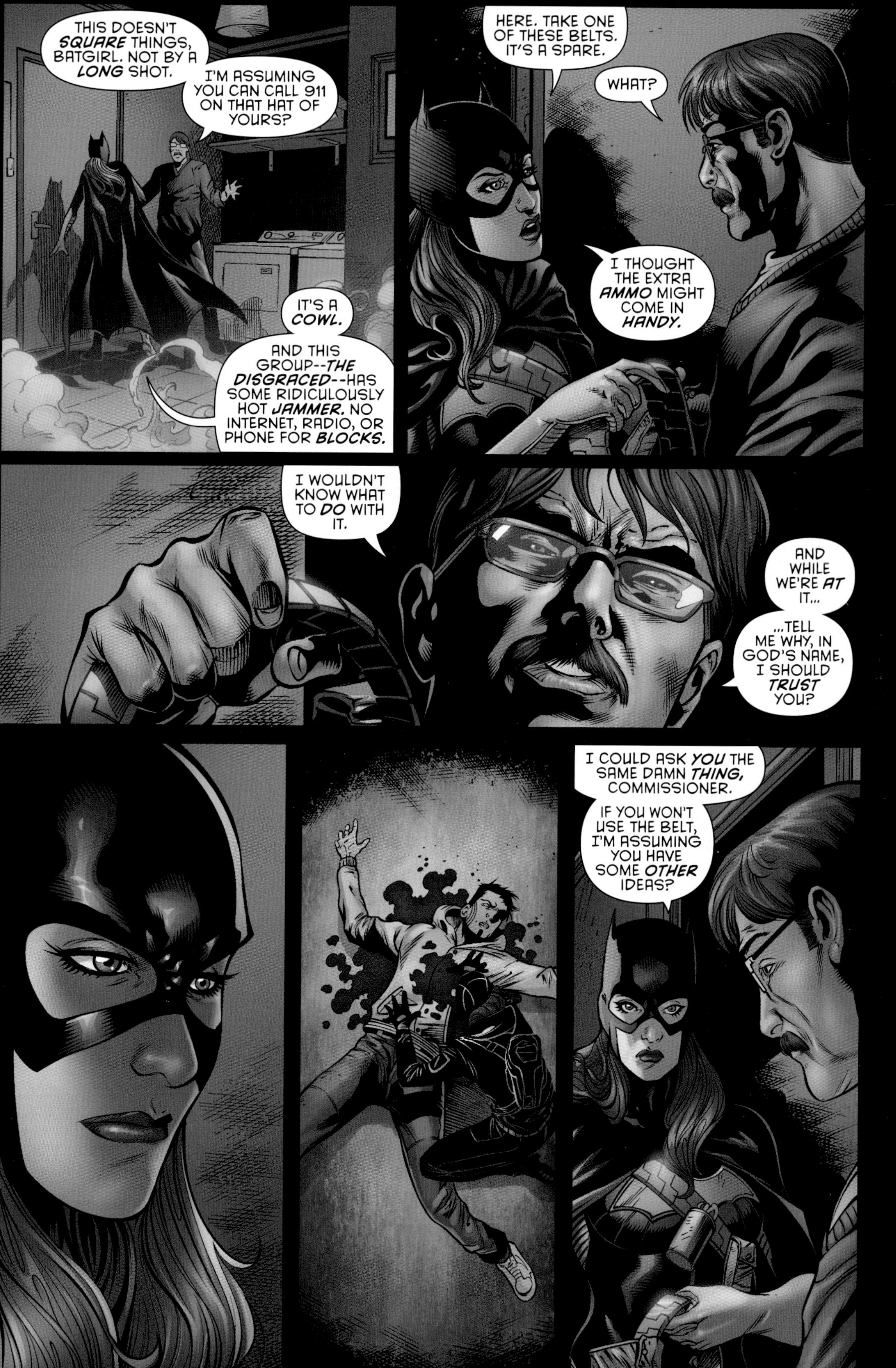
THIS DOESN'T SQUARE THINGS, BATGIRL. NOT BY A LONG SHOT.
I'M ASSUMING YOU CAN CALL 911 ON THAT HAT OF YOURS?
IT'S A COWL.
AND THIS GROUP--THE DISGRACED--HAS SOME RIDICULOUSLY HOT JAMMER. NO INTERNET, RADIO, OR PHONE FOR BLOCKS.
HERE. TAKE ONE OF THESE BELTS. IT'S A SPARE.
WHAT?
I THOUGHT THE EXTRA AMMO MIGHT COME IN HANDY.
I WOULDN'T KNOW WHAT TO DO WITH IT.
AND WHILE WE'RE AT IT...
...TELL ME WHY, IN GOD'S NAME, I SHOULD TRUST YOU?
I COULD ASK YOU THE SAME DAMN THING, COMMISSIONER.
IF YOU WON'T USE THE BELT, I'M ASSUMING YOU HAVE SOME OTHER IDEAS?

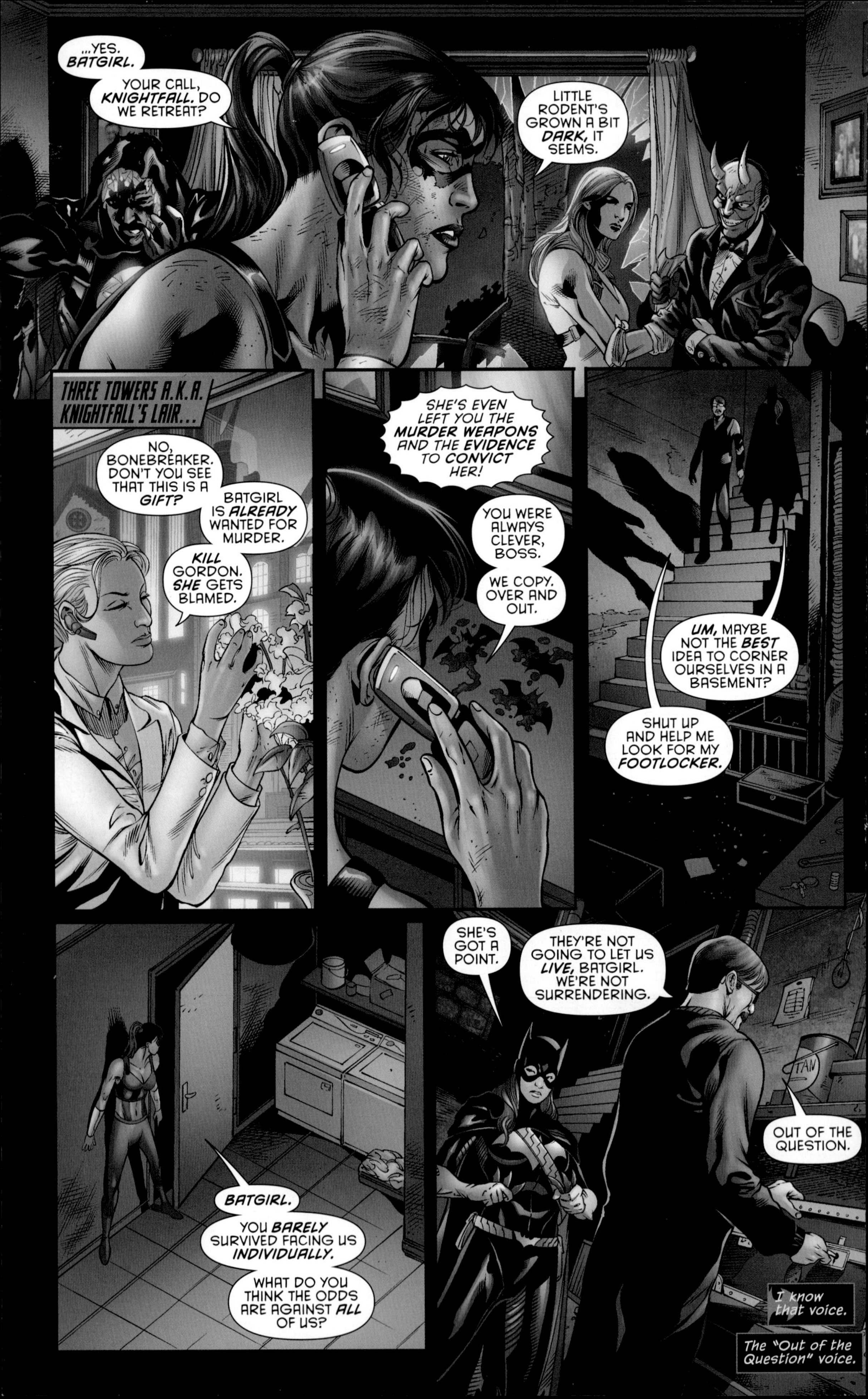

...YES. BATGIRL.
YOUR CALL, KNIGHTFALL. DO WE RETREAT?
LITTLE RODENT'S GROWN A BIT DARK, IT SEEMS.
THREE TOWERS A.K.A. KNIGHTFALL'S LAIR...
NO, BONEBREAKER. DON'T YOU SEE THAT THIS IS A GIFT?
BATGIRL IS ALREADY WANTED FOR MURDER.
KILL GORDON. SHE GETS BLAMED.
SHE'S EVEN LEFT YOU THE MURDER WEAPONS AND THE EVIDENCE TO CONVICT HER!
YOU WERE ALWAYS CLEVER, BOSS.
WE COPY. OVER AND OUT.
UM, MAYBE NOT THE BEST IDEA TO CORNER OURSELVES IN A BASEMENT?
SHUT UP AND HELP ME LOOK FOR MY FOOTLOCKER.
BATGIRL.
YOU BARELY SURVIVED FACING US INDIVIDUALLY.
WHAT DO YOU THINK THE ODDS ARE AGAINST ALL OF US?
SHE'S GOT A POINT.
THEY'RE NOT GOING TO LET US LIVE, BATGIRL. WE'RE NOT SURRENDERING.
OUT OF THE QUESTION.
I know that voice.
The "Out of the Question" voice.

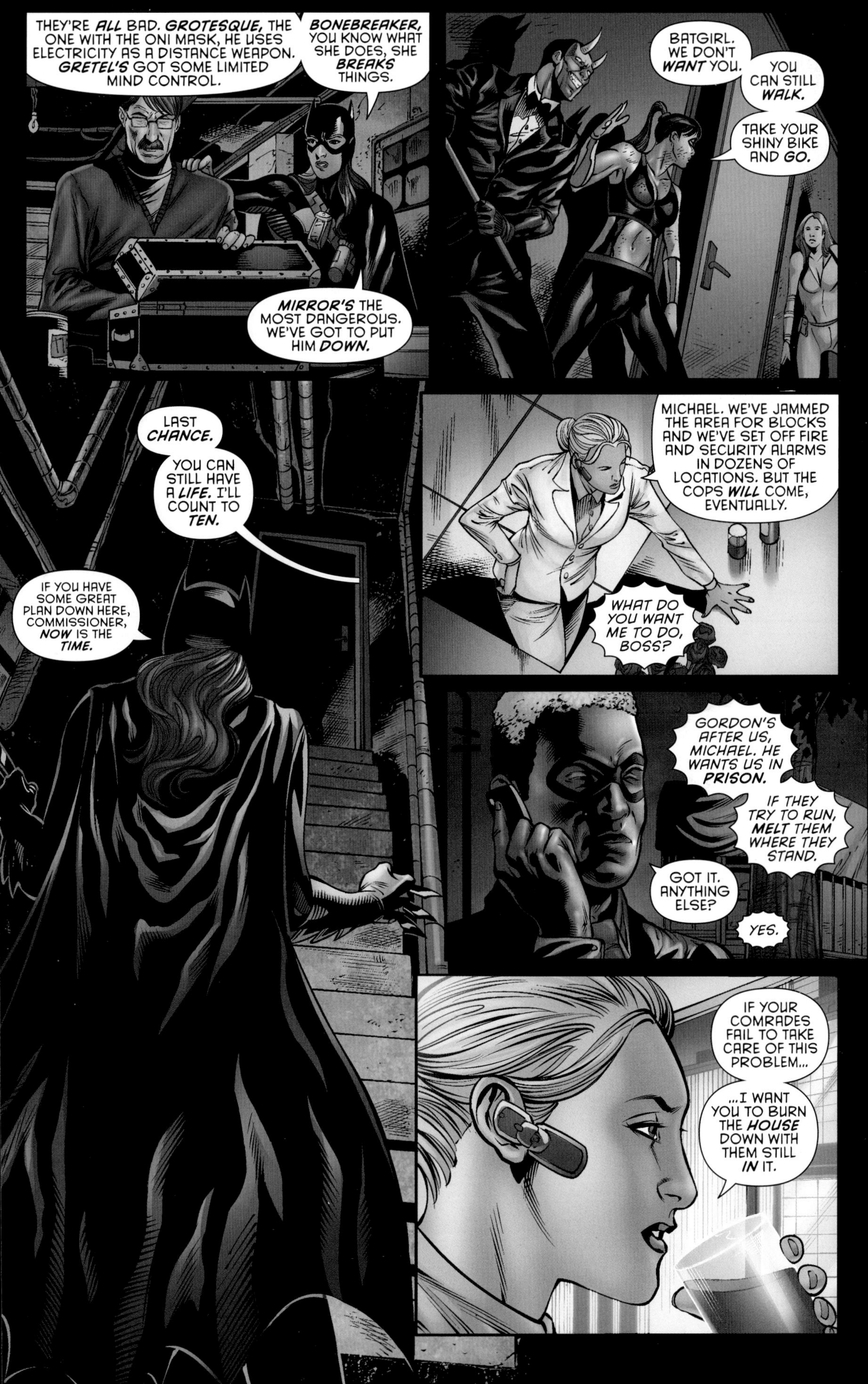
THEY'RE ALL BAD. GROTESQUE, THE ONE WITH THE ONI MASK, HE USES ELECTRICITY AS A DISTANCE WEAPON. GRETEL'S GOT SOME LIMITED MIND CONTROL.
BONEBREAKER, YOU KNOW WHAT SHE DOES, SHE BREAKS THINGS.
MIRROR'S THE MOST DANGEROUS. WE'VE GOT TO PUT HIM DOWN.
BATGIRL. WE DON'T WANT YOU.
YOU CAN STILL WALK.
TAKE YOUR SHINY BIKE AND GO.
LAST CHANCE.
YOU CAN STILL HAVE A LIFE. I'LL COUNT TO TEN.
IF YOU HAVE SOME GREAT PLAN DOWN HERE, COMMISSIONER, NOW IS THE TIME.
MICHAEL. WE'VE JAMMED THE AREA FOR BLOCKS AND WE'VE SET OFF FIRE AND SECURITY ALARMS IN DOZENS OF LOCATIONS. BUT THE COPS WILL COME, EVENTUALLY.
WHAT DO YOU WANT ME TO DO, BOSS?
GORDON'S AFTER US, MICHAEL. HE WANTS US IN PRISON.
IF THEY TRY TO RUN, MELT THEM WHERE THEY STAND.
GOT IT. ANYTHING ELSE?
YES.
IF YOUR COMRADES FAIL TO TAKE CARE OF THIS PROBLEM...
...I WANT YOU TO BURN THE HOUSE DOWN WITH THEM STILL IN IT.

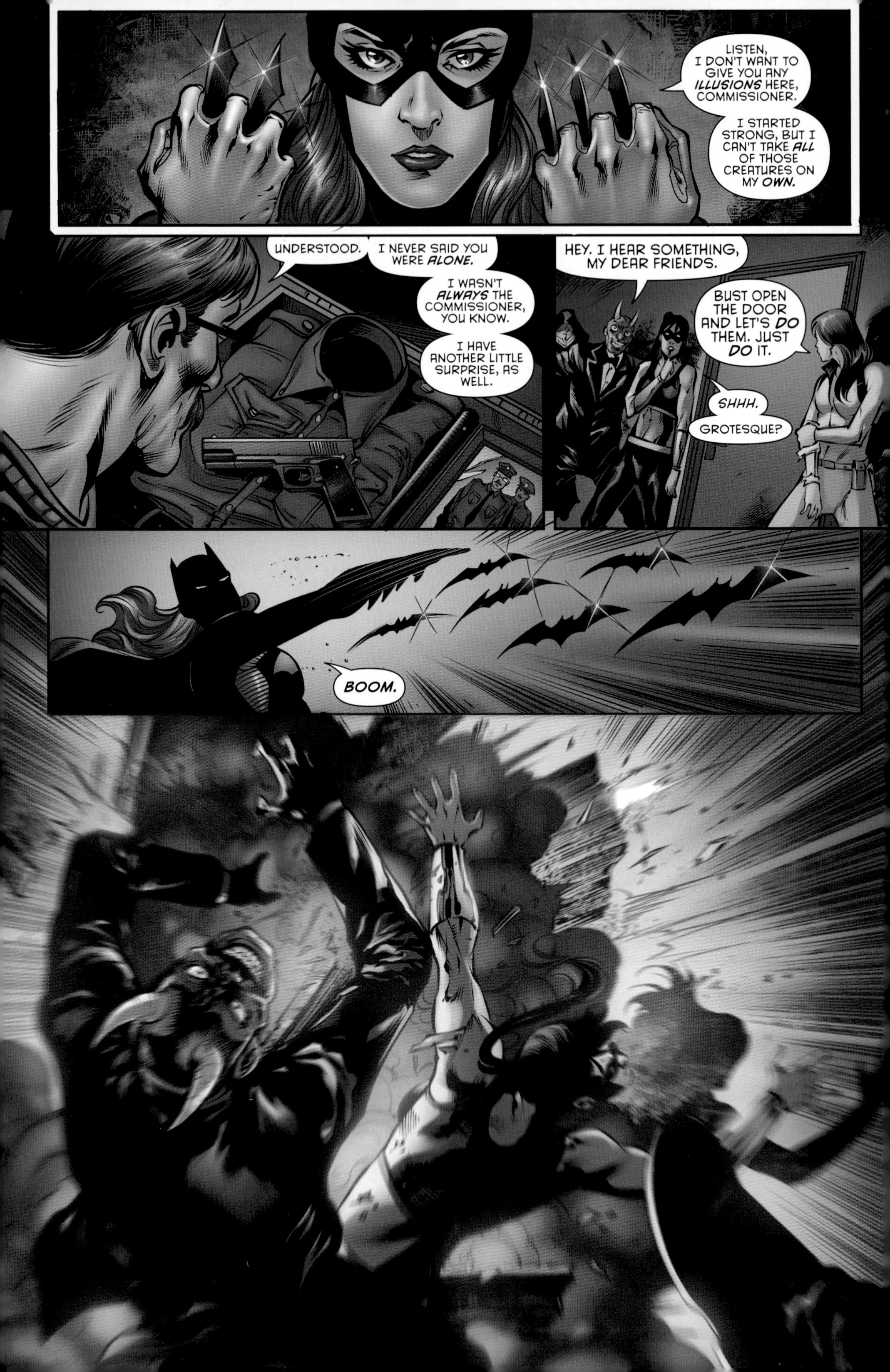

LISTEN, I DON'T WANT TO GIVE YOU ANY *ILLUSIONS* HERE, COMMISSIONER.
I STARTED STRONG, BUT I CAN'T TAKE *ALL* OF THOSE CREATURES ON MY *OWN.*
UNDERSTOOD.
I NEVER SAID YOU WERE *ALONE.*
I WASN'T *ALWAYS* THE COMMISSIONER, YOU KNOW.
I HAVE ANOTHER LITTLE SURPRISE, AS WELL.
HEY. I HEAR SOMETHING, MY DEAR FRIENDS.
BUST OPEN THE DOOR AND LET'S *DO* THEM. JUST *DO* IT.
SHHH.
GROTESQUE?
BOOM.

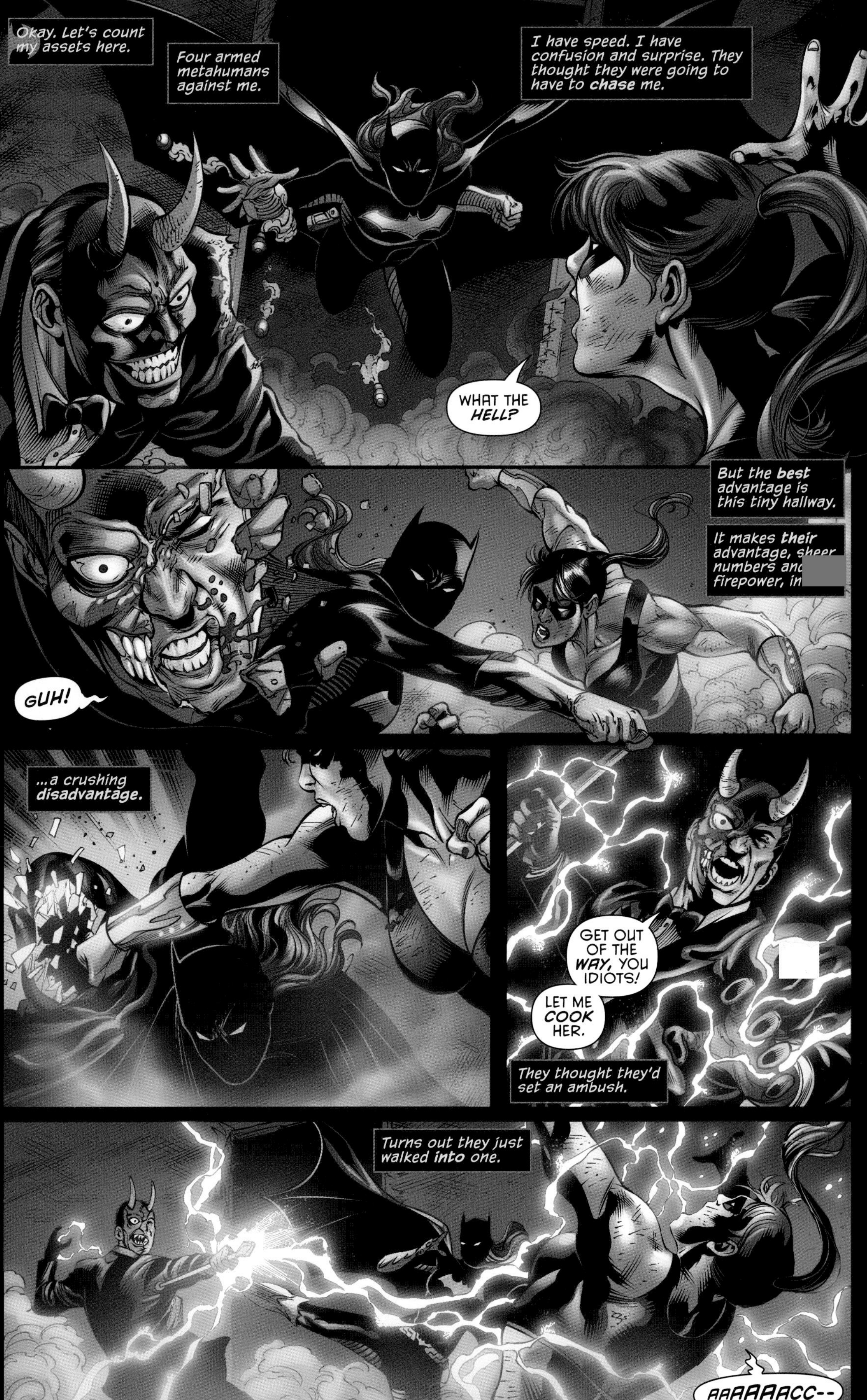

Okay. Let's count my assets here.
Four armed metahumans against me.
I have speed. I have confusion and surprise. They thought they were going to have to *chase* me.
WHAT THE *HELL?*
But the *best* advantage is this tiny hallway.
It makes *their* advantage, sheer numbers and firepower, in
GUH!
...a crushing *disadvantage.*
GET OUT OF THE *WAY,* YOU IDIOTS!
LET ME *COOK* HER.
They thought they'd set an ambush.
Turns out they just walked *into* one.
AAAAAACC--

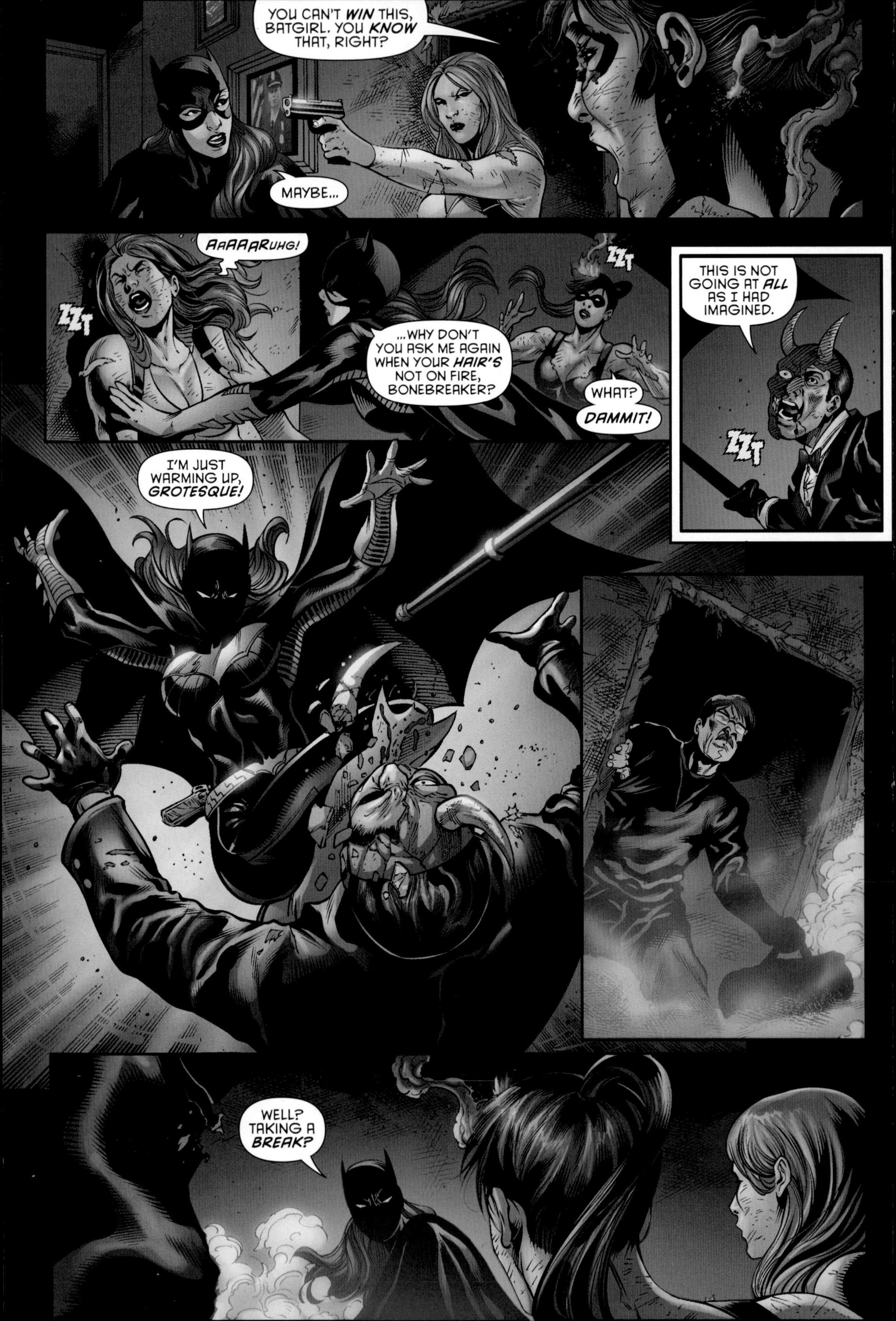

YOU CAN'T *WIN* THIS, BATGIRL. YOU *KNOW* THAT, RIGHT?
MAYBE...
AAAAARUHG!
ZZT
...WHY DON'T YOU ASK ME AGAIN WHEN YOUR *HAIR'S* NOT ON FIRE, BONEBREAKER?
ZZT
WHAT? *DAMMIT!*
THIS IS NOT GOING AT *ALL* AS I HAD IMAGINED.
ZZT
I'M JUST WARMING UP, *GROTESQUE!*
WELL? TAKING A *BREAK?*

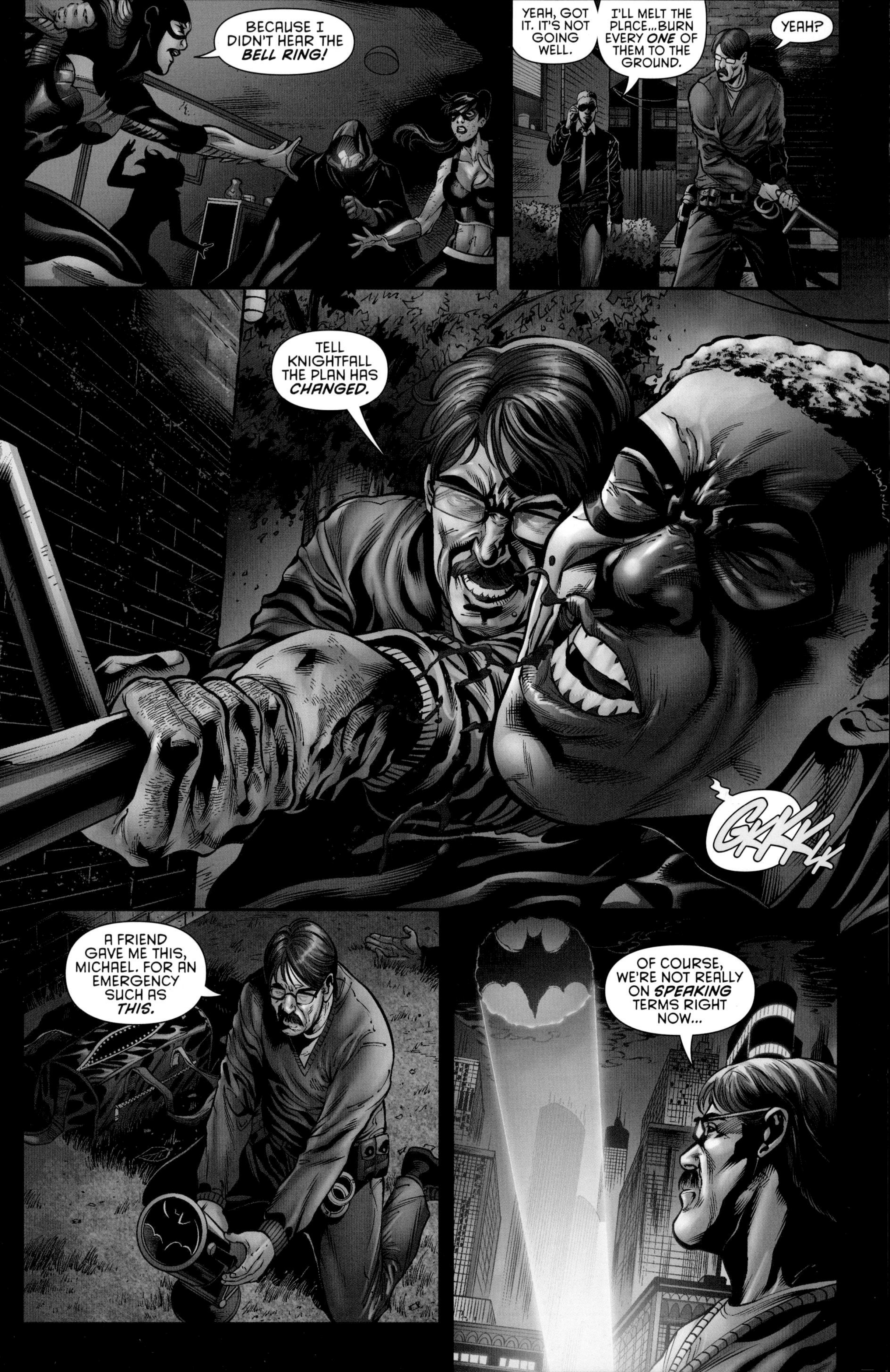
BECAUSE I DIDN'T HEAR THE *BELL RING!*
YEAH, GOT IT. IT'S NOT GOING WELL.
I'LL MELT THE PLACE...BURN EVERY *ONE* OF THEM TO THE GROUND.
YEAH?
TELL KNIGHTFALL THE PLAN HAS *CHANGED.*
GAKKK
A FRIEND GAVE ME THIS, MICHAEL. FOR AN EMERGENCY SUCH AS *THIS.*
OF COURSE, WE'RE NOT REALLY ON *SPEAKING* TERMS RIGHT NOW...

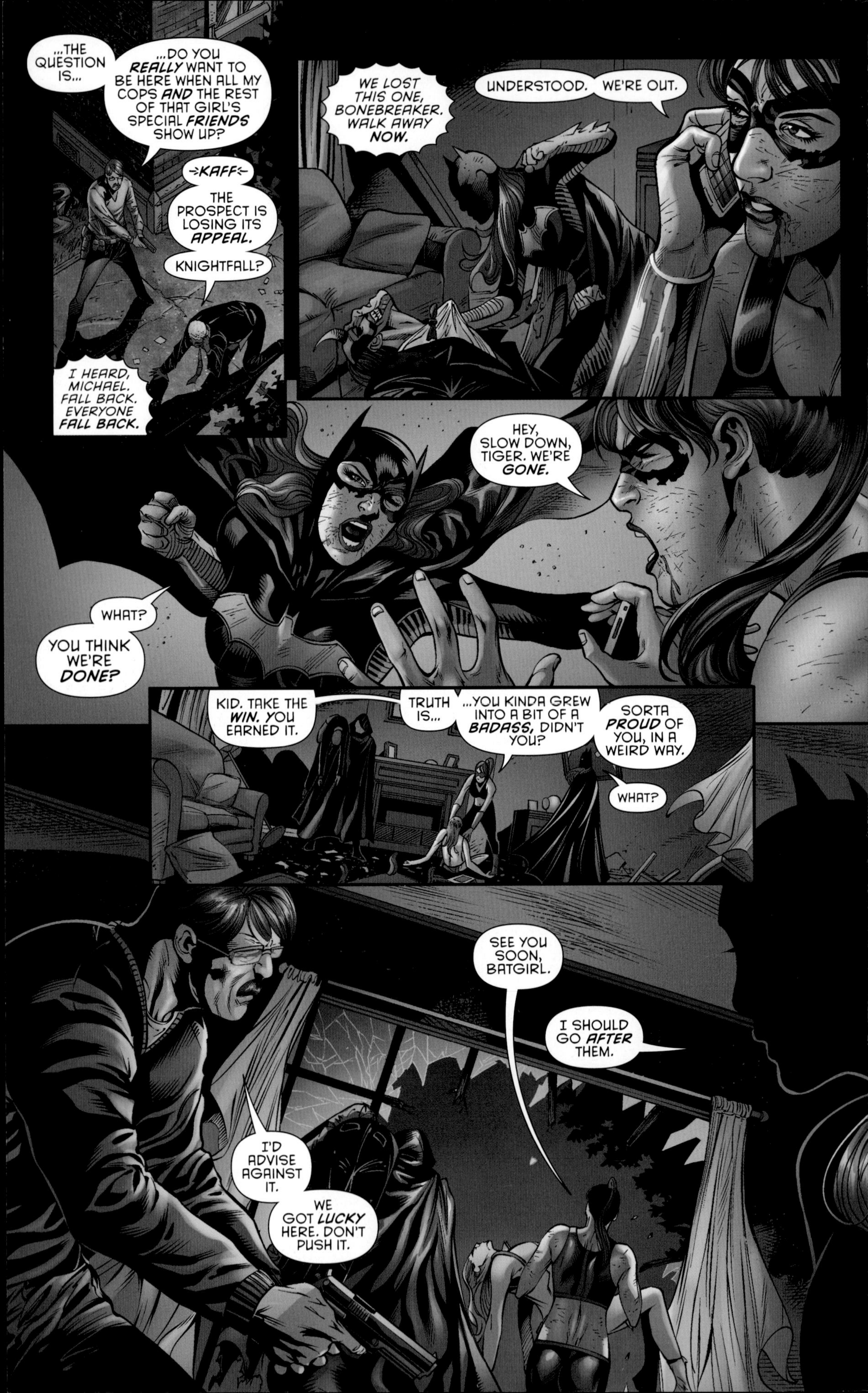
...THE QUESTION IS...
...DO YOU REALLY WANT TO BE HERE WHEN ALL MY COPS AND THE REST OF THAT GIRL'S SPECIAL FRIENDS SHOW UP?
KAFF
THE PROSPECT IS LOSING ITS APPEAL.
KNIGHTFALL?
I HEARD, MICHAEL. FALL BACK. EVERYONE FALL BACK.
WE LOST THIS ONE, BONEBREAKER. WALK AWAY NOW.
UNDERSTOOD.
WE'RE OUT.
HEY, SLOW DOWN, TIGER. WE'RE GONE.
WHAT?
YOU THINK WE'RE DONE?
KID. TAKE THE WIN. YOU EARNED IT.
TRUTH IS...
...YOU KINDA GREW INTO A BIT OF A BADASS, DIDN'T YOU?
SORTA PROUD OF YOU, IN A WEIRD WAY.
WHAT?
SEE YOU SOON, BATGIRL.
I SHOULD GO AFTER THEM.
I'D ADVISE AGAINST IT.
WE GOT LUCKY HERE. DON'T PUSH IT.

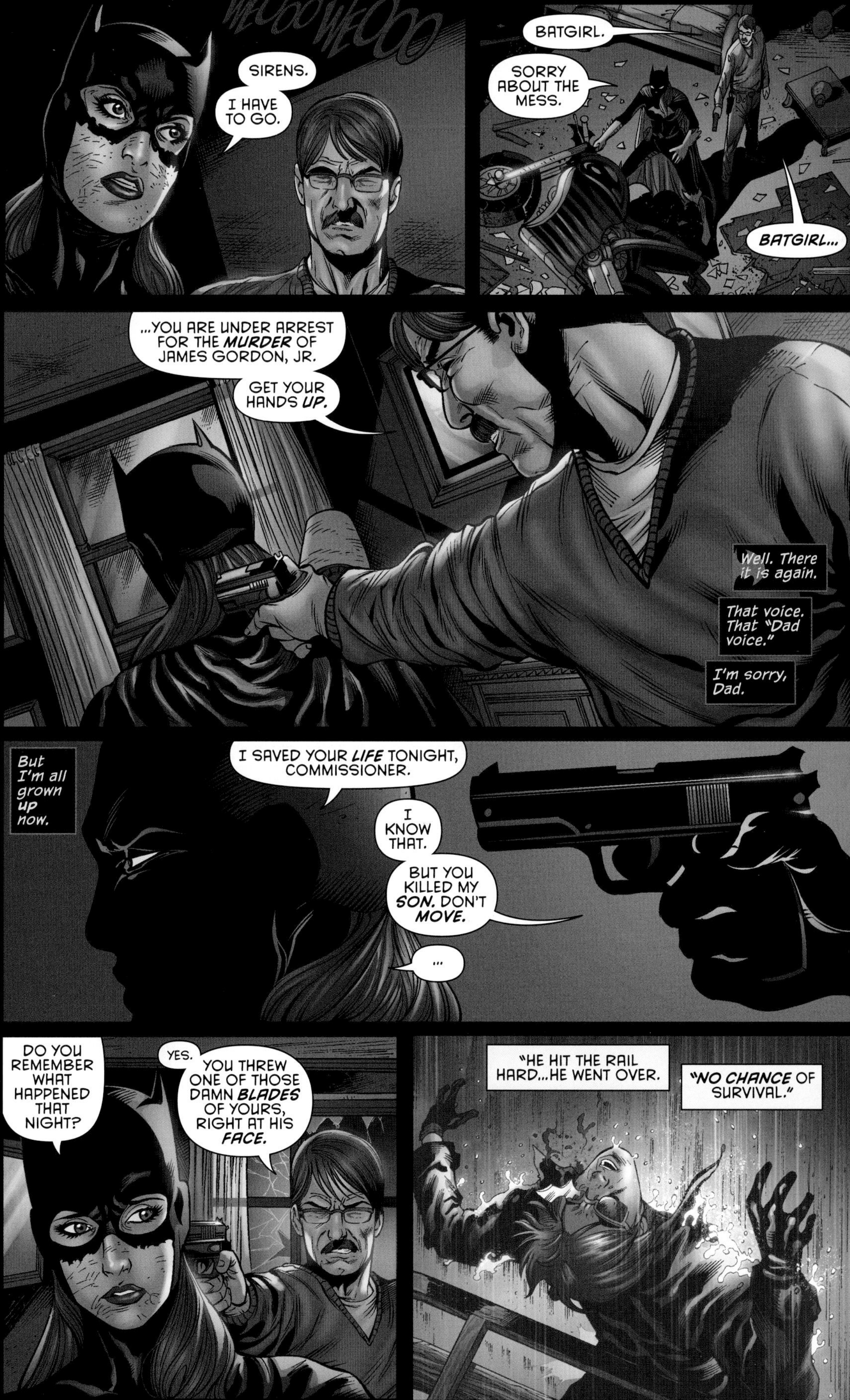
WEOOO WEOOO
SIRENS.
I HAVE TO GO.
BATGIRL.
SORRY ABOUT THE MESS.
BATGIRL...
...YOU ARE UNDER ARREST FOR THE MURDER OF JAMES GORDON, JR.
GET YOUR HANDS UP.
Well. There it is again.
That voice. That "Dad voice."
I'm sorry, Dad.
But I'm all grown up now.
I SAVED YOUR LIFE TONIGHT, COMMISSIONER.
I KNOW THAT.
BUT YOU KILLED MY SON. DON'T MOVE.
...
DO YOU REMEMBER WHAT HAPPENED THAT NIGHT?
YES.
YOU THREW ONE OF THOSE DAMN BLADES OF YOURS, RIGHT AT HIS FACE.
"HE HIT THE RAIL HARD...HE WENT OVER.
"NO CHANCE OF SURVIVAL."

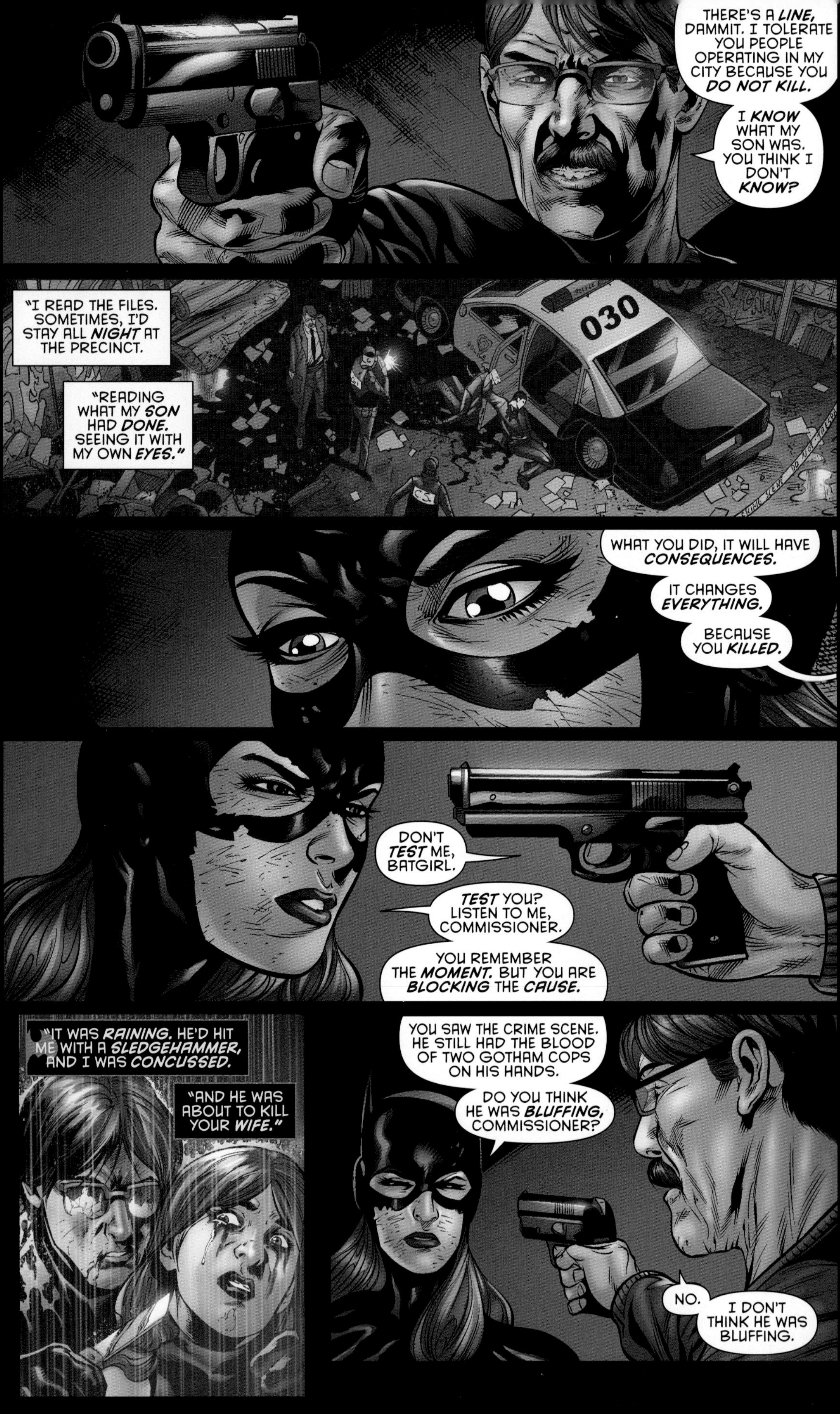
THERE'S A *LINE*, DAMMIT. I TOLERATE YOU PEOPLE OPERATING IN MY CITY BECAUSE YOU *DO NOT KILL.*
I *KNOW* WHAT MY SON WAS. YOU THINK I DON'T *KNOW?*
"I READ THE FILES. SOMETIMES, I'D STAY ALL *NIGHT* AT THE PRECINCT.
"READING WHAT MY *SON* HAD *DONE.* SEEING IT WITH MY OWN *EYES.*"
030
WHAT YOU DID, IT WILL HAVE *CONSEQUENCES.*
IT CHANGES *EVERYTHING.*
BECAUSE YOU *KILLED.*
DON'T *TEST* ME, BATGIRL.
TEST YOU? LISTEN TO ME, COMMISSIONER.
YOU REMEMBER THE *MOMENT.* BUT YOU ARE *BLOCKING* THE *CAUSE.*
"IT WAS *RAINING.* HE'D HIT ME WITH A *SLEDGEHAMMER,* AND I WAS *CONCUSSED.*
"AND HE WAS ABOUT TO KILL YOUR *WIFE.*"
YOU SAW THE CRIME SCENE. HE STILL HAD THE BLOOD OF TWO GOTHAM COPS ON HIS HANDS.
DO YOU THINK HE WAS *BLUFFING,* COMMISSIONER?
NO.
I DON'T THINK HE WAS BLUFFING.

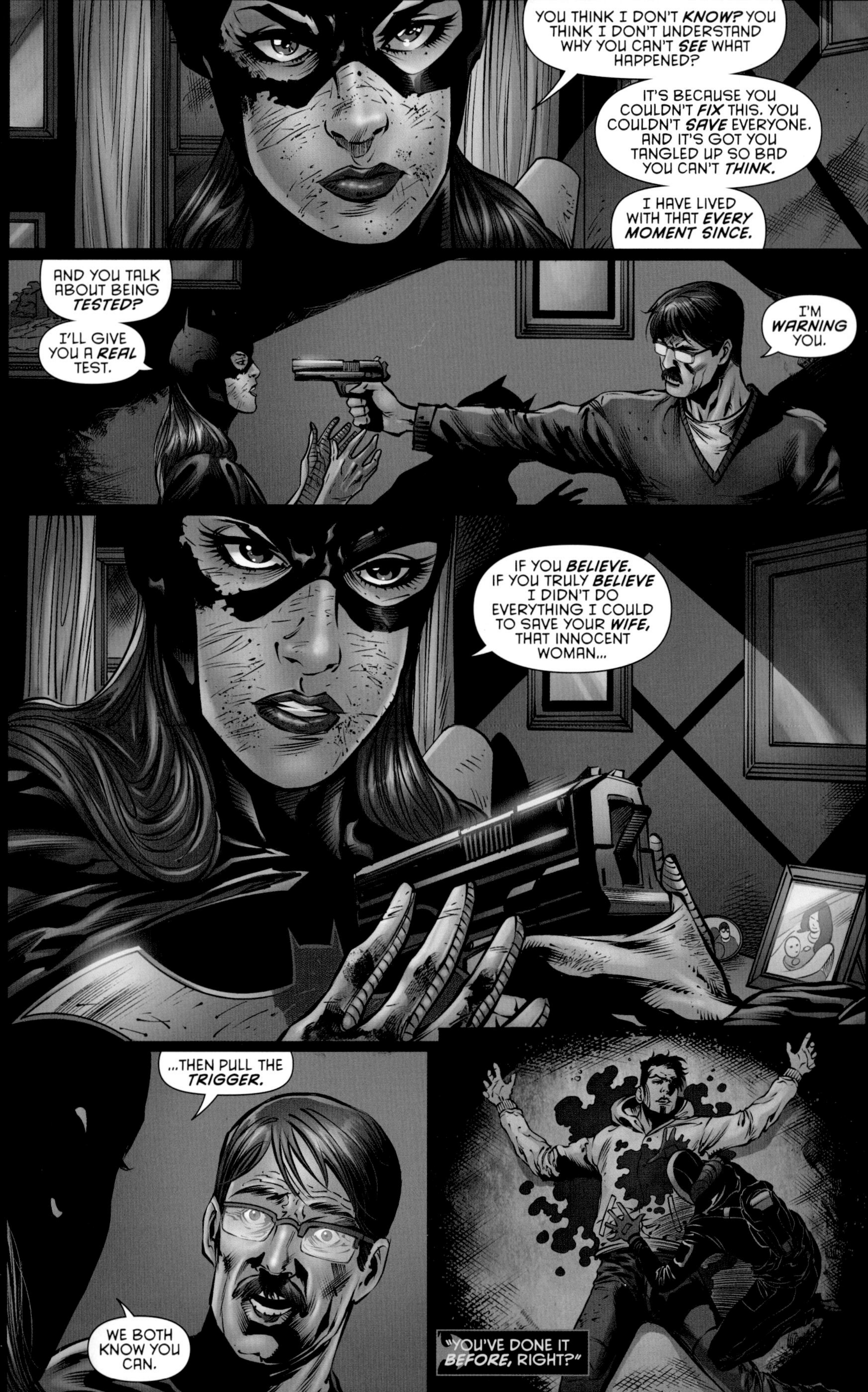
YOU THINK I DON'T KNOW? YOU THINK I DON'T UNDERSTAND WHY YOU CAN'T SEE WHAT HAPPENED?
IT'S BECAUSE YOU COULDN'T FIX THIS. YOU COULDN'T SAVE EVERYONE. AND IT'S GOT YOU TANGLED UP SO BAD YOU CAN'T THINK.
I HAVE LIVED WITH THAT EVERY MOMENT SINCE.
AND YOU TALK ABOUT BEING TESTED?
I'LL GIVE YOU A REAL TEST.
I'M WARNING YOU.
IF YOU BELIEVE. IF YOU TRULY BELIEVE I DIDN'T DO EVERYTHING I COULD TO SAVE YOUR WIFE, THAT INNOCENT WOMAN...
...THEN PULL THE TRIGGER.
WE BOTH KNOW YOU CAN.
"YOU'VE DONE IT BEFORE, RIGHT?"

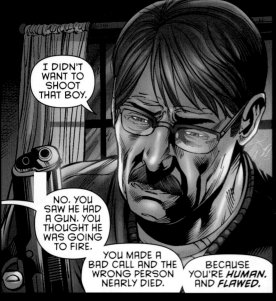

I DIDN'T WANT TO SHOOT THAT BOY.

NO. YOU SAW HE HAD A GUN. YOU THOUGHT HE WAS GOING TO FIRE.

YOU MADE A BAD CALL AND THE WRONG PERSON NEARLY DIED.

BECAUSE YOU'RE *HUMAN*. AND *FLAWED*.

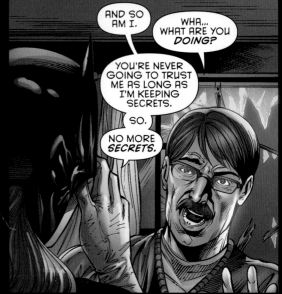

AND SO AM I.

WHA... WHAT ARE YOU *DOING*?

YOU'RE NEVER GOING TO TRUST ME AS LONG AS I'M KEEPING SECRETS.

SO.

NO MORE *SECRETS*.

STOP IT. I DON'T *WANT* TO KNOW.

WHAT?

I DON'T *WANT* TO *KNOW*!

DO YOU THINK I'M A FOOL? I'M A COP. A *GOOD* COP.

IF I'D *WANTED* TO KNOW WHO WAS UNDER ALL THOSE CAPES, I WOULD MAKE IT MY *BUSINESS*.

I'M NOT GOING TO ARREST YOU. FOR NOW.

BUT YOU AREN'T *WELCOME* HERE. EVER.

I...

I should be happy.

GO.

My father no longer thinks I'm a murderer.

But...here I am, ready to share my deepest secret.

Who I really am.

What I really am in the dark.

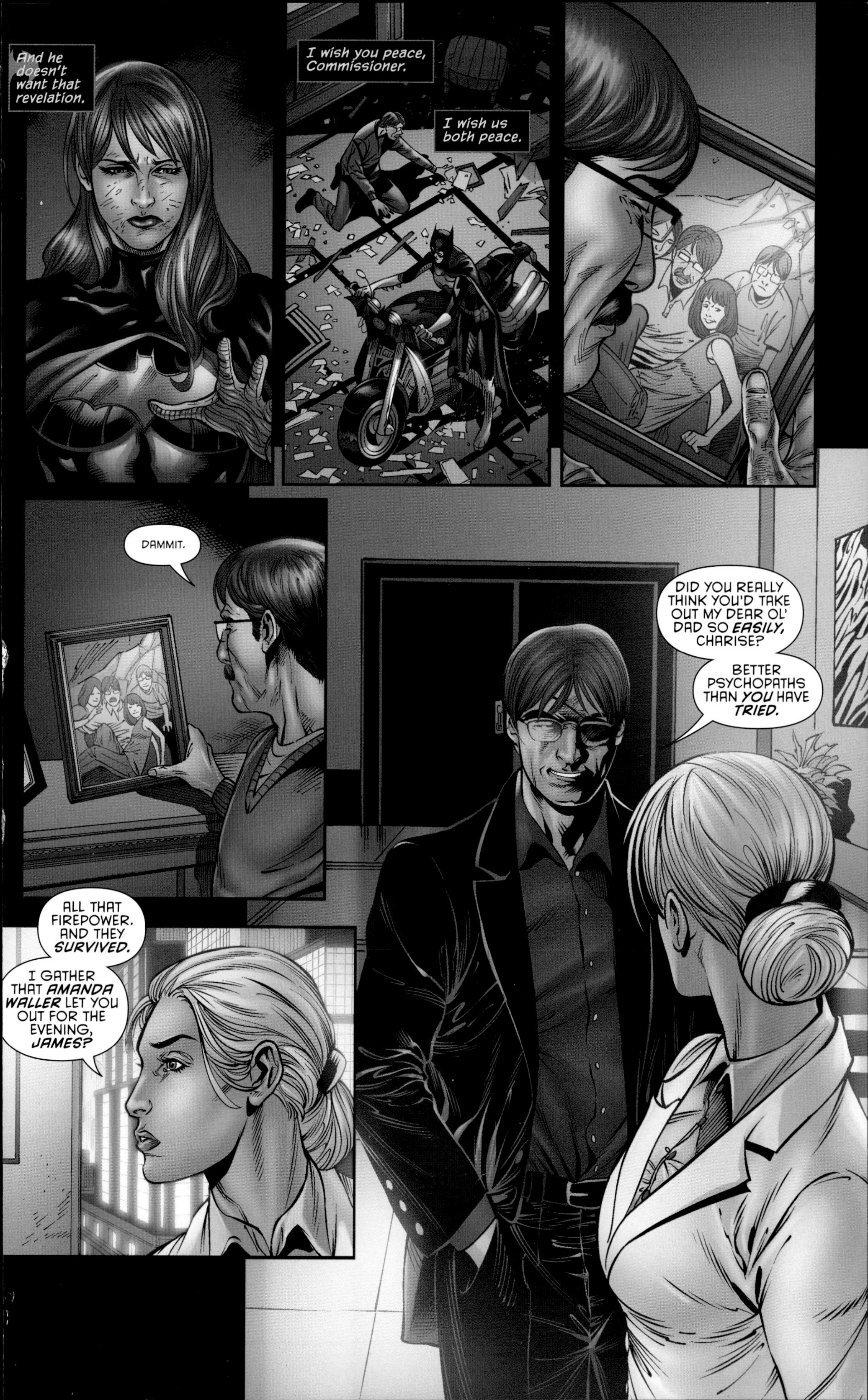
And he doesn't want that revelation.
I wish you peace, Commissioner.
I wish us both peace.
DAMMIT.
DID YOU REALLY THINK YOU'D TAKE OUT MY DEAR OL' DAD SO EASILY, CHARISE?
BETTER PSYCHOPATHS THAN YOU HAVE TRIED.
ALL THAT FIREPOWER. AND THEY SURVIVED.
I GATHER THAT AMANDA WALLER LET YOU OUT FOR THE EVENING, JAMES?

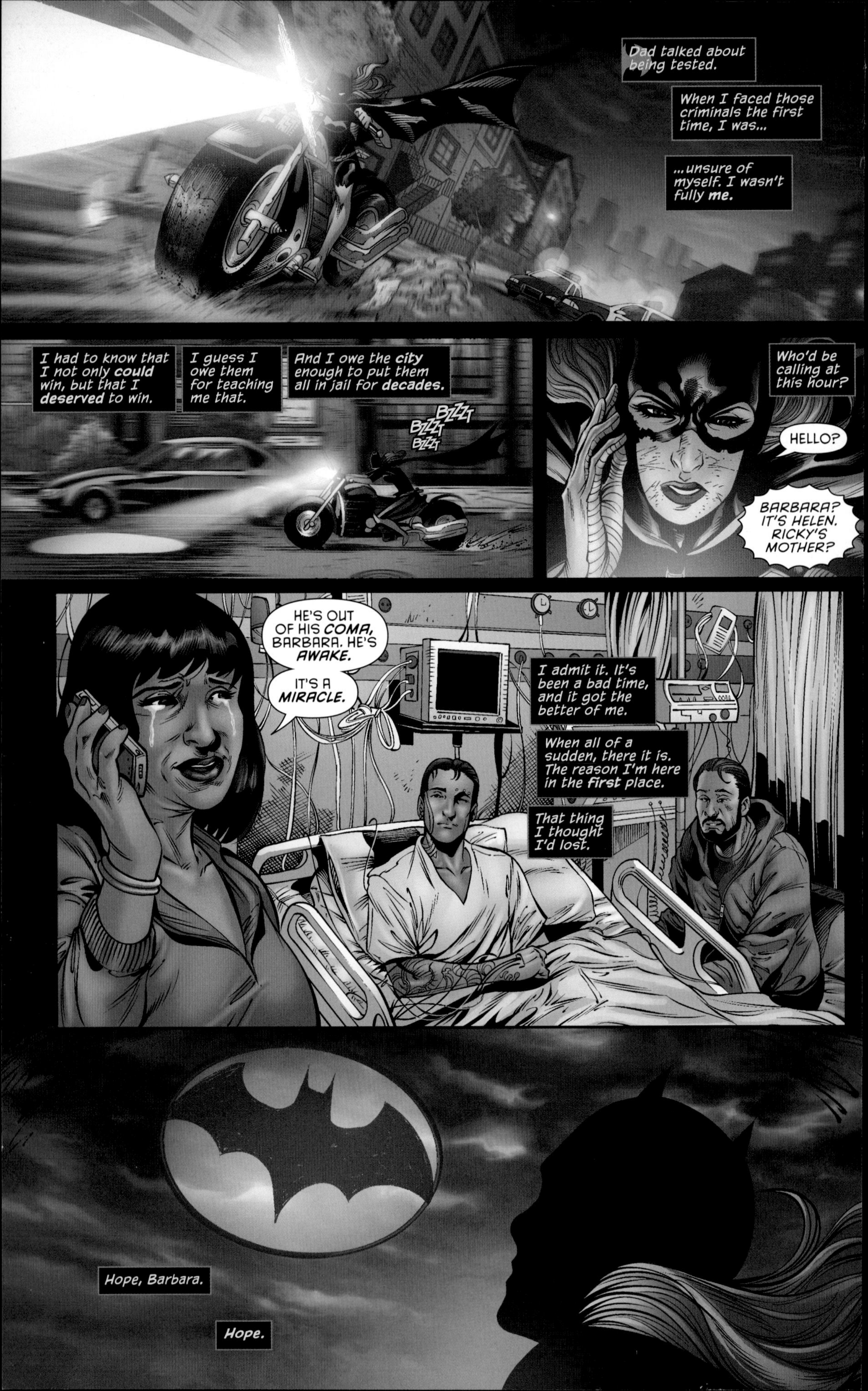
Dad talked about being tested.
When I faced those criminals the first time, I was...
...unsure of myself. I wasn't fully **me.**
I had to know that I not only **could** win, but that I **deserved** to win.
I guess I owe them for teaching me that.
And I owe the **city** enough to put them all in jail for **decades.**
BZZZT BZZZT BZZZT
Who'd be calling at this hour?
HELLO?
BARBARA? IT'S HELEN. RICKY'S MOTHER?
HE'S OUT OF HIS **COMA,** BARBARA. HE'S **AWAKE.**
IT'S A **MIRACLE.**
I admit it. It's been a bad time, and it got the better of me.
When all of a sudden, there it is. The reason I'm here in the **first** place.
That thing I thought I'd lost.
Hope, Barbara.
Hope.

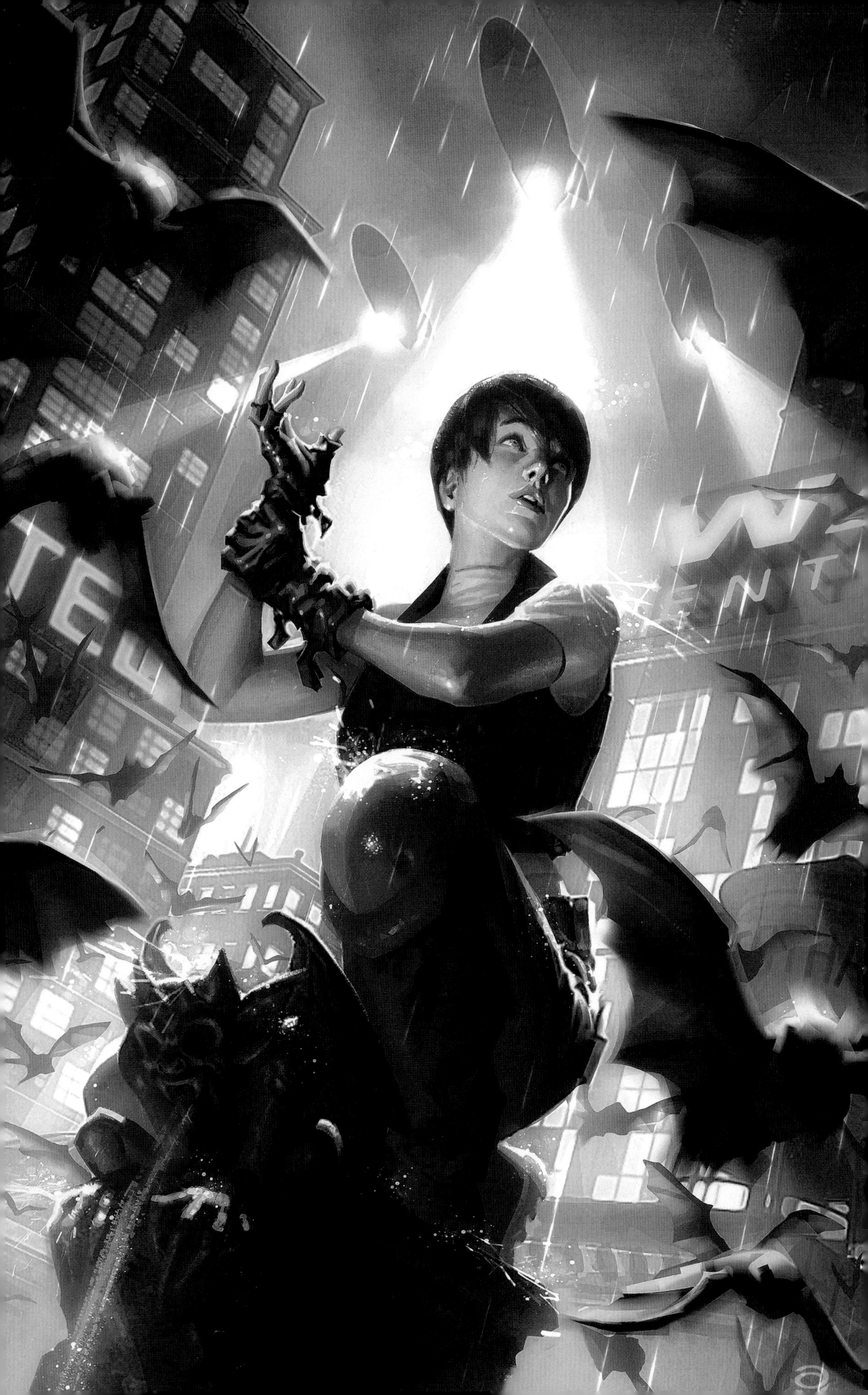

HOMESTEAD

MARGUERITE BENNETT writer **FERNANDO PASARIN** penciller
JONATHAN GLAPION inker **BLOND** colorist cover by **ALEX GARNER**

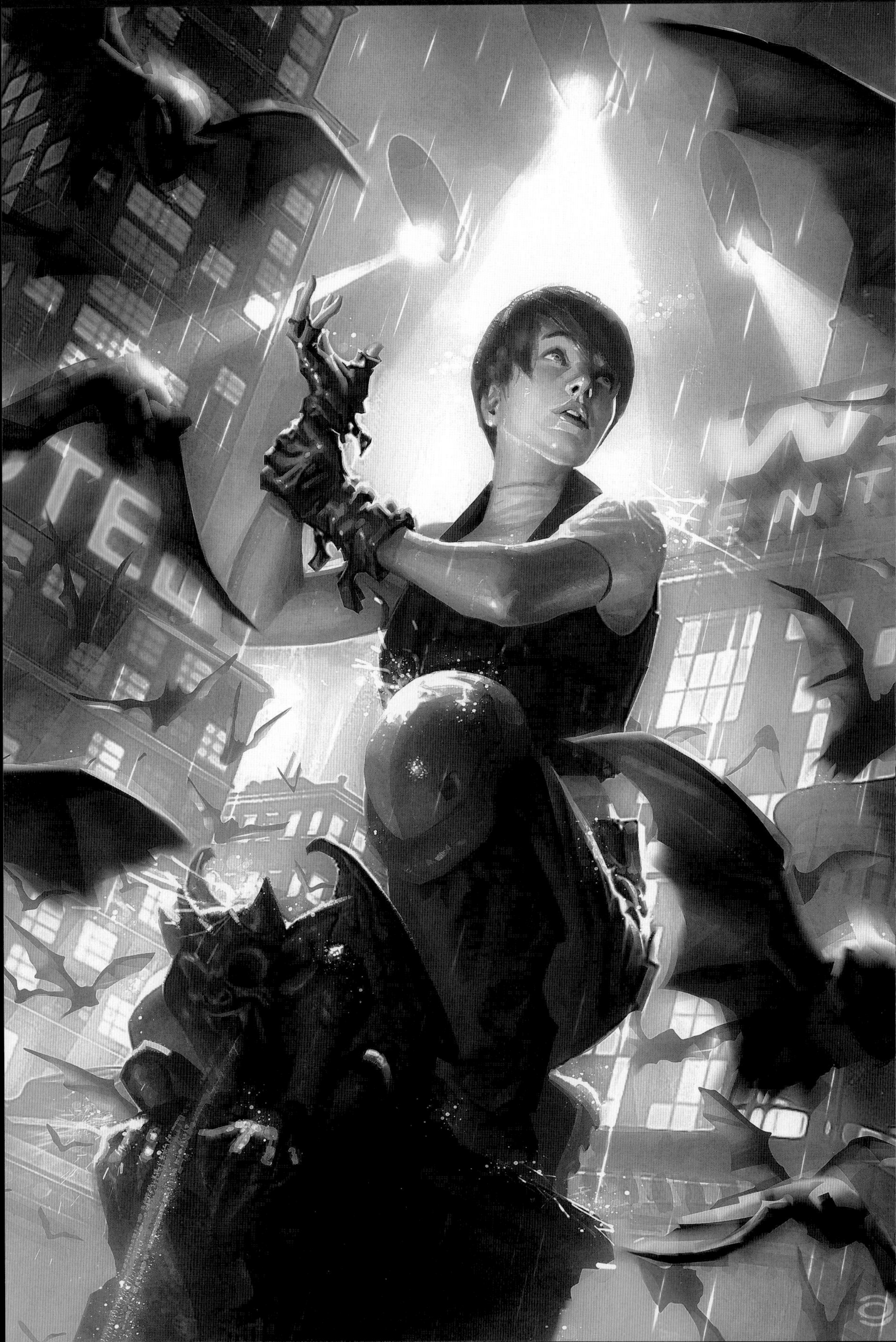

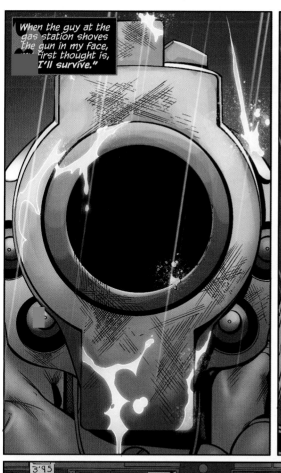

"When the guy at the gas station shoves the gun in my face, my first thought is, *I'll survive.*"

You see, at school, all my friends have these **contingency plans** for disaster.

Coley's

Gasoline Snack Shop

Service Center

Regular

Plus   4.9

   25.45

Premium   26.90

I mean, it's pretty much just action movie disaster scenarios--alien invasion, cars turning into robots, the zombie apocalypse.

You know.

The usual.

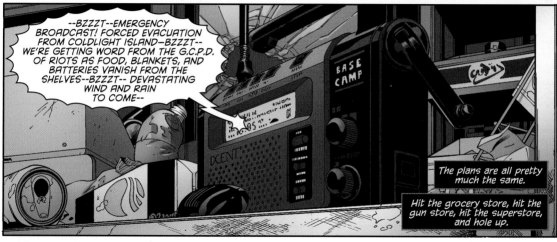

--BZZZT--EMERGENCY BROADCAST! FORCED EVACUATION FROM COLDLIGHT ISLAND--BZZZT-- WE'RE GETTING WORD FROM THE G.C.P.D. OF RIOTS AS FOOD, BLANKETS, AND BATTERIES VANISH FROM THE SHELVES--BZZZT-- DEVASTATING WIND AND RAIN TO COME--

BASE CAMP

The plans are all pretty much the same.

Hit the grocery store, hit the gun store, hit the superstore, and hole up.

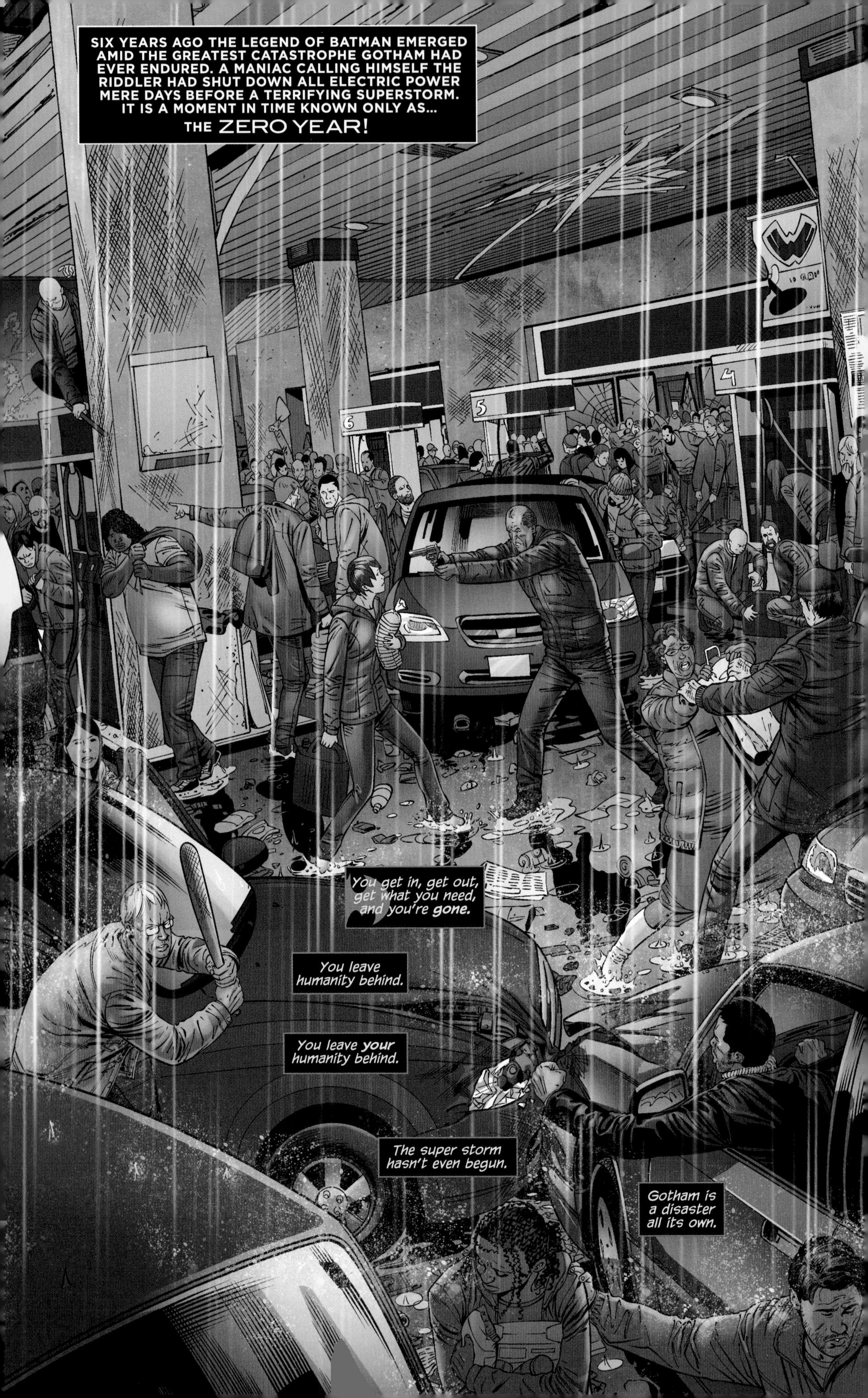
SIX YEARS AGO THE LEGEND OF BATMAN EMERGED AMID THE GREATEST CATASTROPHE GOTHAM HAD EVER ENDURED. A MANIAC CALLING HIMSELF THE RIDDLER HAD SHUT DOWN ALL ELECTRIC POWER MERE DAYS BEFORE A TERRIFYING SUPERSTORM. IT IS A MOMENT IN TIME KNOWN ONLY AS... THE ZERO YEAR!
You get in, get out, get what you need, and you're gone.
You leave humanity behind.
You leave your humanity behind.
The super storm hasn't even begun.
Gotham is a disaster all its own.

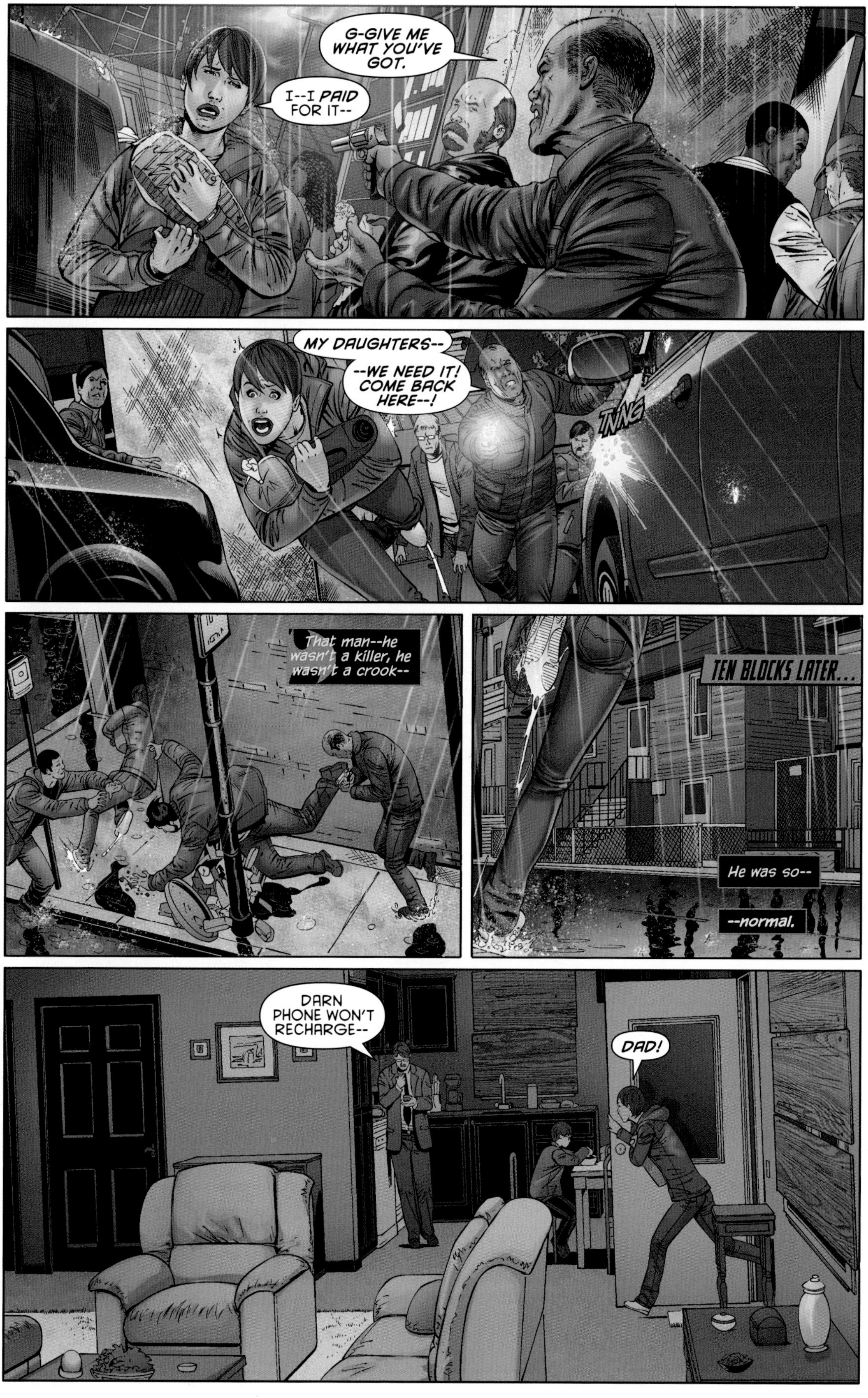
G-GIVE ME WHAT YOU'VE GOT.
I--I PAID FOR IT--
MY DAUGHTERS--
--WE NEED IT! COME BACK HERE--!
TNNG
That man--he wasn't a killer, he wasn't a crook--
TEN BLOCKS LATER...
He was so--
--normal.
DARN PHONE WON'T RECHARGE--
DAD!

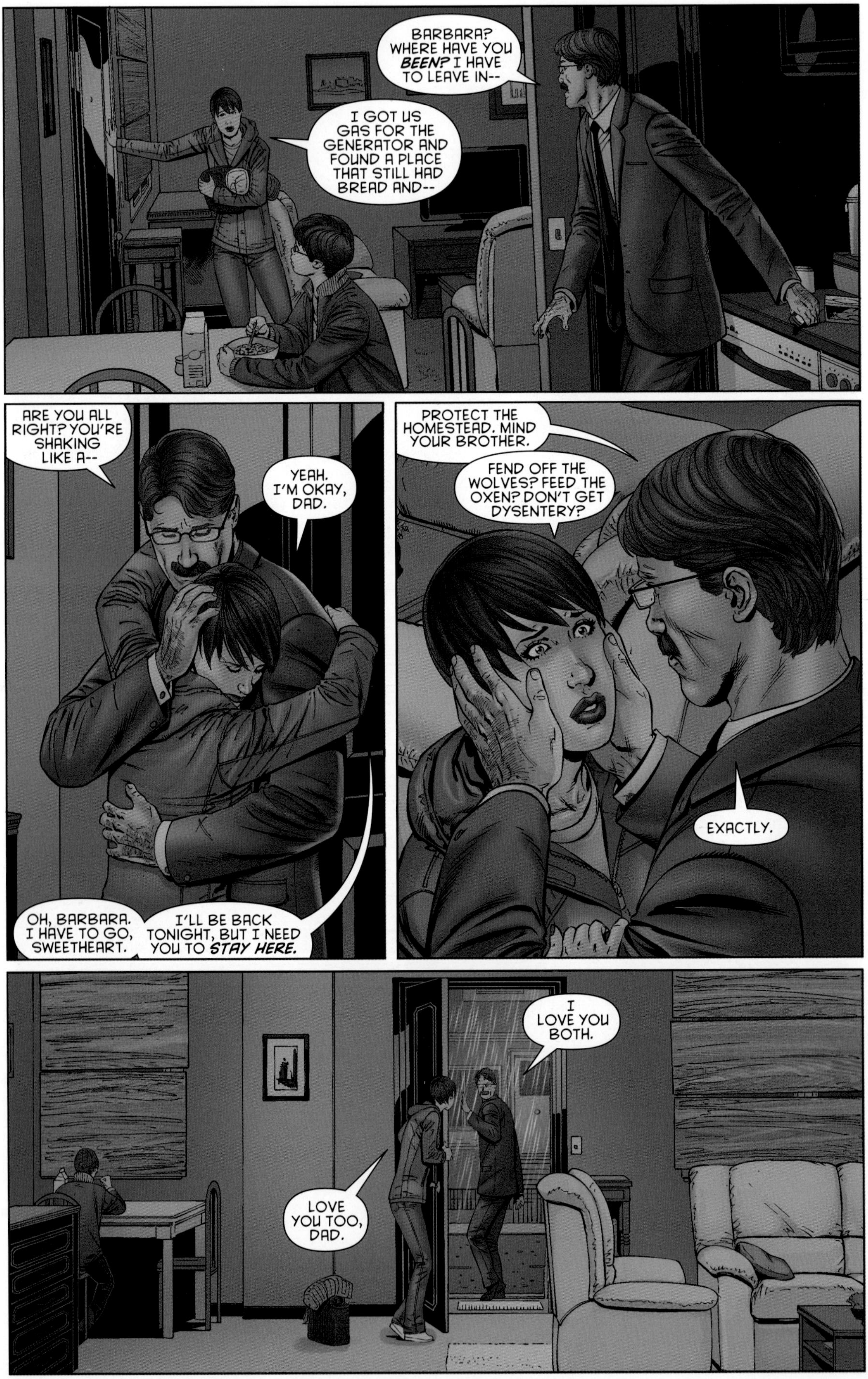
BARBARA? WHERE HAVE YOU BEEN? I HAVE TO LEAVE IN--
I GOT US GAS FOR THE GENERATOR AND FOUND A PLACE THAT STILL HAD BREAD AND--
ARE YOU ALL RIGHT? YOU'RE SHAKING LIKE A--
YEAH. I'M OKAY, DAD.
OH, BARBARA. I HAVE TO GO, SWEETHEART.
I'LL BE BACK TONIGHT, BUT I NEED YOU TO STAY HERE.
PROTECT THE HOMESTEAD. MIND YOUR BROTHER.
FEND OFF THE WOLVES? FEED THE OXEN? DON'T GET DYSENTERY?
EXACTLY.
I LOVE YOU BOTH.
LOVE YOU TOO, DAD.

My contingency plan isn't great, admittedly.

Move everything breakable to the center of the house. Duct tape everything that leaks. Hammer plywood over the windows.

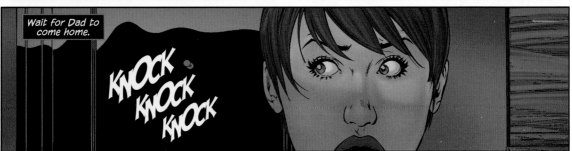

Wait for Dad to come home.

KNOCK KNOCK KNOCK

EXCUSE ME, BARBARA--

OFFICER PETERS! DID MY DAD--?

SORRY, BARBARA, NO.

THE STORM'S ESCALATED, ENOUGH TO PUT YOUR HOUSE IN AN EXTENDED FLOOD ZONE. WE HAVE TO ASK YOU TO EVACUATE TO HIGHER GROUND.

PLEASE GATHER *ONLY WHAT YOU NEED* AND COME OUTSIDE IMMEDIATELY--

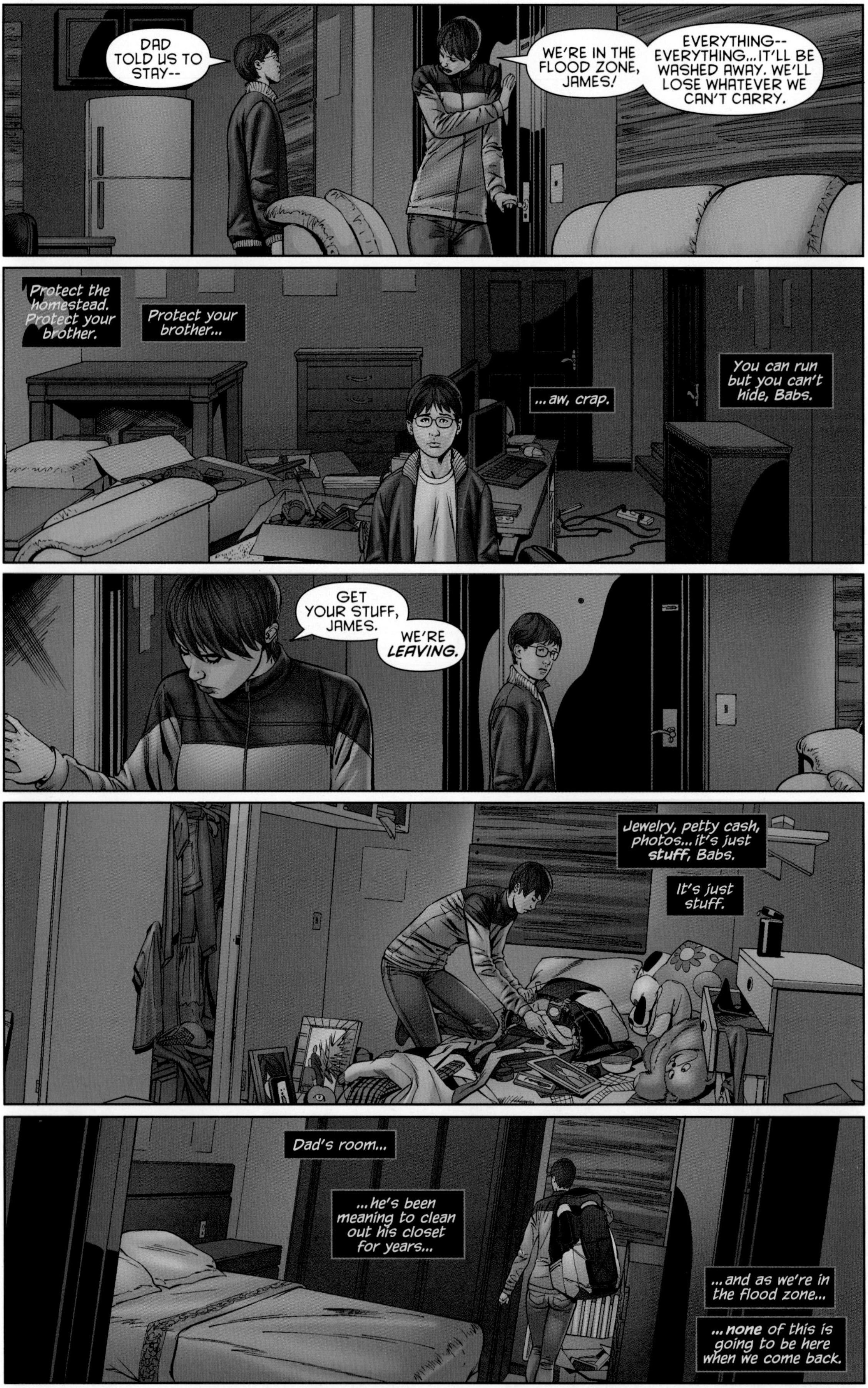
DAD TOLD US TO STAY--
WE'RE IN THE FLOOD ZONE, JAMES!
EVERYTHING-- EVERYTHING...IT'LL BE WASHED AWAY. WE'LL LOSE WHATEVER WE CAN'T CARRY.
Protect the homestead. Protect your brother.
Protect your brother...
...aw, crap.
You can run but you can't hide, Babs.
GET YOUR STUFF, JAMES.
WE'RE LEAVING.
Jewelry, petty cash, photos... it's just stuff, Babs.
It's just stuff.
Dad's room...
...he's been meaning to clean out his closet for years...
...and as we're in the flood zone...
...none of this is going to be here when we come back.

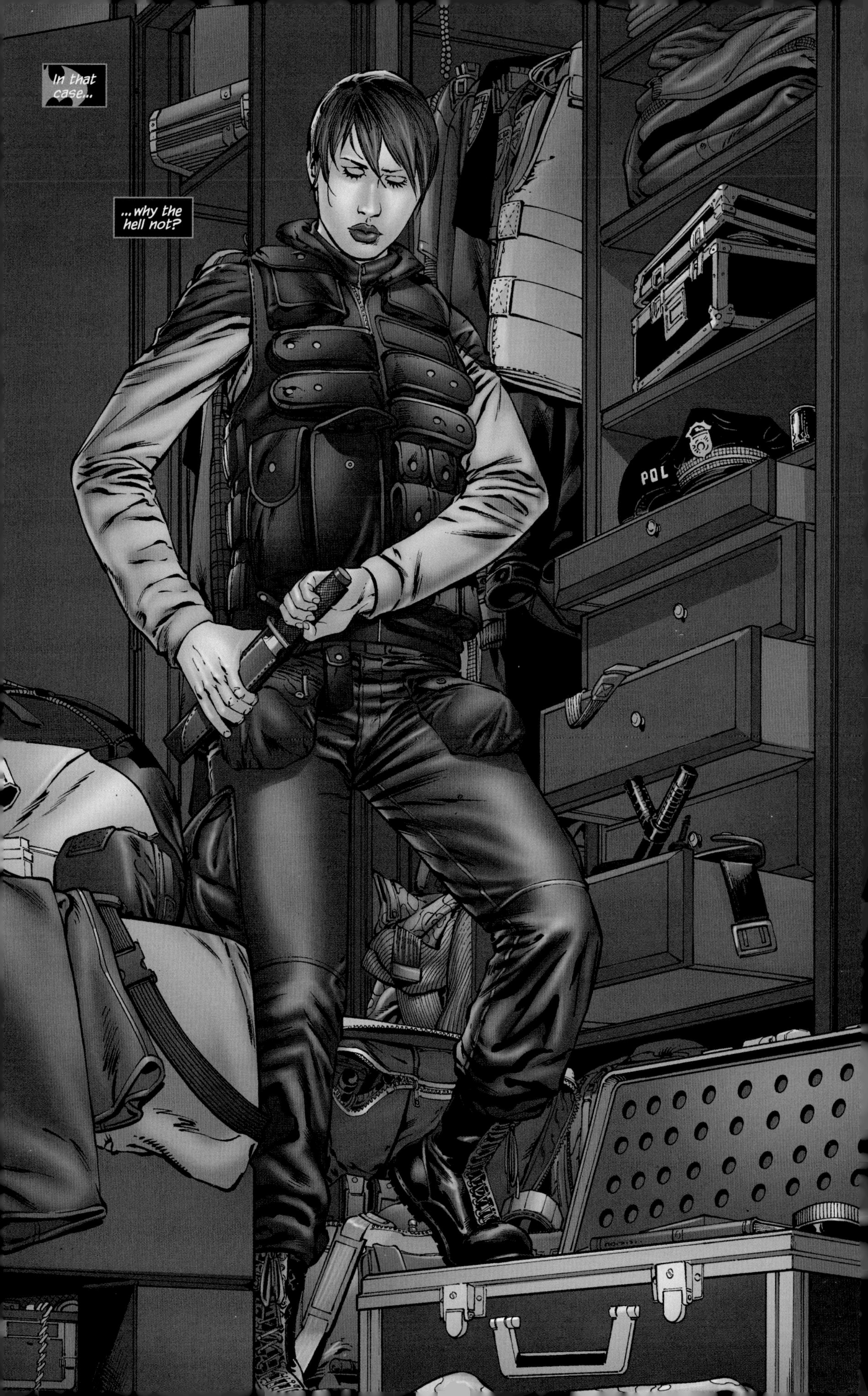
In that case...
...why the hell not?
POL

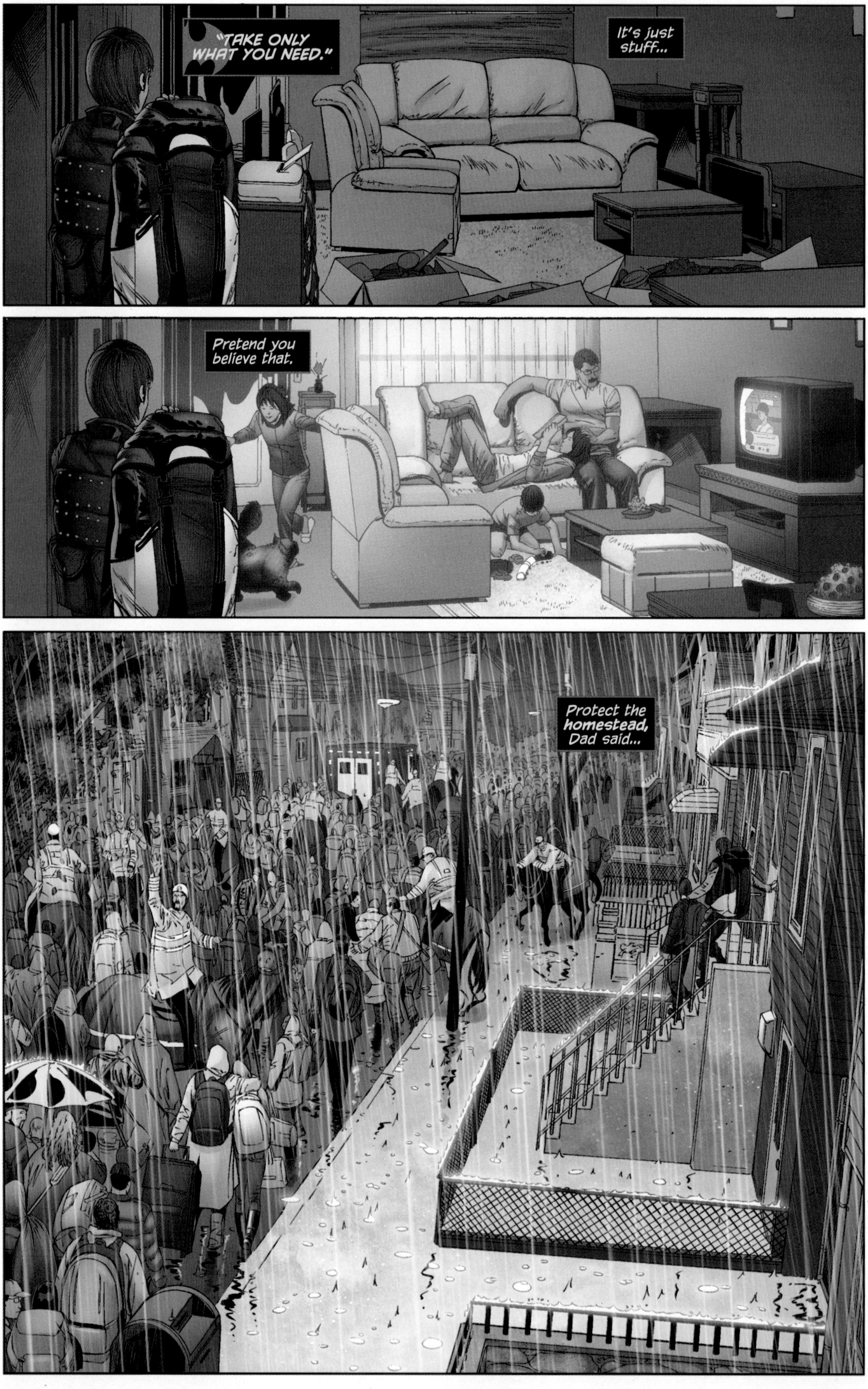
"TAKE ONLY WHAT YOU NEED."
It's just stuff...
Pretend you believe that.
Protect the homestead, Dad said...

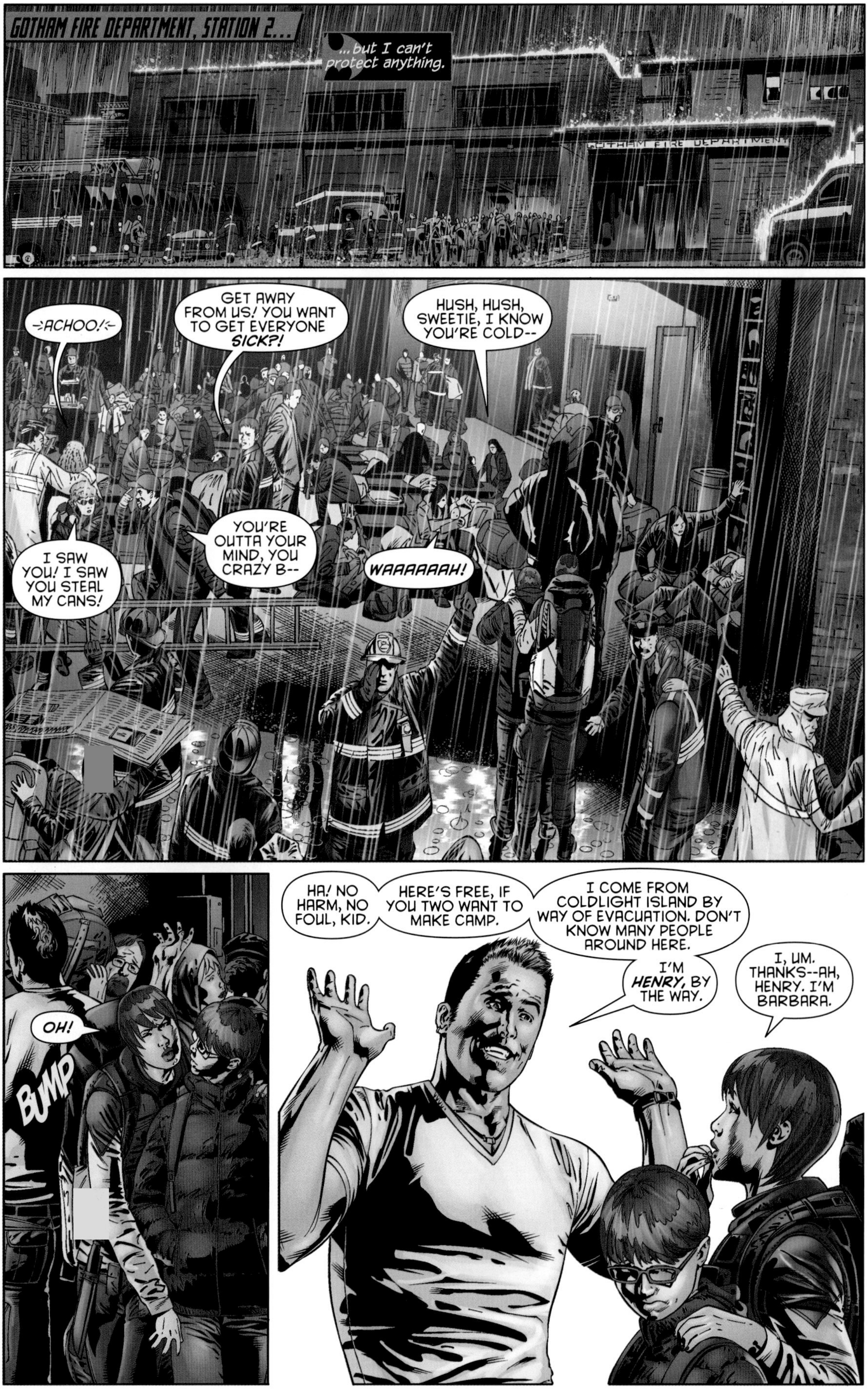
GOTHAM FIRE DEPARTMENT, STATION 2...
...but I can't protect anything.
GOTHAM FIRE DEPARTMENT
-ACHOO!-
GET AWAY FROM US! YOU WANT TO GET EVERYONE SICK?!
HUSH, HUSH, SWEETIE, I KNOW YOU'RE COLD--
I SAW YOU! I SAW YOU STEAL MY CANS!
YOU'RE OUTTA YOUR MIND, YOU CRAZY B--
WAAAAAAH!
OH!
BUMP
HA! NO HARM, NO FOUL, KID.
HERE'S FREE, IF YOU TWO WANT TO MAKE CAMP.
I COME FROM COLDLIGHT ISLAND BY WAY OF EVACUATION. DON'T KNOW MANY PEOPLE AROUND HERE.
I'M HENRY, BY THE WAY.
I, UM. THANKS--AH, HENRY. I'M BARBARA.

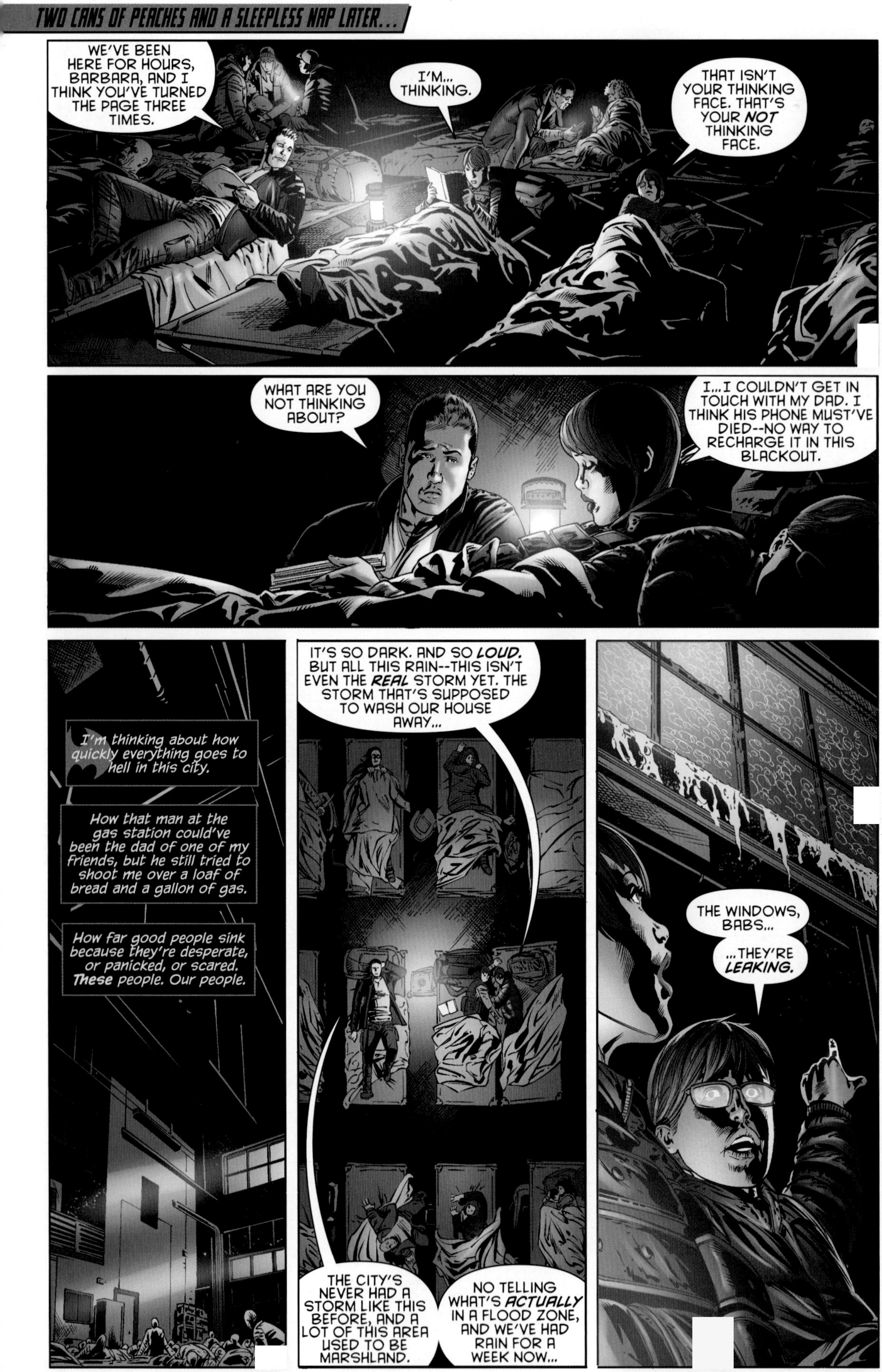
TWO CANS OF PEACHES AND A SLEEPLESS NAP LATER...
WE'VE BEEN HERE FOR HOURS, BARBARA, AND I THINK YOU'VE TURNED THE PAGE THREE TIMES.
I'M... THINKING.
THAT ISN'T YOUR THINKING FACE. THAT'S YOUR NOT THINKING FACE.
WHAT ARE YOU NOT THINKING ABOUT?
I...I COULDN'T GET IN TOUCH WITH MY DAD. I THINK HIS PHONE MUST'VE DIED--NO WAY TO RECHARGE IT IN THIS BLACKOUT.
I'm thinking about how quickly everything goes to hell in this city.
How that man at the gas station could've been the dad of one of my friends, but he still tried to shoot me over a loaf of bread and a gallon of gas.
How far good people sink because they're desperate, or panicked, or scared. These people. Our people.
IT'S SO DARK. AND SO LOUD. BUT ALL THIS RAIN--THIS ISN'T EVEN THE REAL STORM YET. THE STORM THAT'S SUPPOSED TO WASH OUR HOUSE AWAY...
THE CITY'S NEVER HAD A STORM LIKE THIS BEFORE, AND A LOT OF THIS AREA USED TO BE MARSHLAND.
NO TELLING WHAT'S ACTUALLY IN A FLOOD ZONE, AND WE'VE HAD RAIN FOR A WEEK NOW...
THE WINDOWS, BABS...
...THEY'RE LEAKING.

IT'S ALL RIGHT, KID. WE JUST HAVE TO WORRY ABOUT THE ROOF HOLDING--

NO--

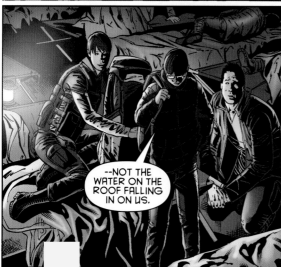

--NOT THE WATER ON THE ROOF FALLING IN ON US.

THE WATER RISING FROM THE *FOUNDATION.*

CRRRRRK CRRRK CRRRRRK

A sinkhole!

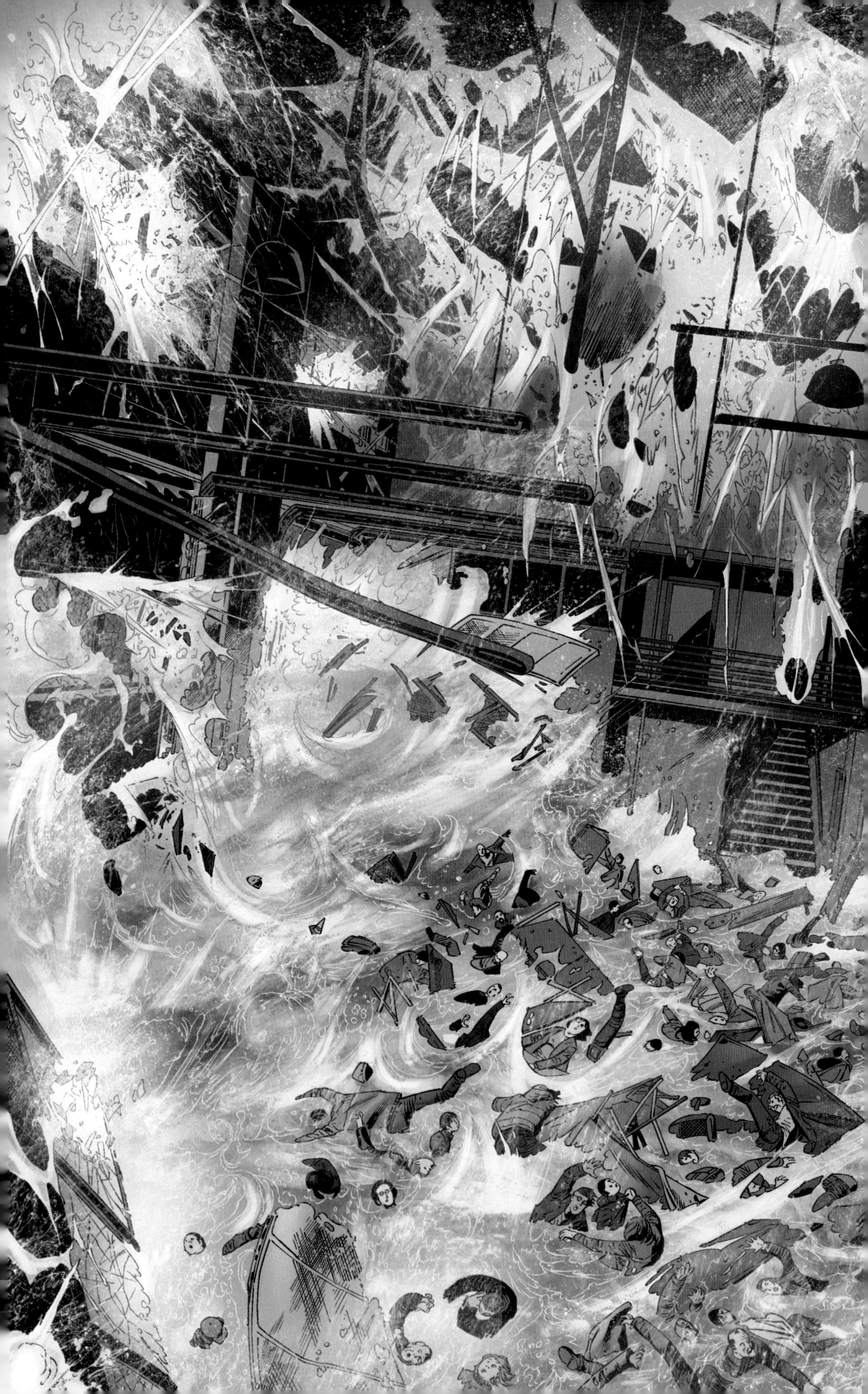

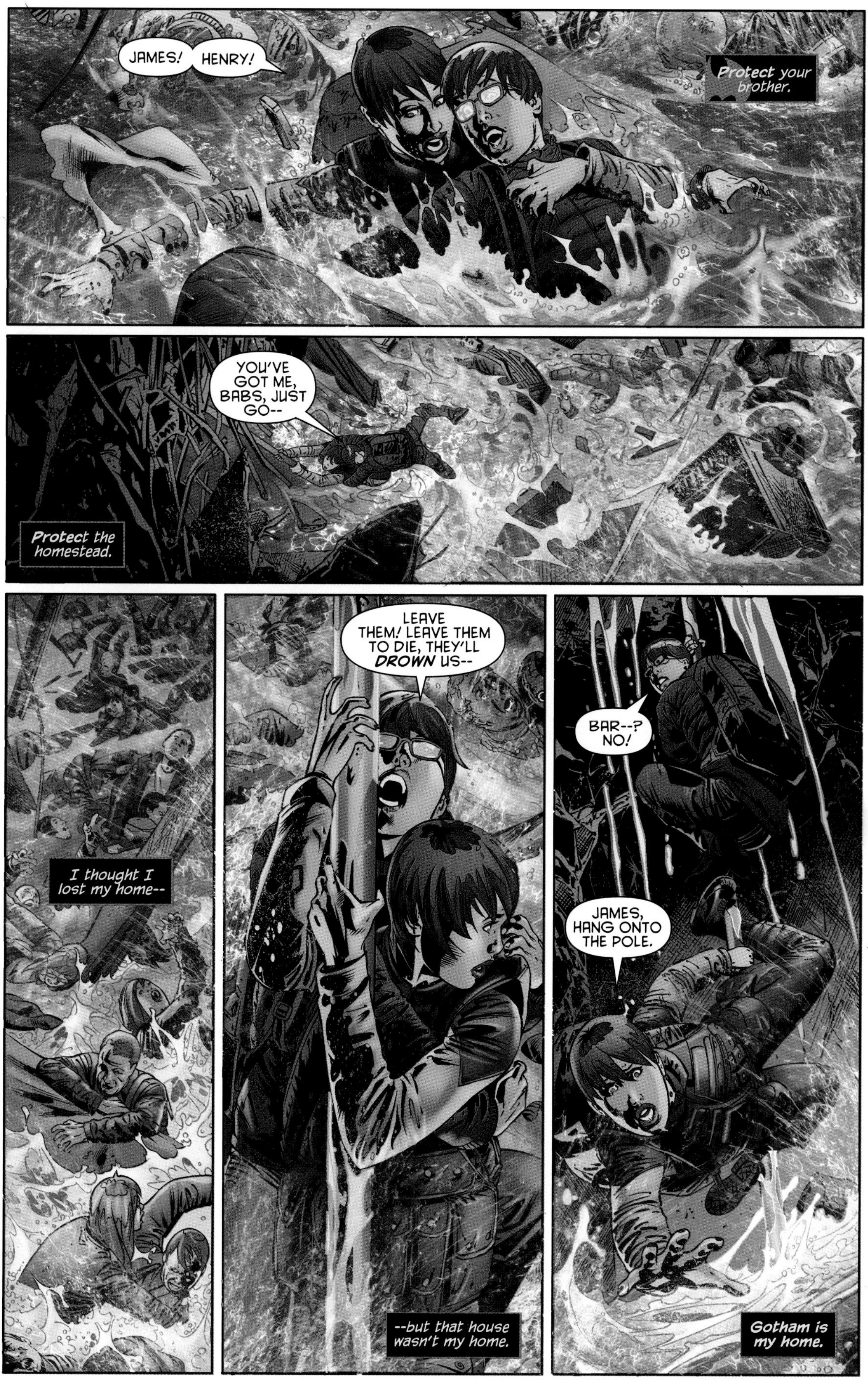
JAMES!
HENRY!
Protect your brother.
YOU'VE GOT ME, BABS, JUST GO--
Protect the homestead.
I thought I lost my home--
LEAVE THEM! LEAVE THEM TO DIE, THEY'LL DROWN US--
--but that house wasn't my home.
BAR--? NO!
JAMES, HANG ONTO THE POLE.
Gotham is my home.

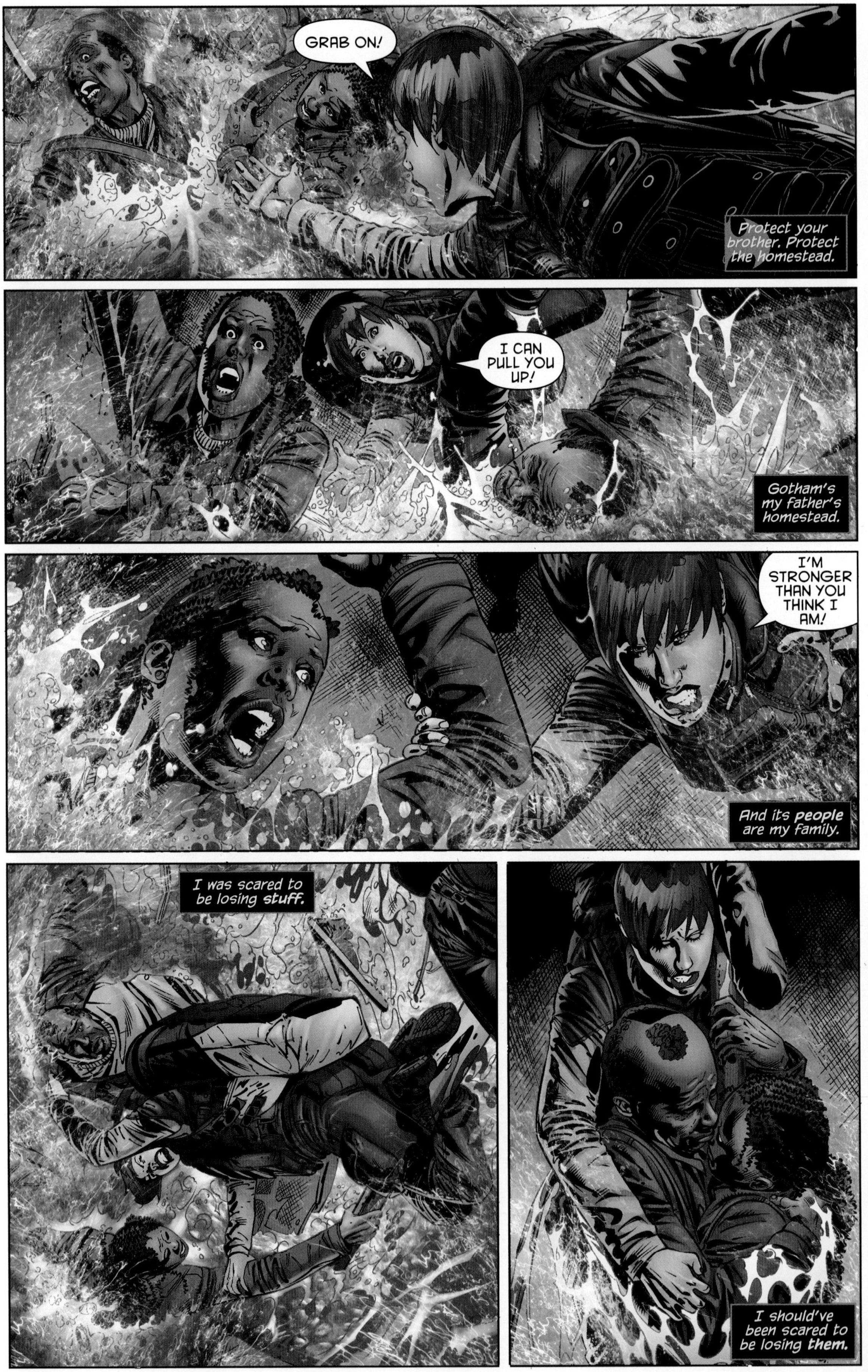
GRAB ON!
Protect your brother. Protect the homestead.
I CAN PULL YOU UP!
Gotham's my father's homestead.
I'M STRONGER THAN YOU THINK I AM!
And its people are my family.
I was scared to be losing stuff.
I should've been scared to be losing them.

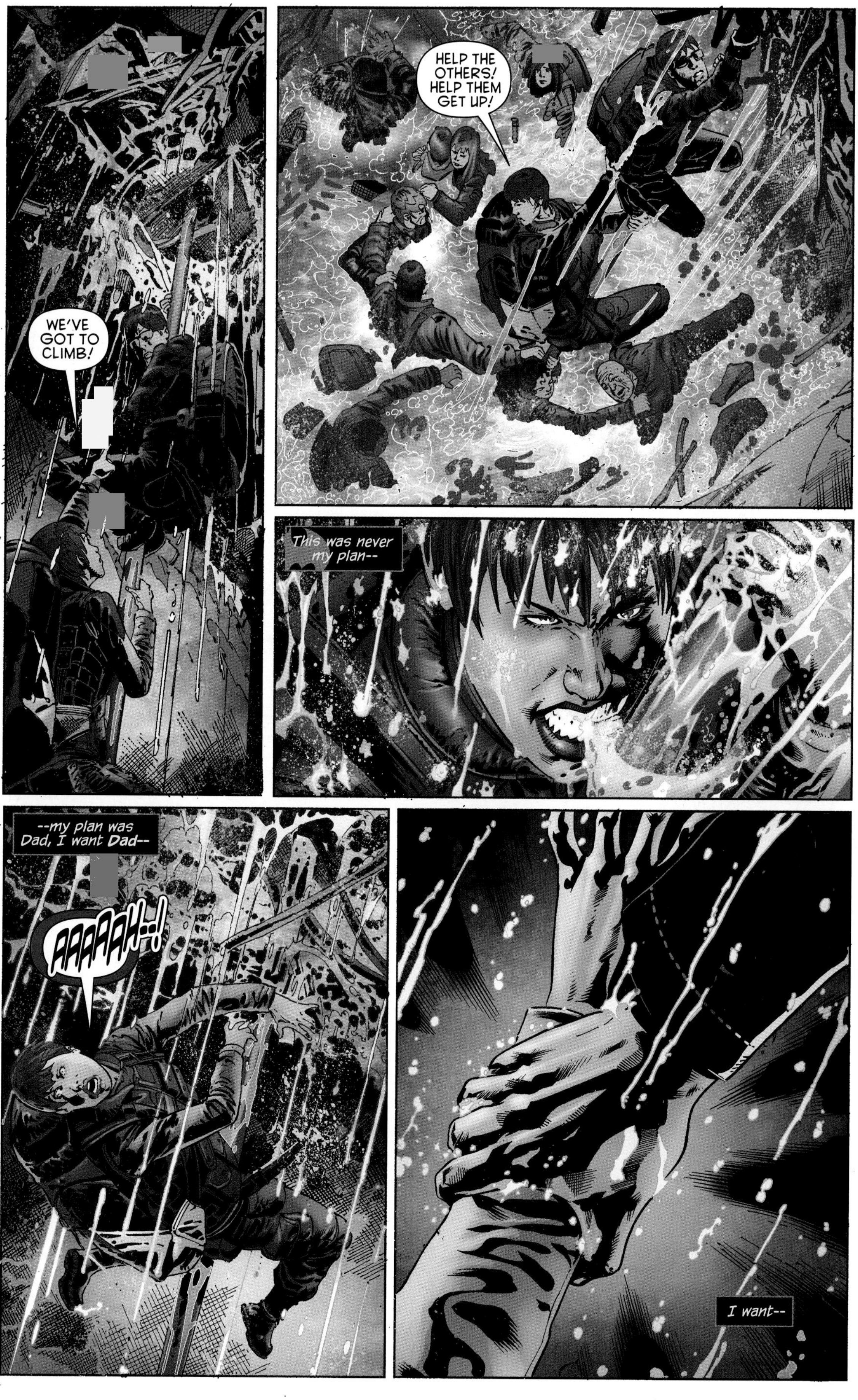
WE'VE GOT TO CLIMB!
HELP THE OTHERS! HELP THEM GET UP!
This was never my plan--
--my plan was Dad, I want Dad--
AAAAAH--!
I want--

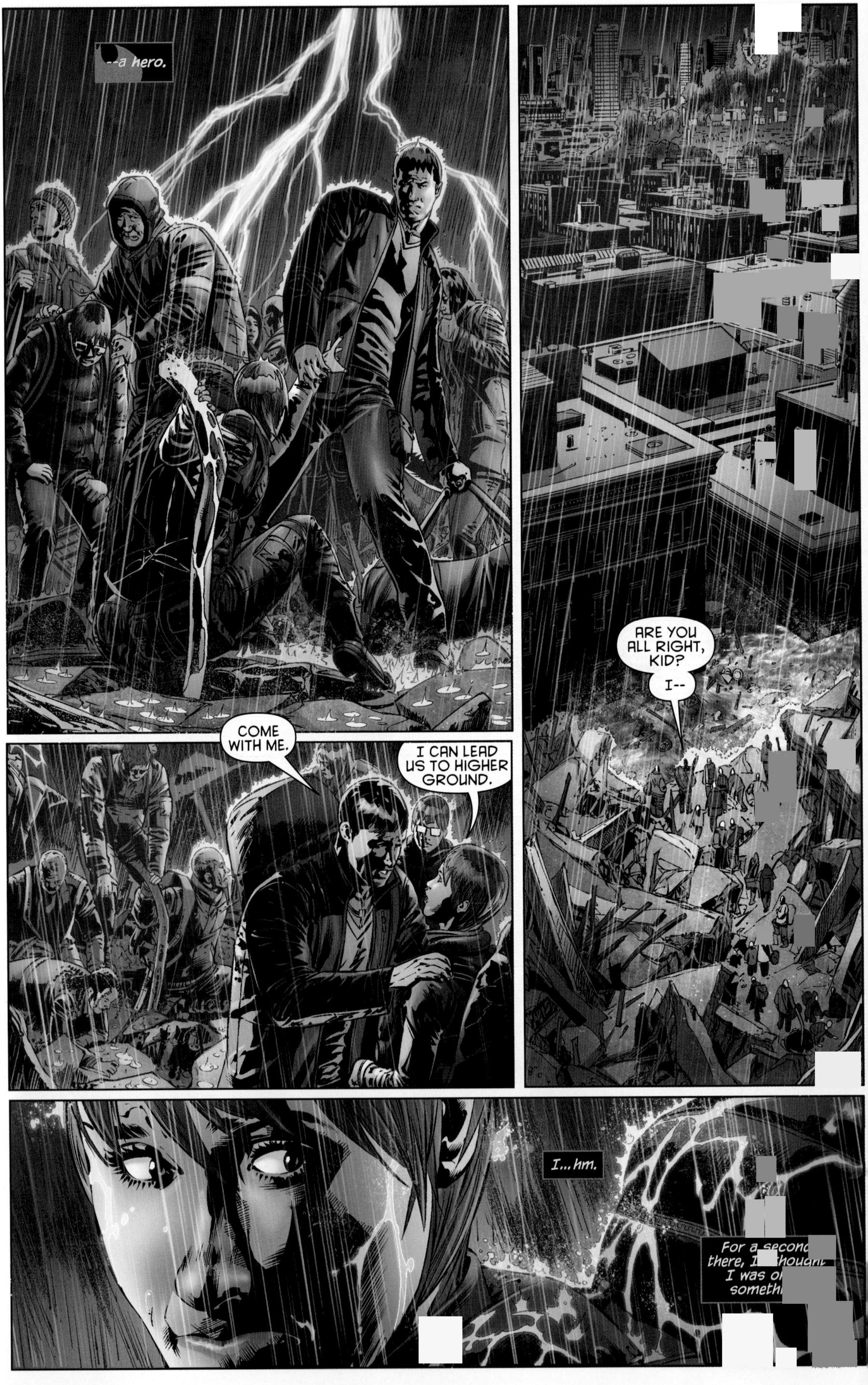
--a hero.
COME WITH ME.
I CAN LEAD US TO HIGHER GROUND.
ARE YOU ALL RIGHT, KID?
I--
I...hm.
For a secon
there, I thoug
I was o
someth

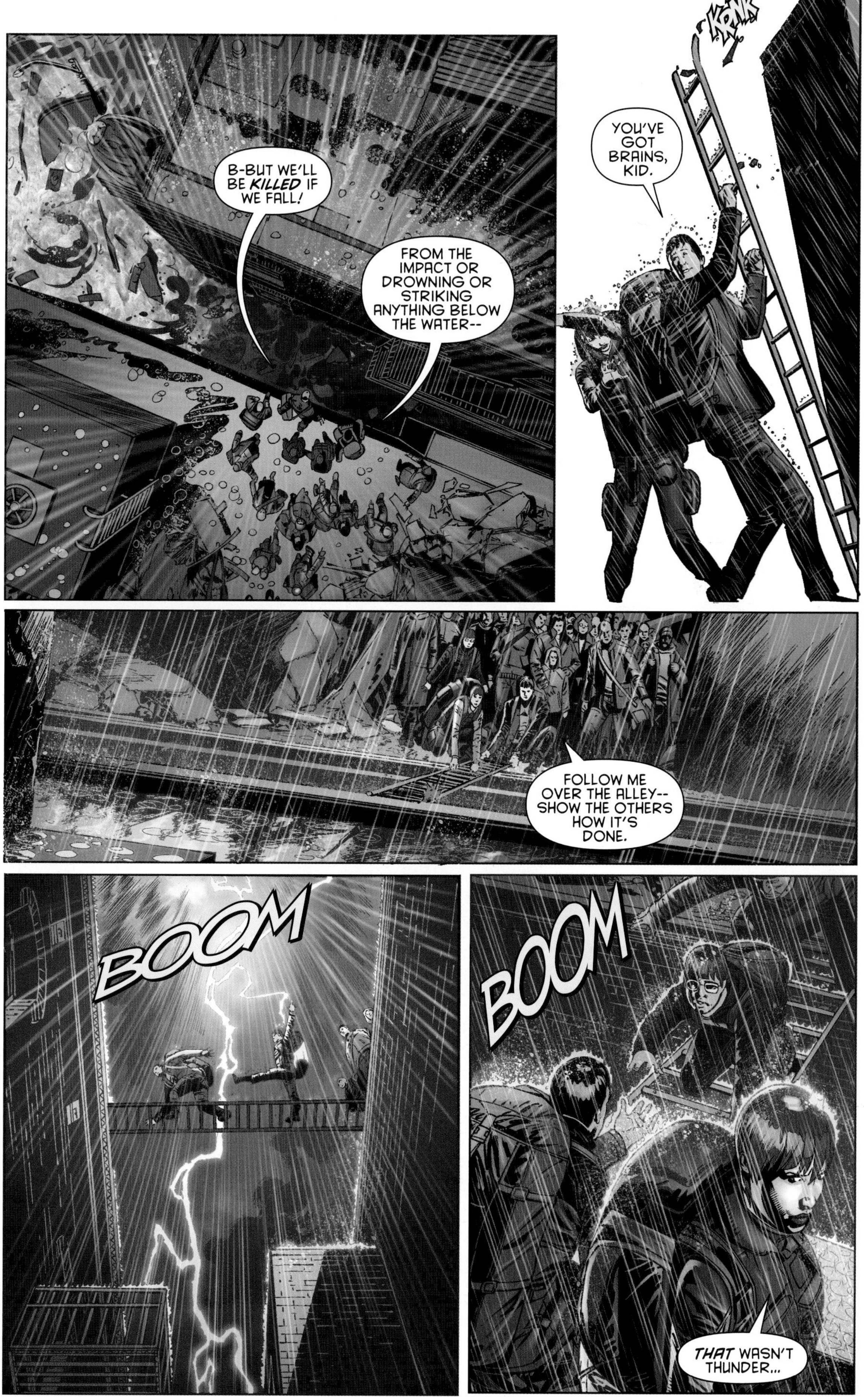
B-BUT WE'LL BE *KILLED* IF WE FALL!
FROM THE IMPACT OR DROWNING OR STRIKING ANYTHING BELOW THE WATER--
KRNK
YOU'VE GOT BRAINS, KID.
FOLLOW ME OVER THE ALLEY-- SHOW THE OTHERS HOW IT'S DONE.
BOOM
BOOM
THAT WASN'T THUNDER...

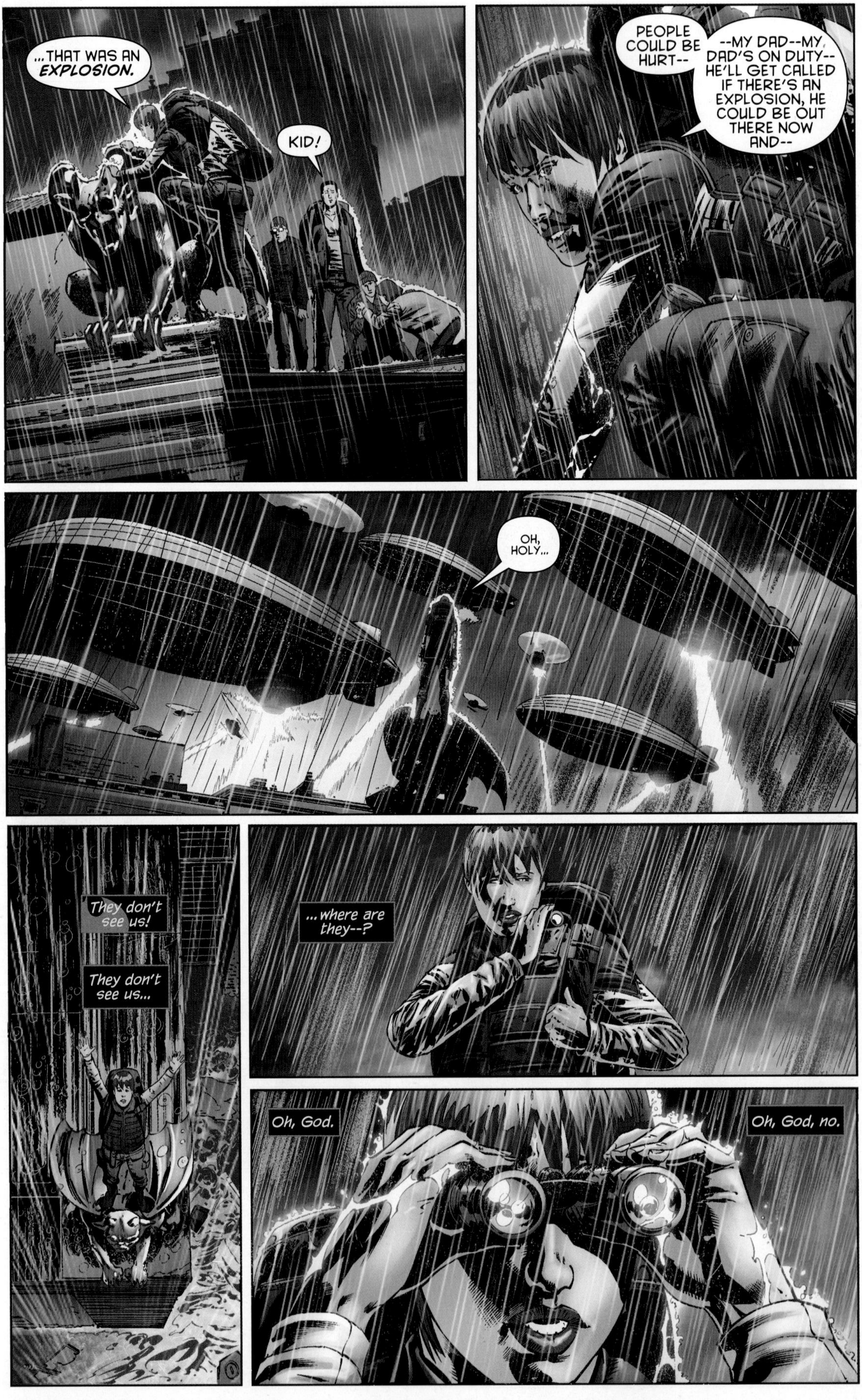
...THAT WAS AN EXPLOSION.
KID!
PEOPLE COULD BE HURT--
--MY DAD--MY DAD'S ON DUTY--HE'LL GET CALLED IF THERE'S AN EXPLOSION, HE COULD BE OUT THERE NOW AND--
OH, HOLY...
They don't see us!
They don't see us...
...where are they--?
Oh, God.
Oh, God, no.

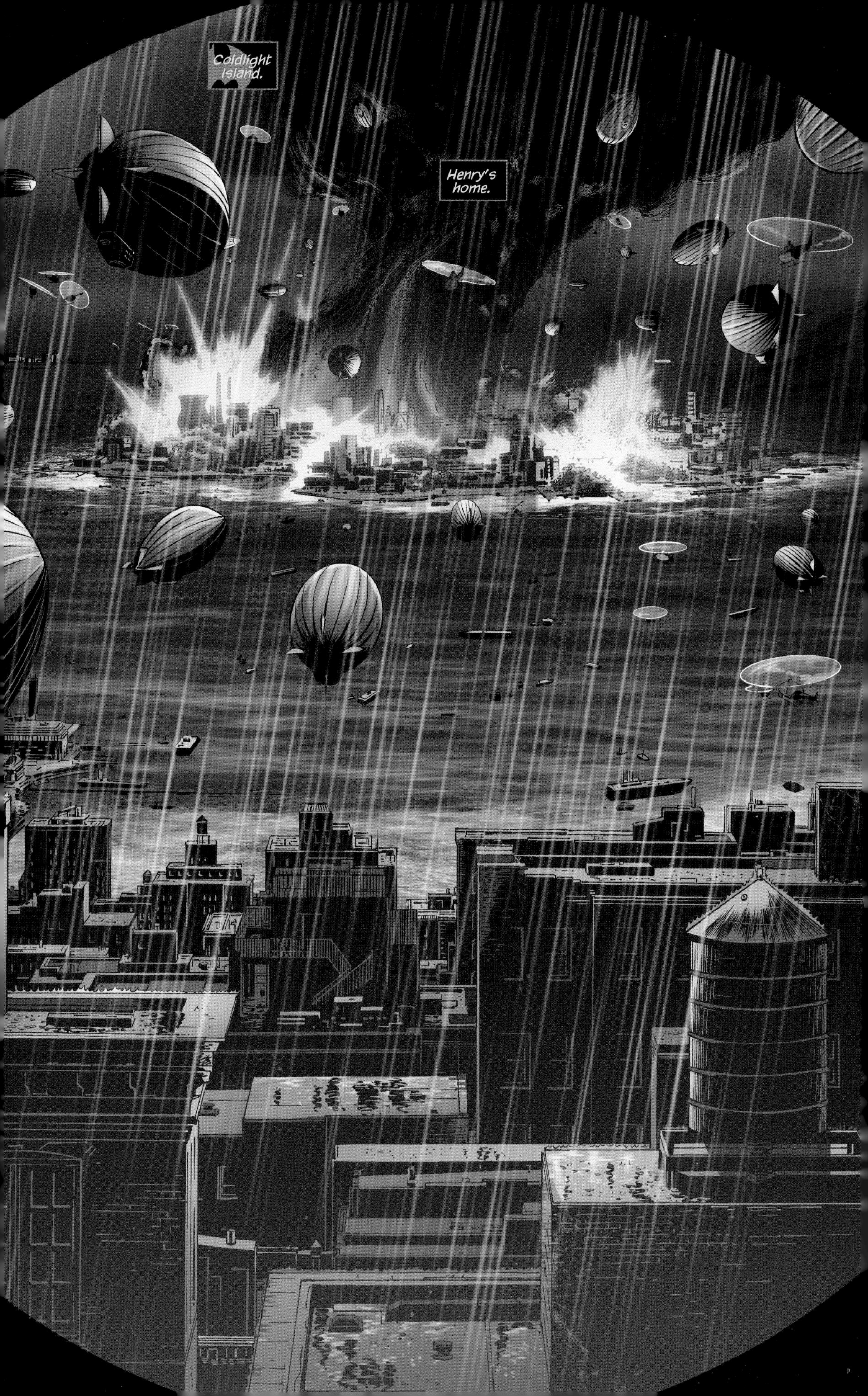
Coldlight Island.
Henry's home.

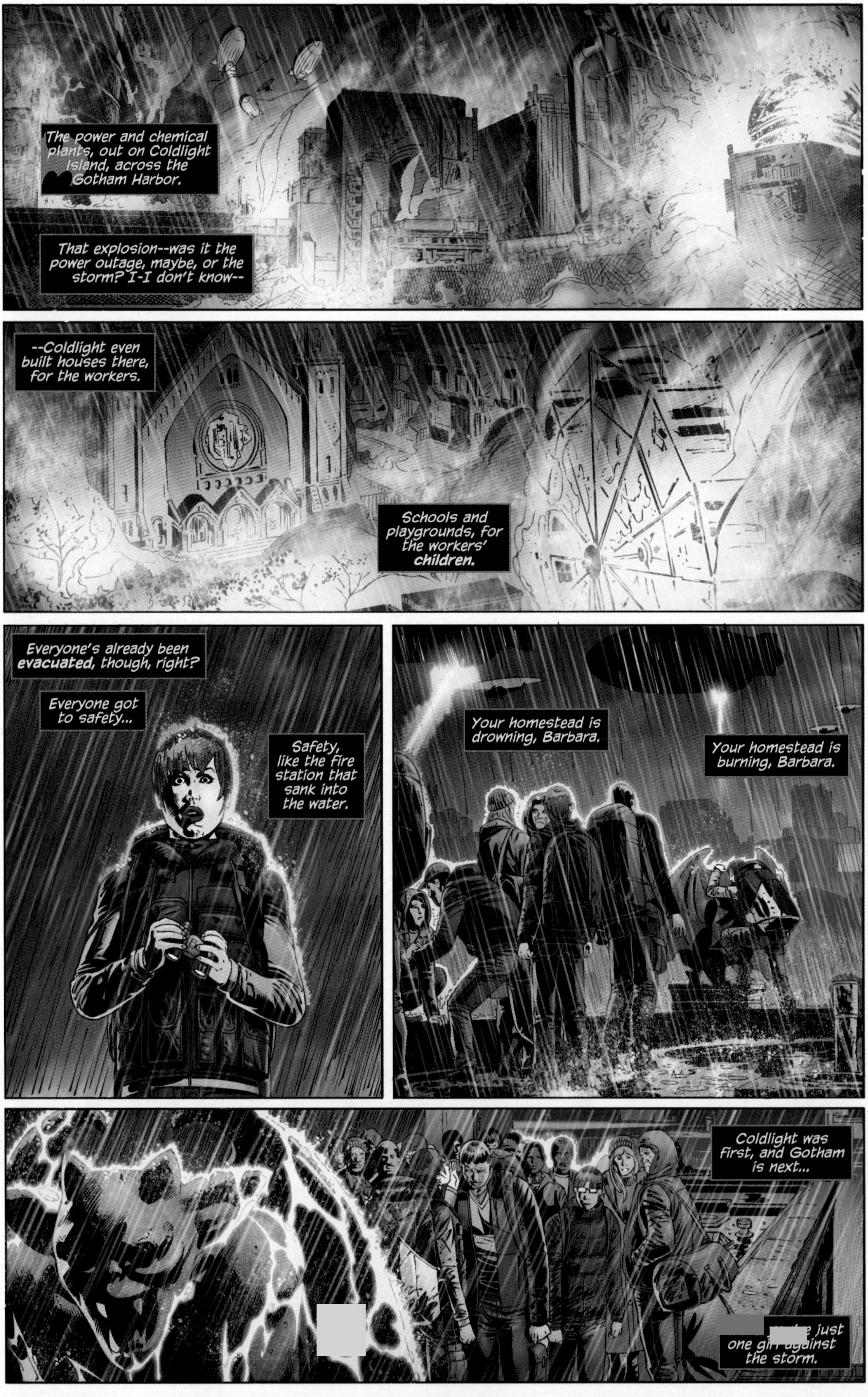
The power and chemical plants, out on Coldlight Island, across the Gotham Harbor.
That explosion--was it the power outage, maybe, or the storm? I-I don't know--
--Coldlight even built houses there, for the workers.
Schools and playgrounds, for the workers' **children.**
Everyone's already been **evacuated,** though, right?
Everyone got to safety...
Safety, like the fire station that sank into the water.
Your homestead is drowning, Barbara.
Your homestead is burning, Barbara.
Coldlight was first, and Gotham is next...
just one girl against the storm.

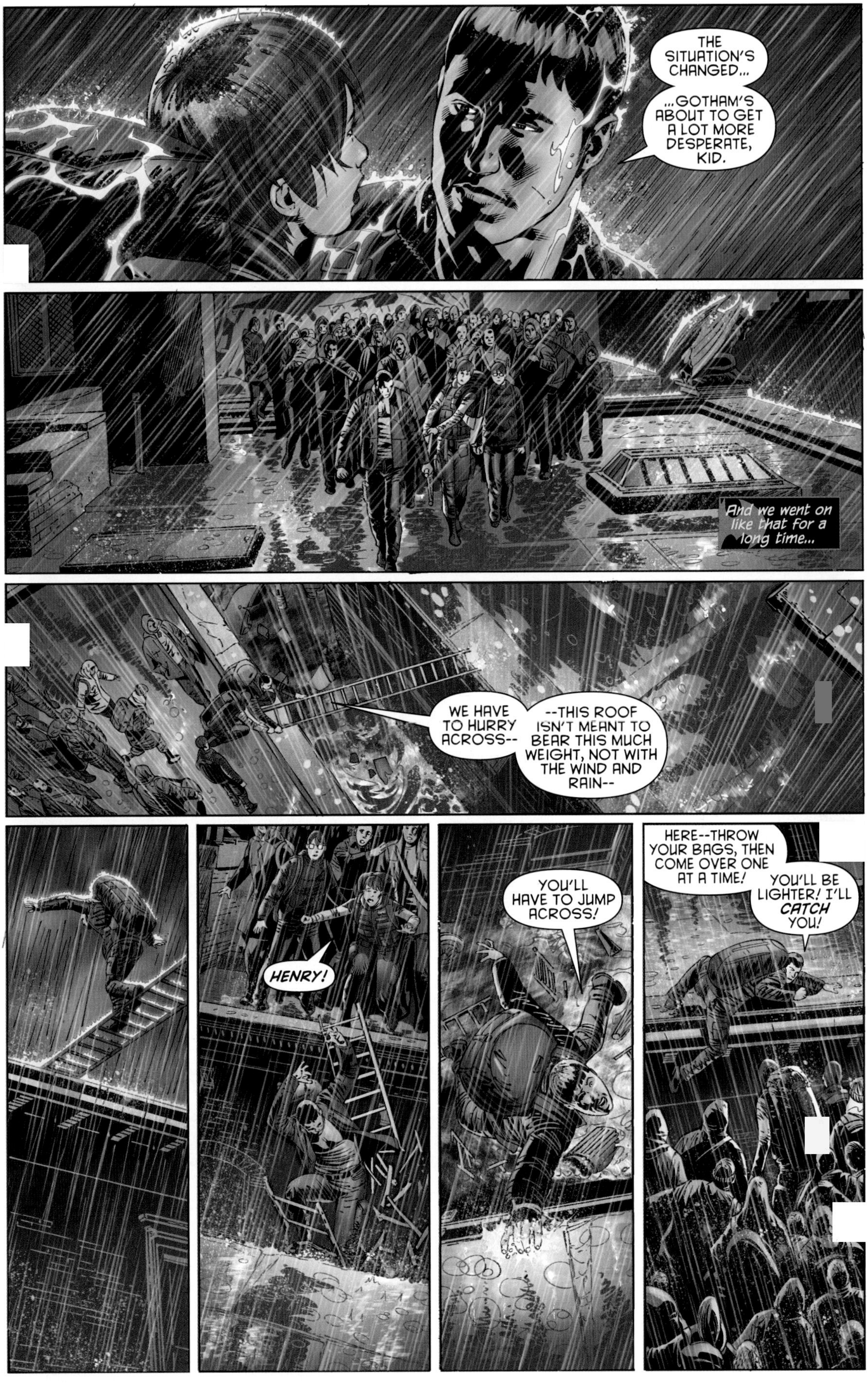
THE SITUATION'S CHANGED...
...GOTHAM'S ABOUT TO GET A LOT MORE DESPERATE, KID.
And we went on like that for a long time...
WE HAVE TO HURRY ACROSS--
--THIS ROOF ISN'T MEANT TO BEAR THIS MUCH WEIGHT, NOT WITH THE WIND AND RAIN--
HENRY!
YOU'LL HAVE TO JUMP ACROSS!
HERE--THROW YOUR BAGS, THEN COME OVER ONE AT A TIME!
YOU'LL BE LIGHTER! I'LL CATCH YOU!

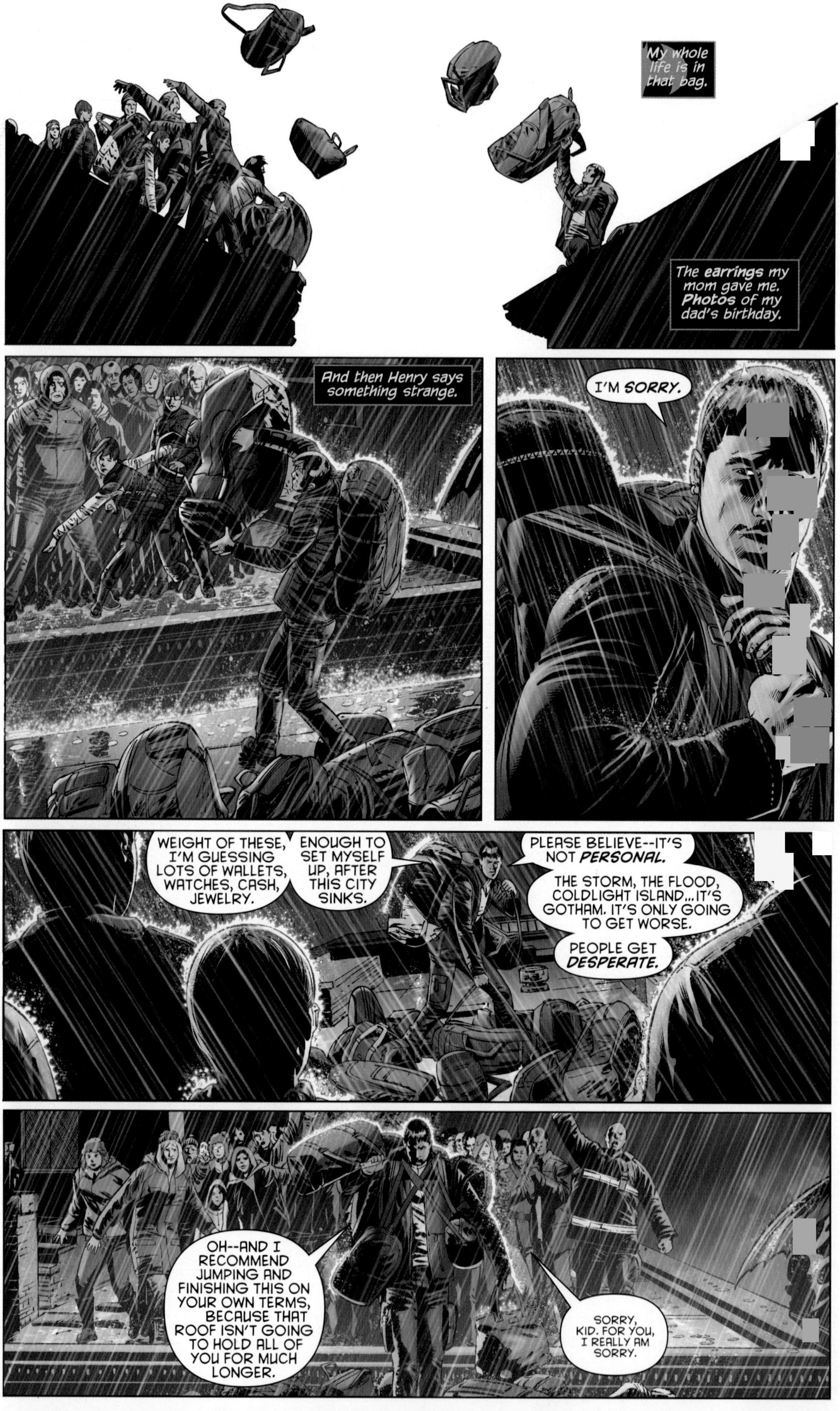
My whole life is in that bag.
The earrings my mom gave me. Photos of my dad's birthday.
And then Henry says something strange.
I'M SORRY.
WEIGHT OF THESE, I'M GUESSING LOTS OF WALLETS, WATCHES, CASH, JEWELRY.
ENOUGH TO SET MYSELF UP, AFTER THIS CITY SINKS.
PLEASE BELIEVE--IT'S NOT PERSONAL.
THE STORM, THE FLOOD, COLDLIGHT ISLAND...IT'S GOTHAM. IT'S ONLY GOING TO GET WORSE.
PEOPLE GET DESPERATE.
OH--AND I RECOMMEND JUMPING AND FINISHING THIS ON YOUR OWN TERMS, BECAUSE THAT ROOF ISN'T GOING TO HOLD ALL OF YOU FOR MUCH LONGER.
SORRY, KID. FOR YOU, I REALLY AM SORRY.

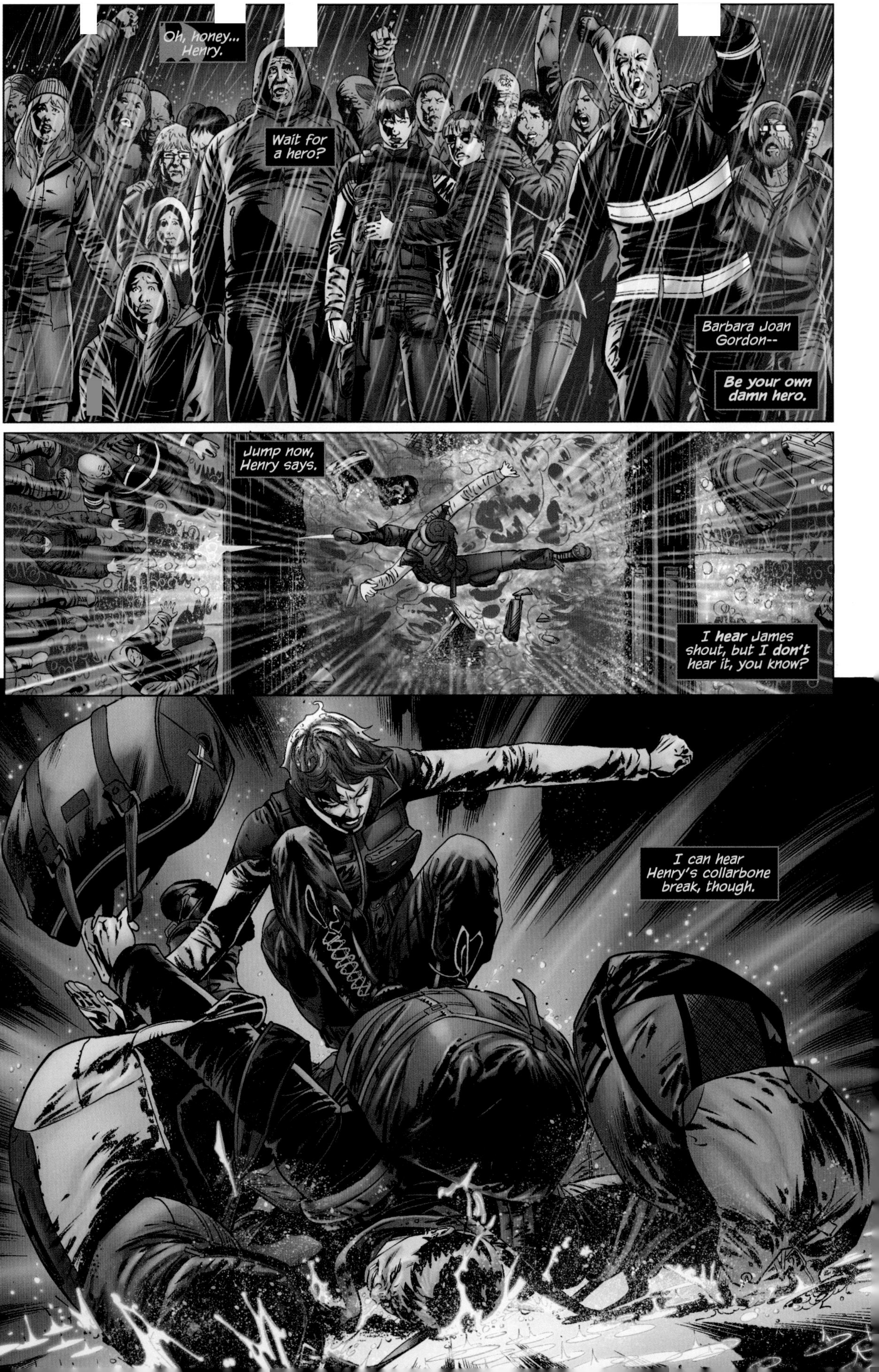
Oh, honey... Henry.
Wait for a hero?
Barbara Joan Gordon--
Be your own damn hero.
Jump now, Henry says.
I hear James shout, but I don't hear it, you know?
I can hear Henry's collarbone break, though.

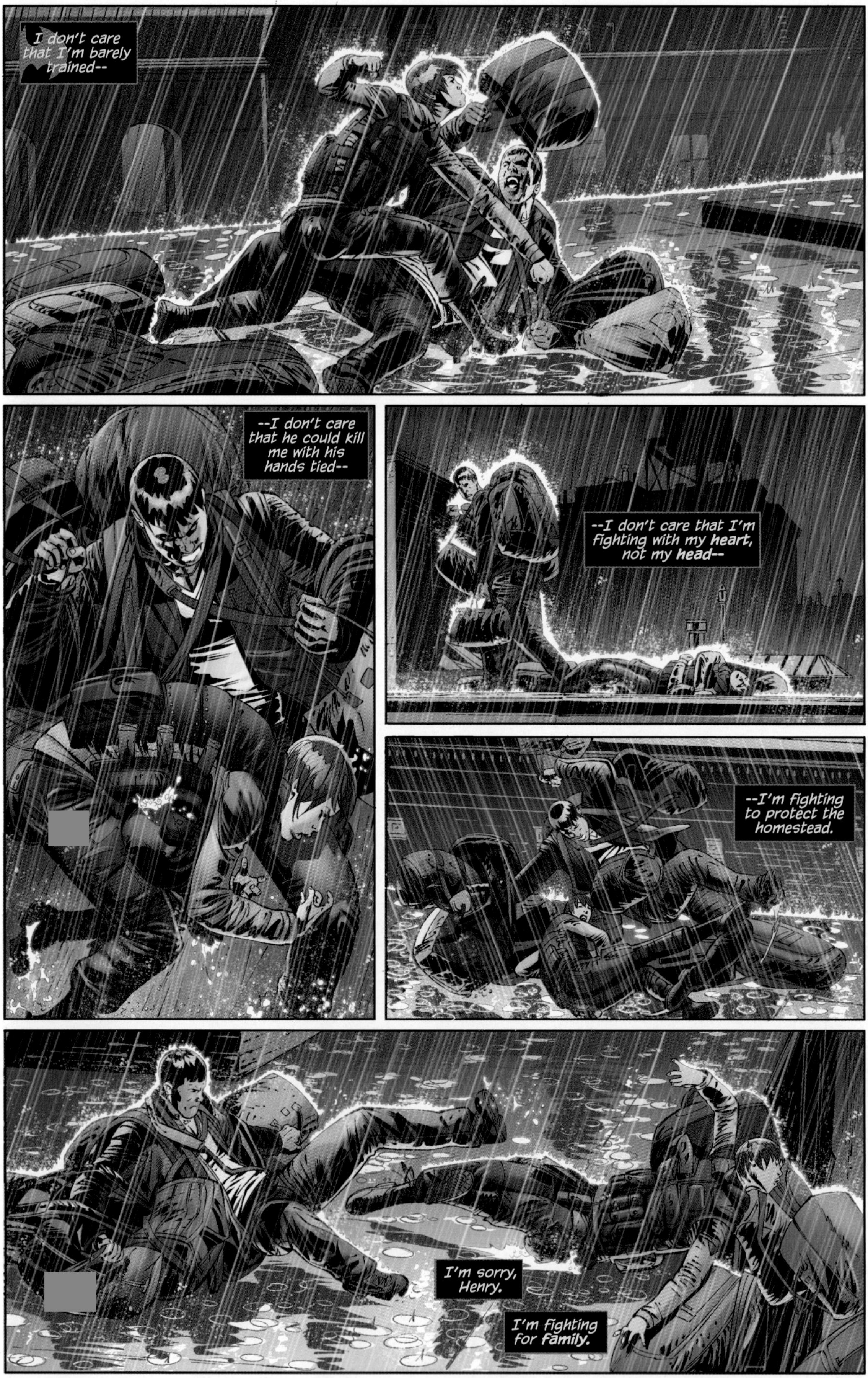
I don't care that I'm barely trained--
--I don't care that he could kill me with his hands tied--
--I don't care that I'm fighting with my heart, not my head--
--I'm fighting to protect the homestead.
I'm sorry, Henry.
I'm fighting for family.

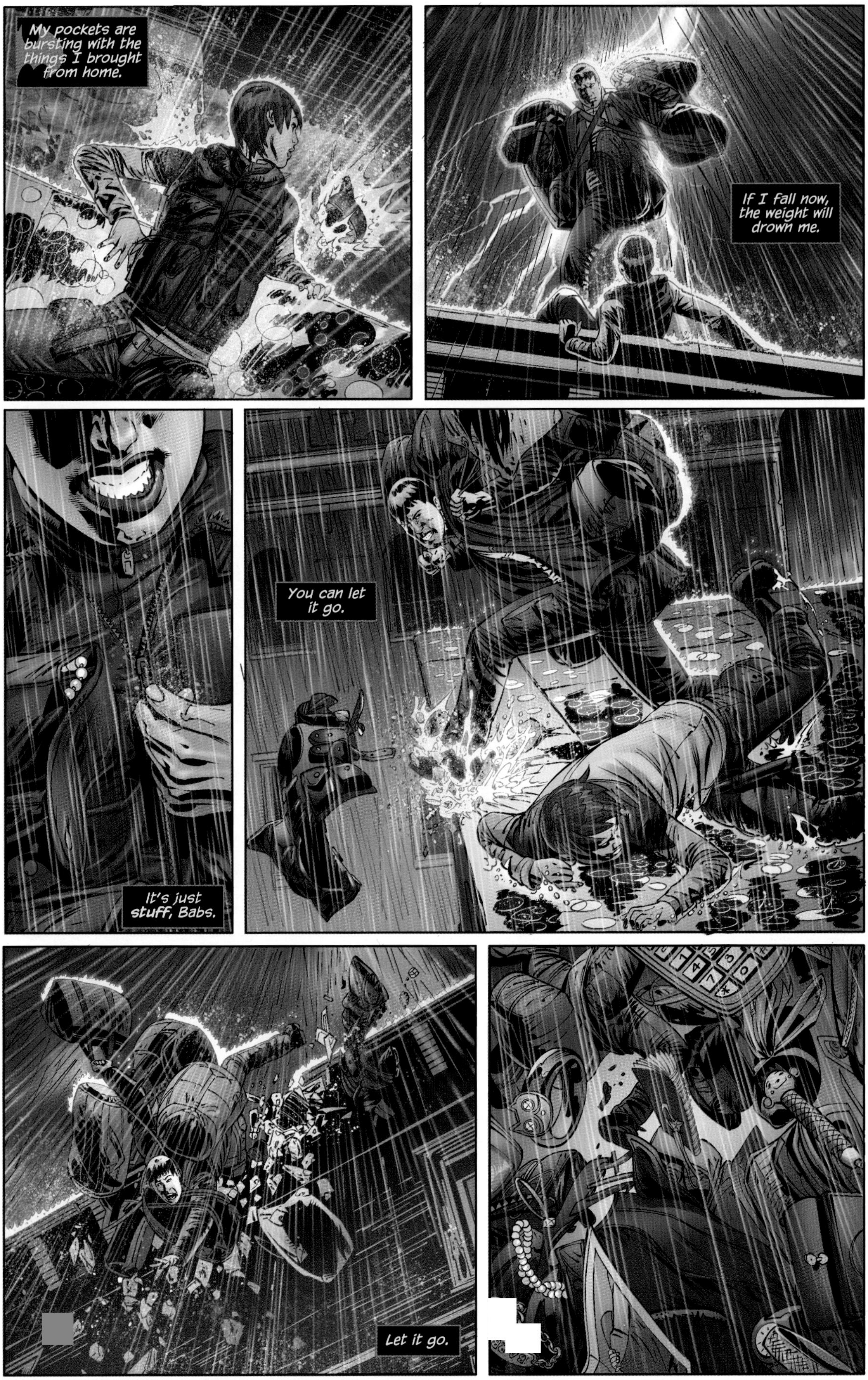
My pockets are bursting with the things I brought from home.
If I fall now, the weight will drown me.
It's just stuff, Babs.
You can let it go.
Let it go.

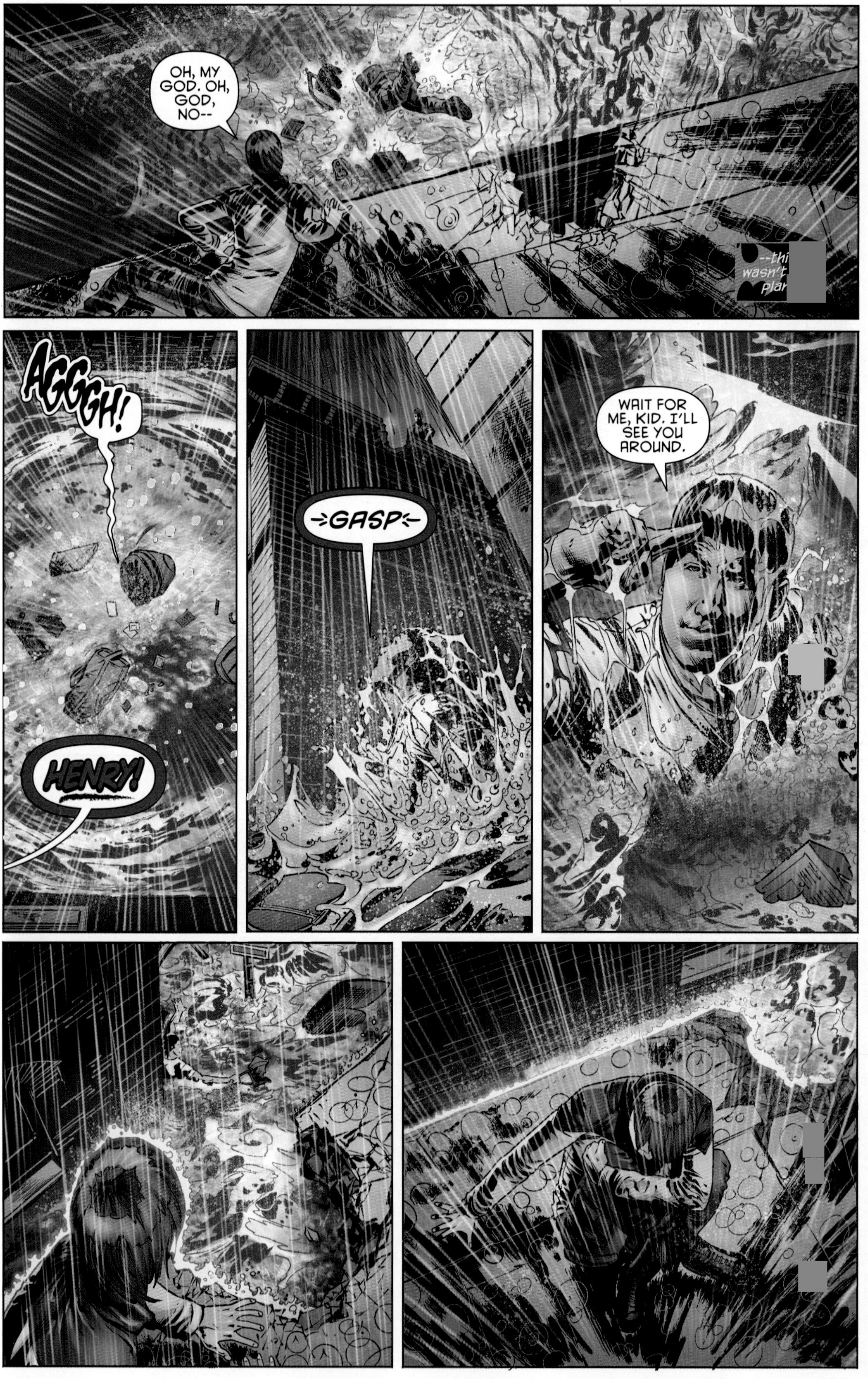
OH, MY GOD. OH, GOD, NO--
AGGGH!
HENRY!
GASP
WAIT FOR ME, KID. I'LL SEE YOU AROUND.

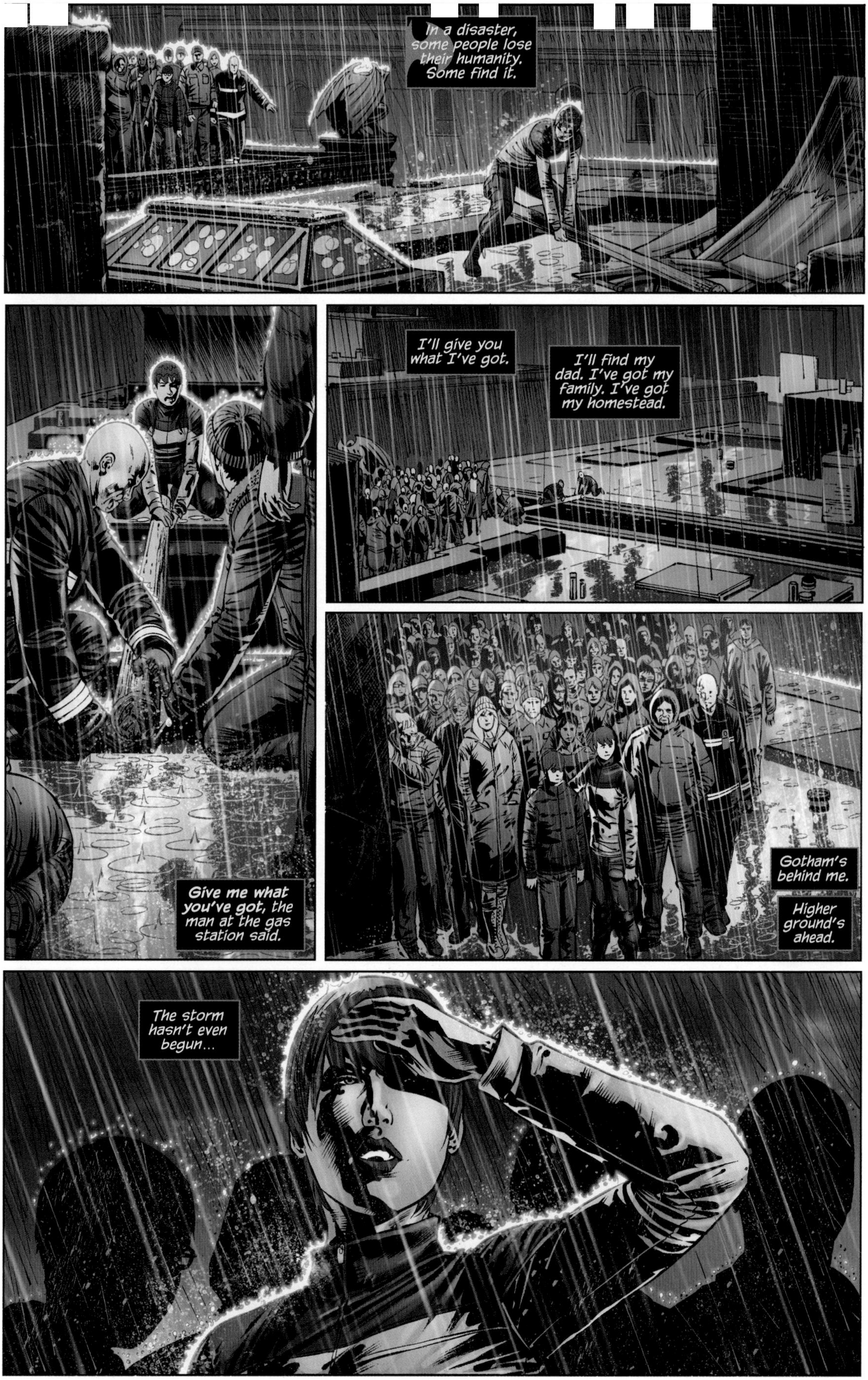
In a disaster, some people lose their humanity. Some find it.
Give me what you've got, the man at the gas station said.
I'll give you what I've got.
I'll find my dad. I've got my family. I've got my homestead.
Gotham's behind me.
Higher ground's ahead.
The storm hasn't even begun...

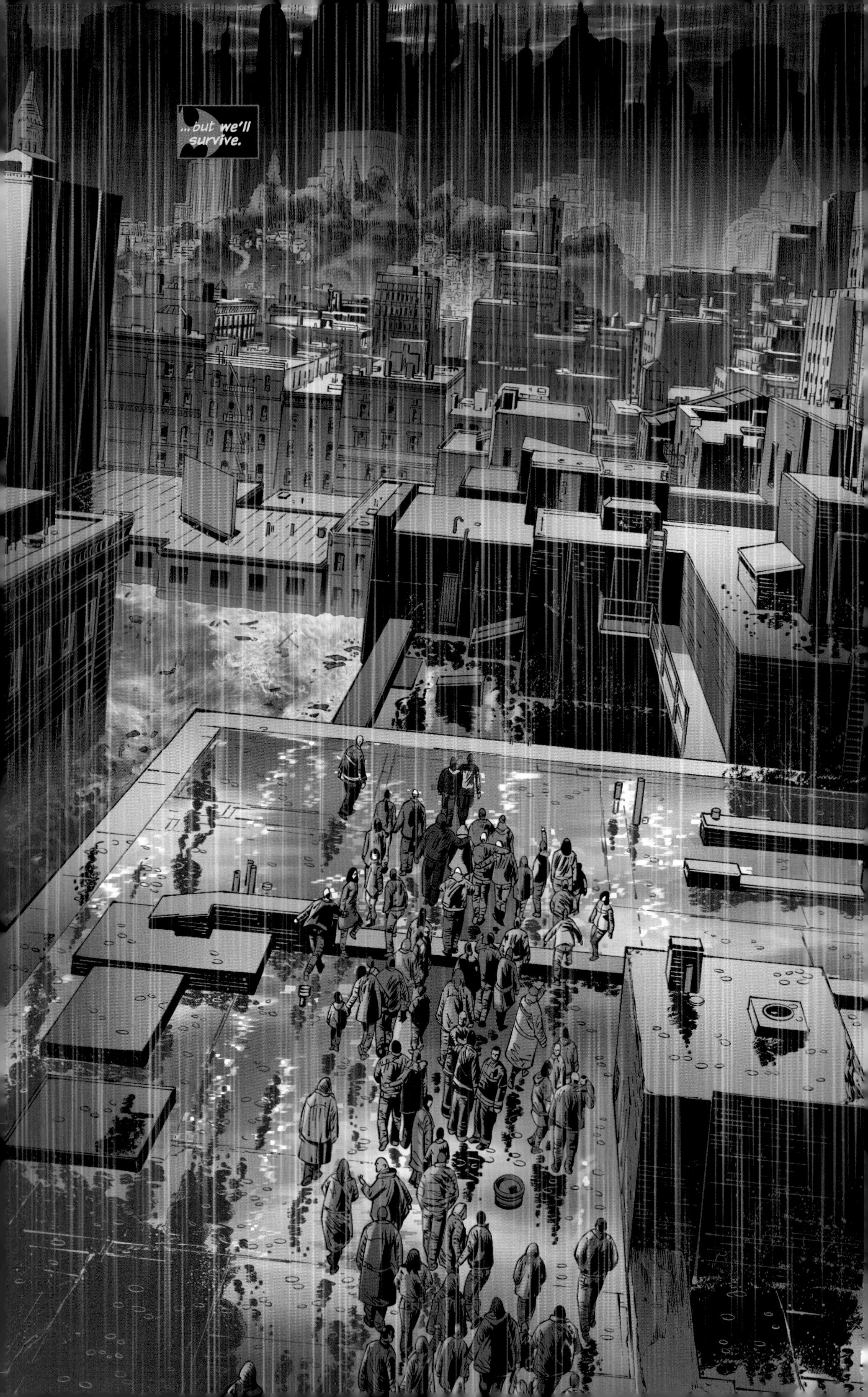
...but we'll survive.

BATGIRL
CHARACTER STUDIES

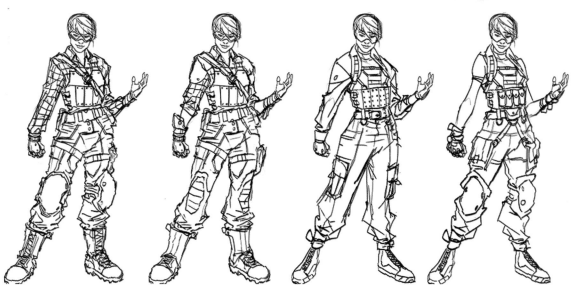

Designs by Alex Garner for Barbara's
Zero Year attire in BATGIRL #25

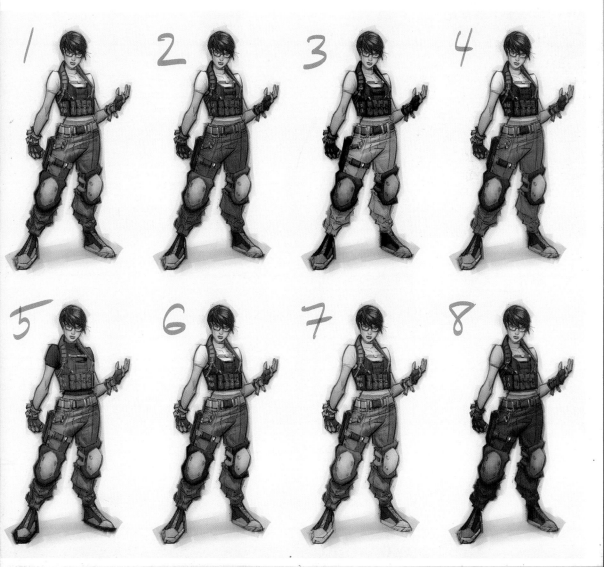

Early design for the Ventriloquist

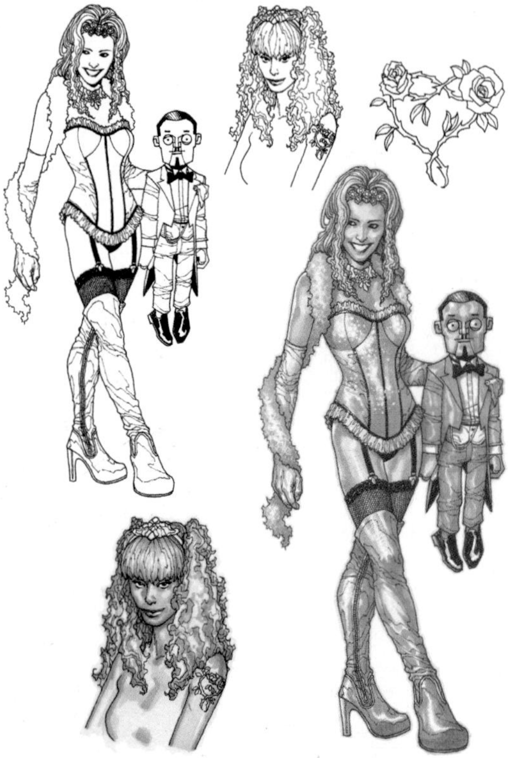

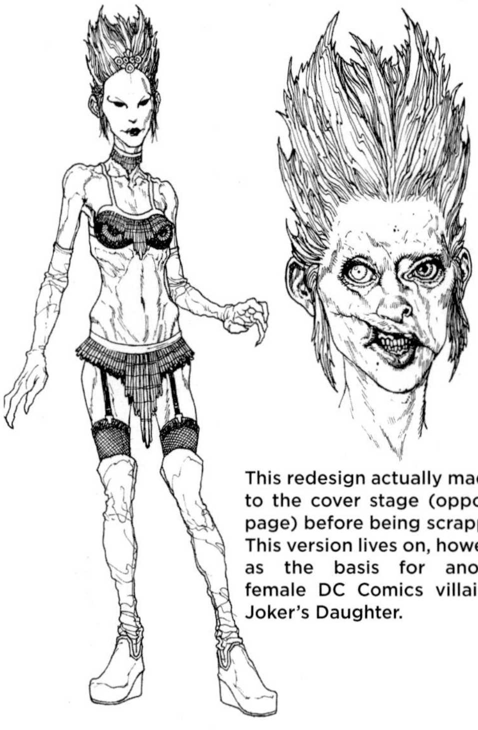

This redesign actually made it to the cover stage (opposite page) before being scrapped. This version lives on, however, as the basis for another female DC Comics villain — Joker's Daughter.

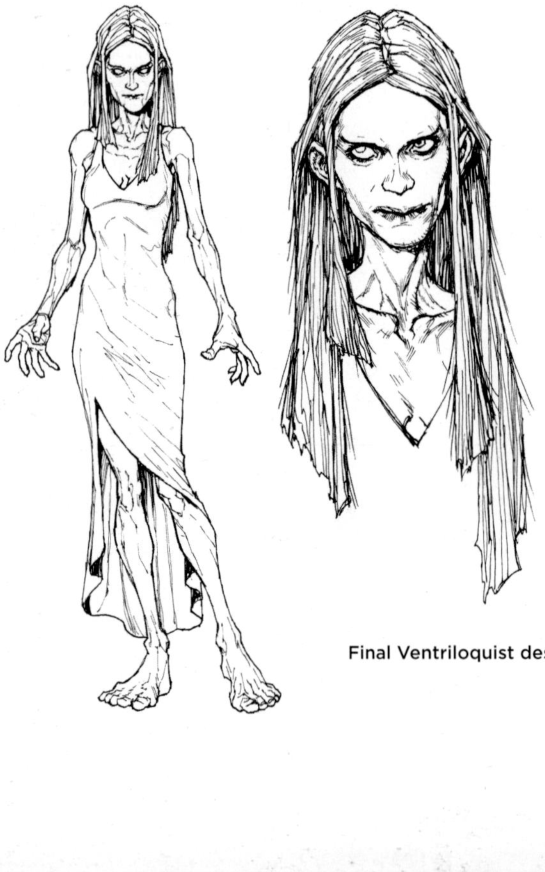

Final Ventriloquist design

Art by Andy Clarke

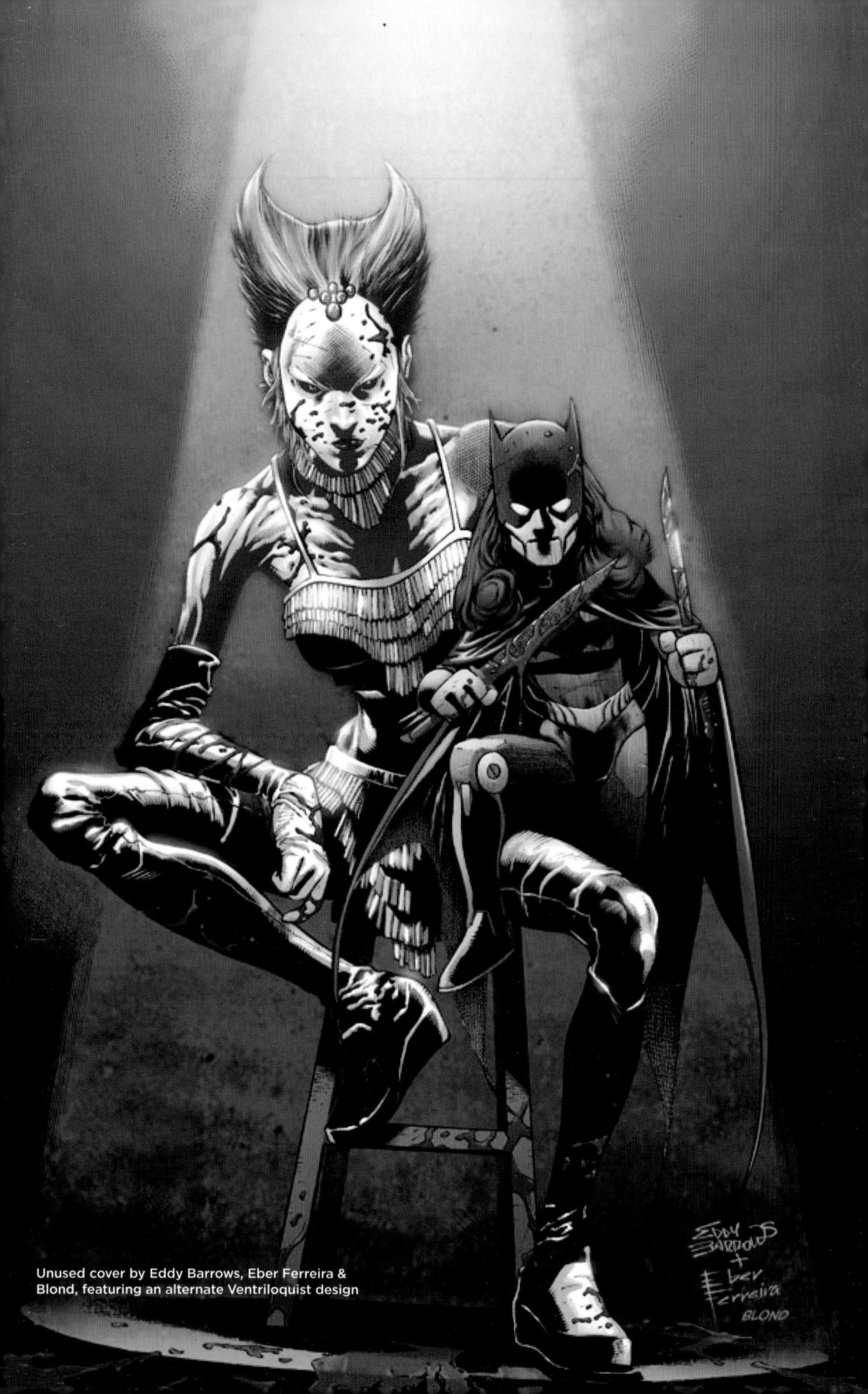
EDDY BARROWS
+
Eber Ferreira
BLOND

Unused cover by Eddy Barrows, Eber Ferreira & Blond, featuring an alternate Ventriloquist design